i

Camp Every County, Washington

and see Washington State from the ground up

Brendan McDonald

campeverycountywa.com

John, Tom, Boca (the dog looking out the tent window), Gary, and Brendan
are the camp-panions of the Camp Every County Crew

COPYRIGHT

TABLE OF CONTENTS

CAMPGROUNDS BY COUNTY

Prologue and Challenge to Camp Every County Washington

Many say there are two Washingtons: Eastern and Western.
In reality, there are 39 Washingtons - one for every county.

Ever notice how most people have one or two favorite campgrounds to which they return year after year, never trying anything new? My three camp-panions and I found ourselves camping on alternate weekends at Manchester State Park and Scenic Beach State Park in Kitsap County. Month after month, year after year, we saw mountains, saltwater, and even our native wild rhododendrons. That was the Washington we knew. We also knew there had to be much more. But I hated traveling far from home since I still worked full time. Gary had a genuine rattlesnake phobia, and it took considerable prodding to get him to camp in Eastern Washington. Tom hated crowds and would camp in only the most private of campgrounds. And John. Well, John hated just about everything (a South Boston thing).

We soon decided to expand our horizons. We bought just about every camping handbook on the market, but rarely found satisfaction. They told us nothing of the experience of camping at these places. We learned how many campsites each campground contained, how much they cost, when they were open, how to get there... but what about the experience of camping? How did it make the camper FEEL? What effect did it have on the camper? Did they have the same briny air that we found at Scenic Beach? The remarkably clear view of Mt. Rainer we found at Manchester? What did the forests smell like? How about the sunsets, if they existed at all? But we got none of that.

The four of us abandoned the camping manuals and set out on a journey over the next five years, eager to discover if the rest of Washington was as beautiful as the one we knew. First, we chose some popular campgrounds far from central Puget Sound -- Steamboat Rock State Park, Mary Hill State Park, and Rasar State Park. Then we explored those less known -- Indian Creek Campground, Battle Ground Lake State Park, and Takhlakh Lake Campground. We were hooked, and soon found ourselves printing out black and white maps of Washington with just the counties outlined, coloring in the "camped counties," and setting out to find campgrounds in the unexplored counties. We finally camped in county #39 (Garfield County) in the summer of 2017. We discovered surprising camping gems along the Snake River and deep in the Umatilla Mountains. We ate mushrooms near Randle, swam in the cool lakes of the Grand Coulee, chased away bears at Spring Canyon, immersed ourselves in ghost towns in the Okanogan, and discovered with awe why remote Palouse Falls was named

Washington's Official State Waterfall. Looking back, this 5-year journey became the adventure of a lifetime, one which we hope to capture in this camping manual.

Take our advice: Step out of your camping box, your comfort zone or, if you will, your rut. We have a great highway system that can get us anywhere in the state within an 8-hour drive. Those favorite campgrounds will still be there when you get back and, more likely, you will have fresh, new adventures that will make you appreciate your old faves even more. Let new parks work their magic on you. Think of them as adventures, treasure hunts, or like Lewis and Clark's Corps of Discovery. This is our challenge to all campers: Hold your maps in one hand, this manual in the other, and set out to go camping in all 39 Washington counties.

Camp Every County Crew dudes Gary, John, and Tom munch on some camp-made Tikka Masala and Pakora at Alder Lake Campground in Pierce County

INTRODUCTION, PART 1

Looking for "The Real Washington"

The State of Washington is a world unto itself, with many distinct regions, habitats, climates, and histories. The million-acre Olympic National Park dominates the northwest corner, with its remote rocky beaches, rain forests, alpine lakes, and picturesque mountains. To the southwest, the North Head lighthouse marks not only the mouth of the mighty Columbia, but also the end of the Lewis and Clark Trail. The Trail then retreats back along the Columbia Gorge, joined by the Snake River flowing to the foothills of the Blue Mountains. In the middle of the state are such natural wonders as the Grand Coulee region, Lake Chelan, Lake Roosevelt, and the Cascade Mountains. In the northeast, mining towns, Indian lands, and spectacular rivers exceed the expectations of visitors. Travelers find that each of these regions is entirely different from the others. In short, one cannot say they have seen the "Real Washington" until they have explored every region of the State.

And yet, campers are complex as well. One camper may view well-manicured lawns and concrete parking pads as camping nirvana, while others may view that as fresh hell. Some campers value primal nature in its purest form as home at last, while others may find it vulgar and off-putting. Some haul large RVs for comfort and protection, while others choose to sleep under the stars. Others view camping as an opportunity to relax, unwind and re-connect with solitude, while others use it as a platform to bike, hike, and boat themselves into total exhilaration and exhaustion. Regardless of who deserves the Most Authentic Camper trophy, it would be a shame to drive 300 miles to an unsuitable campground, one that campers would not have chosen had they known more. For this reason, we have chosen only the best campgrounds in each county and specified the fundamentals that most impacted our camping experience. Furthermore, we have divided the campgrounds into 7 categories that we think will include the widest variety of campers.

1. Most Appealing Campgrounds to the Senses
   Ah yes. Taste, touch, smell, sight, and sound. We all learned those five words in elementary school, until we were mercilessly coerced to think, analyze, then over think, memorize, and be tested until our senses became a distant memory. And so, we end up disconnected from nature, torn asunder from our primal selves, and wondering what happened to that inner child that made us so carefree and willing to play. Get yourselves back to the forest. Pick some mushrooms, add them to your campfire stew, and taste the flavors of nature. Wake up to that dissipating mist on your faces that calls in the new day. Hear the rush of the streams, the gentle breeze stroking the leaves of the cottonwoods, and the birds calling each other into action. Smell the wood burning on the campfire, the menthol balm of the cedar trees, and the salt air of the Pacific. See waterfalls that seem too much like a post card to possibly be real. Welcome home campers! Nature is calling!

2. Most Uniquely Washington Campgrounds
   Washington is not California. Or Hawaii. Or Florida. And I say hallelujah to that. No, Washington is utterly unique unto itself. If you don't instantly know you are in Washington, you have wandered into the cookie cutter

world of generic campgrounds that have succeeded in dulling your senses and disconnected you from nature. Run, don't walk, and choose one of the campgrounds in this manual. They are chosen to show you the best of the magic of Washington State, to let you experience it from the ground up, and to rediscover that inner you that has long forgotten what it feels like to be part of this wonderful land.

3. <u>Best Campgrounds for Entire Families</u>
   This category could equally be called "Most Everybody-Oriented Campgrounds." Certainly, children have certain needs that adults do not. Who doesn't enjoy watching a content child connect with nature? That speaks of real camping. What is not so real, and what the term "family-oriented" often means is campgrounds dominated by a series of complex playgrounds, swimming pools, and ice cream stands similar to those at home. If that's all there is, why not just stay home? No, every good campground should be suitable for children and adults alike. The entire family should be equally engaged in the experience, and not simply adults babysitting the children. It should be a new experience for everyone, and everyone will be happier in the end.

4. <u>Best Equipped/Best Campgrounds for RVs</u>
   There is no denying that trailers, RVs, 5th Wheels, and camping vans have had a huge impact on camping. Even those who still stick to basic tent camping sometimes like access to electricity to recharge cell phones, plumbed bathrooms, running water, and even covered shelters. Some may prefer camp hosts for safety. Boaters prefer boat launches, and swimmers prefer designated swimming areas. And a picnic table or fire grill is always a nice touch and can only add to the camping experience. Just as all campgrounds are not the same, neither are all campers. It's only natural!

5. <u>Best FREE Campgrounds</u>
   Yes, money changes everything, even when it comes to camping. Free campgrounds are not just for the budget minded. No, they tend to draw a different type of camper -- those who come with their hand-crafted camping gear, those who are happy to leave their mobile devices behind, those who provide music via guitars or recorders, and those who prefer to live more deliberately. Pull into Margaret McKinney CG in the Capital Forest and watch the children running with giddy abandon on the grassy loop, coupled by their parents throwing Nerf footballs. Or camp at Big Meadow Lake in northeastern Washington and climb the old fire tower to

watch moose munching on water plants. Or buzz down to the stark Ayers Boat Basin just off the Snake River surrounded by mesas and rock cliffs. Priceless!

6. <u>Best Rustic Campgrounds</u>
Just as FREE is not necessarily rustic, the best rustic campgrounds may charge a modest fee. The emphasis here is natural, untouched, and unmanicured. Want to gather your own firewood? Dip your own water from a pristine stream? Eat when you are hungry and sleep when you are tired? If you have a strong relationship with Mother Nature, you'll be right at home.

7. <u>Best Bike-In Campgrounds</u>
This is Washington. Cities like Seattle and Spokane have bicycle paths everywhere, and it is similar in the rest of Washington. For many, it is the preferred mode of transportation. The San Juan Islands, the Pacific Coast and Olympic Peninsula's Highway 101, southern Washington's Highway 64 along the Columbia River, and Highway 20 along the incredible but little-known Pend Oreille River provide bicycle camping adventures with great access to facilities and supplies along the way. Small towns provide groceries, laundry service, and campgrounds with H/B (hiker-biker) campsites reserved for those traveling light.

Lake Curlew is the prettiest lake in Northeastern Washington, and the best State Park in Ferry County

The following categories can be found exclusively on our website campeverycountywa.com due to space constraints:

8. <u>Best Group Campgrounds</u>
The best experiences of our camping lives have been in group campgrounds with anywhere from 12 to 100 people. The game changes entirely. You can organize activities, play games you haven't played since the "Red Rover" days of your childhood, build crude log cabins out of the fallen limbs of trees, erect natural showers on the tops of old growth stumps, and even have a theme for the entire trip.

9. <u>Best Hike-In Campgrounds</u>
The best nature has to offer is not always accessed by roads. Sometimes you have to hit the trail, literally in this case, and pack your gear into the wilderness. Just get used to tiny butane stoves, thin nylon tents, and freeze-dried foods, as the wilderness areas are a long way from home. But what you'll find is a cleansing of the senses to hear nothing but the sounds of the breeze, birds, and crickets; to see nothing but trees, vegetation and wildlife unaffected by human habitation, and smell smells you didn't know were smells. To paraphrase author Anne Lamott, camping in the wilderness on a clear night "smells like moon." It sure beats the smell of diesel fumes down below.

The Pasayten, William O. Douglas and other Wilderness Areas offer the best opportunities for hike-in camping. But we will leave that type of camping to the wilderness hiking experts, as this is beyond the scope of this book. We will focus instead on the more accessible hike-ins to include the largest number of campers, young and old.

10. <u>Best Boat-In Campgrounds</u>
Last but far from least are those campgrounds accessible only by boat. Most people think this is limited to the western side of Washington. The San Juan Islands, Whidbey Island, and the Puget Sound islands are well-known for boating campers. The Cascadia Marine Trail (CMT) stretches over 140 miles from the Canadian border to Olympia, including 66 campsites in multiple locations for non-motorized beachable watercraft. But don't count out the eastern side. Ross Lake in the NCNP has 25 boat-in campgrounds, Lake Roosevelt has 27, Lake Chelan has 16, and the Greater Columbia Water Trail (GCWT) includes too many to count. You want to see the real Washington? Most of it is accessible by water.

INTRODUCTION, PART 2

Bask in the Complexity of Washington State Campgrounds

Meticulous Washington State Park campgrounds. Spectacular but over-regulated National Park campgrounds. Shaggy but natural Department of Natural Resource campgrounds. Campgrounds given new life in Southeastern Washington by the Army Corps of Engineers. Campgrounds competently and meticulously maintained by various Indian Tribes. Private RV Parks and campgrounds that understand good camping and leaving the land in its natural state. State Forest Campgrounds that allow campers into the world of the working forest. National Park Service campgrounds dotting the shores of Lake Roosevelt. KOA campgrounds that provide more than just added amenities. Membership Camping Club campgrounds that accommodate guests on all but select major holidays. These are all available to those willing to seek them out. Don't dismiss them based on category. If you choose wisely, you may be delighted and have memories that will last a lifetime.

Washington State Parks

There is no denying that our State Parks are under siege. Budget cuts, overuse, and rising vandalism all play a role. We currently have 77 camping State Parks that spread out into 29 of our 39 Washington Counties. On the positive side, this is where you will find most of the State's natural treasures - everything from lighthouses and saltwater beaches to mighty rivers to Old West towns to the State's official waterfall at Palouse Falls. Most are reservable, ensuring you won't be turned away at the gate. All of them have running water, picnic tables, paved roadways, and established campsites. On the negative side, they can be crowded, too manicured for many avid nature lovers, and fairly costly. But they will create memories that delight, educate, and even transform us as residents of this most beautiful of states.

National Park Campgrounds

I stand out as the member of our small band of campers that tends to avoid National Park Campgrounds. In my defense may I say I love our National Parks, but not our National Park Campgrounds. In my camp-panions' defense, these parks often rest in the shadow of not only our greatest natural wonders, but our greatest national treasures. Who could help but fall in love with majestic Mount Rainier, the whimsical Olympic Mountains, or the rugged, unspoiled peaks of the

North Cascades? But while our State Park campgrounds suffer from overuse and budget cuts, the National Park campgrounds suffer even more. They tend to be older, more crowded, more heavily regulated, and typically lack amenities like hookups or a reservation system. Of course, there are a few standouts (Ohanapecosh at MRNP, Colonial Creek at NCNP, and Kalaloch in the ONP). Just choose wisely. That's what it's all about anyway.

National Park Service (NPS) Campgrounds

These are quite a departure from the actual National Park Campgrounds mentioned above. They make up in numbers what they may lack in the way of amenities. The result: less crowding, better availability, and access to the "smaller wonders" that you won't find on the postcards. There are 27 car and boat-in campgrounds on Lake Roosevelt alone, picking up the slack in Northeast Washington (which has but a single State Park campground at Lake Curlew). NPS campgrounds typically offer only running water, parking pads, and picnic tables by way of amenities, but are readily available, less expensive, and can help you discover the real nitty-gritty of what makes Washington such a gem. But don't hurry once you get here. Linger. Take some time. Wander the paths. You may discover the original townsite of Kettle Falls. Or the only Washington State Ferry in Eastern Washington at Keller Ferry. Or even the original buildings of the frontier encampment at Fort Spokane. It's all waiting, and you won't have to stand in line.

Municipal, County, and Regional Parks

These are operated by local governments and fill in many camping gaps in places far from the National and State Parks. These are most prevalent in the more populated counties with larger budgets (King, Snohomish), but also in the smaller counties which otherwise would have few camping facilities at all (Wahkiakum, Whitman). Their biggest strength is that they are all utterly individual. Skamokawa Vista is set in a town once accessible only by a series of natural water canals flowing into the Columbia River. Crow Butte occupies an entire bridged island on the Columbia River, a lush paradise in an otherwise arid country. Kamiak Butte occupies an entire mountain in a series of otherwise random, regularly irregular windswept hills, giving a birds-eye view of this delicately beautiful region. So, don't underestimate these campgrounds. Several of them make our lists of favorite campgrounds in Washington and are places to which we return again and again.

U. S. Forest Service (USFS) Campgrounds

Anyone who has ever camped with me knows that I prefer just about any USFS campground to any other type. Most of Washington is defined by its forests -- in the Olympic, Cascade, Blue, and Selkirk Mountains, on the larger islands of Puget Sound and the Salish Sea, in its many State Forests, and in the Gifford Pinchot, Okanogan-Wenatchee, Colville, Olympic, and Mount Baker-Snoqualmie National Forests. You will seldom find hookups, reservations, paved pads, or elaborate technical equipment. Everything is carved from the forest itself, from picnic shelters, to large canopied campsites, to wooden steps guiding campers down slopes or to the edges of pristine streams. This is the real Washington, the most natural, and the Washington that is easiest to experience from the ground up.

State Forest Campgrounds

These campgrounds are a departure from the rest. They are often set in working forests, where industry and recreation have worked and plotted for decades to peacefully co-exist. Our personal experience is that they have succeeded. In the Capital State Forest, for example, ORVs are permitted in some campgrounds but prohibited in others. Logging occurs far from the designated "quiet campgrounds" such as the marvelous Margaret McKinney CG, allowing many more campers to follow their bliss. This works similarly in Yakima County's Ahtanum State Forest, Okanogan County's Loomis-Loup Loup State Forest, Clark County's Yacolt Burn State Forest, and many others. Don't knock 'em until you've camped 'em.

Department of Natural Resources (DNR) Campgrounds

These may be the most under-appreciated campgrounds in Washington. While they tend to be "shaggy" -- meaning left in their natural state -- they also seem to attract campers who come to recapture their bond with nature. You won't find playgrounds, clubhouses, or souvenir stands here. What you'll discover is how Sitka spruce and Douglas fir grow in their natural states, free of manicuring clippers that want to trim them like Christmas trees. Nope, here they will grow where the sun draws them, the wind makes them retreat, and the bottom branches shed naturally when the tips of the trees reach to the sky. Campers here display homemade camping equipment, formed out of the very elements in which they surround themselves, and children run and play with a genuinely endearing wonderment. This is nature, folks. Sorry if your cell phones don't have 4-bar reception, or your TV reception fades in and out. On second thought, we're not sorry at all.

U.S. Army Corps of Engineers (COE) Campgrounds

The first thing to remember about these campgrounds is that the COE, as any governmental agency, is under a state of constant change. The majority of good campgrounds in southeastern Washington are operated by the COE, many of which were once Washington State Parks. The result: lower costs, better availability, yet operated as well if not better than when run by the State. They have similar amenities, and access to the same local facilities. The 24 COE campgrounds in Washington are found along the Snake River in the region between Pasco in Franklin County and Lewiston Idaho, and along the Columbia River in Klickitat and Benton counties. They are all located on impoundments of both Rivers, dammed into a series of lakes, starting with Lakes Celilo and Umatilla (the Columbia River between eastern Washington and Oregon). The other lakes are formed from the Snake River, starting in the west with Lake Wallula near Pasco, to Lake Sacajawea, Lake West, Lake Bryan, and Lower Granite Lake going east. While some of the COE campgrounds are very basic (Ayers Boat Basin and Nisqually John), others (Hood, Charbonnneau and Fishhook) are more developed and, most of all, all those in Washington are located on great bodies of water.

Bureau of Land Management (BLM)

The BLM has come a long way since its establishment in 1946, formed from the merger of the General Land Office and the U.S. Grazing Service. While we've certainly done our share of "grazing" while camping, these organizations became obsolete with the change in attitudes toward public lands. Over time, the lands that had once been used to encourage homesteading, western migration, and livestock feeding gave way to more complex recreational needs coupled with public land conservation. The campgrounds themselves are among the simplest. Some might not think of them as campgrounds at all, but merely land that permits dispersed camping. Some campers feel more connected to nature in this environment, not just renting a parking space, but being one with the land. Come on, nature lovers, this just might be your ticket.

Bureau of Reclamation and Public Utility District (PUD) Campgrounds

Central Washington, once dubbed the Columbia Desert, has been transformed into a land of blooming orchards, rugged canyons, and a camper's paradise with the introduction of massive, systematic irrigation in this enormous region once dismissed as an uninhabitable wasteland. The Missoula Floods, caused by the melting of ice dams forming Ice Age Lake Missoula, broke loose some 15,000 years ago rechanneling the Columbia River through the region that is now Grant County. Soil was washed away, deep rocky canyons formed, and mesas were defined. By the time the Columbia returned to its original course about 4,000 years later, the land was reduced to a series of scablands, unable to support life apart from scrub brush and bunch grass.

In 1943, the Columbia Basin Project Act was signed, which led to the building of the Grand Coulee Dam, then the largest concrete structure of its kind. It led to the irrigation of over one million acres of arid land. Of course, the most pressing purpose of the Dam was to generate electricity, and the power companies were in turn pressed to create recreational opportunities to replace the land taken by reservoirs. It has now become a camper's playground, featuring State and NPS campgrounds, plus those sponsored by local PUDs. These include Steamboat Rock, Sun Lakes and Potholes State Parks, and Crescent Bar Recreation Area (Grant Co. PUD). Other regions with extensive PUD campgrounds include the Tacoma Power Project (along Alder, Mayfield, and Riffe Lakes in Pierce and Lewis Counties), and numerous campgrounds in Cowlitz County built by PacifiCorp, who dammed the Lewis River to create Merwin Lake, Yale Lake, and the Swift Reservoir. While I personally am not drawn to reservoirs (as the shores have had little time to return to a natural state), these are enormously popular with campers, and families in particular.

Washington Department of Fish and Wildlife (WDFW)

The WDFW is synonymous with conservation, which they would define as preservation of natural environments and the ecological communities, including management for human use. It is not unusual to find more fisherfolk at these campgrounds than campers, or to have the entire campground to yourselves. They are stark, undeveloped, and occasionally delightful. Imagine our delight when we stumbled upon the seep lakes and the Columbia National Wildlife Refuge hidden away in a stark corner where Adams and Grant Counties meet -- a series of small lakes and wetlands in the former "Columbia Desert" -- formed by the seeping of reservoirs higher up raising the water table down below. Imagine our amazement when we laid eyes on our very first Sandhill Crane hovering over little Lyle Lake in an area that was once devoid of life! If this isn't the perfect backdrop for camping, I can't imagine what is.

Kampgrounds of America (KOA) Campgrounds

Sometimes amenities matter. Sometimes on the family vacation, you just need to do laundry, and don't want to spend an entire day driving to the nearest town to do so. Or sometimes a good reliable shower ranks right up there with the best wildlife viewing. And at other times, the wide-open spaces don't seem to be calling your name. We get that and have found many KOA Campgrounds to be a welcome relief from our more primitive camping adventures. Our experience with a handful of them is that they were set among the most representative Washington State locales -- at Willapa Bay, Lyons Ferry, Ellensburg, and Newport, just to name a few. They are tidy, clean, well-equipped, and should not be overlooked.

Specialty Parks

This website includes very few "specialty" parks. By this we mean campgrounds which specialize in a singular activity other than camping: fishing, hunting, dirt biking, power boating, or mere proximity to a local attraction. We have seen fishermen, boaters, hikers, and site-seers leave the campground early in the morning, returning late at night, not noticing or caring that the campsite had no trees, no daytime quiet, and no shade. Other campgrounds seem defined by the roar of ORVs, boat engines, or busy highways. We asked ourselves the question: would we enjoy our experience if we never left the campground? If the answer is no, it may be a good fishing, hiking, or boating experience, but not necessarily a good camping experience.

Choose Your Campsites Wisely

My camp-panions and I have very different ideas about campsite selection. The only thing we agree on is that it's important. I like to mix it up, sometimes socializing with other campers, other times seeking solitude. Tom and John travel with cockatoos. Birds. Noisy, tropical, chomp-anything birds. So, altitude becomes an issue, as it gets too cold at night for them. Their sudden squawks can bother the uninitiated, so bigger sites are necessary. Gary, our most senior camper, feels vulnerable without other campers around him. He is also uncomfortable if he's more than a few yards from the bathroom. John is more comfortable under a full canopy of trees. Our dogs can bark up a frenzy if other dogs come too close to our small campsite -- and if they're not happy, no one is happy. So, we choose our sites very carefully. Factoring in privacy, size, location, vegetation, and even shade versus sunlight can be a vital link in your camping plans. We try to communicate this in words, and include data like elevation, site size, and campsite vegetation, but recommend that you also consult photos from the Washington State Park reservation websites, and more specific websites such as campsitephotos.com.

INTRODUCTION, PART 3
Camping Style

Civilian Conservation Corps (CCC)

From 1933 to 1942, as America rose out of the Great Depression, President Franklin D. Roosevelt organized the CCC to restore the nation's forests, enhance our National Parks, and create a system of state parks. It employed over 3 million people called the "dollar a day men" who built great stone lodges, campsites, roads and trails, all done by hand, pick, axe shovel and wheelbarrow. Many of these are still in existence, adding a distinct style marked by permanence, sturdiness, and hand-hewn determination. Mount Spokane State Park (S.P.) features CCC-built picnic areas, the road to the summit (Cooks Road), and the Vista House. Moran S.P. on Orcas Island is still noted for the CCC's roads and bridges, stone fireplaces, the Log Kitchen Shelter, and the famous Mount Constitution Tower. Deception Pass S.P. still maintains 25 CCC-built structures, including picnic shelters, and the stone and log Bowman Bay Bathhouse houses the Washington CCC Museum. While other groups have built similar structures on a smaller scale, none of them match the powerful vintage character of the CCC.

"Glamping" Versus Camping

"Glamping," for you hard-core outdoor types who've never heard the word, is urban slang for "glamorous camping," or a luxury form of camping which includes expensive equipment, high-class facilities, luxury food and drink, etc. (macmillandictionary.com). It has a negative connotation among the more rugged, traditional campers. But don't worry, glampers, we are your biggest fans. Ever prepare Boeuf Bourguignonne on a single propane burner? We have, and Julia Child would have been proud. We've also doctored up Kraft Mac and Cheese with leftovers and enjoyed that just as much. Ever eaten on a picnic table covered in citronella candles and expensive 'bug zappers" to keep the bugs from sharing your rotisserie chicken and broccoli? Yes, so have we. My single most vivid childhood camping memory is eating "Bug Stew" with the Taylor family at Sun Lakes S.P. It's not the food, or the equipment, or the facilities: it's the experience, the memory, and what it means to be a part of nature. Nature doesn't demand that we be perfect, but mixing a little glamping with your camping, laughing at your own mistakes or self-indulgence, can keep every camping experience fresh and new.

Boondocking

The term boondocking comes from the Filipino/Tagalog word "bundok" (or mountain), adopted by American troops during World War II when they hid in otherwise unoccupied mountain land to remain undetected. It has come to mean a brushy rural location, implying being miles from nowhere. It is applied most often by RV'ers who dry camp alone in undisclosed locations at no cost and with no neighbors. But while the boondocks may have a negative connotation, they can make for the most beautiful, restful, and memorable camping. These sites are most often found along mountain roads between established campsites, or along rivers where campers have direct access to rivers or streams. In our ramblings, the most beautiful boondocking sites are in Barlow Pass on the Mountain Loop Highway (Hwy 92/FR 20) along the South Fork of the Stillaguamish River in Snohomish County. Other great boondocking sites are along Mountain Highway 128 in Garfield Co., and the Tucannon River Road (Hwy 47) in Columbia Co.

Now that You're Chosen a Camp-Worthy Campground, Let's Talk Camping-Compatible Recreation

Some activities are clearly consistent with camping: canoeing, kayaking, hiking, fishing, and even less popular activities like mushroom-gathering, cave exploring, gold-panning, and so on. Other activities... not so much. While I appreciate hunting as an activity, I don't want bullets whizzing through my campground. And for you who enjoy noisy activities like jet skis, Off-Road Vehicles (ORVs), and power-boat racing --- have a good time... in the big lakes, the urban areas, and the logging spurs. We campers are there for the quiet, the connection with the land, and to re-connect with nature. I am genuinely happy when campgrounds are constructed to allow campers and ORVs to peacefully co-exist. The activities listed in this website are quieter, varied, and sometimes a bit peculiar, but they are an add-on to camping itself, not the only reason we're there. Please see Appendix 1 at the back of this manual for more information.

Abbreviations

ADA: Americans with Disabilities Act or wheelchair friendly.

BLM: Bureau of Land Management

Camp-panions: our term for camping companions

Campworthy: worthy of camping

Co.: short for "County, usually in relation to County Parks

CBRA: Crescent Bar Recreation Area

CCC: Civilian Conservation Corps

CMT: Cascadia Marine Trail

COE: U.S. Army Corps of Engineers

DCRS; Douglas Creek Recreation Site

DNR: Department of Natural Resource

GPS: Global Positioning System or, in this case, "directions"

H/B: indicates Hiker/Biker campsites

KOA: Kampgrounds of America (a private campground chain)

K/M: stands for K/M Resorts of America, a private club

MRNP: Mount Rainier National Park

NCNP: North Cascades National Park

NPS: National Park Service

ONF: Olympic National Forest

ONP: Olympic National Park

ORV: Off Road Vehicles

PUD: Public Utility District

Rec: recreational

S.P.: State Park

USFS: United States Forest Service

WDFW: Washington Department of Fish and Wildlife

campeverycountywa.com

An optical illusion at Manchester S.P. in Kitsap Co. causes Mt. Rainier to appear much closer

ADAMS COUNTY (Ritzville, Othello)

Wheat fields, apple orchards, and potato farming in the glacially washed soil left by Ice Age floods dominate this rural and picturesque county. There are few camping options here, with only 7.3% of the County being public land. The majority of land is rolling wheat fields, with a timeless rhythm of its own.

Seep Lakes/Othello Area

The Columbia Basin, or Columbia Plateau to some, was originally designated on maps as the "Columbia Desert." With the coming of the Columbia Basin Reclamation Project in the 1940s, the desert was transformed into rich farmland. High elevation reservoirs and irrigation ditches tended to leak downhill, raising the water table and forming a series of "seep lakes" in the lower lying areas. So, what we have now, on the edges of the farmland, is a desert spotted with many lakes, and with it a wide variety and large numbers of birds, a situation not normally found in nature. And you won't find that anywhere else but in Washington.

Lyle Lake CG (Adams Co.'s *BEST FREE CG* and *MOST UNIQUELY WASHINGTON CG*)
The Adams County seep lakes are on the furthest edge of the desert, away from the Reclamation project and irrigation. This is an opportunity to see what is left of the "Columbia Desert," spotted with many lakes, and close to the well-equipped town of Othello -- to marvel at nature and get the desert experience, without being left high and dry.
Overview: Located 5 miles north of Othello, this area includes 12-acre Lyle Lake, 34.7-acre Herman Lake South, and 12-acre Quail Lake, operated by the WDFW at 934' elevation, open year-round; GPS 46.89540, -119.20274.

Facilities: Lyle Lake has a pit toilet. Otherwise, the campgrounds are primitive with no drinking water. Roads into the area and between lakes are gravel. Quail Lake is accessible by trail only.

Recreation: Fishing for rainbow trout has been restored with the eradication of predator carp in 2012. Duck hunting is very good in season. In March and April, over 35,000 sandhill cranes land here on their northern migrations with their throaty whoops, gangly legs, and giant fluttering wings. The Sandhill Crane Festival is held annually in Othello in mid-March. After April, bird watching remains good for pelicans, Canada geese, mallards and swans. There is a birding trail just 3 miles northwest of Lyle Lake that we recommend for its basalt cliffs and desert stream. Canoeing is good in T-shaped Lyle Lake and square Herman Lake. The prettiest and best canoeing lakes are nearby Shiner and Hutchinson lakes, just 3 miles north of Lyle Lake. Hiking is good in 3 nearby trails: Frog Lake Trail (3 miles onto a mesa with views of the refuge landscape), Marsh Loop (1.8 miles circle two marshes), and the more difficult Crab Creek Trail (one-mile following Crab Creek).

Campsites: Camping is primitive and dispersed on native material and gravel. There are up to about 7 sites, two of which are walk-ins. Use of these lakes is light, so privacy is the norm. Vegetation consists of grasses and sagebrush. Camping is FREE of charge with a Discover Pass. Note that Lyle, Herman, and Quail Lakes lie within one mile of the Columbia National Wildlife Refuge, where camping is not permitted.

Trip Notes: Have you ever noticed how some people look at a purebred dog, let's say an English Bulldog, and think it's crazy ugly while other people think it has unparalleled beauty? Hold that thought. This is an area of extreme stark beauty, but it's not for everyone. People will love it or hate it. It is, however, utterly unique to Washington, part of a designated National Natural Landmark, and its sunsets will win you over -- provided you can appreciate both what it is and what it is not. And if none of that works for you, come in late March or early April when the Sandhill cranes are in migration -- a real experience of the senses.

Local Attractions: The Columbia National Wildlife Refuge covers 30,000 acres and extends well into Grant County. The Wildlife Headquarters is just 1.5 miles from Lyle Lake. The Refuge provides views of ancient lava flows, additional seep lakes, and a wide variety of birds and other wildlife. The Drumheller Channels National Natural Landmark, just 5 miles northwest of Lyle Lake, provides a vantage point to view steep buttes, cliffs, shallow ponds, and sand dunes left behind by ice-age floods.

Ritzville Area

It would be impossible to represent Adams County without giving a nod to the town of Ritzville, with its rich pioneer history. It is the heart of a huge wheat growing area and was once the largest wheat shipping point in the world. Its historic downtown buildings date from the early 1900s, its greatest period of prosperity. The four-square-block downtown area of Ritzville is listed on the State and National Registers of Historic Places and should not be overlooked.

The Cedars Inn (Adams Co.'s *BEST EQUIPPED/BEST CG FOR RVs*)
This moderately rated motel with many amenities extends its services to a pleasant, shaded camping area facing the most modern portion of this historic town.

Overview: Here you'll find camping within the City of Ritzville with good access off I-90. It is adjacent to the Cedars Inn, a full-service motel. The RV Park is open year-round; GPS 47.11858, -118.36508.

Facilities: The motel provides access to showers, full bathrooms, laundry, free Wi-Fi and an outdoor pool.

Recreation: This is a place to both relax and enjoy the sites and history of Ritzville. For golfers, it is close to Ritzville Municipal Golf Course.

Campsites (39 tent/RV sites for any size RV, full hookups 30/50-amp, reservable) The sites are located behind Cedars Inn, protected from the majority of I-90 noise and well shaded, located in the newer portion of Ritzville close to restaurants and services.

Trip Notes: Here's the thing. If you're travelling to Washington all the way from Iowa with six kids, your Uncle Louie and a restless dog, don't make this your destination. Sure, it's definitely the "Real Washington" and it's a lovely site, but it's a very small slice of the pie. Instead, make this a one or two nighter as part of a larger camping trip, or use this as a stopover to a more complex campground. But when you do stay here, pay close attention. The campground faces a beautiful green area that includes a pioneer cemetery and the Ritzville water tower. There is a vibrancy to this small town that is infectious, particularly in this newer section of town, providing more than meets the eye.

Local Attractions: Two museums in Ritzville are heritage tourism destinations: The Dr. Frank R. Burroughs Home (1890) and the Railroad Depot Museum (1910). The downtown area includes the fine Carnegie Library (1907). Historic Ritzville Days, a festival held over Memorial Day weekend, celebrates the community's history and ethnic heritage.

Cow Lake CG (Adams Co.'s *BEST RUSTIC CG* and *MOST APPEALING CG TO THE SENSES*)
Cow Lake is a muddy and shallow lake/reservoir in the rolling sage brush covered hills on the northeast side of Adams County. Cow Creek, which drains Sprague Lake, forms Cow Lake, with cattle lapping at the water on the west end. This is Columbia Basin farm country -- life is very basic here, and so is the camping.

Overview: This 100% rustic campground is located 9 miles east of Ritzville on 199.3-acre Cow Lake, operated by the WDFW at 1753' elevation, open year-round; GPS 47.13471679, -118.1600882.

Facilities: A road and a hand boat launch. Nothing else.

Recreation: There is good fishing for black crappie, bluegill, brown bullhead, grass pickerel, largemouth bass, and rainbow trout. Kayaking and canoeing are excellent.

Campsites (Dispersed tent sites only, no reservations, FREE with Discover Pass) Dispersed camping is most popular along the rocky and muddy shore of the east end of the Lake (the western shores are privately owned). The camping area consists of a small, tight, grassy loop protected from the road by rock outcroppings. There are some 6-12' cliffs, plus a large 9-acre island in the middle of the Lake.

Trip Notes: Our expectations of this were low. Cow Lake? We pictured dodging cow pies through muddy pasture on the way to a murky lake with cattle drinking from the other side. But the lake is beautiful and complex, with many bursts of color and texture. It seems to change and evolve as the sun moves and clouds move in and out. We were impressed by the mere beauty of the place but scheduled an all too short visit on the way to greener pastures. Don't make the same mistake.

The delicacy/subtlety of the desert creates surprising bursts of color and texture.

Sprague Lake

This sprawling 1841-acre lake gives up 673 of its acres to cut across the northeast corner of Adams County. Most people know it only as the lake that parallels Interstate 90 about 35 miles west of Spokane. What they don't know is that it produces some of the best fishing and windsurfing in this part of the State.

Four Seasons CG and Resort (Adams Co.'s *BEST CG FOR ENTIRE FAMILIES*)
This tucked away campground sits on a game reserve, guaranteeing you will see wildlife during every visit. Go fishing with the rest or float your kayak out to the

island just offshore and see what the birds do in this quiet, undisturbed corner of the county.

Overview: This cozy campground is located 6 miles west of Sprague on 67 acres with one mile of shoreline on Sprague Lake, privately operated at 1883' elevation, open April 10 to Oct 1st; GPS: 47.2885, -118.0225.

Facilities: The Resort facilities include bathrooms with showers, running water, picnic tables and fire grills, swimming pool, boat rentals, fish cleaning privy, boat launch, Camp Store, and camp hosts.

Recreation: This west end of Sprague Lake has a consistent low-level wind with gusts up to 20 knots and is the deepest part of the Lake. This gives a big advantage for windsurfing and windsailing, as launching is best here. Additionally, it is great for fishermen, offering shoreline, dock, and boat fishing for bluegill, channel catfish, black crappie, yellow perch, rainbow and cutthroat trout, and largemouth bass. It also faces Harper Island, a designated bird refuge, making good wildlife viewing. Moose and deer also frequent the area. Lake swimming is not permitted due to algae blooms.

Campsites (38 tent and RV sites w/full hookups 30-amp and 4 rental cabins, all reservable): Sites are spacious with ample vegetation. Tent sites are on a sloped hillside overlooking the dock, while the RV sites are side-by-side and well-spaced, all facing the Lake.

Trip Notes: I normally don't list a campground centered around a single activity other than camping, but the camping can be quite good. The proprietor was extremely welcoming, eager to show pictures of the huge trout pulled from 7-mile Sprague Lake by his campers. The grounds were meticulously manicured and watered. The cabins are well-maintained single-wide trailers. It was surprisingly quiet, despite the presence of railroad tracks and I-90 within throwing distance. This could be a good camping experience, but may not be great for young children, although older children interested in fishing or sailing will love it.

For more photos of Adams Co. CGs consult campeverycountywa.com

ASOTIN COUNTY (Clarkston/Asotin/Anatone)

Tucked away in the southeastern corner of Washington State lies the Wild West County of Asotin, with its colorful history as part of the Lewis and Clark Trail and former Nez Perce Indian Reservation. The county is calmer now, part of the Banana Belt of Washington and a county for all seasons with summer sports along the Snake River, year-round fishing on the Grande Ronde River, and hiking and winter sports in the Blue Mountains.

Snake River Region
The Snake River defines the northern and eastern boundary of Asotin Co. with two distinct sections. The portion extending in an east-west direction is a series of lakes, formed by the damming and taming of this otherwise wild and mighty river. The north-south portion of the river flows freely, being undammed, and leading into the remarkable Snake River Canyon, better known as Hells Canyon. Recreation here varies from quiet camping on islands in the Snake River to whitewater rafting on one of the most challenging river runs in the country.

Chief Timothy Park (Asotin Co.'s *MOST UNIQUELY WASHINGTON CG, BEST EQUIPPED/BEST CG FOR RVs* and *BEST CG FOR ENTIRE FAMILIES*)
This glacially formed island is a genuinely "desert" island with its stark desert landscape that will also give you the desert experience while surrounded by lush vegetation and wildlife.
Overview: This 198-acre park is located 8 miles west of Clarkston on 282-acre Silcott Island in the Snake River with a bridge to the mainland, operated by Northwest Land Management for the US Army COE at 807' elevation, open April through September; GPS 46.41550, -117.19422.

Facilities: This well-equipped park includes bathrooms with showers, Wi-Fi, picnic tables, fire pits, a nice playground, volleyball court, boat launch, tie up dock, swimming area, campsite hosts, and an RV dump.

Recreation: The island is all yours -- there are no permanent residents. Enjoy boating, swimming, horseshoes, and nature trails.

Campsites (16 tent sites, 17 tent/RV sites, and 33 sites for RVs up to 40', including 13 with full hookups and 8 with water & electric 30-amp, 4 cabins, reservable): This part of the Snake River forms Granite Lake, situated east of the Little Goose Dam. Sites sit on the lake's calm waters and are grassy and shady with adequate privacy. Parking pads are paved. Much like Crow Butte Park in Benton Co., the campground is the only irrigated part of the island.

Trip Notes: The Park was far lusher and greener than we anticipated. The trouble was that you run out of island pretty quickly, but the staff was so welcoming we felt part of a small close-knit community and wanted to stay much longer. The campground and Day Use Area occupies about half of the land, and the rest is rather arid with little vegetation. It's a great all-around park, and best described as a smaller version of Crow Butte CG in Benton Co., but with a more personal feel.

Washington History: The Park is named after Nez Perce Indian Chief Temuut'su (or Timothy) who saved the lives of Colonel Edward J. Steptoe's troops in 1858, guiding them to safety, after their defeat during an Indian uprising in the Battle of Tohotonimme. Timothy was known as the "Bighorn Chief" because he wore the horn of a bighorn sheep under his arm and remained a friend of the pioneers throughout his lifetime.

Blue Mountain Region

This is the Pacific Northwest's "unknown" mountain range, tucked away in the remote corners of southeastern Washington and northeastern Oregon. It is named for the deep blue hue of its pine trees and known for its deep river valleys and modest peaks, ranging from 1600' to 6500' in height, forming a rampart against Hells Canyon, which plunges over one mile to the Snake River below.

Fields Spring S. P. (Asotin Co.'s *MOST APPEALING CG TO THE SENSES*)

This Blue Mountain beauty sits on top of Puffer Butte with spectacular views of three states, including the Grande Ronde River, the Snake River Canyon, and the Wallowa Mountains. Wildflowers in the spring give way to huckleberries, wildlife and blue skies to match the mountains in the summer, before becoming blanketed with snow for the winter.

Overview: This remote 792-acre park is located 30 miles south of Clarkston and 4.5 miles south of Anatone at 4003' elevation, open year-round; GPS 46.0816, -117.1674.

Facilities: This uniquely equipped campground includes flush toilets, running water, showers, one ADA bathroom, picnic tables, fire grills, playground equipment, and one kitchen shelter with electricity. Rentals include Wohelo Lodge (capacity for 20), Puffer Butte Lodge (capacity for up to 80), Tamarack Cabin (sleeps 4), and two teepees (sleep 8 each). The two teepees combine for a unique and remarkable Group Camp and are available July through Labor Day.

Summer Recreation: Includes 3 miles of hiking trails and 7 miles of biking trails with views that simultaneously include Washington, Oregon, and Idaho. Berry picking is also popular.

Winter Recreation: This groomed Blue Mountain Sno-Park features cross-country skiing tracks, a 9km skating lane, a designated snowshoe route, a tubing hill, designated snow play area, warming huts, and sanitary facilities. This is one of the most extensive sno-parks in the Washington S.P. system. A Sno-Park Pass is required.

Campsites (20 sites for tents and RVs up to 30', no hookups, 2 teepees & 1 cabin & 2 lodges, no reservations): Campsites are private, but awkwardly arranged and hilly. Camping areas are covered with ponderosa pine, Douglas fir, grand fir, and western larch -- a far cry from the dry wheat land plateau in the northern half of the County.

Trip notes: This meandering park is great for dog walking and hiking. The campground itself offers a variety of scenery with farmhouses, cabins, teepees and Tamarack Cabin for rent, retreat houses, and the actual spring, framed with "vintage" rockery and wood planking, reminiscent of the 1940s. We had a short stay, and did not hike the trails, which are a main draw.

Grande Ronde River

This magnificent river forms a giant loop beginning in the Blue Mountains of Oregon. Once flowing through Oregon's rugged canyons, it crosses the Washington border and snakes 40 miles through open, grass covered hills with forested pockets and tributary canyons before flowing into the Snake River at Washington State's southeasternmost point. Around every bend of this serpentine river lies another bend, and with each bend a complete change in scenery. One bend may show only basalt cliffs; another might stumble upon mountain goats dropping down to the water's edge; while yet another may reveal a magnificent vista of wildflowers and mountain peaks. It's all there for the visiting.

Bezona CG (Asotin Co.'s *BEST BIKE-IN CG, BEST RUSTIC CG* and *BEST FREE CG*)
This rustic little campground can boast only of its simplicity, being a quiet getaway, or a launching pad for fishing or boating on the Grande Ronde River.
Overview: This remote and primitive campground is located 31.4 miles south of

Asotin on the Grande Ronde River, operated by the WDFW at 1274' elevation, and open year-round; GPS 46.03511, -117.27360.

<u>Facilities</u>: Vault toilets are the only amenity in this primitive campground. The river water is pure enough for drinking.

<u>Recreation</u>: In short, the campground is about one magnificent river. From September to April it is one of Washington's best steelhead streams. During the summer you can enjoy shore fishing for smallmouth bass, channel catfish, chinook salmon, summer run steelhead, sturgeon, bull and rainbow trout. Whitewater rafting is popular along this entire river. A pleasant 27-mile long stretch of grade II-IV whitewater stretch from Bezona to the river's mouth at Heller Bar on the Snake River. Two put-in sites lie upstream from Bezona at Botts and Cottonwood (great for tube floaters); other put-in/take-outs can be found at Boggans Oasis (also good for tube floaters), Shumaker Grade, Ebsen, and ultimately Heller Bar (all more appropriate for kayakers).

<u>Campsites</u> (several sites for tents or small RVs, no hookups or reservations, FREE with Discover Pass): Sites on gravel pads, partly shady, very flat, and private due to low use.

<u>Trip Notes/Directions</u>: To find the site travelling south on Hwy 128 just south of Anatone you will come to a series of extreme switchbacks. At the base of this hill at Boggan's Oasis turn west on Grande Ronde Rd and drive 1.6 miles. Bezona CG lies on the left of the first of 3 areas marked for "Public Fishing."

The serpentine Grande Ronde River has surprises around every bend

For more photos of Asotin Co. CGs consult campeverycountywa.com

BENTON COUNTY (Prosser/Richland/Kennewick)

Benton County was named for Missouri Senator Thomas Hart Benton (1821-1851), or "Old Bullion," who was a staunch advocate for westward expansion. The County was once sage-steppe desert, but with irrigation from the confluence of the Columbia, Snake, and Yakima Rivers, this county transformed from bunch grass and sagebrush to farm products like wheat, alfalfa, grapes, strawberries, and potatoes, producing much "bullion" to spark the local economy. Later industries included shipping, nuclear power and (Eureka!) tourism and outdoor recreation.

The Columbia River After the Big Bend

The Benton Co. section of the Columbia River downstream from the Big Bend leaves the Tri-Cities (Richland, Kennewick, and Pasco) and turns westward to a stretch of the River that is sparsely populated. The towns of Paterson, Plymouth and a few wineries are all that join the Umatilla Wildlife Refuge, a series of islands formed by the damming of the mighty Columbia. The islands hold many species of ducks, geese, mule deer, quail, pheasants, plus at least 2 good campgrounds from which to appreciate them.

Crow Butte Park (Benton Co.'s BEST CG FOR FAMILIES and *MOST APPEALING CG TO THE SENSES*)
This campground is rated by some as the most popular campground in Washington; local promoters tout it as the "Maui of the Columbia." Silly people, this is desert after all. But it is a well-managed desert island experience that is one of our favorites.
Overview: This utterly unique campground is located 14.5 miles west of Paterson occupying an entire 1500-acre Columbia River island with a bridge to the mainland,

run by the Port of Benton at an elevation of 641', open March 15 - Oct 31; GPS 45.85541, -119.8511.

Facilities: Wonderfully equipped with Day Use and overnight facilities, these include bathrooms with showers, picnic tables and fire pits, a protected swimming area, concession stand, playground, hiking trails, boat ramp, marina, RV dump, and camp hosts.

Recreation: We strongly recommend hiking every trail on the island, as they lead to remote beaches, and sweeping views of the Umatilla Wildlife Refuge to the east, with its many islands. Just watch out for rattlesnakes. Boating, swimming, and fishing are also popular.

Campsites: (50 sites for tents and RVs up to 90' with full hookups 20/30/50-amp, one primitive Group Camp for up to 100 people, reservable): Sites are arranged in one large loop with thorough irrigation -- spacious and grassy with adequate privacy. About half are on the water. The large shade trees provide a cooling effect in an otherwise very hot area. The sprawling, grassy Day Use Area is adjacent to the camping area, with the marina just beyond, making the Park seem much larger.

Trip Notes: Our much-anticipated trip to the "most popular campground in WA" was mostly favorable. The entire greenbelt from the marina through the huge day use area and the spacious camping area were lush and green. Large trees provided shade, and a cool breeze off the Columbia River kept us comfortable most days. This entire strip was meticulous with unobtrusive caretakers. The trails were not well maintained (nor are they irrigated), with sagebrush blocking the paths in several places -- all the while warning of rattlesnakes. Also, the train and highway noise was pretty persistent. The main campground lends itself mostly to large and small RVs, though tent camping would be glorious. The detached Group Camp was not as lush as the main campground/Day Use Area/marina, was somewhat shabby, unused during our stay, and cannot be recommended. However, the bottom line is this fits our ultimate criteria for camping: Would we have been happy staying within the Park without leaving? The answer is a resounding YES, as it is the best of getaways. One word of warning, however. This Park is very remote, and the nearest store is 14.5 miles away in Paterson. Even this has very limited stock, so come prepared and plan to stay put.

Plymouth Park (Benton Co.'s *BEST EQUIPPED/BEST* CG FOR RVs and *BEST BIKE-IN CG*)

No pilgrims at this Plymouth, but the small town and park were named for a huge basaltic rock that projects into the Columbia River, considerably larger than the original Plymouth Rock. The Park has become popular with RV'ers, tenters, and bicyclists who like to rest near this intersection of Highway 12 and Interstate 83, pondering their options in all directions.

Overview: Located 26 miles south of Kennewick near the Columbia River, operated by the US Army COE at 285' elevation, open April 1 to October 31; GPS 45.9332, -119.3481.

Facilities include flush and pit toilets, showers, drinking water, picnic tables, fire grills, laundry facilities, playground, RV dump station and camp hosts. The Day Use Area (located on a small island on Lake Umatilla on the Columbia River) has a swimming beach, boat ramp, and courtesy dock. Although this is regarded as a mostly RV campground, it is good for bicyclers due to its proximity to Highway 14 with amenities and services (albeit limited) in the small town of Plymouth.

Recreation: This includes fishing for chinook, shad, steelhead, sturgeon, and walleye; star gazing, swimming, boating, water skiing and hunting. Mule deer, waterfowl and raptors are commonly seen.

Campsites (32 sites for tents and RVs up to 45', 16 with full hookups and 16 with electric & water 30/50-amp, reservable): This tidy, well-maintained park is covered with tall sage and Russian olive trees for shade, with some sites more exposed. Sites are flat, well-spaced, and mostly pull-throughs, but provide only minimal privacy. There is some road noise.

Trip Notes: This is one of the most meticulous campgrounds around, with all paved roads and parking pads. The grounds are lush and grassy, with a very garden-like atmosphere. The Day Use Area, though popular with fishermen and swimmers, is more arid and brushier.

Local Attractions: McNary Dam and Visitor Center and Lake Wallula are two miles upstream from the campground.

The Lower Yakima River

The Yakima River winds its way to north Richland before taking a U-turn southward to empty into the Columbia River. On this final stretch lies the 19th Century Horn Rapids Dam where fish rushing over the spillway attract flocks of pelicans and bird watchers who enjoy these graceful creatures with their long necks and throat pouches siphoning up nature's bounty.

Horn Rapids Co. Park (Benton Co.'s *MOST UNIQUELY WASHINGTON CG*)

This is Benton Co.'s premier natural area with many unique and eclectic features. Flocks of pelicans ordinarily found near saltwater, gather regularly at the rapids on the Yakima River. Insect lovers come here to visit this renowned sanctuary for the quantity and variety of dragonflies. A model airplane facility run by the Miniature Aircraft Association provides space for remote-control plane flying. That is only the beginning -- they really pack it in here.

Overview: Located 9.9 miles northwest of Richland with 4 miles of Yakima River frontage on 800 acres, operated by Benton Co. Parks at 375' elevation, open May to September; GPS 46.380968, -119.43391.

Facilities include are bathrooms with showers, piped water, picnic tables, fire grills, boat launch, a Day Use Area with a kiosk/gazebo, hiking/biking trails, equestrian facilities, an RV dump, and camp hosts in the summer.

Recreation: This includes fishing for small mouth bass, catfish, trout, and salmon. The area is pending as an "Important Bird Area" by the Audubon Society. Stargazing/astronomy opportunities are good. There is no swimming due to swift currents.

Campsites (16 sites for tents or RVs of any size, full hookups 30/50-amp, reservable): The camping area is one large loop with shade trees on two sides and one towering weeping willow in the middle. The flat and spacious sites have paved pads, average privacy, and are a mixture of pull-throughs and back-ins in a mostly open area with many acres of well-manicured and well-watered lawns.

Trip Notes: Watching the snow-white pelicans lined up underneath the spillway of the Rapids is a site to behold, where these well-fed beauties have found the ultimate "all you can eat fish buffet." There is a gun range close by, and a shooting tournament was in action during our stay, but we heard no noise. The boat launch and fishing area gave a remarkable view of the beautiful Yakima River around the Horn, with its many towering trees, white houses, sea planes, and farmlands beyond. This is, however, a place where you'll have to walk outside your campsite to appreciate the beauty and complexity of this place.

The City of Prosser and Environs

These days, Prosser is known as the Birthplace of Washington Wine. While many foodies across the State are forever grateful, Prosser has long been home to Native Americans who lived here along the Yakima River. They called the region "tap tut" meaning rapids, and the wide-open spaces to the south came to be known as the Horse Heaven Hills that were their hunting grounds for centuries.

Horse Heaven Hills (Benton Co.'s *BEST FREE and RUSTIC CAMPSITES*)
Bands of wild horses once roamed here, in the formerly arid lands between the lower Yakima Valley and Columbia River. Today it is ranked among the most fertile irrigated lands in the U.S. of A, named an American Viticultural Area with livestock, multiple crops, a host of wineries and, if campers look carefully, the occasional campsite from which to view this remarkable area from the inside out.

Overview: Located primarily just south of the area between Prosser and Benton City, operated by the BLM, open year-round; GPS 46.245328, -119.520915.

Facilities: The only area with amenities is the BLM Horse Heaven Vista Unit (don't confuse with Horse Heaven Vista Park in Prosser) and includes a privy, a viewing kiosk, a huge interpretive sign, and a 2-acre parking/camping area. There is no water.

Recreation: There is hiking in the area, including the top of McBee Hill (a 2- mile day hike) and a 6.8-mile round trip hike starting just south of Kiona (trailhead GPS 46.2391, -119.4847). Multiple breweries and wineries in the area include McKinley Springs Winery, Chateau Champoux, Zefina Winery, and Columbia Crest Winery near Paterson.

Campsites (dispersed camping, no water or reservations, FREE of charge): A special note: This area is largely private cropland, which owners must guard for their livelihood. Be respectful of private property and restrict camping to the edges of parking lots and public rest areas that are not marked otherwise.

Trip Notes: We came expecting arid, barren hillsides and dust in our coffee. What we found instead were rolling, verdant farmlands, with better viticultural vistas of the lower Yakima Valley than we have ever seen. We entered from the tiny community of Kiona and drove up west of N.McBee Rd where we looked down on Benton City and the many signs that said NO CAMPING! Just beyond, a gravel side road entered at an angle, creating a small bowl-like camping/parking area (which is also the trailhead for McBee Hill trail). We followed the roads west until we found ourselves above the City of Prosser and pulled into what looked like an unmarked rest stop. Here we found a viewing kiosk with unobstructed views of the valley below, a privy, parking lot, a huge interpretive sign, and a flat area beyond where truckers and campers often stop for the night. While this is not the most remote area in the Horse Heaven Hills, it is certainly the most accessible and the one we chose.

The interpretive sign in Horse Heaven Hills overlooking the City of Prosser

For more photos of Benton Co. CGs consult campeverycountywa.com

Mount Cashmere keeps a watchful eye on Johnny Creek Campground

Wenatchee Confluence S.P. combines campground and Wildlife Refuge

Lake Chelan is synonymous with water recreation

Napeequa Crossing takes you into the wilderness, but stays close enough in for comfort

Camp-panions Brendan and Gary pose before Lake Wenatchee

Entiat Park shows off its "Entiattitude"

CHELAN COUNTY (Wenatchee/Leavenworth/Chelan)

90% of this large county is owned by state and federal governments, providing not only hydroelectric power and irrigation, but many and varied recreational opportunities. From the alpine village of Leavenworth to the grandeur of Lake Chelan, Washington's largest natural lake, you will be drawn in by stunning beauty.

Lake Chelan Region

"Chelan" is a Salish Indian word meaning both "lake" and "blue water." The Lake is the third deepest lake in the U.S. with a depth of 1486'. From the country's most remote resort at Stehekin to the not-so-remote town of Chelan, this 55-mile pristine azure lake will forever change the way you view camping in Eastern Washington.

Lake Chelan S.P. (Chelan Co.'s *BEST CG FOR ENTIRE FAMILIES*)
This is the premier campground of awe-inspiring Lake Chelan, and one of the most "everybody oriented" parks anywhere.
Overview: This most iconic of campgrounds is located 7 miles north of Chelan on 127 acres with 6000' of west Lake Chelan shoreline at 1140' elevation, open Feb.1 to Nov. 1; GPS 47.8716, -120.1961.
Facilities: The Park is well-equipped with bathrooms/showers, fire rings/grills, picnic tables, a playground, a large sandy swimming area, a boat ramp plus 495' of dock, grassy play fields, 0.2 miles of ADA trails, 2 miles of hiking trails, an RV dump, and campground hosts. This is also a stop for Lady of the Lake Ferry.
Recreation: Trout records are often broken here. Fishing is best for Chinook salmon, kokanee, lake and rainbow trout. Swimming is also king, as are boating, jet skiing, and water skiing.
Campsites (146 sites, including 18 with water & electric 50-amp hookups plus 17 with full hookups, reservable): Most sites have lake views. The news is good for tenters and bad for RV'ers. RV sites 1-35 are in full sun (and it gets intense), are

very small and back up to desert vegetation. Newer tent sites (36-76) have been built on the hillside overlooking the Lake. While sloped sites are normally a big negative, these are brilliantly designed, with individual stairways and well-terraced. Some sites have 2 or 3 small landings: one for a tent, one for a picnic table, and one for viewing the Lake. All drop down to a walkway along the water for fishing, boating, or watching the unbelievable scenery. The most popular sites are in the West Loop (sites 72-144) which are shaded and more private, with a few sites lining a small creek. Overall this is still the best of the Lake Chelan campgrounds for children. For alternatives, 25-Mile Creek S.P. (see website) may be a better launching point for activities in the north Lake Chelan Area and better for those with large RVs who need hookups.

Trip Notes: Though we grew up on Willapa Bay, a place surrounded by water, our parents say my brothers and I practically learned to swim at Lake Chelan. We had daily opportunities to swim in rivers, the bay, and the ocean, but we naturally took to Lake Chelan and preferred it. Leave it to kids to declare the obvious.

Local Alternative: Twenty-Five Mile Creek S.P. lies just 2 miles north of Lake Chelan S.P. Some view it as an overflow campground for Lake Chelan CG, but it has its own character. RV'ers are happier here, and this is the preferred CG of the Camp Every County crew. We saw several larger RVs meticulously squeeze into small spaces with good results. Despite having less privacy than Lake Chelan S.P., this might better suit those more interested in camping than the activities available. Sacrifice a little space and privacy for less noise and hubbub? We're in.

Highway 2/Cascade Region

This eastern section of the Cascades is unlike the other eastern slopes -- the same atmosphere that made it very natural for the City of Leavenworth to transform itself into a Bavarian alpine village. That environment permeates every valley, creek, and river in this exceptionally beautiful region.

Lake Wenatchee S.P. (Chelan Co.'s BEST EQUIPPED/BEST CG FOR RVs)

This park is where you can watch a mighty river spring out of a mighty lake both summer and winter.

Overview: This Park is located 20 miles west of Leavenworth on 489 acres with 12,623' of shoreline on Lake Wenatchee at 1473' elevation, only South Camp is open during winter months; GPS 47.812, -120.7222.

Facilities: These include bathrooms with showers, picnic tables, fire rings, 2 kitchen shelters, amphitheater, boat ramp with 16' of dock, 5 miles of horse trails and concessions offering 1 and 2-hour horse rides, 7 miles of biking trails, 8 miles of hiking trails, Camp Store, RV dump, and camp hosts.

Activities: Windsurfing is good here, particularly in June and July. Equipment rentals are available in Leavenworth, with many more in Wenatchee. Fisher folk will have better luck at Fish Lake just one mile northeast.

Winter Activities: In winter the park converts to a groomed Sno-Park featuring 35km of cross-country tracks, 8km of snowshoe trails, skating lanes, a 1.1-mile interpretive snowshoe trail, and a tubing hill. The Day Use Area in the South Camp is also open for winter camping. A Groomed Sno-Park Pass is required.

Campsites (North Camp: 97 sites for tents or RVs of any size w/water & electric 50 amps; South Camp: 100 sites, no hookups, one Group Camp for 20-80 people with tents only, all reservable): Sites are large and spotted with Ponderosa pines allowing average to good privacy. We found the North Loop better overall.

Trip notes: Great for short walks. The Lake is rugged and stunning, framed by mountains. There is an intoxicating "piney woods" smell here very representative of eastern Washington. My dog spent hours leaping like a deer through the underbrush taunting and being taunted by squirrels. Huge boulders dropped by glaciers a few millennia back provided perches to climb and watch the activity from above. The brisk, whistling wind at the lakeshore disappeared like a switch when you stepped away, giving the lake a very foreboding air. Overall, this was an especially good, relaxing camping environment.

Local Alternatives: Glacier View CG is set at the opposite end of Lake Wenatchee, near its head, with 23 non-reservable walk-in sites that sit right on the Lake with killer views, surrounded by towering mountains. Nason Creek is a USFS campground near Lake Wenatchee with 73 sites suitable for tents or large RVs. Both are highly recommended.

Napeequa Crossing CG (Chelan Co.'s BEST FREE CG)
Napeequa is a Salishan word meaning "white water" because the river is nearly white in spring and summer due to glacial melt in this U-shaped trough through which the Napeequa River meanders in this most interesting of valleys.

Overview: This very basic campground is located 31.2 miles northwest of Leavenworth (6 miles beyond Lake Wenatchee) at the junction of the White and Napeequa Rivers, operated by the USFS at 1942' elevation, open year-round, FREE of charge; GPS 47.921, -120.896.

Facilities: Limited amenities include vault toilets, picnic tables, and fire grills. There is no drinking water.

Recreation: Hiking is excellent, the star being dramatic, kid and dog friendly Twin Lakes Trail #1503, which starts at the campground. The 8.4-mile round trip trail into the Glacier Peak Wilderness passes miles of wild ginger with views of Mt. David, wetlands, giant cedars, and of course two alpine lakes. There is one river crossing, so spring and summer are best. Note that that there is no fishing in the Napeequa River.

Campsites (5 sites for tents or RVs up to 30', no hookups or reservations): Sites are on native material, with good privacy due to spacing in this moderately forested campground with black cottonwood, western red cedar, big-leaf maples, Douglas fir, and Ponderosa pine. The site just before the kiosk is huge, with small finger trails leading to other tent sites among the trees and could easily be adapted to fit a multi-family group of friends.

Trip Notes: This was a solo effort on my part, just the dogs and me. The two rivers, especially the White River, provided a backdrop of both visual and audible beauty. This campground has been around the block -- very old, obsolete wooden signs are posted in seemingly random places, though it didn't feel as remote as I anticipated, as a Christian kid's camp was just across the bridge over the Napeequa River. There seemed to be visual surprises as you moved around the area -- unexpected mountain views, trails, and markings that reminded me that a lot of campers have been here before. Just one warning: bring extra bug spray, and even a fogger.

Local Alternative: White River Falls CG, just down the road, is a beautiful alternative that is also FREE. The caution is that viewing is very treacherous, as there is no viewing platform or direct view of the falls. Both injuries and deaths have been reported. This is also walk-in camping with no specified parking area. But it provides quiet forested camping for those who don't want much company.

Icicle Creek/Leavenworth Area

Icicle Creek is not a frozen stream with icicles but derives its name from the native word na-sik-elt (or a-sik-el) meaning "narrow canyon." More to the point, Icicle Creek sits in a long, narrow canyon in the "American Alps" dotted with a wide variety of campgrounds.

Johnny Creek CG (Chelan Co.'s *MOST APPEALING CGs TO THE SENSES*)
Johnny? Who's Johnny? No one seems to know; and while some might assume this translates into "Plain Jane Campground" or "Generic Eastern Washington Campground," the babbling woodland Johnny Creek, the wild water of Icicle Creek, and the towering Washington Alps prove otherwise.

Overview: This Park is nicely located 12.4 miles southwest of Leavenworth near the confluence of Johnny Creek and Icicle Creek, operated by the USFS at 3100' elevation, open April 20 to October 15; GPS 47.5983, -120.8182.

Facilities: Standard USFS touches include vault toilets (ADA), drinking water, picnic tables, fire pits/grills, an RV dump, and camp hosts.

Recreation: Hiking is central here, ranging from easy to very difficult: Icicle Creek Nature Trail (1 mile loop), Icicle Gorge Trail (3.5-mile loop, good for families), Colchuck Lake (9-mile loop, 2000' elevation gain), Fourth of July Creek (12-mile round trip, 4400' gain), and The Enchantments (18-mile loop, 6000' gain). White water rafting comes in a close second, with access points at most Icicle Creek campgrounds. Fishing on Icicle Creek is good for Chinook, Coho and trout. Gold-panning and rock hounding are said to be good. And of course, the town of Leavenworth provides activities for the Bavarian in all of us.

Campsites (65 sites including 5 walk-in sites and 9 double sites, no hookups or reservations): Sites are in two sections - the larger, sunnier Upper Section across the road from Icicle Creek, and a smaller Lower Section with pull-through sites right on Icicle Creek. Best sites are 1, 2, 5, 6, 7, 10, 41, and 116. Pad sites are gravel, sites in the Upper Section can accommodate RVs up to 50'. Sites are shady/partial sun, and medium to large in size with good privacy, particularly in the Upper Section.

Trip Notes: To say "ah-sic-al" is a narrow canyon is an understatement. It is narrow like the edge of a razor blade and seems to suddenly close in on you. Fortunately, it widens slightly by the time you hit Johnny Creek, and is more cozy than confining. Walk-in tent site 41 is typical of the surprising array of campsites. Here, little Johnny Creek divides into two smaller streams forming waterfalls, then rejoins at the far end of the site. Sites along Icicle Creek rest on raging water with a direct view of Mt. Cashmere. It is easy to see why this campground is a favorite among residents of Leavenworth.

Local Alternatives: There are really no bad campgrounds along Icicle Creek Road. Starting nearest Leavenworth and going west, we have Eightmile CG (45 sites for tents or RVs up to 50'), then Johnny Creek CG. Ida Creek CG comes next (10 sites and quieter), then Rock Island CG with the best access to the Alpine Lakes Wilderness, and Blackpine Horse Camp for equestrians. Also sandwiched in are two group camps (Bridge Creek and Chatter Creek).

Columbia River Region

The bad news is that this stretch of the Columbia has been dammed beyond recognition. The good news is that it has been managed very well with great efforts to both restore the River and provide exceptional recreational possibilities.

Wenatchee Confluence S.P. (Chelan Co.'s *MOST UNIQUELY WASHINGTON CG*)

This park was created to reclaim what was lost in the damming of the Columbia, namely, the native natural flora of the shoreline (see Horan Natural Area, below). It achieves that end quite well, plus gives great camping in the middle of a growing city that is dubbed the Apple Capital of Washington.

Overview: This Park is strategically located within the city limits of Wenatchee on 197 acres with 8,625' of freshwater shoreline along the confluence of the Columbia and Wenatchee Rivers at 780' elevation, open year-round; GPS 47.4596, -120.3272.

Facilities: Included are 6 bathrooms with flush toilets (all ADA), 16 showers (8 ADA), a playground, swimming area, boat launch, 4.5 miles of hiking trails, an RV dump, and camp hosts.

Recreation: Bird watching is a given here, with too many species to mention. The most notable are bald and golden eagles, Barrow's goldeneye, black and Vaux's swifts, Calliope and Rufous hummingbirds, Cassin's vireo, common loons, greater scaups, greater white-fronted geese, Hammonds flycatchers, Lewis's and pileated woodpeckers, red-naped sapsuckers, and western bluebirds. Wildlife includes beavers, mink, mule deer, muskrats, otters, and raccoons. The 11-mile Apple Capital Recreation Trail for pedestrians, cyclists, dog walkers, in-line skaters, and joggers circles the Columbia River with 10 miles of asphalt trails. This connects Wenatchee Waterfront Park (with a sculpture garden and narrow-gauge railroad) and Walla Walla Point Park (with sports fields and a swimming lagoon) to the Confluence camping area and Horan Natural Area. Spurs on the Douglas County side of the river connect to Lincoln Rock S.P. and 70-acre Kirby Billingsly Hydro Park. Vegetation within Horan includes a very rare stand of black cottonwood.

Campsites (51 sites with full hookups 30 amps, one Group Camp for 50-300, reservable): Sites are large and grassy, but it is a challenge to balance privacy with adequate shade. The camping area, the North Confluence, has the feel of a very large RV park, but the South Confluence is a man-made wetland area known as the Horan Natural Area. It is a series of canals, small islands, upland vegetation, and wood duck nest boxes, which in turn provide habitat for birds, reptiles, amphibians, and small mammals. Many species of plants are found nowhere else in the world. Visitors can walk the gravel pathways and take this in from 15 viewing sites/kiosks.

Trip Notes: The North Confluence camping area is very bright and cheery, with sufficient room for privacy. It is one sprawling green lawn dotted with mature shade trees, a great place to enjoy the sun without overexposure. The South Confluence/Horan Natural Area has been left in a very natural state, not like a botanical garden, which I appreciated. It provides an opportunity to escape the human world and get back to nature.

Washington History: The Confluence was an important gathering place for Native Americans. It soon gave way to orchards owned by the Horan Family. In 1990, 100 acres were purchased by the Chelan County PUD and converted to a wetland as mitigation for the creation of the Rocky Reach Dam to the north in order to protect native species. Thus, the Horan Natural Area was formed.

Local Attractions: The most intriguing side trip is to Ohme Gardens, a 40-acre Garden Park on top of a craggy bluff overlooking the City of Wenatchee. Here you will find elaborately constructed rock gardens, trails, ponds, and meticulous plantings that make for a great day out.

Entiat City Park (Chelan Co.'s *BEST BIKE-IN CG*)
The City of Entiat, which has been displaced numerous times due to damming of the Columbia River, justifiably boasts of its "Entiattitude," durability, and love of the outdoors.
Overview: This well-equipped and well-appointed campground is located 17 miles north of Wenatchee on Lake Entiat (Columbia River), operated by the Chelan Co. PUD on 40 acres, open year-round; GPS 47.669413, -120.21694.
Facilities: The Park has restrooms with showers (ADA), 2 picnic shelters, an outdoor museum, playground, marina with a 2-lane boat launch, laundry, camp hosts, and an RV dump.
Recreation includes swimming, boating, and fishing on Lake Entiat.
Campsites (26 tent sites and 31 sites for RVs of any size with full hookups 30-amp, reservable, open year-round): The sites are arranged somewhat in the traditional side-by-side RV Park style, but are well appointed and run lengthwise along the river, avoiding the congestion of a large grid. The entire campground is meticulously planted with lawns, shrubbery, and flowers.
Trip Notes: Wow. When did all this happen? 2015, that's when. Everything is new, modern, and inviting. The small amount of traffic noise is nothing when you're right on the water. Entiat has just enough facilities within walking distance to accommodate bicyclers and most other campers. This is the envy of city parks, with its extensive waterfront, rolling Day Use Area, and unique touches that makes it a complete package for everyone from bicyclers to the most ardent RV'ers.

Glacier Peak Wilderness Area
The 566,057-acre Glacier Peak Wilderness features 10,541-foot Glacier Peak, the most remote major volcanic peak in the Cascade Range with more active glaciers than any other place in the lower forty-eight states. Popular with wilderness hikers and campers, there are recreational opportunities of all kinds.

Silver Falls CG (Chelan Co.'s *BEST RUSTIC CG*)
Silver Falls has not just one, but a series of waterfalls extending along a half-mile trail. And the campground is so uniquely appointed by the handiwork of the CCC that the two, the campground and the Falls, fit together to make the perfect camping combination.
Overview: This rustic gem is located 31 miles northwest of Entiat on 26 acres at the junction of the Entiat River and Silver Creek, operated by the USFS at 2400' elevation, open Memorial Day to Labor Day; GPS 47.95806, -120.5375.
Facilities: USFS amenities include vault toilets, drinking water, picnic tables, fire rings, and a camp host (summer only).

The handiwork of the Civilian Conservation Corps and the majesty of Silver Falls combine to make Silver Falls CG one of the best in Washington

Recreation: The amazing Silver Falls National Recreation Trail leads from the campground over a series of hand-hewn bridges and switchbacks to the even more amazing Silver Falls just 0.5 miles away (see more below). Whitewater rafting is also popular on the Entiat River.

Campsites (31 sites for tents or RVs up to 35', no hookups, one group site for 40 people, reservations for group site only): Sites are in two loops, all back-ins, and large with good privacy. Shade comes from White fir, Douglas fir, and Jeffrey pine. Pads are on native materials.

Trip Notes: There is a certain rustic artistic flare going on here. One CCC kiosk seems to have been built only to protect some cut logs they couldn't use elsewhere (art imitating life?), so the campground takes on a very rustic but playful atmosphere. And the Group Camp is second to none -- eclipsed only by the fact that it is not a totally separate entity like Bridge Creek Group Camp on the Icicle River (see website). It's big. It's beautiful. And you're gonna love it.

Local Alternatives: Other USFS campgrounds in the vicinity include Cottonwood CG (25 sites), Spruce Grove CG (2 sites), North Fork CG (8 sites), Lake Creek/Entiat CG (19 sites), and Fox Creek CG (16 sites).

Local Attraction: Silver Falls cascades 140' down the side of a valley, shooting at a 45-degree angle, dropping powerfully onto a jumble of moss-covered boulders and logs. a 0.5-mile walk from the CG!

For more photos of Chelan Co. CGs consult campeverycountywa.com

CLALLAM COUNTY (Port Angeles/Forks)

We have the Klallam, Makah, and Quileute peoples to thank for the character of this county occupying the northern coast of the magnificent Olympic Peninsula. The establishment of the Olympic National Park (ONP), with its 9 Clallam County campgrounds, means this will be preserved. Factor in Cape Flattery, the Strait of Juan de Fuca, and the Dungeness Spit, and you may never want to camp anywhere else.

Sequim/Dungeness River Area
The good news about the City of Sequim (pronounced "Skwim," one syllable) is that it lies in the Olympic Rain Shadow and gets only 17 inches of rainfall annually. The bad news is that, just 40 miles away, the Hoh Rain Forest receives 140 to 200 inches per year. So, if you're in Sequim and want to pop over to the Rain Forest, you should probably grab a jacket.

Dungeness Rec Area *(Clallam Co.'s BEST CG FOR ENTIRE FAMILIES)*
The campground and adjoining Dungeness Wildlife Refuge have a symbiotic relationship. The County runs the campground, the Feds manage the Refuge, and they feed each other. Dungeness Spit is the world's longest sandspit at 5.5-miles long with the New Dungeness Lighthouse (and available lodging) at the end, including a full hiking trail. Be aware that the Wildlife Refuge has a small entrance fee, and that dogs are not permitted (the campground is pet friendly).
Overview: This iconic campground is located near Sequim on a one-mile bluff on 216 acres overlooking the Strait of Juan de Fuca, operated by Clallam County Parks, open year-round; GPS 48.1385, -123.1961.
Facilities: Campers will find flush toilets, coin-op showers, running water, fire rings, picnic tables, a playground, and camp hosts.

Recreation: The Dungeness Spit Trail is a must for all first-time campers. The 5.5-mile sand and rock trail follows the amazing Dungeness Spit far out into the Strait of Juan de Fuca before reaching the New Dungeness Lighthouse. Visitors can become lighthouse keepers for one-week intervals (contact Clallam Co. Parks for details). Along the way, bird watching on both sides of the Spit includes shorebirds of all kinds, as well as all manner of boats and ships to stir the imagination.

Campsites (65 tent/RV sites, 2 ADA sites w/showers, H/B camp with 8 sites, no hookups, 1 large Group Camp, reservable): Sites have above average to good privacy, as they are separated by marine vegetation vs. the old growth forest more typical of the Olympic Peninsula. Sites none-the-less have immediate access to hiking trails, marine views, and wildlife viewing. Best sites are 8, 11, 13, 14, 16, 17 (ADA), 29, 41, 45, 46, 48, 50, 54, 55, 57, 60 (ADA) and 65. Pull-through sites are recommended for large RVs, as the roads are narrow with heavy vegetation right up to the road edges. These include sites 7, 24, 25, and 42.

Trip Notes: While the campground is separate from the National Wildlife Refuge, it is a wildlife sanctuary in its own right. We saw many types of birds we could not identify on the spot. The madrona trees were so large they fooled us, until we looked way up beyond the thick trunks to see the waxy green leaves and the unmistakable red, paper-thin, peeling bark on the smaller branches. Deer seemed to pop up everywhere from the entrance to the bluff and right down to the entrance to Dungeness Spit Trail. Waking up in this campground is met by the distant sounds of the foghorns blowing at the New Dungeness Lighthouse, the misty air, and the briny spell of the ocean. This is a one-of-a kind experience of the senses that sets it apart from all others.

Local Alternatives: Dungeness Forks CG is a forest campground set on the beautiful, explorable Dungeness River. This campground is unsuitable for RVs, but preferable for those who like rustic, wilderness camping with more peace and quiet. It is located 5 miles southeast of Sequim, turn south/left on Palo Alto Road at Sequim Bay S.P. (GPS for Dungeness Forks: 47.972111, -123.11225). Sequim Bay S.P., another popular camping destination, is tight, congested, and awkwardly arranged and, despite its enduring popularity, has long since fallen off of our list of preferred campgrounds.

Lake Crescent/Joyce Area

Lake Crescent is Washington's second deepest lake, reaching a below sea level depth of 600'. It also has species and subspecies found nowhere else, including the Bearslee trout and the Lake Crescent cutthroat trout. But it is the Lake's brilliant blue color, even on a cloudy day, that draws the crowds. *Insider's note: it's not the reflection of the sky, but the lack of oxygen in the Lake, that keeps it blue. But let's keep the tourists guessing.*

Fairholm CG at ONP (Clallam Co.'s *MOST UNIQUELY WASHINGTON CG*)
Certainly, the camping gem of Lake Crescent, this park mirrors the "Lord of the Rings" feel of the ONP, with mountain peaks, oversized maples, and pristine lakes.
Overview: This enchanting campground is located on the western tip of Lake Crescent on 196 acres at 580' elevation, open May-October; GPS 48.067719, -123.916423.
Facilities: National Park amenities include flush toilets, potable water, fire grills, picnic tables, amphitheater, RV dump, camp host, marina, kayak and canoe rentals, camp store and cafe.
Recreation includes the many hiking trails, such as the short hike to Devil's Punch Bowl, the kid-friendly Spruce Railroad Trail, the Moments in Time Nature Trail, a half-mile wheelchair accessible loop, Marymere Falls, Mount Storm King Trail, and Pyramid Peak Trail, a 2,600-foot climb with great views of the Strait of Juan de Fuca.
Campsites (87 sites for tents and RVs up to 21', one ADA site, no hookups or reservations): The best sites per campsitephotos.com are 3, 7, 24, 33, 45, 53, 56 and 69, and these are on point. Large private sites are immersed in rain forest vegetation and views of crystalline Lake Crescent. Not all campsites are flat, but the tradeoff is the views. Note there is some road noise from Hwy 101.
Trip Notes: I expected Lake Crescent to be the star of this campground, and it was spectacular; but it was the trees that made this campground a rival to the Hoh Rain Forest CG in beauty. Great trees plus great Lake makes great camping.

Salt Creek Rec Area *(Clallam Co.'s BEST EQUIPPED CG)*
The area stands adjacent to the once-bustling logging town of Port Crescent, which flourished until the bay was deemed unnavigable. It then turned to tourism, spurred on by its 1.5-mile crystalline blue beach, until it was destroyed by fire and became a ghost town. Camp Hayden, a WWII defense position with sweeping views of the Strait of Juan de Fuca, occupied the site until 1945. All that remains now are the blue beaches, the sweeping views, and a terrific park known as Salt Creek.
Overview: This one-of-a-kind campground is located 22 miles west of Port Angeles on 196 acres, operated by Clallam Co. Parks, open year-round; GPS 48.1641, -123.6979.
Facilities include flush toilets, coin-op showers, fire rings, picnic tables, a playground, on-site host, and a covered picnic shelter.
Recreation: Whale watching is popular along the Strait of Juan de Fuca Whale Trail. Striped Peak Recreation Area, also accessible from the Park, is a premier birding site for bald eagles, Cooper's hawks, merlins, northern goshawks, ospreys, peregrines, turkey vultures, redtails, and sharp-shinned hawks.
Campsites (39 sites in open area w/water & electric 30/50-amp, 51 sites in forested area w/o hookups, all reservable BY MAIL): RV sites are crowded and open, but

with views; the forested sites are larger and private. Despite this, smaller RVs may want to consider the forested loop, even though you may have to park your vehicle away from the campsite and dry camp.

Trip Notes: A large open field greets you as you enter this campground. This is the RV section, which sacrifices privacy for great views of the Strait of Juan de Fuca. This will not win everyone over. Then enter the forest loop. Take in the trail on the bluff and look down at waves crashing over the incredible rock formations. You may begin to wonder why you see no people in the campground, until you take the short walk to Tongue Point, and find them milling about on the rocky beaches, the tall bluffed Island, and the close proximity of Crescent Beach. If you enjoy the outdoors, you will soon fall in love with this place.

Lyre River CG (Clallam Co.'s *BEST FREE CG*)

The river, named for the "music" native peoples said emanates from its flow, doesn't so much "sing" as it makes a gentle sound akin to low level applause.

Overview: This "musical" campground is located 5 miles west of Joyce on 23 acres along the Lyre River, managed by DNR on 23 acres at an elevation of 92', and open year-round; GPS 48.1477, -123.8333.

Facilities: Good amenities as DNR parks go include vault toilets, drinking water, fire rings, picnic tables, a large picnic shelter, and a Fishing/Observation deck.

Recreation includes steelhead fishing in water (starting early Dec.), and cutthroat fishing in late summer. For rock hounds, the river has produced agate, jasper, and petrified wood.

Campsites (11 sites for tents and very small RVs, no hookups or reservations, FREE with Discover Pass): Sites are medium to large, wooded, private and individual in layout, some on the riverside. RVs and trailers are not recommended due to the narrow, curved road into the campground, although many smaller tent trailers are able to make it. Three of the campsites are walk-ins and may be the best sites due to privacy and close proximity to the river.

Trip Notes: We camped in this small, lush campground in the rain, experiencing it at its wettest. We struggled to get our small tent trailer down the sharp-turning road, but we managed. The camp hosts were extremely welcoming. Both the picnic shelter and observation deck were of remarkable quality for a campground this small, giving high marks in my memory. The only potential problem here is the possibility of a single party of rowdy campers who could potentially disrupt the peace and quiet. The camp hosts are well aware of this and keep a friendly but watchful presence. We highly recommend this campground for those seeking to unwind and unplug for a while.

Sol Duc River Watershed

The Sol Duc River flows 78 miles through timberland, forming the biggest watershed in the northern Olympic Peninsula. It begins in the Olympic mountains and flows west through both National Forest and National Park before converging with the Bogachiel and Calawah Rivers in the aptly named City of Forks to become the Quileute River. But along the way camping, hiking, and hot spring adventures await.

Bear Creek CG *(Clallam Co.'s BEST BIKE-IN CG)*
This is frequently listed as among the most popular campgrounds in Washington, due in part to its cost (free), its year-round availability, and its mostly adult appeal. But it's a nice spot above a very pretty river with a great location for weary car and bicycle travelers ready to venture into another section of the Olympic Peninsula.
Overview: This rustic but accessible campground is located 20.4 miles west of Lake Crescent, managed by the DNR at 568' elevation, and is open year-round; GPS 48.0665588 -124.2395630.
Facilities: Familiar DNR facilities include vault toilets, picnic tables and fire rings. A special feature is the Sol Duc River Walk. Note that this campground was founded on the homesteads of several Norwegian families (notably, the Ditlefson family), who built the original roads and bridges. The original Ditlefson homestead is said to be hidden in the forest for those tenacious enough to find it.
Recreation: The River Trail is easily accessible from the campground.
Campsites (12 sites, no hookups or reservations, no potable water, FREE with Discover Pass): Sites are wooded, flat and private with gravel pads, most lying above the Sol Duc River. Its popularity is enhanced because it has no fees, and due to its proximity to the landmark Hungry Bear Cafe, which serves some of the best comfort food on Highway 101.
Trip Notes: DNR campgrounds have their own primitive style, preserving the land but supplying few amenities. I mostly love them, provided I can get one of the best campsites (which we did). There is road noise here, balanced by the quiet beauty of the trail along the Sol Duc River. This campground is not for everybody but will be near perfect for many. Bicyclers find themselves at a crossroads here, where Highway 101 turns 90 degrees, pointing south to Forks, and east to Crescent Lake and Port Angeles. Highway 113 also branches off here toward Ozette, Clallam Bay, and Neah Bay.

Klahowya CG (Clallam Co.'s *BEST RUSTIC CG*)
"Klahowya," a word meaning "welcome" in the Chinook jargon, is reflected in everything from the spacious campsites, to the soothing Sol Duc River, to the

dog friendly Koshe Nanitch Trail. It also has easy access off of Hwy 101, another welcome feature for road weary travelers.

Overview: This Olympic National Forest CG is located 14.6 miles west of Lake Crescent on the South Fork of the Sol Duc River on 32 acres at 800' elevation, and open May-Sept; GPS 48.064011, -124.105278.

Facilities include flush toilets, drinking water, fire rings, and picnic tables, plus Pioneer's Path Trail, a 0.3-mile wheelchair-accessible interpretive trail.

Campsites (53 sites, including 2 w/electric, 2 hiker-biker sites, no reservations): Sites are wooded and big enough to handle big rigs, and fairly well separated by trees and undergrowth. The biggest sites are 14, 31, 37, and 43, and give more privacy than the more crowded ONP campgrounds. It is near the dog friendly Koshe Nanitch Trail, has inner tubing in summer (when water levels are lower), kayaking in spring and fall (when water levels are higher), has no gravel roads to travel (unlike Queets and North Fork), and easy access to Hwy 101. It feels like being in the ONP without the restrictions.

Trip Notes: It is easy to see why Klahowya CG gets overlooked. Its entrance is on a section of Highway 101 that allows logging and looks, frankly, rather shabby. But drive the quarter mile to the park entrance, and you are greeted by old growth forest and a very pretty section of the South Fork of the Sol Duc River. True to its name, it is genuinely welcoming, with no road noise and great privacy between campsites. One older camper posted a sign that said "Kla-Howdy!"

Olympic National Park Ocean Strip (North)

Olympic National Park's narrow 73-mile long coastline is a designated wilderness area that stretches from Cape Flattery in the north to well beyond the boundary of Clallam Co. to the south. The offshore waters are part of the Olympic Coast National Marine Sanctuary, and the islands part of the Washington Maritime National Wildlife Refuge Complex. As such, seals, sea lions, and nesting seabirds are protected for perpetuity. Tread lightly here -- you are not alone.

Mora CG at ONP (Clallam Co.'s *MOST APPEALING CG TO THE SENSES*)
Everyone has tried to claim this area. The native peoples, of course, hold the most credible claim. The Russians tried claiming it, until the wreck of the ship SUV Nikolai on Rialto Beach in 1808 discouraged further Russian exploration. In the 1880s a supply town named Boston was established, later changed to Mora to commemorate owner K.O. Ericson's hometown in Sweden. His hotel/store occupied the spot where the campfire circle in Mora CG is now built.

Overview: This ONP campground is located 13 miles west of Forks and 4 miles north of La Push at the mouth of the Quileute River and Pacific Ocean, open year-round; GPS 47.917482, -124.602888.

Facilities: National Park facilities include flush toilets, drinking water, picnic tables, fire grills, an amphitheater, walking trails, camp hosts, and an RV dump.

Recreation: This includes beach combing or hiking on Rialto Beach (don't miss Hole-in-the-Wall). Birding is excellent at James Pond (reachable by a short walking trail) for bullheads, harlequin ducks, mergansers, red wing blackbirds, sharp-shinned hawks, varied thrush, and many others.

Campsites (94 sites, no hookups or reservations): The campground sits on a bench above the Quileute River in a grove of old growth Sitka spruce and western hemlock. Sites are lush with average to good privacy, though some seemed in disrepair. They are a mixture of pull-through and back-in sites with paved or gravel pads organized into 5 loops, identified by letter: Loop A (sites 1-20) is wooded and well-shaded, but most suitable for tents and RVs less than 21'; Loop B (sites 21-38) is similar to A, but RVs up to 35' can fit into sites 33-37; Loop C (sites 39-57) is similar, but closes in winter; Loop D (sites 58-81) is the largest loop and most sites will accommodate RVs up to 35'; the Camp Every County Crew preferred Loop E (sites 82-94), the smallest loop closest to the ocean surrounded by wetlands and wildlife. We had considerable raccoon activity, but this made the trip (when we heard raccoons in the middle of the night and found Gary's much-boasted but unopened tin of brownies on the ground, John and Gary argued over whether the raccoons were trying to steal it, or whether they didn't like what they found and tried to return it).

Trip notes: This park was a real natural wonder, with the Quileute River emptying into the ocean just below, known only to us by peek-a-boo views and the crashing of the waves. There is a definite rain forest environment, with air that smells like fresh soil in spring, and its vegetation at its most sumptuous late in the season. The real attraction is the short distance to Rialto Beach and the Hole-in-the-Wall, a natural opening in a lava wall cut by the ocean current. At low tide, it can be accessed on foot, including the many tide pools on the north side. While walking 1.5 miles on a pebbly beach can be a strain on the calves and ankles, everyone should put this on their bucket list.

Other Attractions: Don't overlook the pretty town of LaPush, an 11-mile drive to the mouth of the Quileute River. This tribal town is known for beautiful First Beach, and its multiple sea stacks which are frequently shrouded in lacy fog and sea mist. Some stacks are accessible on foot by a land bridge. Second Beach and Third Beach are also short hikes from LaPush with equally stunning profiles.

The offshore islands in Crescent Bay
at Salt Creek Recreation Area

The wooded sites at Klahowya make
you jump up and say Kla-howdy!

The spreading trees at Fairholm CG
give it its "Lord of the Rings" feel

The new lighthouse sits at the end of
5-mile long Dungeness Spit

The rocky beaches and foggy sea stacks make Mora Campground an Olympic
National Park favorite

CLARK COUNTY (Vancouver/Battle Ground)

With the Lewis & Clark Expedition and Hudson's Bay Company dominating this "Cradle of Northwest History," this small southwestern county gets overlooked for its recreational opportunities. Magnificent waterfalls, volcanic lakes, and wild rivers are the real headliners here.

Prairie Region/Klickitat Trail

Little Clark County is outlined by the Lewis River to the north, the 5000' high Cascade foothills to the east, and the Columbia River to the west and south. In the middle you have the prairies – a flat, low-lying region known by pioneers as the Klickitat (or Klikitat) Trail. The Klikitat Indians had a "prairie-oriented" subsistence strategy of moving with the seasons to take advantage of plant resources ripening at different elevations. Today, these diverse plains and prairies are home to the best camping facilities in Clark County.

Battle Ground Lake S.P. (Clark Co.'s *BEST CG FOR FAMILIES*)

This unique park features the perfect fishing, canoeing, and swimming lake that is a 400' volcanic crater/caldera. It may not be Crater Lake but is the centerpiece of an exceptionally campworthy campground.

Overview: This quietly volcanic campground is located 2 miles northeast of Battle Ground on 280 acres surrounding 25.4-acre Battle Ground Lake at an elevation of 509', open year-round; GPS 45.80556, -122.4925.

Facilities: Good facilities include flush toilets, running water, picnic tables, fire grills, equestrian trails, walking/hiking trails, boat ramp and fishing dock (no motors allowed on the lake), a playground, swimming area, concessions, a ball field, camp hosts, and an RV dump.

Recreation: Fishing is popular for many species including bass, catfish, and an emphasis on trout. Horseback riding has also found a home here, with multiple trails surrounding the camping areas and lake.

Campsites (31 sites, some walk-ins, including 6 w/electric & water, 4 cabins, 2 group camps - one for equestrians, and one w/4 Adirondack shelters, reservable): Sites are large and wooded with good privacy, arranged among a series of small hills, yet level. The camping loop includes the cabins, and the best sites are 1, 4, 7, 9, 16, 23, and 27. These include pull-through and back-in sites. The camping spur is a walk-in tent area, also resting above the lake with peek-a-boo views. Wheelbarrows are available for transporting equipment. Best sites here are 31, 37, and 44. The G-1 Group Camp has 4 Adirondack shelters, a covered cooking and meeting area for 25-32 people, but does not allow RVs due to the sloped terrain. Tent camping here is dispersed, but does not detract from the very cozy, close knit arrangement of this best of group campgrounds. The G-2 Group Camp is for horse campers, and includes corrals, and can accommodate 4 equestrian families. All camping areas are set in mature forest with mixed shade and sun.

The gleeful sound of children swimming in Battle Ground Lake
can be heard throughout the State Park

Trip notes: We've camped here in the rain, and we've camped here in the sunshine, and I can tell you that the sun outshines the rain every time. Yes, that may be obvious, but when the sun comes out, the lake erupts with children playing with great abandon, adults proudly unloading their kayaks onto this perfect lake, and cars cruising in and out of the parking lot. In fact, the Park's strength is that, despite this little core of high energy, campers rest high above the banks with great privacy and even seclusion. The noise rising up from that little caldera only serves to keep everyone in the best of moods.

Paradise Point S.P. (Clark Co.'s BEST EQUIPPED/BEST CG FOR RVs and BEST BIKE-IN CG)
Here's the good news for RV'ers: It's right off the freeway. Here's the bad news: The freeway cuts right through the middle of the campground. In truth, the freeway was built long after the Park was established. But though we recommend this

campground with some reservations, it is not paradise lost; just be sure you choose your campsites carefully.

Overview: This tidy, picturesque campground is located 17 miles north of Vancouver and 6 miles south of Woodland, with 6180' of freshwater shoreline on the Lewis River, set on 88 prime acres at 230' elevation, open year-round; GPS 45.865430, -122.704110.

Facilities: This well-equipped campground includes ADA bathrooms with showers, picnic tables, fire rings, 4 miles of hiking trails, an amphitheater, a huge Day Use Area along the Lewis River including a Disc Golf field, and an RV dump.

Recreation: This includes boating (no launch), swimming, freshwater fishing, and hiking within the Park. The secluded 3/4-mile River Walk is by far the best of the trails.

Campsites (58 tent sites, 18 sites for RVs up to 40' with water & electric 50-amp, 9 H/B sites, 2 yurts, most are reservable): In this tiny county, it is difficult to find good RV facilities that feel less like lodging and more like camping. This is where Paradise Point comes in -- it may rest beside the Interstate, but it is definitely campworthy. Campsites are located in two joined loops and a spur. The larger Loop (utility sites 1-20 and tent sites 26-43) is closest to the freeway on grass and among older trees. The smaller loop (non-utility sites 51-68) is heavily forested with good privacy and shade, but some residual highway noise. Most sites are large back-ins with a few pull-throughs. Sites 1-68 are in a partially wooded/grassy area with average to good privacy. The Walk-In Spur Sites (tent sites 71-79) are the most private and quietest in the Park, and especially good for bicyclists. The quaintest sites are those in the small apple orchard (sites 21-24 and 44-50). Here you have more sun and open space.

Trip Notes: Before we camped here, we didn't realize this was set on the EAST fork of the Lewis River. This smaller branch is very slow moving with muddy banks, very reminiscent of the Mississippi, but of course on a smaller scale. As we walked the River Walk Trail, we were taken by the "ole swimmin' hole" where we watched a boy climb the steep bank, grab the rope swing, then hurl himself headlong into the silky waters, flailing his arms and letting lose with a primal, giddy yell. A large woman in a colorful one-piece swimsuit paddled carefree from the middle of a black inner tube until she spotted a "gentleman" on the path and turned shyly away. On the slow-moving waters, paddle boarders stood tall on their tiny vessels, directly themselves in the current with long, colorful poles. Back at the campground, the old apple orchard (the last remnant of the old homestead) reminds campers that this old campground has one foot planted firmly in the past -- a slower, less mechanized time when people were more connected to the land, less self-conscious, and less a part of the incessant noise of the modern age.

Yacolt Burn State Forest

The forest is named for the dozens of wildfires that ravaged Clark and surrounding counties during September 1902. With no organized system for fighting wildfires, the fires spread across nearly 239,000 acres and caused 38 deaths. This led to the establishment of the Washington Fire Protection Association and funded a system of fire wardens and a program of fire prevention on private lands. Now, recreational activities in the Yacolt Burn State Forest include whitewater rafting, horseback riding, off-road vehicle riding, mountain biking, hiking, and, of course, great camping.

Cold Creek Camp (Clark Co.'s *BEST FREE* and *BEST RUSTIC CG*)
This semi-rustic campground is fought over equally by the whitewater rafters along the East Fork of the Lewis River and experienced mountain bikers on the immense trail system of the Yacolt Burn State Forest. The rest of us can just sit back and watch them fight for supremacy.

Overview: The campground is located 26 miles northeast of Vancouver and 10 miles southeast of Yacolt on Cedar Creek, operated by the DNR at 1050' elevation, open year-round with a 7-day limit; GPS 45.76369, -122.34444.

Facilities: Limited amenities include vault toilets, picnic tables, fire grills, tent pads, a large Day Use Shelter, and camp hosts. There is no drinking water, and garbage must be packed out.

Recreation: The Dole Valley Road to the Lewis River stretch of the Rock Creek-Lewis Drainage is 3 miles long and a class II-III+ section of whitewater with a reputation for being unforgiving, even among more experienced whitewater rafters. But mountain biking is king here, and Cold Creek is the most heavily biked section of the 35-mile Tarbell trail system. This strenuous trail, within the Yacolt Burn, definitely produces a "burn" of its own. And, for those who wish to stay closer to the campground, blackberry picking is excellent.

Campsites (8 sites for tents or RVs up to 20', some ADA, one group site for up to 6 people, no hookups, reservable, FREE with Discover Pass): Sites are heavily wooded though not heavily pruned with a rugged feel -- but far more well-appointed than most DNR campgrounds.

Trip Notes: Cold Creek falls well under the radar as one of the most beautiful campgrounds in Washington. The campsites are defined by log borders along most paths and are flat and ADA-accessible. They are well-shaded, large, and very private. But good news -- the Day Use Area is even prettier. Cedar Creek takes on a deep blue sheen along the Cedar Creek Falls Trail and Overlook, leading to the smallish but striking waterfall less than a mile in.

Local Alternatives: Rock Creek CG and Horse Camp are 1.6 miles from Cold Creek. When the pavement ends, simply turn left (instead of continuing on to the odd CAMPGROUND PARKING sign) and drive to the campgrounds.

Sunset Falls CG (Clark Co.'s *MOST APPEALING CG TO THE SENSES* and *MOST UNIQUELY WASHINGTON CG*)

The East Fork of the Lewis River tumbles its way out of the Cascade Mountains and across the Yacolt Burn with 3 successive waterfalls: Lucia, Moulton, and Sunset. Camp at Sunset Falls CG, but don't forget to check out the trifecta of waterfalls.

Overview: This delightful campground is located 39 miles northeast of Vancouver and 10 miles east of Yacolt on the East Fork of the Lewis River, operated by the USFS at 1,041' elevation, open year-round; GPS: 45.818734, -122.250186.

Facilities: Good amenities include vault toilets, picnic tables, fire grills, Day Use Area, garbage service, and camp hosts.

Recreation: Hiking is popular on Sunset Falls Trail #174 and the Silver Star Trail. This stretch of river is also popular with kayakers.

Campsites (18 sites for tents and RVs up to 22', no hookups): Sites are in two sections. The loop (sites 1-10) is car accessible with pull-through sites with paved pads but poor to average privacy. The walk-in section (sites 11-18) consists of more private tent sites. Both areas are very shady with alders, cedars, Douglas firs, and maples. Paths to the River are very steep. All sites are within 200' of the River, while Sunset Falls is 1/4 mile away.

Trip Notes: Of course, it's nice to have an exceedingly beautiful waterfall so near the campground, but you won't spend too much time there. We found the river itself to be more compelling, being more accessible with its more subtle rock formations, pools and privacy. For us, the campground was not so much about the Falls but was about this gorgeous stretch of the East Fork of the Lewis River.

Local Attractions: Moulton Falls County Park is a day-use only park that boasts one of the prettiest waterfalls and one of the best swimming areas anywhere. Lucia Falls County Park is another day-use only park that is a "look but don't touch" situation, as fishing and swimming are prohibited due to the sensitive salmon spawning grounds. However, it is worth checking out the incredible rock formations around the falls.

For further photos of all Clark Co. CGs featured here consult
campeverycountywa.com

COLUMBIA COUNTY (Dayton/Starbuck)

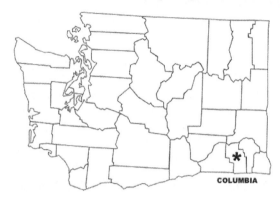

COLUMBIA

Rolling hills and green valleys dominate this small southwestern county that is neither on the Columbia River nor the Columbia Basin. Lewis and Clark passed through here, both to and from the west, leaving their mark in this peaceful place where time stands still.

Dayton Area

This most Americana of Washington towns is surrounded by rolling hills with the long-abiding legacy of Lewis and Clark visible around every turn. Somehow, despite the most basic needs of the pioneers, they saved stands of old-growth forest, historic meadows, rivers, and streams for perpetuity.

Lewis and Clark Trail S.P. (Columbia Co.'s *BEST CG FOR ENTIRE FAMILIES, BEST BIKE-IN CG,* and includes *BEST GROUP CG*)
The land for the Park was first deeded to the Bateman family during the Civil War, who insisted this rare stand of old growth "long-leafed" Ponderosa Pine not be logged for the needs of the settlers. We now have a very natural park, bordered by the Touchet River, with touches from the CCC throughout.
Overview: This historic campground is located 5.8 miles west of Dayton on 37 acres with 1333' along the Touchet River at 1400' elevation, reservable via website. The main campground is open April 1 through Oct. 31, with 17 sites in the Day Use Area remaining open year-round for tents and truck-mounted campers; GPS 46.28833, -118.07083.
Facilities: The CCC of the 1930s have left us vintage bathrooms with flush toilets, running water, and showers. Also provided are picnic tables, fire grills, a ball field, 0.8 miles of hiking trails, an RV dump in the main campground, and camp hosts.
Recreation includes fishing on the Touchet River for rainbow and brown trout. Also take the opportunity to have fun with the history of the area (see below).

Campsites (24 sites for tents and RVs up to 27' in the Main Area, two group camps for up to 100 each, no hookups): Sites are large with great vegetation and excellent privacy. Each site is like an alcove, with high vegetation lending coolness, privacy, and a great noise buffer from the railroads and Highway 12. The mature cottonwood trees shed heavily in late May, sometimes turning the ground entirely white, so allergy suffers should definitely bring their Claritin.

Trip notes: On a positive historical note, this is a FUN place to let the history of the Lewis and Clark expeditions sink in. Five miles away in the town of Dayton, a historical marker points to a small field 2.5 miles off the highway with dozens of life size metal sculptures of all 37 members of the Lewis and Clark Corps of Discovery. Here the pioneers made camp, including blacksmiths, cooks, horses, and the like. On a negative note, it is apparent that the Park itself needs some upgrading, such as replacing signs that are bleached by the sun, the interiors of bathrooms that are less than private, and providing the pamphlets we once received. The staff went to extra lengths to do what they could, providing flags at campsites on Memorial Day Weekend, putting red and white checked tablecloths on tables in the primitive camping sites, and cutting the nettles from the trails, all very personal touches.

Snake River Area

The Snake River is a 1078-mile long tributary of the Columbia River that forms the northern boundary of Columbia County. This section of the Snake has been dammed and transformed into a long series of lakes, taming the wild river but creating a larger camper's paradise.

Lyons Ferry Marina KOA (Columbia Co.'s *MOST UNIQUELY WASHINGTON CG*) Ferries have been used to cross the Snake River since the mid-1860s and were replaced by bridges starting in the 1920s. The Lyons Ferry Bridge is on the National Register of Historic Places, providing vistas of the confluence of the Snake and Palouse Rivers that far surpass those of the old ferry boat days.

Overview: This "elevated" campground is located 7 miles northwest of Starbuck with 5000' of Snake River waterfront at 630' elevation, open year-round; GPS 46.585929, -118.220111.

Facilities include flush toilets, running water, showers, picnic tables, fire rings, shaded picnic sites, a fenced Dog Park, kayak rentals, Kampstore and Snake River Cafe, fish cleaning stations, Wi-Fi, moorage for boaters, outdoor movies on summer nights, and swimming at Lyons Ferry S.P. (2 miles north).

Recreation: Wildlife viewing is accessible in the adjacent 12-acre wildlife area. Boating takes charge here, along with fishing for bass, catfish, pike minnow, rainbow trout, steelhead, and walleye.

<u>Campsites</u> (40 tent sites, 18 RV sites w/partial and full hookups 30/50-amp, reservable): Campsites have poor to average privacy, but are flat, well-engineered, somewhat shaded, and close to all amenities. They can accommodate RVs of any size.

<u>Trip Notes</u>: There we were, on an 11-day tour through 5 counties in southeastern Washington. We had just left Windust, for which we were poorly prepared, having no food with us. It was a great relief to pull into the Snake River Grill at Lyons Ferry Marina, where we could get a late breakfast, batteries for our cameras, and ice for our ice chest. More to the point, there was something very captivating about this environment. We're not fishermen, just campers, yet the busy marina beneath the 2040' Lyons Ferry Bridge and the three-quarter mile-long Joso High Railroad Bridge provided a very cozy, tucked-in feeling that made us want to stay much longer.

Tucannon River Valley

This area is a nice transition between the hilly wheat lands of northern Columbia County and the abject wilderness of the southern county. The River flows through the W.T. Wooten State Wildlife Area, providing just the right balance of nature and civilization that will appeal to most campers.

<u>Dayton/Pomeroy KOA</u> (Columbia Co.'s *BEST EQUIPPED/BEST CG FOR RVs*)
This remarkable KOA Park has been the recipient of the Founder's Award and President's Award on many occasions. Furthermore, it is located on the edge of the Wooten State Wildlife Area with at least 8 small fishing lakes nearby. This Kampground has the look and feel of a finely maintained forest village with happy kampers and wild turkeys everywhere you look.

<u>Overview</u>: Also known as the Blue Mountain KOA and The Last Resort KOA, this meticulous Kampground is tucked away southeast of Dayton on Tum-a-lum Creek near the Tucannon River at 1964' elevation, open March to November; the Park requests that you do not arrive by GPS, and will provide directions upon reservation confirmation.

<u>Facilities</u>: This best-equipped campground features bathrooms with showers and running water, picnic tables, fire grills, a covered picnic shelter, a Meeting Hall, playground, group fire pit, and horseshoe pits, The Last Resort Kamp Store with gas pumps and ATM machine, Wi-Fi supporting mobile devices with on-site tech support, RV dump, propane, firewood, and garbage service.

<u>Recreation</u>: Fishing predominates in the spring and hunting in the fall. Summer features hiking access in the nearby national forest and wilderness areas.

<u>Campsites</u> (6 tent sites, 33 sites for RVs up to 70' with full hookups 30/50-amp, 6 cabins including 5 with kitchens and bathrooms, reservations recommended): The tent sites are better spaced and separate from the more closely placed back-in

and pull-through RV sites. All are forested and shaded with enough vegetation for privacy, with grassy areas in between.

Trip Notes: This lovely KOA Park is a beehive of activity during spring fishing season, but then quickly settles back into the forest and nearby rivers and streams. A summer of early fall visit is recommended.

Tucannon CG (Columbia Co.'s *MOST APPEALING CG TO THE SENSES)*
Calling the Dayton/Pomeroy KOA "The Last Resort" (above) is a bit hasty, because the last and best campground in the Tucannon Valley is 9 miles south on a terrace above the Tucannon River. Tucannon CG isn't quite free, isn't exactly rustic or well-equipped, and has no great Kamp Store -- it is simply the perfect USFS campground on the perfect river before it drops into the wilderness.

Overview: This Umatilla National Forest campground is located about 50 minutes from Dayton, operated by the USFS at 2600' elevation, open early spring to late fall; GPS 46.243, -117.6886.

Facilities include vault toilets, no piped-in water, picnic tables, and fire grills.

Recreation includes multiple hunting and hiking opportunities. Trails lead to Mt. Misery and the Wenaha Wilderness Area, which extends into northeast Oregon.

Campsites (17 sites for tents and RVs of any size, no hookups or reservations, FREE with NW Forest Pass): Sites are well maintained, extremely spacious, private, and lush with vegetation. Four sites are near the River itself. Family members find this a great getaway, despite being best known by fishermen (spring) and hunters (fall). Summer is left to the campers.

Trip Notes: This area was quite different than we expected. First, it was not nearly as remote as reviews indicated. The Tucannon Road was a paved, flat road that extended 29 miles from Highway 12 to the Tucannon CG. The last 9 miles, from the KOA Park to the campground itself, was crowded with at least 8 WDFW campgrounds where people parked/pitched tents randomly in large open areas and crowded the river with fishing gear. Additionally, there were several small ponds stocked with trout for the more fair-weather fishermen. Even the historic Tucannon Guard Station (available for rent) had makeshift campsites filled with fishermen right up to the back porch. In short, we were glad to reach the so-called "fishing campground" of Tucannon to get away from all the fishermen along the way. Take this advice: camp in summertime, not during spring fishing season. The campground itself is lovely, removed from the hubbub, with a great stretch of the Tucannon River and great wooded campsites.

Wenaha-Tucannon Wilderness
This lonely wilderness, stretching down into northeast Oregon, is 176,557 acres of steep-walled river canyons, smooth-topped tablelands, and harsh climate extremes. It is also the land of Rocky Mountain elk, mule deer, white tailed deer, black bears, coyotes, cougars, bobcats, and snowshoe hares. If you climb high

enough, you might even be lucky enough to catch a glimpse of Big Horned sheep.

Godman CG (Columbia Co.'s *BEST FREE* and *BEST RUSTIC CG*)
There is a popular legend that this campground received its name when Lewis and Clark first entered the area and exclaimed, "God, man, where in the [Sam Hill] are we?" Nothing in the Lewis and Clark journals indicates that they ever spoke this way, but it does speak to the remoteness of the area. The last 11 miles of the drive have incredible scenic beauty leading to one of the best rustic campgrounds in Washington, nestled up against the natural beauty of the Wenaha-Tucannon Wilderness.
Overview: This treasure trove of a USFS campground is located 27 miles southeast of Dayton at 6050' elevation, open May through October, weather permitting; GPS 46.099718, -117.786291.
Facilities: Primitive facilities include a vault toilet, picnic tables, fire grills, a group picnic shelter, horse facilities with hitching rails and feed mangers, and a Guard Station (rentable and usually available). There are 1930s touches throughout the campground from early development by the CCC. There is no drinking water, aside from the spring for the horses.
Summer Recreation: The 200-mile network of roller-coaster hiking and equestrian trails in the Wenaha-Tucannon Wilderness are accessible from West Butte Trail #3138, recommended for the more experienced only.
Winter Recreation: You'll likely need a snowmobile to get here, but the snowmobile trails and snowshoeing meadows are popular with sturdy winter sport fans.
Campsites (5 tent sites, plus 3 sites for tents or small RVs, no hookups or reservations, FREE except during hunting season): Sites could be described as "semi-dispersed," with most sites wrapped around the heavily forested ridge at the turn in the road, all with magnificent views available from every site. And at dusk, sunsets remind you of just how beautiful the wilderness can be.
Trip Notes: It takes a little commitment to get here -- a good Forest Service Map, a higher sitting vehicle to maneuver the ruts in the road, perhaps a 4-wheel drive to dodge the limbs overhead, and a watchful eye for wildlife that may never have encountered humans before. That being said, the journey will reward you with a very different feel than closer-in campgrounds. But if you have any trepidations, you might choose Tucannon CG instead.

For photos of Columbia Co. CGs consult
campeverycountywa.com

COWLITZ COUNTY (Kelso/Longview/Castle Rock)

This small but explosive county is dominated by the western flow from the eruption of Mount St. Helens in 1980, which has largely redefined the recreational opportunities where the force and regenerative powers of nature are so evident.

Silver Lake/Spirit Lake Memorial Highway 504

Silver Lake was formed thousands of years ago by an eruption of Mount St. Helens and is now 1424-acres large providing wetland and woodland trails, fishing, and boating opportunities. Spirit Lake, once regarded as the single most beautiful alpine lake in Washington, was all but destroyed in the eruption of 1980, making it inaccessible to current generations for recreational use. But all is not lost: the Johnson Ridge Observatory, the closest driving point to Mt. St. Helens, provides a birds-eye view and details the history of Spirit Lake and the volcano. Furthermore, environmentalists and visitors alike are amazed by the Lake's natural, unexpected regenerative power, making the Observatory a destination in itself.

Seaquest S.P. (Cowlitz Co.'s *MOST UNIQUELY WASHINGTON CG, BEST EQUIPPED/BEST CG FOR RVs,* and *BEST BIKE-IN CG*)

This campground sits safely 30 miles west of the unpredictable Mount St. Helens and is undeniably the best campground for viewing the history and devastating aftermath of its May 1980 eruption.

Overview: This polished Park is located 6 miles east of Castle Rock near Silver Lake on 475 acres at 665' elevation, open year-round; GPS 46.29861, -122.81694.

Facilities: The Park is well-equipped with bathrooms with showers (ADA), picnic tables, fire grills, amphitheater, playground, Mount St. Helens Visitor Center, 7 miles of hiking trails (1-mile is ADA accessible), volleyball field, camp hosts, and an RV dump station. The group camp offers a covered shelter for tables, a fire pit, two braziers, and hose bib.

Recreation: This includes hiking, fishing on Silver Lake, bird watching, walking the forest trails, and visits to the Johnson Ridge Observatory.

Campsites (58 tent sites, 33 utility sites for RVs up to 50' including 17 with electric & water and 16 with full hookups 50-amp, 4 H/B sites, 5 yurts - some pet friendly, one group camp with 3 Adirondack shelters for up to 25 people, reservable): There are 4 loops: the south and two north loops are in a forested setting of secondary old-growth forest, and are spacious with good privacy; the T-loop with full hookups for RVs is a no-barrier area with smaller sites. We especially recommend the sites on the north end of the North Loop (sites 40-48), as these back into the largest green belt. The South Loop is also very good for tenters, but the RV Loop we recommend with some hesitation, as this has a side-by-side field appearance with less privacy. Nonetheless, it remains the best RV option in the County, free of long-term residents, high prices, and remains very campworthy in a forested environment.

Trip notes: This is a very wooded, shady, and great camping park that gives access to Mount St. Helens. The park itself offers wonderful wooded walking trails, and a tunnel under Highway 504 to the Mt. St. Helens Visitor Center and a wetland area on Silver Lake with a 1.0-mile boardwalk trail. It is nice to then leave the wetlands, take the tunnel back into the Park, and find yourself once again in towering old growth forest. The Group Camp sits in the middle of the campground, with some loss or privacy.

Local Alternatives: The Longview North/Mount St. Helens KOA is just 4 miles west (2 miles off I-5 on Highway 504) with premium RV sites, rental RVs, a dog park, a new playground and, best of all, excellent reviews. The Kid Valley CG is a small family-operated facility near the Kid Valley Store and gas station with full-facility sites for tents and RVs. This small campground is located 22 miles east of Seaquest S.P., much closer to Johnson Ridge on Mt. St. Helens, making it attractive to those on bicycle.

Merrill Lake Natural Resources Conservation Area

This area, located at the foot of Mt. St. Helens, is a prime habitat noted for protected animal, plant, fish, and bird species. These include the Cascade torrent salamander, osprey, bald eagle, old growth forest, and brown trout. It is rare to find a campground in such an area, making it a prime opportunity for campers who appreciate nature in its purest form.

Merrill Lake CG (Cowlitz Co.'s *BEST FREE* and *BEST RUSTIC CG*):
Merrill Lake was formed in 1980 when lava flows from Mt. St. Helens blocked the many small streams flowing through this valley, making it the most unique and largest naturally formed lake in the area. It is also proclaimed by many as one of Washington's premier fly lakes and a tent campers paradise.

Overview: This remarkable campground is located 23 miles east of Woodland and 4.7 miles northwest of Cougar on 283.4-acre Merrill Lake on 114 acres, operated by the DNR at 1524' elevation, open April to November; GPS 40.54812, -120.81201.

Facilities include pit toilets, picnic tables, fire pits, a two-mile interpretive trail, a gravel boat launch (electric motors and human-powered boats only), and camp hosts. There is no pumped or piped water.

Recreation: The 2-mile Merrill Lake Old Growth Interpretive Trail is a must for those who enjoy the look and feel of Washington's oldest and most developed vegetation. The Lake is an excellent catch-and-release fishing lake stocked with eastern brook trout, rainbow trout, Yellowstone cutthroat, and, more recently, the protected brown trout. Birdwatching for eagles, ospreys, bufflehead, common goldeneye, and hooded merganser is also popular. Canoeing and kayaking are exceptional.

Campsites (11 sites for tents, no hookups or reservations, but a 3-day stay limit, FREE with Discover Pass): Sites are exceptionally large, most of which could fit multiple tents. They are nicely spaced, allowing optimal privacy. All are forested, but they do not have lake views. The one disadvantage is that all sites are walk-in (albeit, a short distance), so it is limited to tent camping only.

Trip Notes: Wow. We didn't expect this. After visiting hundreds of campgrounds on this 5-year journey, we thought we had a pretty good idea what DNR campgrounds looked like. But this wasn't "shaggy." It was like walking into an old house and finding it appointed with polished mahogany: warm, rich, and inviting. We loved the footbridge over the small stream in the parking lot with its towering rain forest-like trees, the campsite spur on the right, and the Old Growth Interpretive Trail to the left. This trail gives the best views of the Lake. People mistake it for a reservoir, because the shoreline is poorly defined; but the Lake was formed with the 1980 Mt. St. Helens eruption, and nature has not yet had time to work its magic. Tent campers will find magic here -- so much in fact that the DNR limits campers to 3-day stays due to its popularity.

North Fork Lewis River Reservoir Area

Unlike Lewis County to the north, the Lewis River was not named after Meriwether Lewis of Lewis and Clark fame, but for surveyor Adolphus Lee Lewis who took a donation land claim on the river's west bank. These are humble beginnings for a river that drains over 1000 square miles of land, supports three major reservoirs and provides the majority of hydroelectric power for a wide area, not to mention a multitude of recreational facilities for a 95-mile stretch in southern Cowlitz Co. and beyond.

Beaver Bay CG (Cowlitz Co.'s *MOST APPEALING CG TO THE SENSES*)
This is one of the campgrounds founded by PacifiCorp, whose 510-megawatt hydroelectric facilities were built from 1931 to 1958 and located in the shadow of Mount St. Helens and the Cascade Mountains. The campgrounds take every opportunity to connect campers with this world of natural beauty.
Overview: This appealing campground is located 34.5 miles east of Woodland just east of the town of Cougar on 3780-acre Yale Lake (reservoir), operated by PacifiCorp at 512' elevation, open the Friday before the last weekend in April until the end of September; GPS 46.061201, -122.268777.
Facilities include bathrooms with showers, drinking water, picnic tables, fire grills, a Day Use Area, a playground, swimming beach, boat launch, and camp hosts.
Recreation: Here you'll find swimming, fishing for bull trout, coastal cutthroat, and kokanee. Nearby hiking, spelunking, and interpretive opportunities include the Ape Caves Trail #239, leading through the third largest lava tubes in America; the Lava Canyon Trail #184 leads 5 miles through a steep, rugged canyon including lava fields, a swinging bridge, a steel ladder climb, and thunderous waterfalls; and the Windy Ridge Observatory, with eastern-side views of Mount St. Helens, Spirit Lake, and interpretive programs.

Yale Lake is the prettiest of the 3 Lewis River Reservoirs
and is especially popular with the kids

Campsites (63 sites for tents or RVs of any size, one group camp with 15 spots, no hookups, reservable): Sites are divided into two complex loops. Loop A (sites A1-A41) is bisected into 10 rows, some near the shore of Yale Lake (A1-A8 and

A31-A40), while others set back into the forest (A23-A29). This entire loop is reservable. Loop B has 3 rows, one of which sits right on the main road near the Day Use/Swimming Area and is the busiest of the Loops. Privacy is average, sites are large and flat back-ins with parking on natural materials. In between is the Group Camp, which comprises a single cohesive loop. This has relative privacy with a separate entrance.

Trip Notes: We camped in the middle of the A Loop, and confess it took an hour or two to warm up to the place. Sites were occupied by equipment, but devoid of humans. We soon found that the activity and energy of the place is at the far end of the campground at the delightful Day Use and swimming area. Its small "bay" resembles a miniature Cape Cod with its curved arm enveloping a safe and fairly warm natural pool. Kids found logs on which to float, while adults relaxed. We found other campers along the crude banks of the reservoir, relaxing in lawn chairs or launching kayaks. We also discovered the trail that lead all the way to Cougar CG and the town of Cougar. Back at the campground, we found the quiet we needed, a good balance of rest and recreation.

Local Alternative: Cougar CG, also operated by PacifiCorp, is just 1.4 miles west and is like Beaver Bay CG in every way, except slightly less secluded. It has 45 tent sites with restrooms, showers, a boat ramp, and a swimming beach on Yale Lake.

Cresap Bay Park (Cowlitz Co.'s *BEST CG FOR ENTIRE FAMILIES*)
This is the only campground on beautiful Lake Merwin, the largest of the Lewis River reservoirs, and also the newest of the PacifiCorp campgrounds.

Overview: This popular campground is located 27 miles east of Woodland on Merwin Lake (reservoir), operated by PacifiCorp at 441' elevation, open Friday before Memorial Day through end of September; GPS 45.9684, -122.3851.

Facilities include bathrooms with showers and water, picnic tables, fire grills, a Day Use Area, a swimming beach, an amphitheater, a 23-slip marina, a 2-lane boat ramp, a 1.5-mile nature trail, camp hosts, and an RV dump station. The compact Group Camp has a covered shelter with fireplace, sink, and electricity.

Recreation includes hiking, swimming, and boating. Fishing is good for bull trout, Chinook salmon, Coho salmon, Dolly Varden, kokanee, northern pike minnow, sculpin, and tiger muskie. All but bull trout and Dolly Varden are catch and release. Kayaking is magnificent, particularly as the reservoir narrows east, bound on both sides by rock cliffs.

Campsites (56 sites for tents or RVs of any size, no hookups, one group camp with 15 sites, all reservable): The sites are cleverly arranged into 4 conjoined loops, only 3 of which are named, plus a long circle of sites on the periphery. Sites 1T-7T are walk-in campsites right on the water. Sites 2-32, which encircle the 4 conjoined loops, are among the most private, as they back up to green spaces. The A, B, and C loops, in the middle of all this, are still arranged for privacy, are large in size, and flat. Most are back-in sites, with a small number of pull-throughs that favor large RVs (sites 5, 6, 10, 25, and 4B.)

Trip Notes: This is a very tight, well-designed, high energy campground where boys on bikes can simultaneously pursue their adventures on the trails and waterways, kayakers explore the cliff-lined waterways to the east, and camp cooks attempt the perfect stew, soup, or mixed grill, and all get along gloriously. Its popularity can work against it, as the Park can fill to capacity early on summer weekdays when the Day Use Area is free and exceeds capacity, and visitors are turned away. But its popularity also testifies to its wide appeal and "everybody friendly" atmosphere.

Local Alternative: For those campers who prefer the lower energy end of the camping spectrum, Saddle Dam CG is close by. The dam is of the earthen type (not hydroelectric), built to redirect the reservoir waters from seeping away, so waters are calm and still. Camping is in a single dispersed area with access to a very nice swimming and picnicking area just below the Dam. Water, restrooms and showers provided. Use is first come, first served.

The Day Use Area at Cresap Bay is so popular they often turn away visitors by midday

For more photos of Cowlitz Co. CGs consult campeverycountywa.com

DOUGLAS COUNTY (Waterville/East Wenatchee)

This Columbia Basin county is nearly encircled by waterways created by various dams, including the awe-inspiring Grand Coulee Dam just over the county line. The best campgrounds lie along the east side of the Columbia River, but are among the best of the best.

Lake Entiat

Lake Entiat is known by many names, including the Rocky Reach Reservoir, but is the result of the damming of the Columbia River by the Rocky Reach Dam just north of Wenatchee. As such, it stretches 43 miles north, forming the border between Chelan County to the west and Douglas County to the east. The once free-flowing river has been transformed into glass-like waters that provide recreation opportunities including water skiing, sailing, jet skiing, kayaking, wind surfing, and of *course camping.*

<u>Lincoln Rock S.P.</u> *(*Douglas Co.'s *BEST CG FOR ENTIRE FAMILIES* and *MOST UNIQUELY WASHINGTON CG)*
Abraham Lincoln may have never visited Washington State, but nature has carved his profile into the hillside visible across Lake Entiat. In the center of the park a telescope allows campers to get a close up and personal view. The Park far exceeds this novelty, however, with perfect campsites, new cabins, boat docks (some accessible from individual campsites), day use areas, and sports fields. This is where most locals prefer to camp, and we all know what that means -- it's far more than a novelty -- it's the best all-around campground in the area, and one of the best in all of Washington.
<u>Overview</u>: This popular campground is located 5 miles north of East Wenatchee on 75 acres with considerable Columbia River/Lake Entiat shoreline at 1000' elevation, open year-round; GPS 47.5358, -120.2835.

Facilities include 5 restrooms (one ADA) with flush toilets and showers, picnic tables/fire grills, boat ramps/docks, a swimming beach, 2 miles of hiking/biking trails, sports fields, an amphitheater, a Park Store (summer only), an RV dump, and camp hosts.

Recreation includes fishing, swimming, boating, water-skiing, bird watching, and geocaching. The 5-mile paved Rocky Reach Trail connects the Park and the Apple Capital Loop Trail in East Wenatchee and is perfect for pedestrians and bicycles. It is ADA accessible.

Campsites/Trip Notes (94 sites for tents and RVs of any size, including 67 with water & electric 50-amp hookup sites, 12 cabins, reservable): The popularity of this Park lies in its completeness. It has a perfect tent camping loop (Loop A1), providing docks for easy lake access, extremely good shade trees, and easy access to the swimming beach in the Day Use Area. The full hook up loop (Loop A2) accommodates large RVs and has the best view of Lincoln Rock. The quieter, less busy Loop B accommodates both RVs and tents, giving the greatest privacy due to lighter use. This contains four standard cabins available for rent. A group camp and 8 premium cabins are nearby. This is a good all-around campground that is very well laid out and provides something for everybody.

Daroga S.P. (Douglas Co.'s *MOST APPEALING CG TO THE SENSES* and *BEST BIKE-IN CG*)

This is one of the quirkiest, most geographically fractured campgrounds in the State Park System; yet, it is one of our favorites. It consists of a walk-on/boat-in island on Lake Entiat protecting a lagoon; RV sites surrounding a red and white power line tower, and a beach area with a stunning concrete promenade connecting the two. Does quirky work for you? Then get over here! Otherwise, Lincoln Rock S.P. might be more to your liking.

Overview: Located 18 miles north of East Wenatchee on 90 acres with 1.5 miles of Columbia River/Lake Entiat shoreline at 1000' elevation, open year-round; GPS 47.713, -120.2099.

Facilities include bathrooms with showers, picnic tables, fire grills, boat ramps/docks, swimming beach, 2 miles of hiking/biking trails, sports fields, an RV dump, and camp hosts.

Recreation includes canoeing/kayaking, hiking/biking, and fishing. For golfers, nationally recognized Desert Canyon Gold Course is just 2 miles away.

Campsites (45 sites, including 28 with water & electric 50-amp hookups, two Group Camps for 150 people each, reservable): Sites are shady with lots of trees, and grassy with great spacing. Tent sites are walk-in/boat-in only, as they are on an island, and the Group Camp ½ mile south of the RV sites. RV campers rave about this area and its natural beauty.

The Tent Area at Daroga S.P. is an island connected by footbridge

Trip Notes: The power line tower in the RV area is a local icon that fits well into the environment. The campers referred to it as the "Electric Eiffel Tower," as though they would miss it if it were gone. They find it no more intrusive than a huge sugar maple or honey locust tree. The tent camping area is equally unique, with walk-in or boat-in sites on a long narrow island connected by causeways and bridges. Camping equipment must be carried in on aluminum carts (provided by the Park) or via the boat launch. The sites are along the western edge of the island, with poplar trees and windbreak fences constructed to minimize the wind. There is a protected lagoon here that is perfect for quiet canoeing or kayaking. The river side has docks available for powerboating. This is certainly one of the prettiest and most unique parks anywhere.

Beebe Bridge Park (Douglas Co.'s *BEST EQUIPPED/BEST CG FOR RVs)*
This former Columbia River apple orchard was transformed into this newer park as part of a bigger agreement with the local PUD for building the Rocky Reach Dam (downstream) and the Azwell Dam (upstream) to provide recreational opportunities. It is regarded as the best-maintained park in the area, with facilities for RVers, tenters, and especially bicycle campers with easy access off of Highway 97.
Overview: This pristine and well-constructed park is located 37 miles north of East Wenatchee and 4 miles east of Chelan, managed by the local PUD on 56 acres with one mile of Columbia River footage at 856' elevation, open April 1 to Oct. 31; GPS 47.8063, -119.9743.
Facilities include bathrooms with showers, a swimming area, picnic shelters, a 2-lane boat launch and dock, a playground, tennis courts, basketball hoops, soccer fields, and an RV dump station.
Recreation: The River Walk provides a flat, easy walk along the Columbia River accessible to all walkers; fishing and boating are also popular.

<u>Campsites</u> (46 sites for tents or RVs up to 60' with water & electric 20/30-amp hookups, reservable): This very flat area with its spacious sites, some right on the River, are set in a lush grassy spread with shade trees. Parking pads are concrete, with some privacy provided by the spacing of the sites.

<u>Trip Notes</u>: This is the Douglas Co. campground that RV'ers rave about most. The Park is set in the backdrop of the rusty old Beebe Bridge, contrasted by a sweep of colors -- verdant, rolling lawns, and RVs of all shapes, sizes, and brands -- everything from behemoth buses to Teardrop Trailers pulled by VW Beetles. Even the life jackets at the marina popped with color. The swimming area here, similar to that at Daroga, is a very secluded beachy touch to a very nice camping park.

The Waterville Plateau

Once you leave the long oasis along the Columbia River and head east, you begin to climb high up to the much drier land of ancient lava flows and 10,000 years of glacial activity. But this otherwise barren land will tell you its history, as evidenced by haystack rocks, eskers, and basalt cliffs, all waiting for the curious to come and take a long look.

<u>Douglas Creek Recreation Site, DCRS</u> (Douglas Co.'s *BEST FREE* and *BEST RUSTIC CG*)

This camping area is set in dry sage-steppe uplands in a basalt canyon following Douglas Creek with beaver ponds, cascading pools, waterfalls, and smooth boulders that slide right into the crystalline creek -- a place you might call Nature's Water Park, with piped-in music from the songbirds.

<u>Overview</u>: This remote location is 7 miles southwest of Waterville, operated by the Bureau of Land Management (BLM) at 2625' elevation, open March 1 through Nov. 30. GPS: 47.509525, -119.949487.

<u>Facilities</u> are non-existent; but the site is sufficiently isolated for campers to shower in the waterfalls and bath in the pools.

<u>Recreation</u>: The 5-mile Douglas Creek Trail (trailhead GPS 47.4581, -119.8769), just inside the northern entrance of DCRS, is a beautiful, flat interpretive trail that follows Douglas Creek deep into a colorful, volcanic canyon full of songbirds, desert vegetation, and interesting dispersed camping sites. Also popular are horseback riding, hunting, aquatic sports (water slides), and fishing for rainbow trout. This is designated by the Audubon Society as an Important Bird Area of Eastern Washington with black-billed magpie, black-capped chickadee, black-headed grosbeak, Bullock's oriole, lazuli bunting, northern flicker, northern harrier, red-tailed hawk, rock wrens, vesper sparrow, and western meadowlark. The most renowned natural recreation, however, is the quarter-to half-mile stretch of Douglas Creek at the south end of the DCRS that is a series of waterfalls, deep

pools, and overhanging campsites that is a famed and cherished swimming area in both Douglas and Chelan Counties.

Recommended Directions: We strongly recommend approaching DCRS from the north, approximately 5 miles west of the small down of Douglas on Highway 2, then turning right/south onto Rd H SW. The road is long, straight, paved and flat most of the way to the north entrance of DCRS where you will find the trailhead and most of the campsites. Be aware that the road gets progressively worse as you go south, requiring a high-clearance 4-wheel drive vehicle.

Campsites (dispersed campsites, no reservations or hookups, FREE of charge): Sites are set amid cottonwoods filled with songbirds. They are close to the gravel road with dispersed campsites, a rustic but very unique camping experience, an oasis in the midst of a rather barren landscape.

Trip Notes: This trip was a solo effort on my part, just me and the two dogs. We approached from the north, and easily found the entrance. My main objective was to find the famed "Nature's Water Park" and, after exploring the Trail and much of the Creek, I quickly reached the conclusion we had missed it. The road slowly deteriorated, with the Creek spilling over the road many times, and my new focus became connecting with Palisades Road and getting out of the area before dark. Then suddenly it appeared. I slammed on the brakes and did a double take. Yes, this was it -- the natural water park I saw only bits and pieces of in random photos. Waterfall after waterfall, deep pool after deep pool, slippery rock after slippery rock. I bounded down the hillside towards it, my heart racing with unnatural exuberance, shouting "Yes! This is why we do this!" I did a quick look see to make sure there were no "Swimsuits Required" signs (fat chance!), got down to nature, and canon-balled into the first and deepest of the pools. It didn't matter how cool the water was, or who might be watching. Mother Nature had provided me with the object of my desire.

For more photos of Douglas Co. CGs consult
campeverycountywa.com

FERRY COUNTY (Republic/Keller/Boyds)

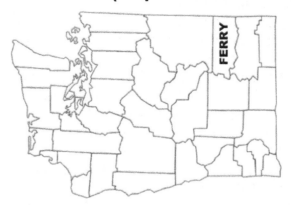

This county has the lowest population density but the best campgrounds and most intriguing tiny towns in Washington. Its history of mining, logging, and farming leave a very earthy stamp on all that you will see and experience.

Republic Area

The quaint pioneer town of Republic, originally called Eureka Gulch, was founded by gold fever in 1896 when the Colville Indian Reservation was opened for mining exploration. Overnight, the valley rang with the sound of pickaxes, shovels, and braying mules. Today, this bustling town is the center of commerce and recreational opportunities up and down the San Poil Valley.

Lake Curlew S.P. (Ferry Co.'s *MOST APPEALING CG TO THE SENSES*)
When does a lake stop being just beautiful and becomes stunning? Answer: When its source is the San Poil River, when it sits mid-way between the towns of Curlew and Republic, and when its shores are spotted with resorts of character that are reachable by canoe or kayak. Yep, that's Lake Curlew!
Overview: This appealing campground is magnificently located 10 miles north of Republic on 123 acres on 921-acre Curlew Lake at 2182' elevation, open April 1 to November 1; GPS: 48.721, -118.6619.
Facilities: Good facilities include bathrooms with flush toilets, running water, and showers; picnic tables, fire grills, a swimming area, 80' of dock, 2 boat launches, 2 miles of hiking/biking trails, an amphitheater, RV dump station, Park Store, and camp hosts.
Recreation: Fishing is best for rainbow trout, but also includes large and small mouth bass and tiger muskies. Rock hounding is popular at the Stone Rose public dig site. Kayaking, canoeing, and water skiing are all excellent.

<u>Campsites</u> (83 sites for tents and RVs of any size, but best up to 35' including 25 with water & electric hookups 50-amp, most are reservable): Sites are large and grassy with poor to average privacy. The RV portion of the park is at the bottom of a "bowl," surrounded by steep hills where white tailed deer come down to feed morning and night.

<u>Trip Notes</u>: Despite a lack of privacy, we extended our stay. The 5.5-mile long lake is exquisite for kayaking and canoeing, with many islands, inlets, and a railroad bridge crossing the north end of the lake. Three small resorts (Tiffany's, Black Beach, and the quaint Fisherman's Cove) are accessible by boat, where you can tie up for a beverage or lunch. Everyone being occupied with fishing or other activities balanced the lack of privacy. The old mining town of Republic and the so-called ghost town of Curlew are well worth visiting and lingering, as both have a strong feeling of history and a lifestyle connected to the land on which it sits.

<u>Local Alternatives</u>: Lone Ranch Park, Beal Park, Peggy Brixner Park, and Matney Park, are all managed in a cooperative agreement between Ferry and Stevens Counties.

Kuehne CG (Ferry Co.'s *BEST EQUIPPED /BEST FOR RVs*)

This is the best equipped and most developed of the campgrounds at County Fairs, and you'll be caught up in the locals' love for this area.

<u>Overview</u>: This remarkable, open campground is located within the Ferry Co. Fairgrounds 3.5 miles northeast of Republic on O'Brien Creek at 2500' elevation, open year-round; GPS coordinates for Republic are 48.6482, -118.7378.

<u>Facilities</u>: In addition to all the Fair buildings, facilities include flush toilets, coin-op showers, running water, and a 100-year old antique carousel (operating ONLY during the Fair).

<u>Recreation</u>: Tiger Trail for hiking or biking extends 3.5 miles to the town of Republic with full services and entertainment.

<u>Campsites</u> (102 RV sites plus additional tent sites, water & electric 30 amps, reservable): Sites are grassy with no barriers, line O'Brien Creek, and are rarely crowded when the Fair is not in operation. This could make an excellent Group Camp if many conjoining sites were reserved. All of the facilities (except the carousel) are located in the campground itself.

<u>Trip Notes</u>: A delightful and unexpected find here. We pulled in out of curiosity, having passed this way many times in the past few years. The grounds were meticulous, with fresh red paint in most places, reports of a 100-year old carousel during the Fair, and sites that back into a perfect sized creek. It's a place where you can't imagine people being unhappy. It's that cheerful, green, and rarely crowded except during the Fair itself (usually the first week of September). You might want to avoid camping here during that time. Kids will love this place. So, did we.

<u>Swan Lake CG</u> (Ferry Co.'s *BEST CG FOR ENTIRE FAMILIES*)
Swan Lake is the largest and prettiest of this small chain of lakes in the Colville National Forest. Long Lake gets the nod from fishermen, but if you are looking for the best camping, this is where you'll want to be.

<u>Overview</u>: This lovely terraced lakefront campground is located 14 miles southwest of Republic on 53.5-acre Swan Lake, one of three campgrounds on four small lakes in a 4-square-mile area, operated by the USFS at 3300' elevation, open mid-May to mid-November; GPS 47.93639, -113.85056.

<u>Facilities</u>: Good and unique facilities include ADA-accessible vault toilets, water by hand spigots, picnic tables, fire rings, hiking trails, a Day Use Area, and boat launches on Swan, Long, and Ferry Lakes. A key feature at Swan Lake is the Swan Lake Kitchen. Built by the CCC in 1936 and restored in 2009, this large covered shelter with a stone fireplace sits right on the lake and invites swimming, boating, and all-day use. The facility can accommodate up to 35 people and is reservable.

<u>Recreation</u>: A variety of possibilities include seasonal huckleberry picking, kayaking, canoeing, swimming, and fishing. Fishing is good for trout, but no motorboats are allowed.

<u>Campsites</u> (Swan Lake: 25 sites for tents and RVs of any size; Long Lake: 12 sites; Ferry Lake 9 sites; no hookups or reservations): Sites are quiet and private. These lakes are used primarily by fly fishermen and, without the intrusion of motorboats, camping is very quiet here. A 0.5-mile trail connects Long Lake with tiny Fish Lake, the smallest of the four lakes. Swan Lake is the largest lake with the largest and nicest campground. Its terraced lakefront sites are the largest, separated in part by hand-hewn log fences. Easy access to the town of Republic is convenient for supplies.

<u>Trip Notes</u>: Long Lake gets the attention due to its superior fishing (although the sites are beautiful, spacious, and shaded), but Swan Lake is the real gem for camping, particularly the lakefront sites. Ferry Lake also has great sites well above the Lake, and a very accessible boat launch at the end of the road. Human-powered boats do well in all 3 car-accessible lakes.

Kettle River Arm of Lake Roosevelt

The Grand Coulee Dam created more lakes than just 130-mile long Lake Roosevelt. It also backed up rivers and streams flowing into the massive lake into a series of "Arms," the largest being from the Kettle and San Poil Rivers.

<u>Kamloops Island CG</u> (Ferry Co.'s *MOST UNIQUELY WASHINGTON CG*)
Sometimes geological oddities make great camping. Just why this beautiful chunk of camping bliss broke off from the mainland seems a mystery. But this is camping, so stop overthinking all that, get out your lounge chairs and have a good time.

Overview: This remarkable little campground is located 2.4 miles south of Boyds with frontage on the Kettle River Arm of Lake Roosevelt, operated by the NPS at 1327' elevation, open year-round; GPS 48.679069, -118.117215.

Facilities: This modestly equipped campground includes vault toilets, picnic tables, fire rings, and a boat dock.

Recreation: Boating and fishing are available, but most campers, captivated by the Island's beauty, prefer to stay put.

Campsites (17 sites, no hookups or reservations): Sites seem scenic but primitive, as the park sits in the middle of the gorgeous Kettle River. The Island sits high above the River/Lake with water always in view, and never more than a short walk away. Even standing on the short bridge is captivating, with a view all the way to the main channel of Lake Roosevelt.

Trip Notes: We'd wanted to camp at this campground for a long time and pitched our tents during the worst drought in 14 years, when the waters of Lake Roosevelt were at an all-time low. As such, Kamloops Island wasn't much of an island at all, but more like a peninsula with a narrow waterway separating it from Highway 395. But it was still gorgeous. There was of course some road noise, but the views were spectacular, and the camping very, very good. With a little imagination, campers can imagine it as completely surrounded by water and far from the hustle of the towns.

Trout Lake CG (Ferry Co.'s *BEST RUSTIC AND BEST FREE CG*)
Tiny Trout Lake CG is used by hikers, fishermen, and hunters, but it gets light use and is one of the quietest camping spots around while still close to services in Kettle Falls.

Overview: Located 40 miles east of Republic and 14 miles northwest of Kettle Falls on 11.2-acre Trout Lake, operated by the USFS at 3087' elevation, open year-round; GPS 48.62389, -118.239845.

Facilities: Limited facilities include a vault toilet, picnic tables, fire pits, boat dock and a boat ramp (non-ADA accessible). There is no drinking water or garbage service.

Recreation includes boating/trout fishing (electric engines only). There is hiking access to Hoodoo Canyon Trail #17, a 4.7-mile hiking trail that intersects the Emerald Lake #94 trail. Wildlife seen in the campground include moose and white tail deer.

Campsites (5 sites for tents and very small RVs, tent pads, non-reservable, FREE with USFS Pass): Campsites are small, private, and located close to the Lake. They are also quiet, being located far from the main road. Vegetation is lush and provides needed shade.

Trip Notes: This is the perfect little Forest Service Campground on the perfect little lake -- and that is the highest compliment any campground will ever get from me.

Local Alternatives: Other FREE CGs in Ferry Co. include Davis Lake CG, Lake Ellen CG, and Little Twin Lakes CG (all USFS).

Colville Indian Reservation

The Colville Indian Reservation occupies the entire southern half of Ferry County. You won't find the big State Parks or luxurious glamping parks, but you will find a series of smaller, utterly unique campgrounds set in pristine forest, and scattered with crystal clear lakes, rivers, and streams.

Keller CG (Ferry Co.'s *BEST BIKE-IN CG*)
This is the most accessible of the campgrounds operated by the Tribe, nestled on a grassy plateau just above the San Poil Arm of Lake Roosevelt. The rising and falling lake levels give it a different look on each visit, but it remains the hidden gem of the Ferry County campgrounds.
Overview: This peaceful campground is located 46 miles south of Republic and 2 miles south of Keller on 4 acres with frontage on the San Poil Arm of Lake Roosevelt, operated by the Confederated Tribes of the Colville Reservation at 1499' elevation, open year-round; GPS coordinates are not established.
Facilities: Good facilities include vault toilets, running water, picnic tables, barbeque pits, a playground, and boating/swimming docks.
Recreation: These include swimming, boating, and pondering the meaning of life.
Campsites (about 20 sites, no hookups or reservations): These beautiful, mostly lakeside sites are grassy and flat with beautiful shade trees and poor to moderate privacy. There is some road noise from Highway 21, which will quiet down after dark.
Trip Notes: This is the Brigadoon of campgrounds. People don't know it's even there, despite passing it many times. It is only accessible from the south, as the entrance road cannot be navigated from the north. Only a small green and white sign saying "campground" (visible only from the south) marks the spot. When you drop down into the Park, there is a certain energy. Everyone I saw was dressed in modern dress, but I couldn't get over the feeling they were native peoples from hundreds of years ago even if my imagination was simply running away with me.

For photos of Ferry Co. CGs or info on HIKE-IN or BEST EQUIPPED CGs
consult campeverycountywa.com

FRANKLIN COUNTY (Pasco/Connell)

This Columbia Basin county is about irrigation and railroads. There is enough space here for campers and railroads to co-exist brilliantly. Box cars carry wheat, hay, potatoes, and sugar beets while the birds, insects, and other wildlife sound off informing you of the richness of this land, until it finally wins you over.

Connell Area

Water destroyed this area during the last Ice Age when torrents of water from Lake Missoula unleashed to scrub away the soil and pluck at the underlying bedrock, resulting in these Channeled Scablands. 13,000 years later, water saved the very same area with irrigation when farms, formerly struggling on sagebrush and sweat, were made green again. The town of Connell now buzzes with prosperity, becoming the prettiest and second largest town in Franklin County.

Scooteney Reservoir CG (Franklin Co.'s *BEST EQUIPPED/BEST CG FOR RVs*)
The reservoir is part of the Columbia Basin Project which also includes Grand Coulee Dam, but the name Scooteney derives from native words meaning "a place to watch fish." You can also catch them, eat them, and brag about them, but mostly this is a place for people to watch nature and enjoy being off the grid.
miles north of Pasco and 10 miles west of Connell on 710-acre Scooteney
Overview: This lovely 1200-acre "dry" RV park and campground is located 36 miles north of Pasco and 10 miles west of Connell on 710-acre Scooteney Reservoir operated by the Federal Bureau of Land Reclamation as part of the Columbia Basin Project at 925' elevation, open year-round; GPS 46.70638, -119.00931.
Facilities: This smart, tidy campground includes bathrooms with running water, picnic tables, fire rings, and a Day Use Area with gazebo. There is a swimming

area but check for closures due to algae. There are also 3 boat launches (one primitive) and an RV dump.

Recreation includes canoeing and kayaking, swimming, birdwatching, and fishing for bass, carp, channel catfish, walleye and yellow bullhead. The reservoir is also popular for ice fishing when conditions allow. It is situated along a major flyway for migratory birds, including sandhill cranes, ducks, geese, northern harriers, American kestrels, merlins, plus great horned owls, barn owls, golden eagles and bald eagles. For fans of vintage boats, Scooteney Reservoir hosts the Annual Antique Boat Races.

Campsites (36 sites for tents and RVs of any size, two ADA sites, no hookups or reservations): All sites are very flat with trees for shade and include paved parking pads. The two ADA sites, with their wheelchair-accessible concrete pads and paths, are the best we have seen. The camping and Day Use areas are irrigated, green, and well-managed

Trip Notes: The charm of this campground is that, while the facilities seem a bit outdated, everything is so well maintained that it's like wearing your favorite old shirt. The reservoir twists and winds, with fingers of land and water intertwining. This makes boating, and especially boating/kayaking, an adventure it itself. It's no wonder that RV'ers love this place, despite lack of hookups or internet technology.

Local Attractions include the Windmill Ranch and Esquatzel Coulee Wildlife Areas for wildlife viewing.

Snake River/Lake Sacajawea

Named after the Shoshone woman, Sacajawea, who was a member of the Lewis and Clark expedition, this 32-mile long lake was formed by the Ice Harbor Lock and Dam on the Lower Snake River. The north bank of the Lake has very few roads to its isolated shores, guaranteeing solitude for those willing to come and find it.

Windust Park (Franklin Co.'s *BEST CG FOR ENTIRE FAMILIES, BEST RUSTIC CG,* and *BEST FREE CG*)

This remote not-so-windy, not-so-dusty park on the Snake River/Lake Sacajawea hums with railroads and bare hills, while mature shade trees and the coolness of the water allow you to relax and watch the world go by.

Overview: This family-friendly Park is located 36 miles northeast of Pasco on 54 acres with extensive shoreline on Lake Sacajawea, operated by the US Army COE at 902' elevation, open year-round; GPS 46.53306, -118.58333.

Facilities include flush toilets, water available seasonally, playground, swimming area with dock, fenced play area, picnic shelter, boat launch, and camp hosts during peak season.

Recreation: Fishing is easy for smallmouth bass, catfish, panfish, and perch. Stargazing is considered good, far from the city lights of Pasco.

Campsites (24 sites, 10 of which are suitable for RVs up to 22' long, no hookups or reservations, FREE of charge): Sites are open on lush grass with mature shade trees, of average size with varying privacy depending on the site, all have lake views. The low use of this park makes up for any lack of privacy. Of the three Parks on this website along Lake Sacajawea, Charbonneau Park has the marina, Fishhook Park has the great campsites, but Windust Park has SOLITUDE.

Trip Notes: We had some preconceptions about this Park before camping there. With a name made up of the words "wind" and "dust," we imagined a "dead zone," a place devoid of much wildlife, plant life, or trees, and where the only sound would be the persistent whistle of the wind. This proved to be quite wrong. Even before pulling into the Park, we shared the road with trucks delivering grain to the Windust Grainery adjacent to the Park (only operational on weekdays). We also heard trains clacking from across the River, doves cooing and crickets chirping, some unidentified ground creatures chattering down small holes, and the low hum of barges pushing their way up the River. Before long, we realized that we were in the heartland of Washington, a desert made to bloom, and the source of much of our food. It was full of life -- sometimes too much, as the birds were noisy all night long (yes, it was breeding season, curse them). It turned out to be a great getaway -- not from nature, but from the more complicated cares of life. One caution: this is a very remote Park, with extremely limited resources for groceries or supplies, so come prepared.

Local Alternative: Devil's Bench CG, just 3 miles north of Windust is a more primitive alternative on 52 acres with 6 sites run by the US Army COE.

Juniper Dunes Wilderness Area (Franklin Co.'s *MOST APPEALING CG TO THE SENSES, BEST HIKE-IN CAMPING AREA*)

The United States Congress designated the Juniper Dunes Wilderness in 1984 to preserve the northernmost growth of western juniper, some of which are 150 years old, along with windswept sand dunes measuring 130 feet in height and 1200 feet in width. This is where you can experience Washington "from the ground up," up close and personal.

Overview: This unique wilderness hiking and camping area is located 18 miles northeast of Pasco, operated by the BLM on 7,140 acres at 750-1300' elevation, open year-round; GPS 46.25708, -118.49523. See special directions below.

Facilities: There is neither water nor facilities, so bring everything you need. Visitors should be well-versed in Leave No Trace ethics and pack out all trash. There are no formal hiking trails within the Refuge. Campfires and mechanized equipment are prohibited, but camp stoves are allowed and recommended. While dogs are allowed (a rarity for Wildlife Refuges), the rugged nature and thorny vegetation of this area may mean it's best to leave them at home.

Recreation: Wildlife viewing includes badgers, bobcats, coyotes, doves, grasshopper mice, hawks, kangaroo rats, lizards, mule deer, owls, partridge, pheasants, pocket gophers, porcupines, quail, rattlesnakes, ravens, skunks, numerous songbirds, and weasels. Vegetation includes old-growth juniper trees, sagebrush, wild rye grass, and wildflowers, including phlox, larkspur, and prickly pear cactus.

Campsites: (Dispersed camping only, FREE of charge with a free overnight permit from the BLM): There are no formal campsites. Leave No Trace Rules are in effect. The entire Wilderness Area is surrounded by private land. Do not travel on random jeep trails without permission from landowners. The only entrance to the Wilderness Area (which is surrounded by a single 15-mile fence) is on an otherwise impassable, sandy ORV road. It may be necessary for hikers to hike an additional 3.5 miles through the Juniper Forest (a nice hike in itself) to the fenced entrance. Some high clearance 4-wheel drive vehicles can make it up this road in the wetter part of the year, but given the area only gets 8 inches of rainfall per year, opportunities are limited. This entrance is at the southwestern end of the Refuge. Hikers/campers entering the southern end of the refuge will find native grasses, which undulate in the hills. Further north, the land becomes hillier with shrubs and tall sagebrush replacing the grasses. The real treasures, of course, are the beautiful, ancient junipers. Birds feed on these bushes in wintertime, when other foraging is at a minimum. Winter is also the time, at least when free of snow, when the land is lush, green, and at its most spectacular.

Trip Notes: The light green and white sandy mosaic of this land make it a delight. Various Indian tribes have relied on the giant sagebrush leaves for a type of spiritual aromatherapy, rubbing the grey-green leaves between their fingers to release a cleansing scent. The juniper berries have been used for centuries to flavor foods, including venison. They have also been used as a soak to treat sore feet and calf muscles. Now if there were only some water out here, it could be put to good use at the end of a long hike.

SPECIAL INSTRUCTIONS/DIRECTIONS: Call the BLM office in Spokane before going out to be sure you can get access: 509-536-1200.

The Palouse River

The Palouse River Canyon defines Franklin Co.'s easternmost border. The Canyon is 1,000 feet deep in places, zigzagging with its high basalt walls directly to the Snake River. This magnificent, meandering river once flowed through the less direct Washtucna Coulee. The Palouse Indian legend states that the formation of the current Palouse River Canyon came when four giant brothers battled a mythical creature called Big Beaver, spearing him five times before he gouged the canyon walls with his massive claws, causing the river to bend and change to its present course. Geologists, wishing no disrespect to Mr. Big Beaver, believe that the Palouse River changed course during the Missoula floods, when Ice Age waters spilled into the Snake River and its tributaries, then receded suddenly, causing the Palouse to cut a more direct path to the Snake River, forming the waterfall and jagged, basalt-walled canyon we know and love today.

Palouse Falls S.P. (Franklin Co.'s *BEST BIKE-IN CG* and *MOST UNIQUELY WASHINGTON CG*)

This park has a unique geology and history, offering a dramatic view of one of the state's most beautiful waterfalls. Palouse Falls drops from a height of 198 feet, higher but narrower than Niagara Falls, with high volumes of water year-round. It was named the official Washington State Waterfall in 2014.

Overview: This iconic campground is located 69 miles northeast of Pasco and 17 miles south of Washtuctna on 105 acres at 784' elevation, open year-round with limited facilities in winter; GPS 46.66694, -118.22278.

Facilities: These consist of pit toilets (ADA), piped water available April to October, picnic tables, fire grills, a 2-acre picnic area with shelter, 0.5 miles of ADA hiking trails, and interpretive panels about Ice Age floods and the creation of the basalt-walled canyon.

Recreation includes nearby Lyons Ferry S.P. (Day Use Only), at the confluence of the Palouse and Snake Rivers, which offers fishing, swimming, and boating opportunities.

Campsites (11 primitive tent sites, one of which is ADA, no hookups, no reservations, payment by cash or check only - no credit cards): All sites (except the ADA site) rest on a knoll and are less than flat. There is shade, but no privacy, and so accommodates only parties who travel very light. Overnight campers have the advantage of being near the falls at sunset, as the light and shadows changing along the canyon walls are magnificent.

Trip Notes: We were most surprised that the waterfall, which was as magnificent as advertised, was so close to the camping area. We expected an arduous hike, when all it took was a short stroll from the parking lot. The trails to the bottom of the falls have been closed due to safety concerns, but the Falls are in full view for even wheelchaired onlookers. Yellow-bellied marmots also scour the area, another source of delight, foraging both the campground and campsites. That being said, the campground is a beehive, with visitors coming and going at all hours. While we loved the park, it is likely best for one-night only stays, particularly for bicyclers.

For photos of Franklin Co. CGs consult campeverycountywa.com

GARFIELD COUNTY (Pomeroy/Pataha)

This key-shaped, southeastern county is the least populated in Washington, covered two-thirds by farms and one-third by forested wilderness in the Umatilla National Forest. If you want nature, you'll find it here.

Snake River/Lake Bryan

Lake Bryan is the reservoir behind the Little Goose Dam on a remote section of the lower Snake River. Here you'll be met with wide-open vistas, steep canyon walls, but few trees. Fish here, swim here, water ski here, camp here, or take a stab at fish viewing at Little Goose or Lower Granite Dams.

Illia Landing CG and Dunes Rec Area (Garfield Co.'s *MOST UNIQUELY WA CG*) With only two arid campsites, this deceptive little campground has a connection to water recreation that can stand up to the biggest and best.

Overview: This smallest and most unique of campgrounds is located 25 miles north of Pomeroy and 4.2 miles northwest of the Lower Granite Dam, operated by the US Army COE on 16 acres at 640' elevation, open year-round; GPS 46.7018261, -117.4710193 (more directions below).

Facilities are limited but include a vault toilet, picnic tables, fire grates, drinking water, a separate drinking fountain, and a boat launch.

Recreation: This otherwise stark campground has access to boating, fishing, and excellent swimming and sun-bathing at the nearby Ilia Dunes Recreation Area (1-mile west).

Campsites (2 tent sites, no hookups or reservations, FREE of charge): Sites are in full sun with privacy guaranteed as you'll probably be alone. Many campers spend the majority of their time fishing or swimming at the Illia Dunes (see the front book cover).

Trip Notes: Stark, yes, but also intriguing. The trees provide no shade but catch the sun in such a way that they appear to have veins running deep into the ground to collect water. Perhaps that is how this primitive campground provides water for the large, stand-alone drinking fountain. Nah, but let your imagination run wild.

Directions: Just east of Pomeroy on SR 12 turn north onto Gould City-Mayview Rd and follow it for 25 miles toward the Lower Granite Dam. The campground is on the right just 3 miles from the Dam. Of note, it may be easier to find this campground from the north by driving to Almota and Boyer Park/Marina (see Whitman Co.), then driving across the Lower Granite Dam (accessible during business hours only, so check before planning to cross).

Illia Landing and the Illia Dunes show the diversity of Garfield Co. camping

Lambi Creek CG (Garfield Co.'s BEST FREE CG)
This shady oasis in the arid lower Snake River Valley provides a cool alternative to the better-known, full-sun campgrounds in the area.

Overview: This cozy campground is located 22 miles north of Pomeroy at the confluence of little Lambi Creek and Lake Bryan, operated by the US Army COE at 640' elevation, open year-round; GPS 46.67944444, -117.50277780.

Facilities are limited to a vault toilet, picnic tables, and fire rings.

Recreation: Fishing is possible from the shore of Lake Bryan. The campground is just 2 miles west of the Ilia Dunes Rec Area for sun-bathing and great swimming.

Campsites (6 sites for tents or small RVs, no hookups or reservations, FREE of charge): Most sites are tucked back into the vegetation or beneath tall trees. None are perfectly flat, but privacy is always likely due to underbrush and light use.

Trip Notes: After traveling the arid countryside of northern Garfield Co., pulling into this campground is much like finding a very old, overgrown apple orchard on the banks of Lake Bryan. Granted, there are no apple trees, only aspen, maple, locust, and lodgepole pine, but the cool shade provides a welcome respite to campers looking to cool their camping heals for a day or two.

Directions: This campground lies just 3 miles west of Ilia Landing (see above).

Pomeroy Area

This quaint, well-preserved town comprises two-thirds of the population of the County, with its historic courthouse, vintage homes, and Main Street shops. This is Americana at its best, with friendly people who live very close to the land, with an unmatched devotion to their community.

Garfield Co. Fairgrounds (Garfield Co.'s *BEST CG FOR ENTIRE FAMILIES, BEST EQUIPPED/BEST CG for RVs*, and *BEST BIKE-IN CG*)

Nothing represents a rural farming community like its County Fair. You won't find roller coasters or shooting galleries (two sure deal breakers for most campers), but you'll find the Eastern Washington Agricultural Museum, and rolling stretches of green grass between farm buildings giving campers a rare opportunity to see rural Eastern Washington and Garfield County "from the ground up." Just one hint: do not visit in mid-September during Fair time.

Overview: These meticulously maintained County Fairgrounds are located 2 miles east of Pomeroy at 1991' elevation, open year-round; GPS: 46.471071, -117.551583.

Facilities: The Fairground facilities are open to campers, including bathrooms with showers and drinking water. There are no picnic tables or fire grills.

campeverycountywa.com

The Garfield Co. Fairgrounds are a prime opportunity to explore Southeastern Washington "from the ground up"

Recreation: The flat, grassy stretches between the well-maintained farm buildings provides unique opportunities for children to explore and play in a safe area all surrounded by chain link fences. It encompasses the Eastern Washington Agricultural Museum with tours available by appointment. For others, it provides close proximity to hiking in the Umatilla National Forest and boating opportunities along the Snake River.

Campsites (10 sites w/water & electric 30-amp, 3 sites have sewer, reservable): This camping area falls off the radar of most conventional campgrounds and RV parks. Sites are flat, back-in, grassy, side-by-side, and back into a steep hillside. The nearby town of Pomeroy can provide all services.

Trip Notes: There is an intimacy to this campground that most lack. At least one towns person camps here at all times to act as campground host. This is the town's showcase, and they open it up to visitors with open arms.

Local Alternatives: For those campers in RVs requiring more complete RV hookups and services, we recommend Pataha RV Park just east of the Fairgrounds on Highway 12. It is a full-service RV Park but does not allow tent camping.

Umatilla National Forest/Mountain Highway

The Mountain Highway, as it is commonly called, is actually three roads. It leaves Pomeroy as Highway 128, veers to the right becoming Highway 107, then switches to Forest Service Road with its cattle grate marking the boundary to the Umatilla National Forest. It then continues perfectly south along the length of the "key" to remarkable wilderness country, where people are outnumbered by mountain goats and coyotes.

Teal Spring CG (Garfield Co.'s *MOST APPEALING CG TO THE SENSES*)
This is the third campground on the Mountain Road, and the most picturesque of all with its spectacular view of the Tucannon Drainage and the Wenaha-Tucannon Wilderness. Fortunately for all of us, spring and summer have few cloudy days to hide these endless vistas.

Overview: This most beautiful of campgrounds is located 23 miles south of Pomeroy in the Umatilla National Forest at 5600' elevation, open year-round; GPS: 46.1886, -117.572.

Facilities: Adequately appointed but rustic, this campground comes with the familiar combination of vault toilet, picnic tables, and fire grates, plus a parking area. There is no water or other services available.

Recreation: Hiking is popular, with the Bear Creek Trailhead just south of the campground. There are some ORV trails in the vicinity, but the remoteness of this area means it gets minimal use. The Clearwater Lookout provides views of the Wenaha-Tucannon Wilderness (just north off
the spur Forest Road 42), which is a delight to both photographers and gawkers alike.

Campsites (7 quaint campsites for tents and RVs up to 35 feet long, no hookups or reservations, FREE with NW Forest Pass, except during hunting season): Most of this area allows camping outside of developed campgrounds up to 300 feet from an open road at no charge. As you progress south on the Mountain Road, the elevation increases with increased chance of snow late in the season, so this will be the last and best stop for most campers.

Trip Notes: The forest here is a remarkable transformation from the rolling farmlands to the north. It is cooler here, with vistas well beyond the next hillside.

Local Alternative: Misery Spring is the southernmost of the four campgrounds on the Mountain Road. RV camping is not advised due to road conditions for the last 2.5 miles. Trails lead to Mt. Misery and the Wenaha Wilderness, which extends into NE Oregon. The best alternative for most is Big Springs CG. To get here, veer left at the Clearwater Lookout Tower onto Hwy 42 (you would veer right following Hwy 40 to get to Teal Spring) and drive 5 miles to the campground. A map of the Pomeroy Ranger District by the USFS is invaluable and recommended

Pataha Creek CG (Garfield Co.'s *BEST RUSTIC CG*)

Pronounced Pa-TAA-Ha, this beautiful spot on the edge of the Umatilla National Forest has a small pond surrounded by meadow, with Pataha Creek running right through the middle. The surrounding pristine pine forest makes for a great getaway without delving into the wilderness.

Overview: This rustic little campground is located 17.3 miles south of Pomeroy, operated by the USFS at 3922' elevation, open year-round, weather permitting; GPS: 46.29224, -117.51387.

Facilities: Limited facilities include a vault toilet, picnic tables, fire grates, and a small day use area; no water or other services.

Recreation: Hiking and fishing are popular. Fish are stocked each spring in Pataha Creek, including rainbow trout and eastern brook trout. Hiking is popular from the Stevens Ridge Trailhead to the south.

Campsites (6 sites for tents or small RVs, no hookups or reservations, fees only during hunting season): The campground is at the National Forest's edge. Once there, the campsites are relatively open on a beautiful meadow near the pond and Pataha Creek.

Trip Notes: This place has a very Appalachian look, first driving on narrow, winding roads along creeks before finding yourself driving to the end of a narrow "holler" along Pataha Creek. You'll be isolated, but you'll also feel tucked in for the night.

Directions: Note that the campground is not on the main north-south Mountain Road/Hwy 128. After driving 7 miles, turn left onto Peola Rd (maps show this as the continuation of Hwy128). Continue for 1.5 miles until you come to the farmhouse, turn left, cross a small bridge, then veer right onto Pataha Creek Road to the campground.

For more photos of Garfield Co. CGs consult
campeverycountywa.com

Brendan climbs to the top of
Steamboat Rock

Quincy Lake is the prettiest of a
series of lakes near the City of
Quincy

There is a real lake in Moses Lake,
and the camping forecast is sunny!

Crescent Bar Island was formed
from swirling eddies in a bend of the
Columbia during Ice Age floods

The hike down to the Ancient Lakes
follows a series of waterfalls

GRANT COUNTY (Ephrata/Moses Lake/Grand Coulee)

The Columbia Basin Reclamation Project has transformed these "channeled scablands" created by Ice Age floods into some of the richest farmland anywhere, while leaving behind lakes, coulees, and other canyonland wonders as reminders of its turbulent geological past. Grand Coulee Dam, Dry Falls, and the Columbia National Wildlife Refuge further meld the past with the future in this best of recreational counties.

Grand Coulee Area

This land was shaped by the Missoula Floods, a series of cataclysmic floods occurring several times over a 2,000-year period between 15,000 and 13,000 years ago. Ice dams formed on the Columbia River, causing it to change course over what is now Banks Lake and the Grand Coulee Area. This explains the unusual patterns of erosion, cutting through basalt deposits, scouring away the soil, creating a landscape we now call the "Channeled Scablands." As the glacial lake retreated and the ice dams eventually broke, the Columbia River resumed its original course, leaving behind such geological wonders as Dry Falls, the Grand Coulee, and Steamboat Rock. 27-mile long Banks Lake later took shape with the building of Grand Coulee Dam, as the Banks Coulee was used to store irrigation water for the Columbia Basin Irrigation Project.

Steamboat Rock S.P. (Grant Co.'s *MOST UNIQUELY WASHINGTON CG*)
Steamboat Rock was once an island in the middle of the glacially diverted Columbia River. Now it looms like a huge battleship in the middle of Banks Lake, towering 800' high and covering over 600 acres. Native peoples and explorers relied on this landmark for directions, and now campers rely on it for the best camping in the entire Grand Coulee Region.

Overview: This indescribable campground is located 56 miles northeast of Moses Lake and 11 miles south of Electric City on 3522 acres with 50,000' of freshwater shoreline on Banks Lake at 1650' elevation, open year-round; GPS 47.8695, -119.0903.

Facilities: The main campground features flush toilets (ADA), running water, showers (ADA), 7 boat ramps, 5 moorage buoys, 320' of dock, a Park Store with concessions, sand dunes, and a great playground.

Recreation: Hiking and boating fight for the main stage here. Steamboat Rock, the basalt monolith that rises straight out of the desert, is the must-do hike of the area. This 4-mile round tripper gains 650' elevation in a very brief distance, and requires considerable scrambling on loose shale, but provides magnificent 360-degree views of the entire area. Dogs and smaller children are understandably not allowed on this trail. An easier trail for hikers, children, dogs, horses, and birdwatchers is the Northrup Canyon Trail, across highway 155 from Steamboat Rock. This canyon has an unusually high density of bald eagles, red-tailed and Cooper's hawks, horned owls, woodpeckers and flickers. The trail eventually passes an abandoned homestead on the way to Northrup Lake. Fishing on Banks Lake yields smallmouth bass, rainbow trout, walleye, and lake whitefish. Ice fishing is popular in the winter. Golfers, particularly those at Jones Bay and Osborn Bay, will enjoy the proximity of the Banks Lake Golf Course.

A birds-eye view of Steamboat Rock CG from the top of "the Rock"

Campsites (26 tent sites, 136 sites w/full hookups 20/30/50 amps, 5 equestrian sites at Northrup Canyon, 3 cabins, reservable): Keep in mind that Steamboat Rock S.P. is actually a complex of campgrounds and lands occupying the upper east side of Banks Lake and vicinity. The main "campus" of the Park (at the base of the Rock itself) are divided into four areas. The Sage Loop (sites 1-50 and

301-312) is furthest from the Rock and Day Use Area, but is also the most private, with sporadic shade trees and grassy surfaces. The Dune Loop (sites 51-100 and 313-326) is similar, but close to activities like the sand dunes themselves, the Day Use Area, and access to the Rock trail. The Bay Loop (sites B1-B36 and Cabins C1-C3) is the busiest of all but has no tent camping. All 3 of these loops accommodate RVs up to 50'. Northrup Canyon (also part of the park) has 5 equestrian sites, which must be reserved. See the website for Jones Bay/Osborn Bay and Ponderosa Point Boat-Ins.

Trip notes: This is my favorite park in Eastern Washington. It reminded me of an adult version of Sun Lakes, with much more space and a less frenetic pace. The children were occupied and happy with sand dunes and a large grassy play park removed from the camping areas. Camping was relaxed and quiet, and the lack of privacy was never an issue.

Local Activities: The Grand Coulee Dam tour is a must for those who have not taken it. The Grand Coulee Dam Observation Rotunda is located on a high ridge where the Dam can be observed from a safe distance. Visits to Dry Falls, the Lenore Caves, and the Sun Lakes are also worthwhile.

Sun Lakes Park Resort at Sun Lakes S.P. (Grant Co.'s *BEST CG FOR ENTIRE FAMILIES*)

Sun Lakes S.P. is a place entirely devoted to fun, but its campground is small and outdated. The Sun Lakes Park Resort picks up this slack, while still very close to the S.P.'s core of activities, adding larger and shadier spaces with room for larger tents and recreational vehicles.

Overview: Located 43 miles northeast of Moses Lake and 26 miles east of Ephrata on Park Lake, privately operated within 4027-acre Sun Lakes S.P. at 1114' elevation, open year-round; GPS: 47.5929, -119.3971.

Facilities: This recreationally equipped Resort offers bathrooms with showers, picnic tables, a limited number of rustic fire pits, laundry facility, marina, boat launch, boat rentals, heated pool, 9-Hole Vic Meyers Golf Course, Camp Store, Ice Cream Shop, Food Store, and more.

Recreation: To the above add sports fields, hiking, miniature golf, boating, golfing, fishing, swimming, mini-golf, and Water Wars.

Campsites (127 sites for tents or RVs of any size, full hookups 20/30/50-amp, 61 cabins, reservable): Sites at the Resort are typically grassy, while State Park sites are on gravel. Some trees provide shade but little privacy. This is a highly popular pair of campgrounds bursting at the seams with people where solitude can be found just minutes away on the trails and on Park Lake itself; but camping at the Resort provides a greener, lusher atmosphere than the starker, State Park campground.

Trip Notes: Sun Lakes S.P. remains a very frenetic park, even within the confines of the Resort, but it is still a magical place for the kids. Adults can enjoy themselves vicariously through their children or find their own peace and more adult recreation opportunities at the Resort, where boating, golfing, and even chilling are very close at hand.

Local Attractions: If your family or group does nothing else while camping at Sun Lakes, you must visit the Dry Falls Visitor Center just two miles north. Here you will witness the dormant Ice Age waterfall that was once 1.5 miles wide and 400' high, easily surpassing Niagara Falls (0.5 miles wide/167' high) and Victoria Falls in Africa (1 mile wide/256' high). When the Columbia returned to its original channel, Dry Falls was left high and dry for exploration.

Local Alternatives: We recommend Coulee Lodge Resort (best), Laurent's Sun Village Resort, and Santiam Resort on Soap Lake.

Crescent Bar Recreation Area (CBRA)

Crescent Bar is one of the famous Ice Age flood sites where giant ripples on top of a huge gravel bar worked their Lake Missoula magic to form giant gravel dunes in the middle of a curved stretch of the Columbia River. The 1.5-mile long gravel island is connected by a bridge to the mainland, making it accessible to those of us looking for yet another tasty slice of Washington in which we can sink our recreational teeth.

Crescent Bar Recreation Area, CBRA (Grant Co.'s *BEST EQUIPPED/BEST CG FOR RVs*)

This area underwent a major renovation in 2017 with the addition of a brand-new campground on Crescent Bar Island and moving the commercial businesses from the Island to the Mainland. All electricity, plumbing, landscaping, and sites are brand spanking new and updated for the future.

Overview: This popular resort area is located 46 miles northwest of Moses Lake and 10 miles west of Quincy on the Columbia River, operated by the Grant Co. PUD at 628' elevation, open April 1st to October 1st; GPS 47.216538, -119.994974.

Facilities: Extensive facilities include bathrooms with showers, sports courts (tennis, basketball, volleyball, pickleball), horseshoes, two boat launches, a swimming area, a picnic shelter, a sun shelter, a playground, a commercial marina, a floating fuel station, multiple beaches, and a 2.5-mile paved walking trail from the mainland to the southern tip of the Island with views of the Gorge.

Recreation: Of note, the Crescent Bar Golf Course extends through the mainland and then across nearly the entire stretch of Crescent Bar Island. Other recreation includes fishing, swimming, exploring the island dunes, and partaking of the sports facilities in the campground. Note that the water between the mainland and the Bar is fairly shallow and gets quite warm in the summer for great swimming.

<u>Campsites</u> (55 sites for tents and RVs up to 54' with full 30/50-amp hookups, some ADA, reservable): Sites come with paved parking pads, gravel tent pads, and are well-spaced. The new campground is located on the old driving range, so is perfectly flat, but has no vegetation. Trees have been planted, but do not as yet provide shade. The best sites are 26, 28, 30, 32, and 34, which are right on the Columbia River and the most private. Some sites have good views of the River.

<u>Trip Notes</u>: Slowly descending the 3 miles from Highway 54 to the "little city" of Crescent Bar is like watching a documentary film on American Recreation. At first you look toward the famous Gorge at George, and layered basalt cliffs just east of Crescent Bar Island. Then the Island slowly unfolds, with its long green lawns and poplar trees. Then you notice the small bridge and the marina and businesses on the mainland. Suddenly you spot some fugly commercial condominiums that seem like scars in the landscape and realize that this place runs the gamut from unspoiled primordial nature to very unnatural manufactured resort life. But as you approach the Island you realize that the CBRA has been restructured to accommodate both campers and jet set resorters. Don't worry campers, the resorters are just afraid of you as you are of them! There is something for everyone here, and both co-exist very well. There is a cherry orchard on the mainland whose cherries ripen in mid-June with just enough overhanging branches that wily campers can steal a taste of the local cuisine. The paved walkway to the end of the Island provides a great getaway, while the layered basalt cliffs allow the campers to sit back and reflect.

<u>Crescent Bar Alternative</u>: The Crescent Bar RV Resort (a Thousand Trails Resort) is nearby on the mainland of CBRA.

<u>Geological History</u>: Between 6 and 17 million years ago, this area was engulfed in layer after layer of molten lava (basalt) from volcanic eruptions to the east. These layers are visible from CBRA campground, and identify the various lava flows over 11 million years. Ironically, life flourished between these layers, representing a very long period of this land's history. Crescent Bar itself was formed from swirling eddies during the last Ice Age, due to the short, sudden bend in the Columbia River, forming the gravel island on which the CBRA partially rests.

Quincy Lakes Area

The 15,266-acre Quincy Lakes Wildlife Unit is composed of 2 smaller recreational units: The Quincy Lakes Area, with its 4 large fishing lakes (Stan Coffin Lake, Quincy Lake, Burke Lake, and Evergreen Reservoir), all reachable by motor vehicle; and the hike-in area known as the Ancient Lakes.

<u>Quincy Lake CG</u> (Grant Co.'s *BEST FREE CG*)

This is not the largest of the 4 lakes in the region but is the most popular for both camping and fishing, each in its own season. The sunsets here will be etched on your memory long after the sleeping bags are rolled up and the fishing poles return home.

Overview: This reservoir/lake campground is located 4.6 miles south of Quincy, operated by the WDFW at 1174' elevation, open March through October; GPS: 47.1409 N, -119.926 W.

Facilities: Primitive facilities include vault toilets and a concrete plank boat launch.

Recreation includes fishing for rainbow trout, kayaking and canoeing.

Campsites (dispersed, no hookups or reservations, FREE with Discover Pass): Sites are primitive but flat with good lake access. Shade is non-existent, and privacy is at a premium, except a few more dispersed sites up from the main area; it gets better after March when fishing season ends, and crowds decrease. The camping area is elevated above the Lake with a panoramic view of the area and the many flocks of birds that frequent this and nearby lakes. There is also camping at nearby Burke Lake, but not Stan Coffin Lake or Evergreen Reservoir.

Trip Notes: This intriguing lake has just enough small arms and secluded bays to make kayaking a real pleasure, plus the views of mountains and basalt cliffs in the distance make it visually appealing. The bullfrogs can be loud at dusk, but they tend to settle in as the night goes on.

Directions: Follow the directions to the Ancient Lakes (below), but continue straight ahead at the second parking area, and drive approximately one mile.

Ancient Lakes Hike-In Campsites (Grant Co.'s *BEST RUSTIC CG*)
This portion of the Quincy Lakes Wildlife Unit is the product of erosion from lava flows by glacial flood waters, leaving many layers of exposed basalt in 800-foot cliffs, isolated mesas, surreal waterfalls in the desert, and potholes. These potholes are actually seep lakes from higher elevation reservoirs, leaving wetlands in the desert, where campers can rest at lakeshores with sweet and smoky sagebrush-scented prairie while listening to coyotes and crickets lull them to sleep at night. Yep, this is what clichés are made of.

Overview: Located 5 miles south of Quincy at 826' elevation, managed by the WDFW, accessible from March until September; GPS 47.1604 N, -119.9808 W (more directions below).

Facilities: none, except the parking lot at the trailhead.

Recreation: Many hike in, then drop their packs and continue exploring the various trails up the hillsides and to Dusty Lake. Fishing is fair in the lakes for yellow perch, crappie, smallmouth bass, largemouth bass, and rainbow trout.

Campsites (dispersed campsites, no hookups or reservations, FREE with Discover Pass): There are several small campsites located around the 4 Ancient Lakes (Ancient Lake South being the largest at 8.7 acres), several isolated sites along the Ridge, and several more along 41.3-acre Dusty Lake. Most prefer camping in the spaces around the 4 Ancient Lakes, and particularly next to the waterfall located nearby. The sites on the Ridge and Dusty Lake require an extra 90-minute hike, but some prefer the desolate but more private Dusty Lake.

Trip Notes: This instantly became one of my favorite hike-in camping areas. Boca (my trusty canine) and I hiked this one alone, choosing to take the more strenuous but spectacular upper entrance near Quincy Lake and follow the waterfalls down to the camping area. A small pond signaled the first such waterfall, which could be crossed on foot, with trails beyond. The second two waterfalls were lined with shale and slower going, but a treat to stand before the free fall of the third and final waterfall. We struggled a bit over small boulders to the barren hills to the camping area, where we could finally take a deep breath and take it all in. We were surrounded on three sides by basalt cliffs, with a direct view of the stream and 3 waterfalls right before us. Now this is camping!

Directions: From George, take SR 281 north towards Quincy/Wenatchee for 5.6 miles. Turn left/west on White Tail Rd. Drive another 3 miles to the public fishing sign and turn left/south. Continue 0.3 miles on the gravel road to the second parking area on the right, where you will find the trailhead.

Moses Lake Area

Most Washingtonians think of Moses Lake as the city, but there is a lake of the same name. The natural shallow lake was dammed in the early 20th century to create a larger lake with multiple arms and islands. Despite the arid atmosphere, the Lake was not named for the biblical Moses, but for tribal leader Chief Moses, aptly nicknamed the "Sun Chief."

Cascade Park CG (includes Grant Co.'s *BEST BIKE-IN CG*)

This is the City of Moses Lake's premier outdoor camping area, located on its namesake lake. This is sun country, and one of Washington's nicest small cities located on one of its prettiest and least known lakes.

Overview: This sun-drenched 30-acre campground is located in the City of Moses Lake on 6,728-acre Moses Lake, operated by Grant Co. Parks & Recreation at 1050' elevation, open April through September; GPS 45.6032975868, -122.508064634 (see more below).

Facilities: The Park is well-equipped with bathrooms/showers, picnic tables, fire grills, picnic shelters, a playground, soccer and T-ball fields, boat launch, camp host, and an RV dump.

Recreation: Fun-in-the-sun activities include swimming and boating. Fishing is good for fishing for black crappie, bluegill, carp, channel catfish, lake whitefish, and rainbow trout.

Campsites (33 tent sites, 42 RV sites with water & electric 20/30-amp hookups, one 10-site Group Camp for up to 60, reservable): Sites 1-33 are tent sites, including one ADA site along the lakeshore. These are flat, with good privacy and ample shade. Sites 34-75 are RV sites on an elevated bench above the others. They are flat with less shade and average privacy. Sites 76-85 comprise a single Group Camp near the soccer fields and lake. In this case, you might forget about privacy and shade and focus on the group experience!

Trip Notes: The Group Site was so fun and crazy busy we wanted to jump in and join the crowd. Both the RV and tent areas are more conventional with equally good lake views. We were impressed with this one -- but admit we would have felt more comfortable in the well-shaded lakeshore tent area than the elevated, partial-sun RV area.

Directions: From I-90, take Exit 176 north onto Broadway. Turn left at the 3rd traffic light (Broadway & Stratford), cross the lake, and turn left at the next traffic light (Valley Road). Continue through two traffic lights and a flashing yellow warning light and down the hill. The Park is on the left.

Potholes Reservoir Area

The Potholes Reservoir, also known as Lake O'Sullivan, is the crowning example of the transformation of the Columbia Basin. As water was pumped from the Columbia River to the north side of the O'Sullivan Dam, the 43.44 square mile Potholes Reservoir was formed. Consequently, an organized plan of irrigation unfolded, both agriculture and wildlife were transformed, and what was once a wasteland become the perfect coulee playland.

Potholes S.P. (Grant Co.'s *MOST APPEALING CG TO THE SENSES*)
The potholes themselves are actually kolk-carved depressions carved during the Ice Age floods. As the floodwaters gouged troughs in the basalt, swirling eddies of water (or "kolks") plucked out chunks of rock from these channels. Subsequent floods widened them, leaving the area full or large deep holes or "pock marks" in the desert. These later filled with water as the O'Sullivan Dam (forming the Potholes Reservoir) raised the water table in the area, and water seeped through cracks in the basalt bedrock, forming the many seep lakes beyond the reservoir itself.

Overview: Located 18 miles southwest of Moses Lake on 640 acres with 600' of freshwater shoreline on the Potholes Reservoir at 1047' elevation, open year-round; GPS 46.969475, -119.309807.

Facilities include bathrooms with showers (2 ADA), running water, picnic tables, fire grills, sheltered picnic area, 2 volleyball fields (bring your own equipment), boat dock, 4 boat ramps, 3 miles of hiking trails, and an RV dump station.

Recreation: Fishing, of course, is the thing here. Boat and fishing equipment rentals are available nearby. Fish commonly caught here include largemouth bass, rainbow trout, smallmouth bass, and walleye. The creek running adjacent to the Group Camp is also good for trout and bass. Water birds capture the attention of bird watchers, including the American wigeon, Bullock's oriole, Caspian terns, dusky flycatchers, eared grebes, ferruginous hawks, Savannah sparrows, warbling vireos, yellow-rumped warblers, and many others. Swimming, water-skiing, jet skiing and hiking are also popular.

Campsites (121 sites for tents and RVs up to 50', 60 with full hookups 50-amp, 5 cabins, reservable, open year-round): Note that none of the campsites border the Reservoir itself. The sites start in large irrigated hubs (sites 1-60), fanning north and east toward the Reservoir. Those on the outer edge (sites 61-126, plus the cabins) tend to be dusty and dry late in the season, with sagebrush and other desert vegetation. The sites close to the hub are lush and green (all of the hookup sites are here). The hub also contains many conifers and deciduous trees, including Big Leaf Maples, Russian olive, and poplars providing some shade. There is very little shade in the rest of the park, however, and people should bring their own sun tarps or shade umbrellas.

Trip Notes: Approaching Potholes S.P. from the south, I asked the driver, "What town is this? I don't see it on the map anywhere." That was not a town, it turns out, but the many resorts crowded together at the south end of the Potholes Reservoir: Mar Don Resort, O'Sullivan Sportsman Resort, and many others. These provide the services, rentals, and even fishing licenses for many at the State Park. The fishing fever here was certainly contagious, and at the campground most people were indeed fishing on the Reservoir. While I liked the lush irrigated portion of the campground, the dry, dusty, sage-brushy tent sites were rather off-putting. But fishing aside, there are enough other good things about the campground -- the birds, the desert animals, the sand dunes and trails to the Pothole lakes, and even just staring at the tiny islands in the northern part of the Reservoir.

Local Attractions: The Columbia National Wildlife Refuge, just south of the Reservoir, is a scenic mixture of rugged cliffs, canyons, lakes, and arid sagebrush grasslands that attract migrating and wintering waterfowl, nesting birds, and the famous Sandhill Crane.

For more photos of Grant Co. CGs, HIKE-IN, BOAT-IN, or GROUP CGs, consult campeverycountywa.com

GRAYS HARBOR COUNTY
(Montesano/Aberdeen/Ocean Shores)

Most recreation in this coastal county revolve around 95 square mile Grays Harbor, the ocean beaches, the Olympic National Forest, and Lake Quinault to the north. While the communities battle the loss of once-flourishing logging and fishing industries, the campgrounds thrive and are, frankly, very underrated.

Olympic National Forest/Quinault Rain Forest
Glacier-fed Lake Quinault is the centerpiece of the Olympic National Forest in Grays Harbor Co. But other less known destinations -- Wynoochee Lake, the Colonel Bob Wilderness, and the West Fork of the Humptulips River -- rival Lake Quinault in rain forest beauty, old growth forests, and especially camping.

<u>Campbell Tree Grove CG</u> (Grays Harbor Co.'s *BEST FREE CG*)
This is considered one of the most beautiful stands of old growth forest in the Olympic National Forest, kept pure by its isolation. Stand back you slick, modern campgrounds -- this is the real thing.
<u>Overview</u>: This rustic gem is located 47 miles northeast of Aberdeen, operated by the USFS at 1100' elevation, open late May to early September; GPS 47.480983, -123.690177.
<u>Facilities</u>: Limited facilities include vault toilets, picnic tables, and fire pits. There is no running water.
<u>Recreation</u>: Hiking is king here. West Fork Humptulips Trail #806 takes hikers into the incredible Colonel Bob Wilderness including Stovepipe and Moonlight Dome peaks. This is a difficult 17-mile climb which requires fording the river several times but is hailed by experienced hikers. Fishing is also available from the campground for cutthroat trout.

Campsites (11 sites for tents or RVs up to 16', no hookups or reservations, FREE with Northwest Forest Pass): The forest floor here is covered with temperate rain forest plants. Sites are located in a thick grove of 500-year old Douglas fir and western red cedars, making for great privacy and an old-growth forest experience. Parking aprons are gravel and grass. Most sites are located on the West Fork of the Humptulips River (for those from out of state – Humptulips is a real place. We think it's pretty funny, too). Note that a camp host is present in the summer months – a good thing, since this campground is 27 miles from the nearest services.

Trip Notes: This beautiful unpruned, under-cultivated, and unspoiled campground is well worth the 22-mile drive off of Highway 101 to get there. (Half of those 22 miles are paved roads, the other half is a gradually narrowing gravel road, so be mindful of the hidden potholes that can wreak havoc on vehicle axles). Long before you enter the campground, high views of the West Fork of the Humptulips River from one-lane bridges will draw you in to the beauty of this lesser known rain forest area. Small trailers such as Scamps, teardrops, or the smallest pop-up trailers may work here, but this one is primarily a paradise for the tenters. One note regarding the number of campsites: a camper and former Forest Service employee at the campground informed us that until the budget cuts of 2007-8, there were plans to build two loops of 10 sites each. One of the loops roads was even built but plans to add more campsites will not likely happen in the near future.

Coho CG (Grays Harbor Co.'s MOST *APPEALING CG TO THE SENSES*)
On the edge of the Olympic rain forest, behind the remote Wynoochee Dam, sits a campground that was kept pristine and isolated for many decades due to a poorly accessible gravel road filled with loud, aggressive logging trucks and the last remaining logging camp in Washington. The logging camp is gone, and the logging trucks are quieter, and now the road has been beautifully paved all the way from Highway 12. Wilderness camping is just a short drive away.

Overview: Beautifully located 35 miles north of Montesano on 8 acres on the southwestern shore of 1140-acre Lake Wynoochee, managed by Wilderness Adventures LLC under a USFS Special Use Permit at 800' elevation, open mid-May to early October; GPS 47.45806, -123.60222.

Facilities include flush toilets, drinking water, picnic tables, fire rings, boat launch, a dock in the Dam's Day Use Area, swimming beach, an RV dump, and camp hosts. Showers and laundry are available 3-miles away at Satsop Center.

Recreation: Hiking, fishing, boating, and swimming are the mainstays. The half mile long Working Forest Nature Trail extends north from the campground. The 12-mile long Wynoochee Lake Shore Trail #878 encircles the Lake. Waterfall seekers should try the many sub-trails off the Lakeshore Trail, including those to Spoon Falls, Maidenhair Falls, and Wynoochee Falls (see below). Fishing is primarily for rainbow trout, with a 12-inch minimum size and 2 fish per day limit. Note that there is no marina for launching larger boats.

Campsites (46 sites including 8 ADA-friendly walk-in sites and 1 group site for up to 12, no hookups, 3 yurts, reservable): Sites are level, both asphalt back-ins and pull-throughs. Thick vegetation provides excellent privacy. Sites will accommodate any size RV, while the tent walk-in sites (adjacent to the yurt area) are wheelchair-friendly and have limited views of the lake. Some Loop B sites also have partial lake views. Loop A sites are first come, first served. Trees are a variety of conifers, such as hemlock and Douglas fir, and hardwoods including alders and maples. The adjacent Wynoochee Dam provides a dramatic vista outlook, plus a huge Day-Use Area that gives additional lake access for the campground.

Trip Notes: Stunning. Pristine. Awe-inspiring. Everything about this campground exceeded our expectations. The lake water is pure, clear, and crystal blue. The dam itself is like part of the campground. This is in every way a hidden treasure at the southern entrance to the Olympic Mountains that we cannot recommend too highly.

Local Alternative: Satsop Center CG is an historic Forest Service work center 3 miles east of Coho CG with 4 tent sites, 8 sites for RVs up to 36', some with hookups, and one group site for up to 50 people.

Willaby CG (Grays Harbor Co.'s *BEST RUSTIC CG*)
This campground sits right Lake Quinault but is best known for the amazing hiking opportunities right from your campsite. Lace up your hiking boots for the day (or overnight) and prepare to stare out of that glacier-fed beauty of a Lake when you get back.

Overview: This Olympic National Forest gem is located on the south shore of Lake Quinault on 14 acres at 200' elevation, open year-round; GPS 47.4485, -123.8037.

Facilities: One flush toilet, potable water, picnic tables, fire rings, one large covered shelter built by the Civilian Conservation Corps (CCC) in the 1930s, boat ramp, and camp hosts.

Recreation: Trails in the area include the Willaby Creek Trail (1.3 miles), the Rain Forest Nature Trail Loop (0.5 miles), and the Quinault Lakeshore Trail Loop (3.5 miles). A short distance from the campground are the Big Spruce Tree Trail, Forest Service Nature Trail, Kestner Homestead Trail (1.5 miles round trip), and the Gatton Creek Trail (part ADA accessible). Pete's Creek Trail #858 is more difficult, gaining 1800' in 2.4 miles, where it joins Colonel Bob Peak Trail #851. The latter is gains over 4,200 feet in 7.2 miles to the summit of Colonel Bob. The Mulkey Trail Shelter is reached in 4.0 miles. There is limited camping space at Mulkey Shelter and Moonshine Flats for overnight camping.

Back at Lake Quinault, note that the south shore lies within the Olympic National Forest, not the Olympic National Park, so dogs are allowed on all trails. Boat and kayak rentals are available at Quinault Lodge. Be mindful that the Lake is part of the Quinault Indian Nation, and tribal fishing permits and boat decals are required.

Campsites (24 sites for tents or RVs up to 40', no hookups or reservations): Sites seem rather small, but lush and more private than Falls Creek. Best sites are 13, 14, 15. This is the best choice on Lake Quinault for those who value privacy.

Trip Notes: The park's strength is its direct, elevated views of Lake Quinault. Hiking access is excellent. That being said, it is a fairly ordinary park on an extraordinary lake. The bottom line is this: if you are looking for the rain forest experience, you will need to hike the trails, visit Falls Creek CG to the east, or visit the Hoh Rain Forest to the north.

Falls Creek CG (Grays Harbor Co.'s *MOST UNIQUELY WASHINGTON CGs*)
You would expect this campground to be about Lake Quinault, as it sits on a small peninsula jutting out into the glacier-fed, crystalline Lake, but this is among the prettiest rain forest campgrounds anywhere.

Overview: This small campground is located on the south shore of Lake Quinault on 3 acres, operated by the USFS at an elevation of 200', open summer months only; GPS 47.4696, -123.8454.

Facilities include bathrooms with flush toilets (ADA), drinking water, picnic tables, fire grills. one shelter built by the CCC, and a boat launch.

Recreation: swimming, boating (with license and decal), hiking on the Quinault Lakeshore Trail. Keep in mind that the south shore of Lake Quinault sits in the National Forest, not the National Park, so dogs are allowed on all trails.

Campsites (3 acres, 21 sites for tents or RVs up to 16' plus 10 walk-in tent sites, no hookups, reservable): Most of the sites are tiny and close together, but all are under a heavy umbrella of towering cedars, firs, and spruces, making all sites seem much larger. Site 20 sits right on Falls Creek with a direct view of the falls, while a bridge across Falls Creek takes campers to the more private walk-in sites.

Trip Notes: Falls Creek is clearly the most beautiful Lake Quinault campground, though it is somehow squeezed into just 3 acres. It seems much larger as it is adjacent to both the Lake and the grounds of Lake Quinault Lodge. The bridge also connects campers to the Quinault Lakeshore Trail, once again making the campground seem larger than life.

Washington History: Since Teddy Roosevelt visited the Olympic Peninsula in 1903, controversy raged about how much logging, mining, and private exploration should be allowed in the old growth forests. Loggers said the idea of a National Park was too extreme, while conservationists said more land should be set aside. President Franklin Delano Roosevelt visited the Olympic Peninsula in 1937 to quell the controversy. After lunching at the Quinault Lodge, he was taken on a tour. Upon seeing a section of clear-cut timber, he said to his guide, "I hope the son-of-a-bitch responsible for this is roasting in hell," not knowing the SOB in question was standing right beside him. The rest is history: the Olympic National Park was established and, after the last parcel was added by Harry Truman in 1953, came to occupy 922,650 acres, making it the fifth largest national park in the lower 48, and one of the few wilderness national parks.

North Beach Region

This stretch of ocean beach starts with the soft, shifting sand of Ocean Shores in the south, and slowly evolves to the rocky shores of Ruby Beach and the ONP to the north.

Pacific Beach S.P. (Grays Harbor Co.'s *BEST EQUIPPED/ BEST CG FOR RVs*)
This is Washington's only state park with camping right on the beach. But be mindful -- you'll have lots of company -- so plan accordingly.
Overview: Located within the City of Pacific Beach on 10 acres with 2300' of Pacific Ocean shoreline, open year-round; GPS 47.2058, -124.2022.
Facilities: Two bathrooms with showers (ADA), Day Use Area, RV dump station, camp hosts. No fires permitted in campsites, but fires are allowed on the beach. The town of Pacific Beach provides groceries, propane, ice cream, prepared food, and beach town shops.
Recreation: Kite flying, beachcombing, and bird viewing are prime.
Campsites (18 tent sites, 42 sites for RVs up to 60' with 30-amp electrical hookups, 2 yurts, reservations recommended): Sites have no shade, no protection from the wind, and little to no privacy. That being said, every site has a direct, head-on ocean view.
Trip Notes: Yes, this small park is about the beach, but what a glorious stretch of beach it is! The explosion of color from the myriad windsocks and kites seem to pay homage to the sand and water below. The stream, pilings, and rocks divide the park from the houses perched above, plus a 20-20 view of the endless stretch of beach. That's the good news. The bad news is that it's still crowded, noisy, and frenetic. I would prefer this for a short beach party weekend, or if travelling through on a bicycle. Otherwise, Ocean City S.P. to the south outclasses this popular park when it comes to pure camping.

Ocean City S.P. (Grays Harbor Co.'s *BEST CG FOR ENTIRE FAMILIES*)
Great dunes, great vegetation, great saltwater marshes, great beach access. This makes it a must see, must camp experience.
Overview: This beach campground is located 21.2 miles west of Aberdeen just north of the City of Ocean Shores on 170 acres with Pacific Ocean beaches at minimal elevation, open year-round; GPS 47.0325865 -124.164064.

<u>Facilities</u>: This comes well-equipped with bathrooms, flush toilets, showers, running water, an RV dump, campsite hosts, and short trail to the Pacific Ocean.

<u>Campsites</u> (178 sites, including 29 with full hookups 30-amp, two group camps for 20-30 each, reservable): Sites are level, small to medium in size with poor to average privacy, but are lush with easy ocean beach access. See campsitephotos.com for the best sites. For me, the most Loop 4 is the prettiest, with sites surrounded by windswept, mature vegetation

<u>Trip Notes</u>: The popularity of this park works against it, as sites are smallish, and the park congested. This visit reminded me, however, how very beautiful are some of the sites (especially Loop 4), and how nice it might be to camp here during the week, or during a less busy time. The ocean access is a great draw, where you will see horseback riders and kites decorating the blue-gray sky. Overall, this campground is a real class act.

<u>Nearby Attractions</u>: The City of Ocean Shores has restaurants, a casino, and cycle rentals. Razor clam digging is available in season at Copalis, Iron Springs, and Mocrocks (Moclips) beaches. An appropriate fishing license is required. Check with the WDFW before setting out.

campeverycountywa.com

Ocean City S.P. has wonderful marine vegetation and beaches

South Beach Region

Notably quieter than Florida's infamous South Beach, this is a gray sandy stretch of beach that ends near the seaport town of Westport to the north, with just enough festivity to spice up your camping experience.

<u>Twin Harbors S.P.</u> (Grays Harbor Co.'s *BEST BIKE-IN CG*)

The land on which this campground rests was once a military training facility, and is irregularly arranged, but remains one of the most versatile and best campgrounds on Washington's Pacific Coast.

<u>Overview</u>: Located 19.2 miles west of Aberdeen and 4 miles south of Westport on 172 acres with extensive Pacific Ocean shoreline, west camp open year-round; GPS 46.855972 -124.1081.

<u>Facilities</u> include bathrooms with flush toilets (one ADA bathroom), showers (all ADA), running water, an RV dump, and campground hosts.

<u>Recreation</u>: Here you'll find Shifting Sands Interpretive Beach Trail and other beach trails, razor clam digging in season (fishing license required), kite flying, plus saltwater fishing in Westport. Birding is excellent at nearby Bottle Beach S.P. featuring 6500' of Grays Harbor shoreline with 130 species of shorebirds for the viewing (and hunting in winter, so be mindful). Surfing is popular at Westhaven S.P. near Westport, although wetsuits are the norm.

<u>Campsites</u> (265 sites, including 42 with full hookups 30 amp, 4 H/B sites, 2 ADA sites, 1 group site for up to 60, 2 yurts, 5 cabins, reservable): Sites vary from no privacy (RV sites) to good privacy (tent sites). Sites closest to the ocean lack privacy, while those on the east side are more private and framed by high marine vegetation and leafy trees. Best sites are 193, 215, 217, 227, 230, 265, 275, 281, 299.

<u>Trip notes</u>: Coastal Highway 105 divides park in two, with the more private sites lying on the eastern side. There is very little road noise, as Highway 105 is lightly travelled. We found the RV sites rather small, congested, and lacking privacy. For RVers who need hookups, we recommend the more modern Grayland Beach S.P. (see Pacific Co.) 4.5 miles to the south. The most interesting sites, in my opinion, are those just inside the western entrance (sites 285-307). The loop closest to the beach (sites 308-299) has a few good sites on the outside of the Loop with 2 yurts and 5 cabins for rent. Overall, we enjoyed out camping experience in the eastern loop (sites 86-190) and recommend these sites above all. All sites have good beach access and are within walking distance for most.

<u>Local attractions</u> include Westport Lighthouse S.P., with a 135-step climb to the top of this 100' structure, giving great views of the Pacific Ocean, Grays Harbor, and the fishing town of Westport. The town of Westport itself features many shops and restaurants, plus a viewing tower that provides more great views. A similar viewing tower is located at nearby Westhaven S.P.

For photos of Grays Harbor Co. CGs, or HIKE-IN, BOAT-IN, or GROUP CGs, consult campeverycountywa.com

ISLAND COUNTY (Coupeville/Oak Harbor/Camano)

Whidbey Island and Camano Island are homes to 5 camping state parks and more shoreline than you will ever have time to explore. Unless you get started now, of course.

Camano Island

This 18-mile long island is connected by a land bridge to Stanwood in Snohomish County, making it more accessible to the greater Puget Sound Area, but removed from its counterpart Whidbey Island -- except for the killer views of Whidbey across Saratoga Passage.

Camano Island S.P. (Island Co.'s *MOST APPEALING CG TO THE SENSES* and *BEST CG FOR ENTIRE FAMILIES*)

This Park is unique in the State Park System in that it is "a community initiated and supported park." It was established in 1949 and now maintained by hundreds of volunteers from Stanwood and Camano Island who recognized its potential long before most other Washington State Parks were established.

Overview: Located 14 miles south west of Stanwood on the southwest shore of Camano Island on 134 acres with 6700' of saltwater shoreline on Saratoga Passage, open year round; GPS 48.1236, -122.488.

Facilities include bathrooms with showers, drinking water, picnic tables, fire pits, 2 community BBQs, and a fire circle; the North Beach Picnic Shelter for up to 12 people; the Lowell Point Kitchen Shelter with a sink, wood stove and electricity for up to 44 people; 2 boat ramps, 1 mile of biking trails, 3 miles of hiking trails (including a trail to Cama Beach S.P.), an amphitheater, large ball field, and camp hosts.

Recreation includes hiking, bicycling, fishing, clamming, crabbing, boating, waterskiing and sailboarding. Golfers will find an 18-hole golf course is nearby.

Campsites (87 sites for tents or RVs up to 40', one group site for up to 100, 2 H/B sites, 5 CMT sites for boaters, 5 cabins, no hookups or reservations): Some sites have great waterfront views. Campsites are nestled among cedar, Douglas, fir, hemlock, spruce, yew, alder, apple, cherry, maple, and poplar trees. They lie in an Upper and Lower Loop. Some sites in the Upper Loop are run down and roped off. This is regarded as the best Loop for RVs, but the better-maintained lower loop may be better for all but the biggest rigs.

Trip Notes: We are probably spoiled by the fastidiousness of the State Park System, which generally keeps all camping parks well-maintained. Maintenance by the community is both this Park's strength and weakness. On one hand, many details in the park are unique, from the entry sign to the hand-hewn fences along the shoreline in the day use area, to the handmade furniture in the cabins. On the other, some aspects of the park are run down. The natural settling of the land has created fissures in the roadways (something beyond anyone's control). In truth, we loved the Day Use Area, the trails to Cama Beach, and the campsites in the lower loop nearest the water. Besides, you can't escape the abject beauty of this place, its uniqueness, and the way it makes you feel you can see the entire world from here.

Local Alternative: Cama Beach S.P. is a restored 1930's fishing resort that rents cedar waterfront cabins and bungalows, allowing no motorized vehicles in the camping area. No tents or RVs are allowed. Personal gear is wheeled down from the upper lots by aluminum carts. The buildings are restored to their 1930s simplicity, though the inside of public restrooms/showers are quite upscale. The "camp" includes the working Center for Wooden Boats, where you can watch actual boat restoration or rent one for yourself. It also has a cafe, a camp store, an information center, and many other facilities. The cabins have unobstructed views of Saratoga Passage, while the Park has 15 miles of hiking trails, some of which connect to Camano Island S.P.

Whidbey Island

This 45-mile long island is connected to Fidalgo Island in Skagit County by the scenic 2-span Deception Pass Bridge in the north, and to the mainland by the Clinton-Mukilteo Ferry in the south. It is the largest island in Washington, and the fourth largest island in the contiguous United States. The Island has a diverse landscape, with equally diverse recreational opportunities.

Cranberry Lake CG at Deception Pass S.P. (Island Co.'s MOST UNIQUELY WASHINGTON CG)

Deception Pass S.P. includes 3 campgrounds - Bowman Bay CG north of the Bridge in Skagit Co., and Quarry Pond and Cranberry Lake CGs south of the Bridge in Island County. Cranberry Lake CG is located on the northernmost tip of Whidbey Island between North Beach, West Beach, and Cranberry Lake. It is visually stunning, with bluffs and rock formations at every turn, making it one of the most iconic campgrounds in the Washington State Park System.

Overview: Located 8 miles north of Oak Harbor on the northernmost tip of Whidbey Island on 4134 acres at 116' elevation with extensive saltwater shoreline, open year-round; GPS 48.3931, -122.6473.

Facilities include bathrooms with showers (some ADA), drinking water, picnic tables, fire pits, , amphitheater, 3 picnic shelters for 50-300 people each, 40 miles of hiking trails through the Park, camp hosts, RV dump.

Recreation includes swimming for kids in Cranberry Lake, fishing, beachcombing, hiking, and viewing Deception Pass and its islands from the amazing 2-span Deception Pass Bridge.

Campsites (147 tent sites, 83 sites with electric & water hookups 50 amps for RVs of any size, 3 primitive Group Camps for 25-50 people each including one with Adirondack shelter, Ben Ure Cabin, reservable): Sites are large, wooded, and shady with good privacy, although so heavily forested that it can be too cool, even in mid-summer. Sites are both back-ins and pull-throughs. Tent pads are on native material. The Forest Loop sites are the best for camping, but also the furthest from the swimming area on the West Beach of Cranberry Lake. The Forest Loop, as well as the H/B sites, have good access to the North Beach underneath the bridge, which is the most scenic. Otherwise, the campground is remarkably quiet for the crowd, allowing campers to relax. And if you're more adventurous but want some luxury, rent Ben Ure Cabin on its own island in Cornet Bay. You'll have to bring your own boat.

Trip notes: This is arguably the most scenic campground we've experienced. The shoreline and bridge over the Pass are spectacular. The biggest complaint by far was the military planes from Oak Harbor that regularly passed over, drowning out all conversation for several minutes, and being a deal breaker for at least one of our campers. Yet, it is possibly the most visually appealing campground in Washington. Be aware that the waters are treacherous here, and children should be very closely watched (limit their swimming to the very safe Cranberry Lake). But this campground, as well as its counterpart Bowman Bay CG across the bridge in Skagit Co., should be on everyone's camping bucket list. They're not perfect, but they're unforgettable.

Fort Ebey S.P. (includes Island Co.'s *BEST EQUIPPED CG* and includes *BEST GROUP CG*)
This former World War II gun emplacement site has given way to a little-known campground filled with grasslands, bluffs, paragliders, surfers, and killer marine views. This is Whidbey Island in slow motion, stripped down to its bare essentials.

Overview: This peaceful, sweeping park is located 6 miles west of Coupeville on 645 acres with 3 miles of saltwater shoreline on the Strait of Juan de Fuca at 82' elevation, open November 1st to April 1st; GPS 48.2226, -122.7632.

Facilities: These include restrooms with showers, picnic tables, fire rings, 28 miles of hiking trails, 25 miles of biking trails, Beach Picnic Shelter for 50 people, Gun Battery Picnic Shelter for 150 people, 2 BBQ grills, a surfing beach, 2 primitive sports fields, an amphitheater, sports fields, and a Park Store. Vista Group Camp, located on a bluff down Partridge Road includes a vault toilet and running water, with flush toilets and showers a 5-minute walk away.

Recreation includes hiking, surfing, paragliding, limited fishing on Lake Pondilla, and exploration of WW2-era concrete military bunkers. The Park features the bluff walk which gives breathtaking views. This is a double bonus, as the park is adjacent to the Kettles Trail System which includes over 30 miles of hiking and mountain-biking trails. Paragliders also gravitate to the bluff here and provide great visuals.

Campsites (39 tent sites, 11 sites w/water & electric hookups 30/50 amp for RVs of any size, 6 H/B walk-in sites near Lake Pondilla, one marine trail campsite, one group campground (Vista Group Camp) for up 20-60 people, reservable): Sites are very large with good vegetation, some of the trees and shrubs being windblown and smaller, as the campground sits on top of a large bluff overlooking the Sound towards Port Townsend. The heavy vegetation provides a windbreak and some relief from rainfall. The very pretty, compact Vista Group Camp is decorated with large shade trees and natural vegetation.

Trip Notes: Step up to the grassy, barren shelf on the bluff just beneath the military bunkers, and you suddenly find yourself immersed in a reflective, contemplative, even Zen environment. This is the launching place for many a paraglider, and you can almost imagine the Karate Kid practicing his karate kicks under the tutelage of Mr. Myagi. It is so different from the more popular Deception Pass S.P., with its many rock ledges, scenic beaches, sea life and, to its own detriment, throngs of visitors and noise from military planes. Fort Ebey is stripped away Whidbey Island, relaxing and less known. The heavily forested campsites protect you from the wind and rain, the beautiful Vista Group Camp gives you the best view of the Straight anywhere, and the trails will lead you over the entire central portion of Whidbey Island -- so underrated, so peaceful, so inviting.

Local Alternative: A good alternative for select people would be nearby Fort Casey S.P., with extensive military bunkers and batteries which pre-date World War I, plus, for lighthouse fans, the Admiralty Head Lighthouse, which is open to visitors. However, the campsites sit on the pebbly beach near the Keystone Ferry, are subjected to exhaust fumes from the boats, have limited boating due to the wakes created by the ferries, and have little privacy.

Rhododendron Co. Park (Island Co.'s *BEST BIKE-IN CG*)

This bicycle campground, also popular with car campers and hikers, is centrally located on Whidbey Island with its own complex trail system, plus access to trails and roads all over the Island.

Overview: Located 1.5 miles southeast of Coupeville on 192 combined acres at 200' elevation, operated by Island Co. Parks, campground open April 1 to Nov. 1; located 20265 SR 20, Coupeville, WA.

Facilities include vault toilets, BBQ's, picnic tables, fireplace rings, fresh water, connection to Rhododendron Park Trails and picnic area, 3 athletic fields, playground and picnic shelter.

Recreation: Bicycling is king here, in one of the best bicycling counties in Washington.

Campsites (12 tent sites, 3 sites for any-size RVs with water hookups only, all first come, first served): Sites are large, flat, and heavily forested with good privacy. They are especially picturesque when the wild rhododendrons bloom in late spring and early summer (slightly later than commercial rhododendrons).

Trip Notes: This is a lovely campground, regardless of whether you are biking, hiking, or driving. This may even rival Fort Ebey S.P. for the quietest campground on the Island. I can picture whole families, from tykes to grandparents, all on bicycles exploring the ball fields, playgrounds, and forests away from the campground proper.

campeverycountywa.com

Bicycling is the thing at Rhododendron Co. Park, but car campers love it too

Other CAMPGROUNDS: Island County has no RUSTIC or FREE CGs that we can recommend at this time.

For more photos of Island Co. CGs, or more on BOAT-IN CGs, consult
campeverycountywa.com

JEFFERSON COUNTY (Port Townsend/Kalaloch)

Jefferson County stretches from Puget Sound, across the Olympic Peninsula, all the way to the Pacific Ocean. But with 95% of this county's population living in the far northeastern corner, there is plenty of space for pure recreation: start with the amazing Kalaloch Beach, the Hoh Rain Forest, Mount Olympus, and the pristine waters of Hood Canal.

Port Townsend/Quimper Peninsula

It is rare that an entire community, especially one as large as Port Townsend, is on the National Register of Historic Places. Not only that, but continue around the Quimper Peninsula, and you'll find 58 other locations on the National Historic and/or the Washington State Registry. But that doesn't mean this northeast corner of Jefferson County is on historical lock down. On the contrary, this peninsula, surrounded by Puget Sound, the Strait of Juan de Fuca, and Discovery Bay is home to far too many quality campgrounds to feature in this guide. But the historic aspect makes the camping come alive!

Fort Flagler S.P. (Jefferson Co.'s *BEST EQUIPPED/BEST CG FOR RVs* and *BEST BOAT-IN site*)
A sign at the entrance to the Island states, "Marrowstone: A Tiny Island Nation Slightly Off the Coast of America, where the living is easy, the water is sweet, and ALL the beaches are clothing optional." Local law enforcement begs to differ. You decide which laws have authority here.
Overview: This expansive campground is located 8 miles south of Port Townsend on 1,454 acres on Marrowstone Island with 19,100' of saltwater shoreline at 150' elevation, open year-round; GPS 48.094, -122.6973 (more below).
Facilities: These include flush toilets, showers, running water, 5 miles of hiking/biking trails, 2 boat ramps with 256 feet of dock and moorage, a military

museum with gift shop, camp hosts and an RV dump. Rentals include the Engineers House (sleeps 4), the Hospital Steward's House (sleeps 4), the non-Commissioned Officer's Quarters North & South (sleeps 4 per unit), and the Waterway House (sleeps 8). Camp Hoskins, Camp Richmond, and Camp Wilson each contain multiple buildings and can accommodate 180-273 people each.

Recreation: Viewing the extensive military buildings and trails within the campground will occupy most for multiple days. Kite-flying, hang gliding, clam digging, oyster harvesting, fishing, and boating (motorized and human-powered) are popular. Marine birds are plentiful for viewing, including black-bellied plovers, black turnstones, Bonaparte's gulls, Brants, California gulls, Caspian and common terns, double-crested cormorants, glaucous-winged gulls, Hermann's gulls, horned grebes, long-tailed ducks, mew gulls, Pacific loons, pelagic cormorants, pigeon guillemots, red-breasted mergansers, red-necked grebes, Thayer's gulls, and western sandpipers.

Campsites (117 sites for tents and RVs from 25 to 50', including 57 w/full hookups 50-amp, two H/B sites, one Cascadia Marine Trail site, 5 military "houses" and 3 larger military group camps for up to 250 people, two small group camps, and a Scout Camp, reservable): The Upper Forest Campground (sites 1-47) is heavily wooded, and relatively flat with good privacy. RV length is limited to 25'. This is the best camping option for tenters due to wind protection. Included are 2 primitive walk-in H/B sites. The Lower Beach Campground (sites 48-116) is near the beach with little shade, limited privacy, and windy. Sites are, however, all flat and very popular with longer RVs. The larger group sites are very close to the main clusters of buildings and staging area with a rather "classroom" feel and are best suited for school age groups or historical societies. The one lowly Cascadia boat-in site is right on the beach with adequate separation/privacy from the other beach campsites.

Trip notes: We never expected to enjoy this park as much as we did. I spent countless hours walking with my dog through the flat, wooded trails to the military facilities at the end of the bluff , the marine research facility, many military batteries hidden in the woods, encountering small bands of deer feeding in the open areas, and watching the activities in nearby Port Townsend from afar. Camping was relaxing and quiet in the upper campground, although the lower less wooded RV campground did not seem appealing.

Historical Note: Fort Flagler was once part of the "Triangle of Fire" (made up of Fort Flagler, Fort Worden and Fort Casey) that was the primary military defense of Puget Sound in the 1890s through the 1950s when Fort Flagler was closed. The property was purchased as a state park in 1955.

Abandoned military buildings pop up all along the trails of Fort Flagler S.P.

Fort Townsend S.P. (Jefferson Co.'s *BEST BIKE-IN CG* and *BEST GROUP CG*)
The fort was used sporadically between 1856-1895 to provide "protection" to the promising town of Port Townsend from a Native American "threat" that never materialized. The wooden barracks and fort burned to the ground in 1895 and were never rebuilt. The land was not used again until WW2 when a torpedo-defusing station was built in what is now the Group Camp. This is the only structure still standing and is believed by many to be haunted. Hmm. Sounds like the perfect
Overview: Located 3 miles south of Port Townsend on 367 acres with 3,900' of saltwater shoreline at low elevation, open year-round; GPS 48.0748, -122.7896.
Facilities include flush toilets, 1 shower, running water, 3 picnic shelters, 6.5 miles of hiking mountain biking trails. Rentals include the "Friends Barn" for up to 100 people for weddings, family reunions, etc.
Recreation: Hiking and mountain biking are popular inside the campground, as is beach combing, clam and oyster harvesting, crabbing, and saltwater fishing.
Campsites (44 sites, no hookups, 4 H/B sites, 1 group camp for 80, reservable): Best are 1, 7, 16, 24. Sites in the wooded loop are in average size, private, and very wooded with lush vegetation. However, the road is difficult to navigate with larger vehicles (heed their warning for trailers > 21'). The sites in the RV strip are just that -- side-by-side parking with two gravel roads that border both the front and back of each site. These will not be for everybody. The H/B sites are excellent, and even have their own set of toilets.
Trip Notes: This park is unlike the other parks in the area built on old forts (Fort Warden S.P., and the wonderful Fort Flagler S.P.). It leaves the modern mind wondering why the fort ever existed at all. It is only until you explore the 6.5 miles of trails, stumble upon the abandoned cemetery, and realize that lives once both flourished and ended here. But it is the trails themselves, perfect for mountain

bikers and walkers, and the almost 4000' of beach front with its straight-on views of Port Townsend, Whidbey Island, and the waters of Puget Sound that finally grabs you. My favorite part was the Group Camp itself, with the seemingly haunted Torpedo Tower. I can imagine inviting all my friends, young and old, to camp out and tell ghost stories. The building is perfect for ghoulish pranks that people are likely to remember for a long time.

Local Alternative: Fort Warden S.P. is likely the most popular of the area's three State Parks. The camping, however, is more exposed to the elements than even the Lower Beach Campground at Fort Flagler and has less privacy. For those of you who love it --- follow your bliss! We just can't recommend it over Fort Flagler or Old Fort Townsend.

Hamma Hamma, Duckabush and Dosewallips Rivers

These three short but wild rivers flow out of the eastern slopes of the Olympic Mountains, and all flow east before emptying into Hood Canal in quick succession along Hwy 101. Three vintage, concrete bridges are listed on the National Register of Historic places, and rank among the most iconic sites along this stretch of highway. What the rivers also provide is quick and deep access into this lesser-known side of the Olympics for recreation of all varieties.

Collins CG (Jefferson Co.'s BEST *RUSTIC CG*)

Sometimes you want rain forest, and at other times you want freedom from the restrictions of the National Parks. Eureka! Here you can have both. This out-of-the way campground on the ethereal blue-green Duckabush River takes campers away from the bustle of Highway 101 and into the over-the-rainbow world of the Olympic National Forest.

Overview: This campground is nestled on the Duckabush River 43.5 miles south of Port Townsend and 4 miles southwest of Brinnon on 4 acres at 200' elevation, open mid-May to late Sept.; GPS 47.6831, -123.0216.

Facilities: Limited amenities include vault toilets, picnic tables, and fire rings. There is no drinking water.

Recreation: Note that the Duckabush River has access to the Duckabush and Ranger Hole Trailheads (each about 1 mile from the park), and close access to Murhut Falls (3 miles from campground) with a 0.8-mile hike to the dramatic falls. Interrorem Cabin, just 1.5 miles before the park, is available for rent. Duckabush Trail #803 is a 10.6-mile round trip trail that leads to the Brothers Wilderness and the vistas of "The Big Hump."

Campsites (16 sites total, 6 for tents only and 10 for tents or RVs up to 21', no hookups or reservations, no drinking water): Sites vary in size, 6 of the 16 being walk-in tent only sites. Several sites are close to the Duckabush River (8, 9, 10, 11, 12, 13, 14), but its soothing flow can be heard from every campsite. All sites are medium to large, have heavy vegetation, and excellent privacy. Parking pads are mixed gravel and native materials. For RVs, we recommend sites 1, 3, 14, 15.

Trip Notes: Pulling into Collins CG can be likened to Dorothy, Toto, and the Scarecrow following the Yellow Brick Road past the wicked, talking, apple-throwing trees from the Wizard of Oz. The trees here loom over the campsites, each with their own personality, moss hanging low, their limbs pointing at us with narrow, craggy fingers, as if following our every move. But they've become friendly in their old age, providing a soothing canopy for campers to unwind while the river lulls them to sleep at night.

Local Alternative: Dosewallips S.P. is a popular destination for campers who also enjoy the pursuit of the famous molluscan geoduck. Deal breaker for us: Hwy 101 runs right through the middle of campground. Enjoy it if you will, but you'll find us at Collins CG.

The trees at Collins CG resemble the wicked apple-throwing trees
from the Wizard of Oz

Lena Lake Hike-In CG (Jefferson Co.'s *BEST CG FOR ENTIRE FAMILIES*)
This is Washington's most popular hike-in campground. Not just with families. Not just with the young. Not just with the old. Everybody. The Lake was formed 1300 years ago by a log jam on Lena Creek. Now it has given way to some of the most diverse camping in the area.

Overview: The trailhead for the 3.2-mile hike-in is located 5 miles east of Eldon on 55-acre Lena Lake (more below), operated by the USFS at an 1800' elevation, FREE with a Northwest Forest Pass, open spring through fall; GPS 47.37205, -123.09728.

Facilities: These include picnic tables, fire grills, and a picturesque but nonfunctional composting toilet sitting on the edge of a steep bank. You may want to bring a portable toilet and water purification tablets.

Recreation: For those who need even more to do after reaching Lower Lena, Upper Lena Lake (also with campsites) is just 3 miles beyond. A boulder blocks the trail and must be scaled, so children and dogs are prohibited on Upper Lena.

Trailhead: From Olympia head North on Highway 101 for 51 miles. You will pass through the towns of Shelton, Hoodsport, Liliwaup, and Eldon. Turn left at the brown and white sign that indicates the Hamma Hamma Recreational Area. This will be Forest Road 25. (If you come to the town of Brinnon, you have gone too far). Continue for 8 miles until you reach Lena Creek Campground and trailhead.

Campsites (29 sites, no drinking water or reservations): Sites are scattered around the lake, providing space and privacy. Some sit at the base of Lena Creek as it flows into the Lake, others sit high on the Lake's banks, while others are tucked into little "hollers" along the way. If you follow the trail around the Lake to its absolute end, you will find a large, flat sandy area that few ever find, which is also the best campsite on the Lake.

Trip Notes: As I watched the small children in the crowded trailhead parking lot, each strapped into their tiny Hello Kitty and Spiderman backpacks, I knew immediately what this trip confirmed: that this is an "everybody-oriented" campground that any child, adolescent, or adult would love. The trail is an ingenious series of switchbacks, some with bridges to cross, and others crossing under rock outcroppings. Once at the Lake, I saw people everywhere. A dad and his three young children seemed to spend hours simply throwing rocks into the Lake. On Lunch Rock, teenagers seemed spellbound by the floating logs near the log jam. On the opposite side, teenage girls in bikinis could be heard giggling from a hundred yards away, though they quieted when they saw me on the trail. In short - everyone seemed to be rediscovering how to play. I think anyone who camps here will turn out to be a lifelong outdoorsman.

Local Alternative: Lena Creek CG (GPS: 47.598306, -123.151361) is a small but campworthy spot on the Hamma Hamma River just past the Lena Lake Trailhead. Its greatest feature is the Living Legacy Trail constructed by the Civilian Conservation Corps in the 1930s. #Note that Lena Creek CG is in Mason Co., while Lena Lake CG crosses into Jefferson Co.#

Olympic National Park Ocean Strip (South)
While the northern border of the 73-mile ONP Ocean Strip begins at Cape Flattery, it ends at the more accessible southern border of Jefferson County. Ruby Beach, Destruction Island, and the Kalaloch Lodge are among its most iconic locations.

<u>Kalaloch CG at ONP</u> (Jefferson Co.'s *MOST APPEALING CG TO THE SENSES*)
The word Kalaloch (pronounced CLAY-LOCK) in the Quinault language means "a good place to land." It features the best walking beach on the Peninsula; but beware, in the stormy winter weather it becomes treacherous with drifting logs.

<u>Overview</u>: This popular campground is located 45 miles south of Forks on the ONP Ocean Strip at 75' elevation, open Memorial Day weekend to late Sept.; GPS 47.61306, -124.37472.

<u>Facilities</u> include with flush toilets, drinking water, picnic tables, fire rings with grates, garbage collection, fish cleaning stations, a one-mile hiking trail along Kalaloch Creek, camp hosts, and an RV dump. There are several stairwells providing access to the beach 40' below.

<u>Recreation</u>: Birding is terrific here. So terrific, in fact, there are too many bird species to name. Some of the more unusual include the black oystercatcher, chestnut-backed chickadee, dark-eyed junco, fox sparrow, golden-crowned sparrow, marbled murrelet, ruby-crowned kinglet, spotted towhee, and the occasional puffin.

<u>Campsites</u> (168 sites for tents and RVs up to 21-35', including 4 ADA; no hookups, one group tent site, reservable): Sites sit on a high bluff above the Pacific Ocean, organized into 6 loops. The A, B, and C loops are conjoined, the A loop encircling the B and C loops. Many sites seem overgrown, small, and awkwardly placed, especially in Loop F.

<u>Trip notes</u>: I would rank this among the best beach campgrounds, particularly where Kalaloch Creek joins the ocean between the park and the lodge. It sits high over the Pacific, with tide pools, bird watching, and endless walking. The iconic floating tree has roots that reach both sides of a deep but narrow ravine, and high enough that even the tallest person can stand under it. The vistas from the bluff are so sweeping it makes you want to explore forever. Kalaloch means "a good place to land." It certainly was that.

<u>Local Attractions</u>: Rugged and rocky Ruby Beach, located 10 minutes north of Kalaloch, is a readily accessible beach filled with offshore sea stacks, whale sightings, and ruby-colored crystals in the sand. The Olympic National Park's "Big Cedar, located" 4 miles north of Kalaloch, is believed to be over 1000 years old. Note that it partially collapsed in a storm during March of 2014, so if you want to see this behemoth beast before it is you late, you should come here soon.

Hoh Rain Forest

Everyone knows about the tropical Amazon Rain Forest. The Hoh Rain Forest, by comparison, is one the world's largest temperate rain forests. Its dew, fog and mist alone contribute 30 inches of "wet" per year. All told, it receives 14 feet of rain in 12 months-time. But when you dry off your glasses and zip up your GorTex, you will find yourself in the most carefully preserved rain forest in the northern hemisphere, which has remained unchanged for thousands of years.

<u>Hoh Rain Forest CG at ONP</u> (Jefferson Co.'s *MOST UNIQUELY WASHINGTON CG*)
What would it take to get you to visit a campground that gets 140-170" of rainfall per year? The answer is simple: Hoh, Hoh, Hoh.
<u>Overview</u>: This ONP campground is located 40 miles northeast of Kalaloch along the picturesque Hoh River at 581' elevation, open year-round; GPS 47.857977, -123.93207.
<u>Facilities</u> include flush toilets, running water, picnic tables, fire rings, an amphitheater, camp hosts, and an RV dump.
<u>Recreation</u>: The park has access to many easy walking and longer hiking trails, including the Hall of Mosses Trail (.8 miles), the Spruce Nature Trail (1.2 miles), and the Hoh River trail, which leads 17.3 miles to Glacier Meadows, on the edge of Mount Olympus.
<u>Campsites</u> (88 sites for tents and RVs from 19 to 35' with a couple for larger, no hookups or reservations): Sites are small to huge with average to good privacy with paved parking pads, heavily shaded and often wet. Vegetation includes huge Sitka spruce, some reaching 250 feet in height and 30 to 60 feet in circumference (note you can stay dry if camping under one of these); Douglas fir, many more than 100 years old; western hemlock and western red cedar; moss-covered big leaf maples; stair-step moss; groups of sword ferns that grow up to your waist; and, growing from the limbs of trees are licorice ferns, cattail moss, and hundreds of species of lichens, lungwort, and liverworts forming a thick canopy over many campsites. Sites are arranged in three loops. The A Loop (sites 1-35) has larger sites nestled against the River; Loop B (sites 39-56) has some larger sites, but is away from the River, and may have the driest sites; Loop C (sites 60-89) has smaller sites, but sites sit in a saddle surrounded by the River and is the preferred loop for tenters. Best sites are 5, 8, 19, 23, 29, 44, 63, 65, 68, and 69.
<u>Trip Notes</u>: I travelled to this park several times in college, and even camped along some of the trails, but had never camped in the campground itself. What struck me now is how gloriously wet everything is. I don't mean dripping wet, just rich and verdant and flowing. The waters of the milky Hoh River make me want to dip my feet for hours and wait for wildlife to come to me. The moss hangs from the tree limbs like billowing, delicate scarves in a chic boutique. This isn't just a rain forest, this is fairyland.
<u>Local Alternatives</u>: There are four smaller but campworthy campgrounds in the immediate vicinity, all of which are FREE. Minnie Peterson CG sits right on the Hoh River on the edge of the rain forest. It has large sites, but also some road noise. The popular Hoh Oxbow CG is situated on a bluff overlooking the River It comes with both a boat launch and road noise. Willoughby Creek CG is situated

where this creek joins the Hoh River. It is more rustic with 8 sites for tents and RVs less than 25'. Cottonwood CG comes with a boat launch and is free of road noise. It includes a group camp for up to 10 people and is popular with anglers and hunters.

Coppermine Bottom CG (Jefferson Co.'s *BEST FREE CG*)
This hidden campground occupies a nice stretch of the shallow, pebbly-bottomed Clearwater River, a tributary of the Queets River. The campground gets its name from its location on the floor or "bottom" of the River, plus copper mines that long ago occupied the area. It represents one of the best getaways in this area, known largely only by locals, with an abundance of marshland vegetation and wildlife.
Overview: This secluded campground is located 33.6 miles south of Forks and 84.1 miles north of Aberdeen near Queets on the Clearwater River, operated by the DNR in the Bert Cole State Forest (adjacent to the Hoh Rain Forest) at 1317' elevation, open year-round; GPS 47.6554451 -124.1882553.
Facilities: Primitive facilities include vault toilets, picnic tables, fire pits, a Day Use Area with group shelter, and hand boat launch. There is no drinking water.
Recreation: An added bonus of this campground is its excellent salmon and steelhead fishing, due largely to a unique dory-launch, enabling flat-bottomed boats to launch into shallower water.
Campsites (10 sites for tents or RVs up to 16', no hookups or reservations, FREE with Discover Pass): The sites swing in an arc around a turn in the Clearwater River, ranging in size from large to XXL. Vegetation is heavy with cottonwoods along the River. Pads are on native material, with sites secluded from one another, each with paths leading to the River.
Trip Notes: Much like Klahowya CG to the north, and Campbell Tree Grove CG to the south, Coppermine Bottom is overlooked due to its "assumed" similarities to the logging lands and primitive roads that surround them. But this is not a case of "getting there is half the fun." In this case, the last mile of the ride (the only graveled portion) can be off-putting. But once you arrive, you are away from the city, away from crowds, and nested down into one of the most pristine and secluded campgrounds anywhere. If seclusion is what you seek, your paradise awaits.

For photos of Jefferson Co. CGs, or more on Hike-In, Boat-In, or Group CGs, consult campeverycountywa.com

KING COUNTY (Seattle/Federal Way/Enumclaw)

This, the most populous county in Washington, is much more than the Space Needle and the Seattle sports stadiums. It is a very diverse place, with its beginnings in logging, fishing, coal, and hops. These have largely been supplanted by such companies as Starbucks, Boeing, and Amazon.com. But outside the big population centers -- near the farms of Enumclaw, the railroad towns of the Skykomish Valley, the raging waters of the Green River Gorge, the sandy beaches of Dash Point, and the Cascade Mountains of Snoqualmie Pass -- are surprisingly remote campgrounds that make better attractions than you'll ever see on television or the Fortune 500.

Puget Sound Region
Federal Way, the largest city in southwest King County, began as a trading post along a north-south Indian trail. The trail become a government road, informally known as the "Federal Highway," the first between Tacoma and Seattle. Seven small communities grew along this "Federal Way," but those along the Puget Sound shoreline avoided the ensuing suburban sprawl, giving way to parks, a scout camp, retreat centers, conference centers, a live theater, and one of the nicest sandy beaches in all of Puget Sound.

Dash Point S.P. (King Co.'s *BEST CG FOR ENTIRE FAMILIES*)
This park has become defined by "the ravine" and "the beach," but high above it all is good camping that allows campers to enjoy the best of three worlds.
Overview: Located between cities of Tacoma and Federal Way on 398 acres with 3,301' of saltwater shoreline on Puget Sound at 184' elevation, open year-round; GPS 47.317, -122.4065.
Facilities include bathrooms with showers, picnic tables, fire rings/grills, amphitheater, 2 covered shelters in Day Use Areas, an RV dump, and camp hosts.

The beach at Dash Point S.P. is always a big draw, rain or shine

<u>Recreation</u> includes beachcombing, hiking, windsurfing, swimming, and 11 miles of hiking trails. Clamming is not recommended.

<u>Campsites</u> (141 sites, including 27 with full hookups 30 and 50 amps, one group camp for 80 with 10 smaller sites within the camp, reservable): Sites have been recently updated with the addition of sewer hookups for RV sites. However, this is an old park, originally built in the country, and the sites are of average size with fair privacy, but good vegetation. The Park is intersected by Marine View Drive, yet there is very little road noise, that being the click-clack of cars crossing the bridge over the ravine. No sites are on the saltwater beach but sit high on a forested plateau. The Group Camp is closer to the beach but has less than total privacy. The larger Day Use Area is quite crowded, but the smaller Picnic Point is extremely private. This is still superior camping to that of nearby Salt Water S.P., which has an equally good day use area, but limited camping.

<u>Trip Notes</u>: This Park has a suburban setting but sits in nearly 400 acres of a heavily forested ravine whose stream leads to Puget Sound. With full services available just 15 minutes away in the village of Browns Point, campers can stay insulated from the suburban sprawl that surrounds the park.

<u>Local Attractions and History</u>: The West Hylebos Wetlands Park lies deeper in the heart of Federal Way on 120 acres, named after a Belgian-born priest who established many hospitals and churches in the area. The wetlands are equal parts wildlife refuge, ecological and hydrological conservatory, and nature trail. It includes the Denny and Barker cabins (early pioneers of South King Co.), a 1.7-mile trail with one mile of boardwalk, interpretive signs, and a 'Deep Sink', one of a very few remaining peat bogs in the area. More than one hundred bird species frequent the park, including great blue herons, red pileated woodpeckers, orange-brown warblers, and violet green swallows.

Green River Valley

Most know the Green River as a slow, meandering canal through the City of Kent, where it has been subdued by dikes and re-channeling. Closer to its source in the Cascade Mountains, however, it flows through a gorge where it tears through ravines, tumbles over smooth moss-covered boulders, and challenges to be tamed. And this is where our camping adventures begin.

Kanaskat-Palmer S.P. (King Co.'s *MOST APPEALING CG TO THE SENSES*)
The Park is named for two tiny communities (Kanaskat and Palmer) of the North Pacific Railroad in this coal-mining district of east King County. This stretch of the Green River is a premier spot for expert whitewater kayakers, and campers who love to sit and watch them pass by from the comfort of their lawn chairs.
Overview: Located 10.4 miles north of Enumclaw on 320 acres with 2 miles of shoreline on the Green River at 761' elevation, open year-round; GPS 47.3197, -121.9053.
Facilities include bathrooms with showers (some ADA-accessible), picnic tables, fire rings/grills, 4 fire circles, 3 covered shelters in Day Use Area, and camp hosts.
Recreation: Whitewater rafting and kayaking (experts only, Class III-IV) is the Park's biggest draw. Fishing is great for steelhead. You will see tubers and swimmers here, but the water is treacherous, and caution is advised. There are also 3 miles of hiking and biking trails. The most popular trail is the River Walk, which follows the Green River for over a mile, running the entire length of the campground.
Campsites (50 sites, including 19 w/water & electric 30-amp, 2 ADA sites, 1 group camp for up to 80 people, 6 ADA-accessible yurts, reservable): Sites are spacious and wooded with average to good privacy. The Group Camp has two great Adirondack shelters, a dining shelter, and consists of a labyrinth of interconnected campsites. While it claims to accommodate 80 people, I would be more comfortable with 30-40 people, given the close proximity of the shelters and tent sites.
Trip Notes: Here's the thing – this park is located at the base of the Cascades, and when it rains it dumps enough rain to damage equipment and the spirits of even the happiest of campers. That being said, the park is gorgeous, with beautiful walks along the Green River Gorge. The group camp is inviting, with wooden bunkhouses in vintage style. Great dog walking, forests and river. Camp here on a sunny stretch of days!

South Fork Skykomish Valley (Highway 2)

Highway 2 starts in Everett and follows the old railroad towns of Sultan, Startup and Gold Bar (Snohomish Co.) before dipping down into the King County towns of Baring, Grotto, and Skykomish. And this is where the River changes from all too ordinary to strikingly beautiful, with camping to boot.

<u>Money Creek CG</u> (King Co.'s *BEST BIKE-IN CG*)

The stream from which this campground gets its name was first explored for its mineral wealth. In fact, Money Creek was named because of a large sum of money sent by eastern stockholders to develop a mine and other resources of the stream. Fortunately, the mining was a bust and the campground is a keeper.

<u>Overview</u>: Located 2 miles south of Skykomish with extensive South Fork Skykomish River shoreline, operated by the USFS at 833' elevation, open late May to mid-September; GPS 47.7292, -121.4075.

<u>Facilities</u> include vault toilets, picnic tables, fire rings, running water, and camp hosts.

<u>Recreation</u>: Fishing is good for steelhead and rainbow trout. Two swimming holes provide informal swimming. There is no hiking within the campground, but nearby opportunities include Iron Goat Trail #1074.

<u>Campsites</u> (25 sites including 4 ADA/wheelchair accessible sites, no hookups, reservable): Sites are large, well-spaced, and wooded. They all lie across the South Fork of the Skykomish River from busy Highway 2. The spur has sites along the River, is sunnier, and has double-wide parking aprons, but a tight turn around, so large RVs are not recommended here. The loop is in old growth forest of cedar, Douglas fir, and big leaf maple. It is shadier and better for larger RVs. The sites in the loop have less road noise, but possibly more railroad noise.

<u>Trip notes</u>: I preferred the sites on the spur due to prettier and better river access. The big drawback is the trains, which pass through and blow their whistles hourly. Railroad lovers like me find it comforting, others find it annoying -- but if you want to experience this part of Washington "from the ground up," it will include railroads. Those desiring more quiet may want to consider nearby Beckler River CG in Snohomish Co.

Snoqualmie Valley

This majestic valley is situated between Seattle and the foothills of the Cascade Mountains. The quaint towns of Duvall, Carnation, and Fall City have a traditional main-street look, melding pastoral beauty with arts, culture, and some of the most unique recreation touches anywhere.

<u>Tall Chief CG/RV Park</u> (King Co.'s *BEST EQUIPPED CG*)

This campground has more than enough amenities, is close enough to the attractions in Seattle, and yet is wooded and quiet enough to appeal to entire families. And not just young families with kiddies -- extended families with restless teenagers, excessively energetic school kids, your Aunt Sophie who hasn't been camping since 1492, and the entire gang. If you don't like this campground, you probably don't like camping.

Overview: Located 4 miles west of Fall City and 25.6 miles east Seattle on 70 acres, operated by Encore RV Resorts at 300' elevation, open year-round; GPS 47.5986, -121.942.

Facilities include bathrooms with showers (ADA-accessible), a playground, outdoor pool, hot tub, a Clubhouse, a billiards/game room, mini golf, sports courts, horseshoes, library, laundry, Wi-Fi, walking trails, camp hosts, and RV dump services 3 days per week.

Recreation includes swimming, forest walks, and birdwatching.

Campsites (172 RV sites, most with water/electrical hookups 30-amp, 6 designated tent sites, 6 cabins, 2 yurts, reservable, open year-round): Sites are above average to large, all wooded, private, many configurations, no street noise. Best sites are 85-98, built out over the edge of a forested hill with small ravines between each site.

Trip notes: We were lucky to set up before the rains came but spent most of the first two days in our dry campsites under awnings and pop-ups. My first impression was that it was a typical, representative forested campground, better than many. But, for the purposes of this website, "good enough" is not good enough to be included. Once I had the opportunity to move around and talk to other campers, it clicked. The vast majority of campers were from out-of-state. For them, this otherwise "typical" forest was nothing less than amazing. Most also came to see such nearby attractions as the Experience Music Project and the Space Needle in Seattle, the Microsoft Campus, and the Amazon.com building. For us native Washingtonians, these are simply local icons -- but for them, the out-of-staters, this is a necessary stepping-stone to experience "the real Washington." And for us, the fall foliage here delighted us and kept us happy campers.

 Local Attraction: Snoqualmie Falls and Lodge are not to be missed.

Tolt-MacDonald Park (King Co.'s MOST UNIQUELY WASHINGTON CG)
Whenever I hear people complain that all Western Washington Parks are the same -- a refrain with which I categorically disagree -- I recommend this campground. Three-sided cabins? Mountain bike trails? An A-frame amphitheater? Cabins made from shipping containers? Suspension bridges? I rest my case.

Overview: Located 24 miles east of Seattle in the town of Carnation on 574 acres at the confluence of the Snoqualmie and Tolt Rivers at 82' elevation, operated by King County Parks, open year-round; GPS 47.6439, -121.9246.

Facilities include flush toilets, running water, showers, picnic tables, fire pits, a playground for small children, and camp hosts. Most notable are re-purposed shipping containers fashioned into eco-friendly "cabins" with radiant heating, LED lighting, tables, benches, cupboards, and futons bunks plus a futon chair/bed. There is a 500' suspension bridge over the Snoqualmie River leading to the west camping area. Two large picnic shelters and a beautifully restored barn are also available for larger day-use groups. Nearby are a playground, soccer field and two ballfields.

Recreation: The park contains an extensive set of mountain biking trails on the Ames Lake Plateau, plus 12 miles of hiking trails. Bicyclers have access to the 27-mile Snoqualmie Valley Trail to view local farms and forests.

Campsites (44 sites, including 16 RV sites w/water & electric 30 and 50 amps, 6 yurts - 2 ADA, two 3-sided cabins, reservable by phone): The west camping area, across the suspension bridge, has 11 walk-in sites, the yurts, and the 3-sided cabins. There is also one large group site with a picnic shelter and raised fire pit for up to 60 people. A smaller group site includes an A-framed amphitheater and 2 fire pits for up to 40 people. Wheelbarrows are available to move equipment from the parking lot. The east camping area comprises the RV loop. All sites are pull-throughs with paved pads. This is spacious and grassy with shade trees on the periphery. It includes a spur with 12 tent sites that are somewhat small and less than perfectly level, so come prepared.

Trip Notes: Nothing is typical here. The beach was the big surprise, with its sandy shores on the Snoqualmie River. Sunbathers, kayakers, and inner tubers were having a ball. The 3-sided cabins were more like rustic 3-1/2-sided modified Adirondack shelters. What struck me were the number of Day Use visitors who came out just to walk around this spectacle and add some spice to their day. Camping was even spicier.

North Bend/Western Slope of Snoqualmie Pass

This part of Washington is extremely fortunate to have one of the most accessible and beautiful mountain passes so close to the State's largest metropolitan area, giving quick access to the entire interior of Washington State. The snow-capped peaks, the fragrant conifers, and even the split-lane, high-rise construction of Interstate 90 are nothing short of spectacular. The downside is overcrowding, overuse, and freeway noise. King County, always the innovator, has provided some very innovative camping alternatives.

Middle Fork CG (King Co.'s *BEST RUSTIC CG*)

Sometimes campgrounds get built because they are close to a natural wonder, an outdoor tourist site, or because an overnight stop is needed along a busy highway. Then there are the good ones -- those that get built out of a grass roots need from campers. In this case, another campground was needed on the western slope on Snoqualmie Pass, both to ease the overused existing campgrounds and bring law enforcement into an area inundated with increased illicit activity. This campground was opened in 2006 and upgraded in 2014 to meet that need, providing the best (and quietest!) camping in the area.

Overview: This busy, forested campground is located 12 miles northeast of North Bend at the junction of the Middle Fork of the Snoqualmie and Taylor rivers, operated by the USFS at 1145' elevation, open May - September; GPS 47.5532378791, -121.538198048.

Facilities: Less rustic than in the past, amenities now include vault toilets, picnic tables, fire grills, and running water.

Recreation: The first thing you'll notice about the Middle Fork Valley is the plethora of trailhead signs. They're everywhere, on the 12-mile drive to the campground, the "hiking spur" across Taylor River, and in the campground itself. These include the Middle Fork Trail #1003 (25.3 miles in and back), the Pratt River Trail #1035, and the CCC Trail (upper and lower), with access to the Iron Horse Trail.

Campsites (38 sites for tents or small RVs up to 40', plus one group site for up to 35-40, no hookups, reservations recommended): Sites are large, flat, and shady beneath a canopy of cedars, Douglas fir, and western hemlock. The best sites are the higher priced sites, particularly sites 10, 14, and 28.

Trip Notes: First, a word of warning. When you see the Middle Fork C.G. sign, turn left. Do not cross the Taylor River Bridge, and do not drive to end of this hiking spur road. It is treacherous, and you may not be able to turn around, especially on weekend mornings when the hikers show up.

That having been said -- this is the real thing here. We immediately felt that calming USFS campground affect and were presented with more places to explore than time. The mountains here are phenomenal! Some rise straight up from the ground like giant sea stacks, but lush and forested. The Middle Fork River in particular had a green translucent quality one moment, then breaks into a wall of small rivulets the next. There was a need here, and it has been met. If you camped here in the past, come back. The upgrades have made all the difference.

Nearby Alternative: The best local alternative is Denny Creek CG, which regrettably rests below and between the east and westbound lanes of Interstate 90. The good news is that it is heavily forested, well laid out, well-equipped and very accessible. The road noise surrounding the campground is surprisingly muffled but creates a persistent white noise. If you need a stopover, however, this is your best and most accessible choice, but you may want to head out first thing in the morning.

OTHER CAMPGROUNDS: There are no FREE Campgrounds in King Co. that we can recommend at this time.

For more photos of King Co. CGs, or more on HIKE-IN or GROUP CGs, consult campeverycountywa.com

KITSAP COUNTY (Port Orchard/Bremerton)

This spade-shaped county, sitting in the middle of Puget Sound, is over 90% surrounded by water. It gives both the best views of Mount Rainier and the Olympic Mountains, both in the distance. But the saltwater campgrounds make this one of the most overlooked counties in Washington.

Puget Sound

This section of Puget Sound faces east toward Vashon Island, Blake Island, Bainbridge Island, and the City of Seattle, with an unobstructed view of Mt. Rainier. It is far from the madding crowd of the east Puget Sound shoreline, keeping more than just a physical distance with its own unique rural character.

Manchester S.P. (Kitsap Co.'s *BEST EQUIPPED/BEST CG FOR RVs* and *BEST GROUP CG*)

Overview: This, our favorite campground, is located 5 miles east of Port Orchard on 111 acres with 3400' of saltwater shoreline on Puget Sound, open year-round; GPS 47.5773, -122.555.

Facilities: Generous facilities include flush toilets, showers, running water, picnic tables, fire rings, 2 covered shelters, and the old torpedo warehouse which is big enough for weddings and other large events.

Recreation: This includes 1.9 miles of hiking trails which pass abandoned military batteries and sheds, plus views of Vashon and Bainbridge Islands with views of downtown Seattle and Mt. Rainier. Good blackberry picking within the campground (not the preferred black caps). This is part of the Cascadia Marine Trail with kayak access.

Campsites (49 sites for tents and RVs up to 60', including 15 with water & electric 30-amp hookups, one group site for up to 130, 3 H/B and kayaking sites, reservable): Sites are large, wooded and private on a well-terraced and gentle hillside. The Group Camp includes a large fire circle, 12 RV hookups, a covered shelter with eight picnic tables, electricity, several unsheltered picnic tables and braziers. There are two unisex ADA restrooms and showers.

Trip notes: Of all the campgrounds we have visited in Washington State, this our personal favorite. This is odd, since in two of our six visits, it rained so hard that it actually toppled trees and blocked both the entrance to and our exit from the Park. Despite this, we found it not only invigorating, but stayed dry and had the best camping experiences of our lives. This is due to the thick forest and carefully terraced sites, which soak up the rain as quickly as it hits. At dusk, you can hear the sea lions on the docks of the nearby Naval Supply Center. There are great walks on the bluff looking across at downtown Seattle and Vashon Island, and the Park even supplies blackberry picking in late summer. And just for the record, we had just as much fun when it was sunny.

Blake Island S.P. Boat-In CG (Kitsap Co.'s *MOST UNIQUELY WASHINGTON CG* and *BEST BOAT-IN CG*)

Most people know Blake Island for Tillicum Village, a Washington-flavors dinner location with Native American-themed stage performances. Few know there is much more here including peaceful trails, fishing, clam digging, and camping, complete with magnificent sunsets over the Olympic Mountains.

Overview: This campground is located on 476-acre Blake Island (between the south end of Bainbridge Island and the north end of Vashon Island) with 5 miles of saltwater shoreline, open year-round; GPS 47.53833, -122.49222.

Facilities: These include restrooms with showers (May through October) or vault toilets in off-season, picnic tables, fire grills, a playground, two picnic shelters with fire circles (Group Camp), an Adirondack Shelter (Group Site), 7.5 miles of bike trails, 8 miles of hiking trails, 1500' of mooring dock, 24 mooring buoys, and a marine dump station. Tillicum Village is a licensed concessionaire that provides transportation to the Island plus a Camp Store, longhouse, totems, and meals, Native American story-telling and traditional dance, plus educational programs on the Island.

Recreation: Kayaking, canoeing, and/or motor boating are a given. Scuba diving is popular at the south end of the Island, and bird watching is popular throughout.

Campsites (44 tent sites plus 3 boat-in only sites, no hookups or reservations): The island is a triangle shape with the tip pointing straight down/south. The three Cascadia Marine Trail sites are located in the northwest corner close to mooring, and rests on open beach, but are the most private sites. The West Point

Campground is just south of the marine sites, and consists of six beach sites, sheltered by towering madronas. They are also very private, and are best for kayaking from the mainland of Kitsap Co. The Main Campground is located near the northeast corner, just south of Tillicum Village. Privacy is minimal here, being in the shadow of considerable activity. The Group Camp, which can accommodate up to 100 people, is adjacent to that. Most campers in the Main and Group campgrounds arrive from the Argosy Cruise boats out of Seattle. Additional dispersed campsites are in the South End Campground on the southern tip of the Island. These are also protected by tall madronas, primitive, and very private.

Trip Notes: The best thing about camping on Blake Island is having the luxury of choosing sites ranging from total seclusion to total inclusion in the activities and dining at Tillicum Village. There are no other boat-in campgrounds quite like it in all of Washington. Its proximity to populated areas allows quick, spontaneous island adventures to a large number of people. This is a great addition to the already complex and diverse array of campgrounds available to boat-in and all other types of campers in Washington.

Getting There: The shortest paddle to Blake Island is from the Manchester city dock (just north of Southworth), or Manchester S.P. (about 2 miles). Others launch from Fort Ward S.P. or Eagle Harbor on Bainbridge Island. Seattle kayakers typically launch from Alki Beach Park at 1702 Alki Ave. S.W. (4 miles). Most power boats launch from the Don Armeni Boat Ramp and Viewpoint at 1222 Harbor S.W. in West Seattle/Alki Beach. Most campers arrive by Argosy tour boats which leave from downtown Seattle from March to October. Campers can catch the 9:00 a.m. boat for campers only, which returns in 24 hours. For more information on Argosy Cruises see:

https://www.argosycruises.com/argosy-cruises/tillicum-excursion/

Washington History: Blake Island was an ancestral camping ground of the Suquamish Indian tribe. According to legend it was the birthplace of Chief Sealth, for whom the City of Seattle was named. The earliest European settlers knew it as Smuggler's Island (it was also a hot spot for bootleggers during prohibition), until 1841 when it was named after George Smith Blake, the officer in charge of the United States Coast Survey (1837-1848). It was completely logged in the early 1900s and purchased in 1917 by Seattle millionaire William Pitt Trimble. He established Camp Sealth, an influential Campfire Girls camp that moved to Vashon Island upon the tragic death of his wife in 1929. She established the island as an ad hoc bird and wildlife sanctuary, but the island was abandoned after her death. In 1959 the Washington State Board of Natural Resources set aside all of Blake Island for a park. It became a State Park in 1960 with the inclusion of Tillicum Village.

Local Alternative: The best alternative for boat-in campers in Kitsap Co. is the Cascadia Marine Trail sites at Fay Bainbridge S.P. (see below).

campeverycountywa.com

Blake Island S.P. offers campsites ranging from total seclusion to total inclusion

Hood Canal

The Kitsap County view of Hood Canal faces due west with a direct shot of the Olympic Mountains. They'll both be right at your feet, those mystical peaks and magic waters.

<u>Scenic Beach S.P.</u> (Kitsap Co.'s *MOST APPEALING CG TO THE SENSES* and *BEST CG FOR ENTIRE FAMILIES*)

This rhododendron and madrona-clad campground is strategically located to look straight up Hood Canal from a lush peninsula separating Hood Canal from Seabeck

Bay. It has the feel of an island garden surrounded by mountain peaks to the east and west.

<u>Overview</u>: This campground is beautifully situated 19.3 miles northwest of Bremerton and 2.4 miles west of Seabeck on 88 acres with 1500' of saltwater shoreline on Hood Canal, open year-round; GPS 47.6466, -122.8468.

<u>Facilities</u>: These include bathrooms with flush toilets and coin-op showers, running water, picnic tables, fire rings, a playground, horseshoe pits, a volleyball area, a kitchen shelter that can accommodate 100, a wheel-chair accessible country garden, gazebo, and bridge at the historic Emel House, camp hosts, and an RV dump.

<u>Recreation</u>: Campers come here with recreation on their mind but typically end up staying put in the campground and enjoying the views. Bird watching and beach exploration are popular.

124

Campsites (52 sites, no hookups, one group site for 20-40, the Emel House for rent, one Adirondack Shelter in the Group Camp, reservable, open year-round): Sites are either pull-throughs or long narrow sites divided by wild native rhododendrons that provide privacy as well as space. There are no bad sites.

Trip notes: This beautiful park rests on the eastern shore of Hood Canal with our favorite waterfront view, looking north toward Dabob Bay and the Olympic Mountains. There is a large common area, access to the rocky beach, and the historic Emel House with its English gardens that have been restored and maintained. Spring is the best time, as the flowers are in bloom. We have visited here multiple times and are never disappointed. If nothing else, drive over and get a shot of that VIEW. If that doesn't get you, the rhododendrons will. Just keep one thing in mind: We learned the hard way that the native, wild rhododendrons bloom much later than the commercial, nursery rhododendrons. It's only natural, of course. But if you come to see the rhodies, look to late May or early June.

Bainbridge Island

This residential island is ten miles long and 5 miles wide, protecting most of the inland bays in Kitsap County. It is an island of parks, bicycle trails, hills, secluded beaches, and vibrant villages available by ferry, all with a rural character that make camping both accessible and extraordinary.

Fay Bainbridge Park (Kitsap Co.'s *BEST BIKE-IN CG*)
There was never anyone named Fay Bainbridge; rather, the State purchased the land from the estate of Temple S. Fay, a noted neurosurgeon. His children sold the land to be a State Park on the stipulation that they always retain the name "Fay." When budget cuts came in the late 2000s, Bainbridge Island Metro Parks purchased the Park and made capital improvements, and camping is better for the change.

Overview: This park is discreetly located 5 miles east of Poulsbo on Bainbridge Island on 17 acres with 1420' of Puget Sound shoreline, operated by Bainbridge Island Metro Parks and Recreation District, open year-round; GPS 47.70194, -122.50639.

Facilities: Generous facilities include bathrooms with flush toilets, showers, and running water, picnic tables, fire grills, a playground, a regulation-size sand volleyball pit, very spacious picnic sites, two beach boardwalks, a rain garden, 3 kitchen shelters (reservable), 2 mooring buoys, and camp hosts.

Recreation: This might possibly be the best bike-in campground in Washington, with only a 7-mile ride to the campground from the ferry terminal in Winslow, and many other metro parks to visit on the Island. It is also part of the Cascadia Marine Trail, with a large site set aside for kayakers, and mooring buoys for other boaters.

<u>Campsites</u> (10 tent sites, 26 sites with water-only hookups for RVs up to 30', one group site for up to 16, all reservable, plus 3 H/B sites and one kayaker site, all non-reservable and one-night-only): This campground has two decided parts: the large, flat beach area, and the "grassy knoll" above the beach that includes the tent and group sites. These have a very layered look, with grassy sites, with conifers and deciduous trees intertwined -- a delight to the eye in autumn. Sites are medium in size and very shady, with a rather "snug" but private feeling, hemmed in by windswept trees and hillsides. The beach area has a natural look with boardwalks giving passage through the driftwood to the sandy beach. The beach area has panoramic views of Puget Sound, looking north to the south end of Whidbey Island, and south towards Edmonds and North Seattle, with views of Mount Baker and Mount Rainier beyond. The RV sites are small to medium, and are side-by-side, but have a much larger feel due to the openness of the huge beach area. RV sites are well shaded and up against the hillside, whereas the H/B and kayak sites are more exposed.

<u>Trip Notes</u>: This former State Park seems to have flourished under the management of Bainbridge Island Parks, who began operations of the Park in 2011. I have been here on both sunny days and stormy days. While true Washingtonians are seldom deterred by the rain, and even feel that the rain brings out the "real Washington," sunny days have a big advantage at this campground. The beach area can take a full on hit from weather fronts, good for storm watchers, but making the marvelous beach area less accessible. Non-storm watchers will find the grassy knoll more protected and enjoyable.

<u>Local Alternative</u>: The only other camping alternative on Bainbridge Island is for kayakers only at Fort Ward Marine Park on the south end of the Island. This former state park is 137-acres on Rich Passage and is part of the Cascadia Marine Trail.

Green Mountain State Forest

This 6,000-acre State Forest is adjacent to the Tahuya State Forest in Mason County and is part of an extensive network of working forest lands that provides revenue for county services, state universities, and local schools. It includes its namesake Green Mountain, giving views of the entire Puget Sound Region, the Olympic and Cascade Mountains. You'll have to get here on foot, mountain bike, or horseback, but camping at the end of the trail will be well worth the effort.

<u>Green Mountain Horse Camp Hike-In/Ride-In</u> (Kitsap Co.'s *BEST RUSTIC* and *BEST HIKE-IN CG*)
This multiple-approach campground adds credence that Kitsap County is best known for its views -- and these great views are from the highest point in the County.

Overview: This campground sits on top the Green Mountain State Forest of Central Kitsap County, managed by the DNR at 1639' elevation, open Memorial Day weekend through mid-September; GPS 47.57849884, -122.7925415.

Facilities include vault toilets, picnic tables, fire grills, group shelter, and corrals for horses. There is no drinking water.

Recreation: The many trails and viewpoints provide almost endless possibilities. A trail map of the Green Mountain State Forest is strongly recommended.

Campsites (14 tent sites, no drinking water or reservations, FREE with Discover Pass): This is one of the most diverse campgrounds on this site. There is limited drive-in access off Tahuya Lake Rd on most weekends from Memorial Day to Labor Day, making it accessible to horse trailers and bicyclists, although its 3.4-mile graveled, uphill forest road will not agree with most touring bikes. Otherwise, hiking and equestrian access is best from Wildcat Trailhead. This campground is hosted by the Backcountry Horsemen of Washington. Our experience with horse campers is that they are the most respectful and least intrusive of any campers, making this even more inviting for everybody.

Wildcat Trailhead: To reach the trailhead, take the Seabeck Hwy Exit off of Hwy 3 in Silverdale and head west. Drive the entire 3.1 miles of Newberry Road until it ends at Seabeck Hwy NW and turn left. Continue for 2.0 miles and turn right onto NW Holly Rd (this occurs at the roundabout). Drive 1.8 miles, just past Wildcat Lake. The trailhead is on the left.

Trip Notes: This well-maintained, unspoiled campground is a real gem for equestrians and hiking campers alike. We expect working forests such as this to show more signs of logging, but none is evident from the campground. The logging roads to the vistas provided viewing at the higher elevations. The hiking/equestrian trails themselves pass mature forests, meadows, and beaver ponds. Forest roads lead to vistas of the Olympic Mountains, Hood Canal, Puget Sound, the Seattle City skyline, and Mount Rainier. While long stays are inviting, there is a 7-day limit for each 30-day period. Hikers will want to pack light on equipment in order to bring their own water.

OTHER CAMPGROUNDS: There are no FREE Campgrounds in Kitsap Co. that we can recommend at this time. For more photos of Kitsap Co. CGs consult
campeverycountywa.com

KITTITAS COUNTY (Ellensburg/Cle Elum)

This Central Washington county stretches from Snoqualmie Pass to the Columbia River. It has its beginnings as a stop-over for cowboys driving their herds north to Canada and northwest to the Puget Sound Area. Anyone who has driven I-90 through the county knows it still retains this character. But the outlying areas diversified with the completion of a wagon road over Snoqualmie Pass (1867), the discovery of gold at Swauk Creek (1873), coal mining by French companies near Cle Elum (1883), and the completion of the Yakima River Irrigation Project (1932). Now campers will find frontier mining and railroad towns, orchards, petrified forests, green valleys in the desert, recreational lakes, rodeos, and wind farms.

Eastern Slope of Snoqualmie Pass
As eastbound drivers pass the ski resort at Hyak and begin their descent, the land slowly takes on Ponderosa pine, less rain, more sunshine, and mountain camping on or near the reservoirs of the Yakima River.

Lake Easton S.P. (Kittitas Co.'s *BEST CG FOR ENTIRE FAMILIES*)
This is a compact State Park beside an even more compact railroad town that has the best camping among the reservoirs in the headwaters of the Yakima River.
Overview: Located 1-mile northwest of Easton on 516 acres with 24,000' of frontage on 205-acre Lake Easton at 2169' elevation, open year-round; GPS 47.2437, -121.1862.
Facilities include bathrooms (ADA), showers (ADA), fire pits/grills, a play shelter and playground, boat launch and 20' of dock, 6 miles of bike trails, 6.5 miles of hiking trails (some ADA accessible), excellent swimming area, amphitheater, basketball court, RV dump, camp hosts.

<u>Summer Recreation</u> includes swimming, boating (motorboats limited to 10mph), hiking, and limited fishing.

<u>Winter Recreation</u>: The Sno-Park is located in the Day Use Area (Sno-Park Permit required), plus cross-country skiing, snowshoeing, dog sledding, and a skate track on the John Wayne Pioneer Trail.

<u>Campsites</u> (135 sites, including 45 with hookups 30/50-amp, 2 H/B sites, one group camp, reservable): The tent area has 90 sites on the Yakima River with tent pads, and is well wooded and spaced. The RV area has 45 sites above Lake Easton, is also well wooded and spaced with good privacy. Parking pads are on gravel. The walk-in group camp for tents can accommodate up to 50.

<u>Trip notes</u>: This well-maintained State Park packs a lot into a relatively small area. We explored every square inch before the trip was over, and found all of it fascinating: hills, marshes, hiking trails, a dam, the Yakima River, and even the town itself. The Iron Horse Trail (giving access by bicycle or horseback) is just across the lake, with other walking trails giving views of the lake and dam. On the town's MainStreet the gal running the store will cook you a hamburger if you ask; on the other side of the freeway you can dine with friendly (yes, I said friendly) bikers. When you're done, the lake is perfect for boating and swimming.

<u>Nearby alternative</u>: Those interested in water skiing, jet skiing, or speed boating might find Lake Kachess Campground more suitable. Disadvantages are noise, crowds, and extremes in water levels later in the summer.

Cle Elum River Valley Region

This beautiful valley is part of the Irrigation Project, with the creation of reservoir Lake Cle Elum now at center stage. The French influences are evident here, as prime investors in the coal industry. Native influences are reflected in place names (Cle Elum, for instance, is a Salish term for "swift water," no doubt referring to the once swift Cle Elum River). This valley leads into the incredible Alpine Wilderness Area, with plenty of good camping along the way.

<u>Salmon La Sac CG</u> (Kittitas Co.'s *MOST APPEALING CG TO THE SENSES*)
The name comes from a French description of a native fishing technique whereby they employed woven cedar bark baskets to catch the salmon. It is French in name, but the beauty of the place speaks for itself in any language.

<u>Overview</u>: Located 16 miles north of Roslyn between the Cle Elum and Cooper Rivers, operated by the USFS at 2360' elevation, opens the weekend prior to Memorial Day, closes according to winter weather; GPS 47.4033, -121.0992.

<u>Facilities</u> include vault toilets, drinking water by hand pump, picnic tables, fire rings/grills, vintage fireplaces, a picnic shelter, and camp hosts.

<u>Summer Recreation</u>: Hiking, fishing, swimming, horseback riding and mountain biking are among the possibilities. Native blackberry picking is available right in the

campground. Hiking trails include the Cooper River Trail (7.8 miles round trip), Pete Lake Trail (15 miles round trip), and Lake Waptus Trail (18.8 miles round trip).

Winter Recreation: The Sno-Park has 6km of tracks and a skate lane that is shared with snowmobilers; it also has scenic views and sanitary facilities.

Campsites (69 sites for tents and RVs up to 38', no hookups, reservable): Campsites are large enough to accommodate larger parties, spaced well enough to provide privacy, and wooded enough to provide shade in the summer, where campers like to sit on sun-warmed rocks on the banks of the two rivers. Those along the Cooper River are better shaded and have vintage CCC fireplaces. Those along the Cle Elum River are sunnier, with many double sites and concrete parking pads. The foliage in both is alpine transitional, between the full hemlock, spruce, and Douglas Fir forest of Snoqualmie Pass and the Ponderosa pine forest that begins in earnest to the east.

Trip Notes: The left side of my brain wants to call this place "Shangri-La-Sac," after the mythical paradise of Shangri-La, but then the right side of my brain reminds me that we're really just on the edge of paradise here. This campground isn't perfect, but pretty close, bordering the Alpine Lakes Wilderness and all it contains. The Cle Elum River in particular draws you in the longer you are there.

Local Alternatives include Red Mountain CG and the single site portion of Cle Elum River CG to the south. Red Mountain is quite beautiful, sitting right on the Cle Elum River at the base of a high, red topped mountain. The problem here is that unofficial campsites just across the River in the French Cabin and Poverty Flats Areas are extremely noisy, and the USFS is unable to enforce quiet hours or control their activity. Cle Elum River CG is quieter, but unexceptional, and best used as an overflow area for Salmon La Sac CG.

Local Attraction: The nearby town of Roslyn, a one-time company town for Northern Pacific Railroad's subsidiary coal mines, stands remarkably unchanged from the time of its peak coal production in the late 1800s and early 1900s. Landmarks include the huge company store (still in operation), the Brick Tavern with its famous 20-foot spittoon, and its "segregated" cemetery, representing its one-time fraternal lodges and ethnic diversity. The town was later used as the backdrop for the popular television series "Northern Exposure."

Washington History: In 1912 French investors backed the Kittitas Railway and Power Company, eager to exploit coal reserves further up the Cle Elum River. Here they built an impressive steep-roofed log structure intended as a railroad depot to transport coal from Salmon La Sac to Yakima. The investors backed out in 1913 with the threat of World War I in their French homeland. The company went bankrupt and were sued by the Forest Service for unlawfully cutting government timber. The depot was handed over to the USFS in payment and was used as the ranger district headquarters for over 60 years. It was placed on the

National Historic Register of Historic Places in 1974. It stands proudly in the Salmon La Sac area as a testament to the past.

Owhi CG (Kittitas Co.'s *BEST RUSTIC CG*)

This rugged little campground (pronounced OW-high), named after a famous Indian Chief, is a few miles beyond where the pavement ends at Salmon La Sac. Yes, you can drive there on a rough gravel road, but most people hike in on the Copper River Trail from Salmon La Sac. Once there, you're not just near the Alpine Lakes Region, you're smack dab in the middle, and camping on one of the prettiest alpine lakes in the Cascade Range.

Overview: Located 27 miles Northeast of Cle Elum on 130-acre Cooper Lake, operated by the USFS at 2788' elevation, open late May to early June depending on snow melt; GPS 47.4244, -121.17.

Facilities: vault toilets, picnic tables and fire grills. There is no potable water.

Recreation: The Lake allows no motors, making for good kayaking and canoeing. The fishing here is good enough to make up for the marginal fishing at Salmon La Sac and Cle Elum Lake: brook trout, brown trout, bull trout, kokanee, and Westslope cutthroat are commonly caught. Many can fish right from their campsites. Most popular hikes are to Pete Lake (4.5 miles each way) and of course the Cooper River Trail (7.8 miles round trip) which starts at Salmon La Sac C.G., and loops through Owhi C.G. This is a perfect hike for beginning hiker-campers, as the elevation gain is only 400'.

Campsites (22 walk-in tent sites, no hookups or reservations): You may have to walk a bit to get to these scattered sites, many on the wooded shore of Cooper Lake; others are further back and in groups. Privacy is a given, as usage is very low. Old grown Douglas fir and western hemlock add still more privacy. Visible to the north are extraordinary views of the craggy summits of Chikamin Peak and Lemah Mountain. For those who prefer to slow down, unplug, and decompress, Cooper Lake itself is one mile of alpine purity, where most people prefer to poke around for days in kayaks, and explore the unspoiled forest.

Trip Notes: Cooper Lake both surprised and wowed us. This is the perfect lake for canoeing and kayaking. Finding all the individual sites was an adventure in itself, but they are there, tucked away in the deep forest of the lake shore. RVs should not come here (there is no RV parking), although there is ample parking for cars and trucks. Clearly, this campground is best hiked in, but you might want your camp-panions to transport your kayaks in by car or truck.

Tucquala Meadows CG/Fish Lake CG (Kittitas Co.'s *BEST FREE CG*)

The campground is officially called Fish Lake CG, but it seems prudent to call it by its lesser known name of Tucquala Meadows CG, since there is no Fish Lake and Tucquala "Lake" is really a widening of the beautiful upper Cle Elum River in a broad meadow in the Alpine Lakes Wilderness Area on the eastern slopes of Snoqualmie Pass.

Overview: Located 29 miles northwest of Cle Elum and 9.9 miles north of Salmon La Sac near 20-acre Tucquala Lake, operated by the USFS at 3,379' elevation, open year-round depending on weather conditions; GPS 47.521654, -121.072553.

Facilities are limited to a vault toilet and fire pits.

Recreation: Hiking starts at the Tucquala Meadows Trailhead and leads into the Alpine Lakes Wilderness, including the Paddy-Go-Easy Pass Trail, Deception Pass Trail, Squaw Lake Trail, and the Cathedral Trail #1345 which includes Deep Lake, Michael Lake, and Waptus Lake. Other activities include berry picking, fishing, birding, and wildflower viewing, especially in early July.

Campsites (an estimated 20 sites dispersed over one mile, FREE with NW Forest Pass): the best sites occur before you see the Fish Lake Guard Station, where they are on dirt roads away from the Lake and are used primarily by hunters in the Fall. The best sites are clearly along the Lake, starting just before Scatter Creek up to the Fish Lake CG sign.

Trip Notes: "Ah wilderness, where paradise enow!" I don't remember exactly where I first heard that quote, or just what "enow" means, but I do know that wilderness can be paradise sometimes. After 10 miles of rough, narrow, winding roads, and driving across Scatter Creek that still spilled over the road in mid-July, we saw it: beautiful, delicate, gentle Tucquala Lake. So why is the campground called "Fish Lake?" Turns out, according to the Cle Elum Ranger Station, the European settlers didn't know how to pronounce the native word Tucquala (almost sounds like Tukwila) and they decided to give an unexceptional name to a nice campground on an extraordinary body of water. It is serene, still, and calming. If you get lucky enough to find a campsite right on the Lake, it will be "enow".

Blewett/Swauk Pass

The mountain pass on which this campground sits was originally a dirt road built over a series of Indian trails to access the gold mines. Over time, and many reincarnations, including rerouting from Blewett to nearby Swauk Pass to accommodate modern traffic, confusion grew over the name. Locals still prefer to call it Blewett Pass, due to its long colorful history, and most campers are fine with that.

Swauk CG (Kittitas Co.'s *BEST BIKE-IN CG*)

You want to have the gold mining camping experience "from the ground up?" You've come to the right place. The campground is as primitive as the old gold miners, with few amenities and many remnants of their gold-seeking ventures. Glampers beware.

Overview: Located 27 miles east of Cle Elum on Swauk Creek off Highway 97, operated by the USFS at 3130' elevation, open weekend before Memorial Day through Tuesday after Labor Day; GPS 47.328, -120.6617.

Facilities include vault toilets, drinking water, picnic tables, fire rings, picnic shelter, a small ball field, and nature in its purest form.

Summer Recreation: The best hiking/walking trail is at Sculpture Rock #1397 (2 miles), but there is no fishing. Ghost towning in the nearby sites of Blewett and Liberty are remarkable. Gold panning and sluicing are regular activities in the vicinity.

Winter Recreation: The nearby ungroomed Sno-Park contains 92kg of marked trails for cross-country skiing and snow shoeing. A Sno-Park Permit is required.

Campsites (22 sites for tents and RVs up to 30', no hookups or reservations): Sites are in a mixed forest of Ponderosa pine and Western larch, which muffles road noise from Highway 97. But noise insinuates itself from the backside, as Off-Road Vehicles (ORVs) are permitted. Privacy is good here, with tent areas on native material and large paved parking aprons, and not perfectly flat (RVers, bring leveling blocks). The sites are in a single loop with two tent spurs. The Civilian Conservation Corps (CCC) built a stone fireplace in the Day Use Area and stone ovens in some sites, all still useable.

Trip Notes: It's good to disobey the rules sometimes. In this case, we disobeyed the sign that said, "no RV Turn Around" and drove up the spur to sites one and two, which are clearly the best sites in the campground. Very spacious, stone fireplaces built by the CCC, and great alpine forest made this trip pretty swell. We were far from the road noise of Highway 97 and had complete privacy. The rest of the campground, however, does have the road noise and less private sites. Be bold, campers. And for the record, we were able to turn our trailers around just fine

Washington History: Liberty is the oldest mining townsite in Washington dating back as early as 1850 in its various incarnations. The Liberty Historic District has been placed on the National Register of Historic Places, with some structures still visible: the former Meaghersville Hotel (a private residence), the Thomas Meagher cabin, an ore flume, a dredge pond/barge, and interpretive signs. Other buildings are owned by the remaining residents of this "ghost town," so be considerate. The original townsite of Old Blewett, one of the most violent mining camps in history, has all but disappeared. Remnants include remains of the 20-stamp mill and a well-preserved old mining arrasta, a donut shaped stone used for ore grinding.

Ellensburg/Prairie Region

The bunch grass here can come up to your knees, and the highest structures will be the wind turbines on the high desert ridges. But strap on your cowboy boots and spurs, because camping can be good here, provided you know where to look.

<u>Ellensburg KOA</u> (Kittitas Co.'s *BEST EQUIPPED/BEST CG FOR RVs*)
KOA parks can be so crowded and so kid-oriented that you feel like you're dodging herds of lemmings on their way to the swimming pool. They can also be compact, well-equipped and well-placed oases that represent camping at its best. You've arrived in the lemming-free zone.
<u>Overview</u>: Located just west of Ellensburg with shoreline along the Yakima River at 1542' elevation, open February 21 to Nov. 15. See below for directions.
<u>Facilities</u>: Extensive amenities include bathrooms with showers, picnic tables, fire grills, badminton, horseshoes, volleyball, basketball, 2 playgrounds, swimming pool (open 5/22-9/15), laundry, Kamp Store, a dog park, cable TV, Wi-Fi, and an RV dump.
<u>Recreation</u> includes fishing (catch and release) and rafting on the Yakima River.
<u>Campsites</u> (28 tent sites plus tent village, 80 sites for RVs up to 70' with many pull-throughs, full hookups 30 and 50 amps, 4 cabins, 3 group sites, reservable): Sites are well shaded with towering willows, big leaf maples, firs, spruces, and wind-breaking arborvitaes.
<u>Trip Notes</u>: Pulling off of I-90 in the blazing sun with very little vegetation to counteract the heat, it is refreshing to pull into this nicely appointed KOA with its many shade trees and the spray of the Yakima River. Yes, it's compact, as most KOAs are, but it remains a good camping experience for those who need to be close to CWU and Ellensburg. <u>Directions</u>: From I-90 just west of Ellensburg take Exit 106. If coming from the west, you'll drive right past the campground. If exiting from the east, go left from the off-ramp.
<u>Local Attractions/Washington History</u>: The Ellensburg Rodeo (Labor Day Weekend) and Central Washington University (CWU) are Ellensburg's biggest draws. Olmstead Place Historical S.P. is a 217-acre day use park just east of Ellensburg, a living historical pioneer farm named for the family that founded it. Walking trails pass an old log cabin and farmhouse in operation long before modern mechanization. Also on display are farm implements, tools, and clothing, with guided tours available.

Columbia River Gorge

The wind in this region, just south of the "Gorge at George," can rip the glasses right off your face, but when it calms, you'll find yourself in an idyllic oasis. Yet, schedule your trip around the concerts at the Gorge unless you want to end up in the mosh pit slam-dancing with heavy metal fans. But you already knew that slam-dancing and camping don't mix.

Lake Wanapum/Ginkgo Petrified Forest S.P. (Kittitas Co.'s *MOST UNIQUELY WASHINGTON CG*)

They've made the desert bloom here and placed it just south of one of the most fascinating national historic preserves in the nation.

Overview: Located 3 miles south of Vantage on 7,470 acres with 27,000' of freshwater shoreline on Lake Wanapum/Columbia River, at 663' elevation, open year-round; GPS 46.9041, -119.9917.

Facilities include bathrooms with showers (both ADA), metal picnic tables, fire grills, an excellent swimming area with an outside shower and sandy beach, picnic area, 3 miles of hiking trails, 2 boat ramps, Park Store, camp hosts, and an RV dump.

Recreation: Fishing is known for bass, crappie, walleye, catfish, sunfish, and lake trout.

Campsites (50 sites for tents and RVs up to 60', all with full hookups 20/30/50 amp, reservable): Sites 1-31 are huge and grassy with adequate privacy provided by their mere size, plus adequate shade provided by leafy trees. Sites 32-50 are not irrigated, a little smaller, and are terraced with desert vegetation, and less shade, with basic desert landscape. Sites are both back-ins and pull-throughs.

Trip notes: This Park gets my vote for prettiest park with a "deal breaker" – in this case, the WIND. It's all or nothing: either the wind whips up early or the morning, or it is perfectly still. If the wind does start, it lasts all day and is intense. Having said that, it is the most manicured, perfect camping we have experienced. It looks directly over Lake Wanapum (the Columbia River behind the Wanapum Dam). It has separate boating and swimming facilities, both excellent. Most fascinating for us were the nearby wind turbines run by Puget Sound Energy. I would say camp here only with an enclosed trailer, not a tent or tent trailer, unless you're willing to pack up and leave when the wind starts up. Note also that this campground is reachable by bicycle or horseback using the Iron Horse Trail (see King Co.).

Nearby attractions: Ginkgo Petrified Forest Interpretive Center is 3 miles from the campground. It offers views of the Ice-Age floods basalt landscape.

For more photos of Kittitas Co. CGs, or more on GROUP CGs or HIKE-IN CGs, consult campeverycountywa.com

KLICKITAT COUNTY (Goldendale/White Salmon)

As you look across the Columbia River from Hood River, Oregon toward Bingen/White Salmon on the Washington side, you see the clear line of demarcation: the end of the wet, forested western side of the Cascades, contrasting the bald rolling hills of the eastern side. The name of the county derives from the Chinook Indian word for "beyond." Indeed, this is the other side of the Columbia Gorge: the dry, laid back, old world side that will take you to a time and place you may never knew existed.

Columbia River Gorge National Scenic Area

Thanks to the Columbia River Gorge National Scenic Area Act of 1986, 290,000 acres along the border of Oregon and Washington have been saved from the impending sprawl of Portland and Vancouver. The Washington side of the Columbia is a little slower, with highways instead of freeways, and smaller towns with more pioneer charm that will remain a wonderland of thousand-foot cliffs, thundering waterfalls, and epic views up and down the vast river.

Maryhill S.P. (Klickitat Co.'s *BEST EQUIPPED/BEST CG FOR RVs* and includes *BEST GROUP CG*)

This campground is located in Sam Hill's country, a wealthy and accomplished railroad executive, financial manager, and investor. He is responsible for building roads into areas so rural others could only ask, "Where in the Sam Hill is that?" The "castle" he built for his wife Mary is now a world class art museum that looks down on the tiny orchard town of Maryhill and the State Park of the same name.

Overview: Located in Maryhill (across the bridge from Biggs, OR) and 13 miles southeast of Goldendale on 99 acres at187' elevation, open year-round; GPS 45.68306, -120.82583.

Facilities: This facility-ready campground includes bathrooms with showers, picnic tables, fire pits, two picnic shelters, four horseshoe pits, two boat ramps, over 200' of dock, a swimming area, 1.1 miles of hiking trails, interpretive kiosks, an RV dump and camp hosts.

Recreation: Sailboarding and windsurfing is excellent here, a preferred place for more experience surfers. Rentals are available in The Dalles, OR. Freshwater fishing, water skiing, and bird watching are also popular.

Campsites (70 sites for tents or RVs up to 60', including 51 with water & electric 50-amp hookups, one group site for up to 200 people, reservable): Sites are large, flat and grassy with shade trees but poor to average privacy. Parking pads are concrete. There is some railroad and highway noise.

Trip notes: This trip was a last-minute switch due to snow in the mountains. The park rests right on the Columbia, nestled against the tiny orchard town of Maryhill. It was a clean, interesting stopover, with many local attractions. Personally, I preferred walking the streets of the tiny town of Maryhill, with its old church and quaint businesses, including a shop to repair horse buggies, to the better-known tourist sites. All the remaining buildings were frozen to about the year 1920. The world must have seemed much larger then when a town of just 40 people was the center of these people's universe. Check it out. Eat s'mores, wander through the local orchard, wade in the Columbia, and imagine that you're at the center of the universe.

Local Alternative: Adjacent to Maryhill S.P. is Peach Beach Campark, with 70 sites for tents or RVs. There are 12 dry tent sites, 21 sites with full hookups, and 49 with water & electric 50 amp only.

Local Attractions: A full-scale replica of Stonehenge is located one mile from the park. The Maryhill Museum of Art is nearby. The Goldendale Observatory is13 miles away for star gazers.

The Maryhill Art Museum is a world class museum near Maryhill S.P.

Columbia Hills Historical S.P. (Klickitat Co.'s *MOST UNIQUELY WASHINGTON CG, BEST CG FOR ENTIRE FAMILIES, MOST APPEALING CG TO THE SENSES* and *BEST BIKE-IN CG*)

This massive State Park is an amalgam of the old Horsethief Lake State Park, the Dalles Mountain Ranch (an historic homestead ranch), and the Crawford Oaks hiking area. The campground itself was the historic site of a Wishram Indian village near the famed Celio Falls (often mentioned in the Lewis and Clark journals). What remains is an area of "terrible beauty" marked by yellow flowers of arrowleaf balsamroot, purple lupine, pockets of gnarled oaks and Osage orange, Indian petroglyphs, and the towering Horsethief Butte that towers over everything like a beacon.

Overview: The historical and magical campground is located 26.5 miles southwest of Goldendale and 4 miles east of Dallesport on 3338 acres with 2 miles of Columbia River shoreline on 90-acre Horsethief Lake at 3200' elevation, open year-round; GPS 45.64556, -121.10389.

Facilities include flush toilets, running water, showers, a swimming area with a natural wind break in the huge Day Use Area, kayak rentals, 12 miles of hiking trails, and camp hosts.

Recreation: Excellent windsurfing opportunities are available at Doug's Beach S.P. near Lyle. Rentals are available in Hood River, OR. Rock climbing is popular on Horsethief Butte. Hiking Horsethief Butte and the Crawford Oaks Trail is a must. And don't miss the opportunity to view the amazing Indian petroglyphs and take the guided tour.

Campsites (20 sites for tents and RVs up to 60', including 8 utility sites with water & electric 30 amp, 4 walk-in tent sites, 2 H/B sites, 1 teepee, 2 platform tents, reservable): Sites lack privacy, and line the back edge of a huge Day Use Area that makes them seem much larger. The camping area sits on spit in the middle of Horse Thief Lake surrounded by water on 3 sides, a true "oasis in the scrubland ". Most inviting is the 14' diameter Plains Indians style teepee, and the two 10' x 12' furnished platform tents, all for rent.

Trip Notes: It becomes immediately apparent that this campground occupies the site of an ancient Indian village: the petroglyphs are on display just a short walk away, but sadly, the Temani Pesh-wa Trail is closed due to vandalism. Guided tours are available just twice weekly. Two problems were train noise and the wind. The swimming area had a natural wind break, while many of the campsites had both trees and wind break panels to minimize the wind. The Day Use Area also had rows of popular, lodgepole pine, and locust trees to minimize the wind. Horseshoe Butte was an easy hike, providing great views, rock climbing and (though we missed them) more petroglyphs. The Dalles Mountain Ranch is putting more efforts into constructing hiking trails to connect to the Crawford Oaks. While nostalgic, most of the individual displays were closed without explanation. Bottom line: we loved the compact camping and Day Use Area with its access to the petroglyphs and great view of Horsethief Butte. The "RV Park style" camping setup was more than compensated by its openness to the Day Use Area.

Columbia Hills S.P. is a desert surrounded by water in the shadow of Mt. Hood

Klickitat River Area

The 75-mile long Klickitat River was designated as a Wild and Scenic River in 1986. This 2-mile wide canyon boasts dramatic scenery along steep 1500' columnar basalt cliffs. In places, chunks of basalt have fallen into the river from the walls. Wildflowers grow everywhere from spring through midsummer. These are a delight for whitewater rafters, tube floaters, and campers alike, a virtually unknown lush paradise in an otherwise very arid county.

Leidl South CG (Klickitat Co.'s *BEST FREE CG*)
This is the most established campground along the Klickitat River, sitting roughly midway between its headwaters near Mt. Adams and rivers' end at the Columbia River town of Lyle. All along the way, there are trails for hikers, gentle rapids for tube floaters, canoers and kayakers, fish for the fisherfolk, and campsites for all varieties of campers.
Overview: This sandy campground is located 13 miles east of Glenwood and 32 miles west of Goldendale on the Klickitat River, operated by the WDFW at 920' elevation, open year-round; GPS 45.93694277, -121.1187269.
Facilities: This primitive site has two pit toilets, a few picnic tables, a boat ramp, and stone fire pits in places.
Recreation: Boating access sites for canoers and kayakers are located all along the river: to the north at Summit Creek near the Steel One-Lane Bridge, and to the

139

south at Icehouse Public Access in the town of Klickitat. Keep in mind that the river is less treacherous downstream as it heads to the Columbia River. Rafting from Leidl CG to Icehouse Public Access includes 40 class 1 rapids and a few class 2 rapids, offering plenty of action for open canoers and beginning kayakers. The Pitt Hang Gliding Area is between the towns of Wahkiakus and Klickitat. The Klickitat Trail is a 31-mile hiking, biking, and equestrian trail that follows an old railroad bend, stretching from Lyle to Warwick. A 10-mile section from Lyle to the hamlet of Pitt follows the Klickitat River.

Campsites (35 primitive sites for tents or small RVs, no hookups or reservations, FREE with Discover Pass): The larger section (left side as you arrive) has 23 dispersed sites, 2 of which have tables and rock fire rings. The boat launch is located here, with a few sites on the river. The smaller section (right side as you arrive) has 12 dispersed sites with rock fire rings but no tables. Most of these sites are on the river in a grove of Ponderosa pines and are rather close together. Each of these two sections has its own pit toilet. Both areas are flat and lightly forested for shade. Of note, there are a few boat-in only campsites downstream from Leidl South CG that, to our knowledge, represent the only boat-in only campsites in the county.

Trip Notes: So sandy! That was our first impression, like a giant set of sand dunes, but flat. And as you explore, you will find a network of small arms filled with campsites of all kinds -- some on the River filled with rafters and kayakers, others nestled between the Ponderosa pine, Scotch pine, and scrub oaks. The River surrounding it on two sides makes it less desolate, and the high banks, rocky but tree-topped, provide more for the eye to see. This is a deserty, beachy riverside campground with diverse activities in all directions. Stay awhile, and it will grow on you.

Local Alternatives: There are primitive campsites at the Icehouse Public Access and Stinson Flats Access (15 campsites here). The boat launch at Stinson Flats has been washed out due to river erosion, so check before setting out. Other small campgrounds with boating access on the Klickitat include Turkey Hole and Mineral Springs Campsite.

Outlet Creek CG (Klickitat Co's *BEST RUSTIC CG*)
This rustic but striking campground is set on Outlet Creek, which dumps its water into the Klickitat River in the form of an exceptional 69' waterfall which is its real centerpiece. It is the closest camping facility to the Conboy Lake Wildlife Refuge with all of its sights and sounds, teaming with wildlife.

Overview: This most rustic of campgrounds is located 3.5 miles east of Glenwood and 30.9 miles east of Goldendale, on WDFW land managed by Hancock Forest Management at 1822' elevation, open year-round; GPS: 46.015816, -121.219841.
Facilities: Sparse facilities include 2 vault toilets, 3 picnic tables, and fire rings. There is no piped water.

Recreation: This includes hiking, fishing, swimming, and whitewater paddling on the nearby Klickitat River. A 2.5-mile hiking trail is accessible at Conboy Lake Refuge. An Outlet Creek/Klickitat River viewpoint is 2 miles east of the campground A short but steep trail to Outlet Falls begins at the northeast corner of this lookout.

Campsites (10 sites for tents or small RVs, no hookups or reservations, FREE with Discover pass): Ruddy- barked Ponderosa pines provide the piney-woods smell here, providing plenty of shade and privacy. The entrance to the campground is unmarked but located 3-4 miles east of Glenwood just east of the bridge over Outlet Creek. The best site is right on the quiet Glenwood Highway with a view of Mt. Adams. The campground is primitive, and you'll need to leave your campsite to see much of what the area offers.

Trip Notes: It's a rough campground, with roads to nowhere, flat bare spaces that appear to have once been campsites, and lots of fallen branches. This will appeal to some, primarily those who value privacy, but will be too little for most. It is, however, perfect for those seeking seclusion, and those who dare take the steep hike to the Falls, lined by 200- granite banks, where the creek water freefalls for 69' into a magnificent pool. In the winter, icicles hang from the rocks, creating palatial images along the rock faces.

Local Attraction: Conboy Wildlife Refuge at 6,500 acres was created in 1964 to preserve the Camas Prairie. It was a place where Native Americans harvested bulbs of the camas plant and camped for thousands of years during migrations between harvests of salmon in the Columbia River and huckleberries in the mountain. Visitors will find groves of quaking aspen and breathtaking views of Mt. Adams, with stunning sunsets to match. What you won't find is a lake, during summer months at least, but instead a seasonal marsh, providing sanctuary to 10,000 migrating geese and ducks, breeding grounds for trumpeting sandhill cranes, and the last stronghold of spotted frogs, colorful dragonflies, and purple camas.

For more photos of Klickitat Co. CGs consult
campeverycountywa.com

LEWIS COUNTY (Chehalis/Centralia/Packwood/Pe Ell)

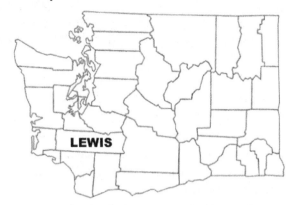

This "mother of counties" once contained half of present-day Washington and British Columbia. Now it is but a long narrow strip stretching from the Willapa Hills to the Cascade Range, but still includes old growth forests, mountain peaks, lakes, and even part of MRNP.

Southeast Mount Rainier National Park (MRNP)

The southeast corner of MRNP occupies the northeast corner of Lewis Co. The most beautiful rivers and scenery (apart from Mt. Rainier itself) are found here, including the best camping in the National Park.

Ohanapecosh CG at MRNP (Lewis Co.'s *MOST UNIQUELY WASHINGTON CG*)
The snow-fed Ohanapecosh River could be a National Park in itself -- it is that beautiful. The name Ohanapecosh derives from the Taidnapam Indian word for "standing on the edge." This is very telling, as camping alongside this river, sitting high on its rocks and staring down into the crystalline blue waters could become a wonderful obsession.

Overview: This exceptional campground is located 82 miles east of Chehalis and 12 miles northeast of Packwood in MRNP at 1914' elevation, open late May to late September, weather permitting; GPS 46.731100, -121.570280.

Facilities: These are good as National Parks go, including both vault and flush toilets (no showers), picnic tables, fire rings, drinking water, an amphitheater, hiking trails, a Visitor Center, camp hosts, and an RV dump.

Recreation: Nearby are popular hikes to Silver Falls and the Grove of the Patriarchs. The latter is a 1.5-mile loop just up Highway 123 in the middle section of the Ohanapecosh River where thousand-year-old evergreens rule the sky. This hike is nearly flat, and good for all ages.

<u>Campsites</u> (188 sites for tents or RVs up to 32' in 8 loops, both back-ins and pull-throughs, plus 10 walk-in sites, no hookups, reservable): Sites are large, well-spaced, shaded, and on asphalt parking pads. Among the best are four of the G Loop walk-in sites (18–21), which provide a natural sound barrier despite the 100-yard downhill walk. Other best sites include the E Loop, where generators aren't allowed giving more daytime quiet. Vegetation is thick, including old growth Douglas fir, western hemlock, and spruce.

<u>Trip Notes</u>: The campground is quite complex, with much of the scenery and activities overshadowed by the beauty of the Ohanapecosh River. The hot springs are worth the walk, though they are leaking rivulets of hot, colored mineral water, not soaking tubs, so check your expectations. The trail to Silver Falls is accessible from Loop B in the campground, but shorter hikes to the same can be found just 1.6 miles north of Ohanapecosh on Highway 123 (hike is only 0.6 miles). Another shortcut to Silver Falls is the Stevens Canyon Road just west of the Stevens Canyon Entrance, across from the Grove of the Patriarchs trailhead (hike is 1.2 miles). Camp away, but don't forget these very accessible recreation options.

<u>Local Alternative</u>: La Wis Wis CG sits at the confluence of the Ohanapecosh River, the Clear Fork of the Cowlitz River, and Purcell Creek. This is one of the oldest USFS parks in Washington, with vintage details in picnic tables and shelters. Campsites are large but hemmed in by old growth forest, which provides partial shade but limits maneuverability. While the old growth forest of Douglas Fir, western hemlock, western red cedar, Pacific yew, and big leaf maple may cause fits for the maintenance crew, it is the park's biggest draw, rivaled only by the park's 3 beautiful rivers.

Packwood/Goat Rocks Area

Packwood may not be the largest town in Lewis Co., but it has the most influence where recreation is concerned. It is the gateway to White Pass, lies in the heart of volcano country, and sits on the edge of the 108,023-acre Goat Rocks Wilderness. In such an area where mountain goats outnumber people, recreation is an inseparable part of the mountainous landscape.

<u>Walupt Lake CG</u> (Lewis Co.'s *BEST CGs FOR ENTIRE FAMILIES*)

What can you say about a remote campground that requires a 21-mile drive on dusty, pot-holed, washboard gravel roads, but is still one of the most popular in Washington? Read on, campers.

<u>Overview</u>: This Gifford Pinchot National Forest campground is tucked away on 381.6-acre Walupt Lake located 92.7 miles southeast of Chehalis and 23.3 miles southeast of Packwood at 3900' elevation, open mid-June through late September; GPS 46.42306, -121.47361.

<u>Facilities</u>: Mixed rustic facilities include pit toilets, fire rings, piped water (for drinking only!), thick beveled picnic tables (a real plus), garbage service, a Day Use Picnic Area, a primitive boat launch, hiking trails, and camp hosts in summer.

<u>Recreation</u>: Swimming, fishing and hiking are the draws here, particularly with the campground's proximity to the Goat Rocks Wilderness Area. Walupt Lake Trail # 101 is an easy hike along the northern edge of the lake. The Nanny Ridge Trail # 98 is steep but offers great views of the Goat Rocks Wilderness. Be sure to fill out a Wilderness Permit before entering the Wilderness. Fishing is mostly for rainbow and cutthroat trout. Swimming is popular, particularly with families.

<u>Campsites</u> (42 sites for tents or RVs up to 40', including 6 walk-in and 3 group sites, no hookups, most sites reservable): Sites here are all back-in and heavily forested, shady, and divided into two loops. Site size is remarkable: many are so large that there are several "rooms" where campers can set up multiple tents, screen rooms, sitting areas, etc. All are flat, with the exception of the waterfront walk-ins (Sites 37-42), with parts of sites on multiple levels. Parking is on gravel surrounded by sub alpine silver fir, cedar and hemlock. Most sites are deserted during fishing and hiking hours, making an otherwise busy campground much quieter during the day.

The safe swimming shores of Walupt Lake make it a family favorite

<u>Trip Notes</u>: As you enter the campground, the Lake seems much smaller than its actual size. Be sure to hike the first 1.5 miles of Walupt Lake Trail to the northeast corner of the Lake for an appreciation of its full breadth. Here, we found boat-in campers with children, an excellent and easy place for first timers. This half of the Lake crosses into the Goat Rocks Wilderness, so permits are required for overnighters. The Lake itself provides good swimming for families, as a "shelf" extends out all along the north shore, giving shallow water for the first 50' out, where parents can supervise their kids with less worry. The line for the deeper

water is very visible. When the sun shines directly down, the water shimmers from the sand and rock beneath the surface, increasing its appeal. As for boaters, the shallow shore waters keep away the larger boats, and human-powered and smaller motorboats co-exist beautifully. The reflections from the surrounding mountains on the Lake add the cherry on top.

Directions: From I-5, drive 62 miles east on Hwy 12 (to about 2.5 miles west of Packwood) and turn right/south on FR 21. Follow 21 south, past the Johnson Creek Sno-Park, to FR 2160. Follow 2160 east to the campground. Directions are well-marked.

Chambers Lake CG (Lewis Co.'s *BEST RUSTIC CG*)

For those who want their camping rustic, quieter, and less gravel road to drive, Chambers Lake CG is a decommissioned USFS campground on the same road as Walupt Lake, but a few miles closer to Packwood. The fragile, placid, verdant lake has a quiet charm for canoers/kayakers, as well as a base camp for experienced hikers.

Overview: This forest campground is located 83.7 miles southeast of Chehalis and 14.3 miles southeast of Packwood on 14.4-acre Chambers Lake at 4465' elevation, open weather permitting; GPS 46.4678937, -121.5373064.

Facilities: This most rustic of campgrounds has homemade fire pits, a few fire grills, and a very nicely constructed vault toilet. There is no drinking water.

Recreation: Canoeing/kayaking are excellent for those who take it slow. Hikers are in close proximity to the Berry Patch Trailhead with hiking access to the Goat Rocks Wilderness via Goat Ridge Trail #95, Jordan Creek Trail #94, and Lily Basin Trail #86. Swimming and motor boating are not allowed. Fishing is not recommended.

Campsites (14 sites for tents and smaller RVs, including one double site, no hookups or reservations, FREE with a NW Forest Pass): All sites are arranged in a single loop, as though the USFS still maintained the campground! Sites range from the very simple, with nothing more than a fire pit of rocks, to large flat spaces with lake access. Lush vegetation includes grand fir, hemlock, and cedar.

Trip Notes: There is a quirkiness to this campground that invites a vast variety of campers yet remains quiet enough for equestrians to trust that their prized horses won't be spooked by the neighbors. Those looking for rest can float all day on tiny Chambers Lake, while the more pent up can spend their days conquering some of the most difficult hiking trails in the area.

Directions: Take the same FR 21 toward Walupt Lake and drive 12 miles before turning left/east onto FR 2150 and follow it to the campground.

<u>Soda Spring Forest Camp</u> (Lewis Co.'s *BEST FREE CG*)

It takes a small natural wonder to stand behind a small natural campground. The cold-water spring was once the source of carbonated water for bygone industries. The old bottling facility is long gone, but the orange-tinted cold-water spring is now surrounded by this compact forest campground. Note: Don't confuse this with the Soda Springs CGs on Bumping Creek in Yakima Co., on the Little Wenatchee River in Chelan Co., or on the Soda Springs Wildlife Unit in Klickitat Co.

<u>Overview</u>: This Wenatchee National Forest campground is located on the far west side of White Pass 13.5 miles northeast of Packwood at 3200' elevation, open mid-May to October; GPS 46.7031685, -121.4809193.

<u>Facilities</u>: A bit on the rustic side and isolated, this campground has one old-style double vault toilet, picnic tables, and fire grills. There is no potable water or camp host.

<u>Recreation</u>: Campers should take the short walk to see Soda Spring (see below). The Cowlitz Trail #44 Trailhead (located in the campground) accesses the William O. Douglas Wilderness for hiking and exploration.

<u>Campsites</u> (6 rustic sites plus 2 dispersed sites along Summit Creek for tents and truck campers, no hookups or reservations, FREE): The campground is a single loop on a plateau above Summit Creek, and heavily forested with Douglas fir, western hemlock, and silver fir. Privacy is optimal due to dense vegetation and spacing of the sites. Note that Summit Creek is not visible from the upper campsites. Trailers should not attempt camping here, as the last hundred yards has some tough, problematic ruts.

<u>Trip Notes</u>: This compact USFS campground is a smaller version of some of our favorites. Just listen for the sound of gurgling water, then climb down a steep 60-yard trail past maidenhair ferns, huckleberry bushes, and bunchberries to the colorful, bubbling soda spring. It is contained in a stone cauldron, with a perfect stone spout where the orange tinged mineral water splashes down onto a long flat mineral bed, forming wide striped ribbons trickling down to Summit Creek below. This spring far outshines the soda springs in the other 3 counties mentioned above.

<u>Local Alternative</u>: Campers will pass Summit Creek CG on the way to Soda Spring. This less private campground, however, is exposed to road noise, and has little privacy between sites. Yet, the Creek itself is quite pretty and draws more campers than Soda Spring.

<u>Directions</u>: From Packwood, continue on Hwy 12 for 9 miles to FR 45 and turn left/north. Drive 0.35 miles to FR 4510. Drive an additional 4.2 miles and bear right on FR 4510 052 past Summit Creek CG all the way to Soda Spring Forest Camp.

Randle Area

This major recreational crossroads in the center of Lewis Co. connects the wilderness areas of the Gifford Pinchot National Forest down Highway 131 with the Cowlitz River reservoirs and White Pass ski area along Highway 12. The town itself is mostly a long stretch of RV parks, restaurants, gas stations, and a Ranger Station, and the local high school, but provides the services for campers for a very large and varied region.

Iron Creek CG (Lewis Co.'s *MOST APPEALING CG TO THE SENSES*)
This campground gets kudos from nearly everyone for its moss-covered old growth trees, ferns that are among the largest in Washington, and the utter stillness of this exceptional stand of forest.

Overview: This Gifford Pinchot National Forest campground is located 61.9 miles southeast of Chehalis and 12 miles south of Randle at the confluence of Iron Creek and the Cispus River at 1200' elevation, open mid-May through late September; GPS 46.431, -121.984.

Facilities: In true USFS fashion, facilities include vault toilets, potable water, picnic tables, fire grills, and camp hosts.

Recreation: Fishing is good for cutthroat trout, rainbow trout, and whitefish. Family-friendly hiking is plentiful. Iron Creek Old Growth Trail #87 (0.3 miles) begins at the Iron Creek Picnic Area and winds through exceptional old growth forest with views of the Cispus River. Iron Creek Campground Loop Trail #187 is a wide, level trail that circles the entire campground (1.5 miles). Woods Creek Watchable Wildlife Trail #247 is just north of the campground, and loops through five ecological areas with interpretive signs. Other nearby hiking trails include Camp Creek Falls Trail #260, a short hike up a steep slope leading to the 20' waterfall; Kraus Ridge Trail #275, a good 4.4 mile early season hike with views of the Cispus River and Tower Rock; and Layser Cave Trail #290, a 0.25 mile walk to a cave where animal bones and stone tools found on the floor of the cave enabled archaeologists to piece together a 7,000 year history of human habitation.

Campsites (98 back-in and pull-through sites for tents and RVs up to 40', some doubles, no hookups, reservable): These nearly perfect sites are arranged in 4 camping loops - large, wooded, private, and with asphalt parking pads. Many spots back up to the Cispus River. Vegetation includes hardwoods, old growth Douglas fir, western red cedar and hemlock. The best sites are 10, 14, 22, 37, 38, 39, 57, 61,66, and 81. This campground is often overlooked for the better-known lakeside campgrounds like Takhlakh Lake and Walupt Lake, but offers terrific forest camping that rivals anything in the area.

Trip Notes: This campground carries that old familiar USFS charm. We did not have time to walk the trail around the campground which has several access "beaches" to the Cispus River.

Local Alternative: A nearby alternative is Tower Rock CG, which is smaller and less scenic than Iron Creek.

Local Attraction: The Windy Ridge Viewpoint at Mount St. Helens is approximately 20 miles away.

Mayfield Lake

This beautiful spider-webbed 2,023-acre lake/reservoir was the first formed by damming the Cowlitz River, in this case with Mayfield Dam. Among its multiple fingers, arms and islands, the lake is spotted with many public parks, private resorts, and accesses, making this a water lover's dream.

Ike Kinswa S.P. (Lewis Co.'s *BEST EQUIPPED/BEST CG FOR RVs*)
This remarkable Park is named after John Ike Kinswa, a Cowlitz Indian who homesteaded this area as a way of settling up with settlers from the east. The developers of Mayfield Lake relocated some Indian graves, leaving others on discreet display within the park.
Overview: The park is located 28.5 miles east of Chehalis and 3 miles west of Mossyrock on 454 acres on Mayfield Lake at 656' elevation, open year-round; GPS 46.5518, -122.5294.
Facilities: These include bathrooms with showers, picnic tables, fire grills, an accessible island, good cell phone service, horseshoe pits, 40' of dock, 1.5 miles of hiking trails including a 0.5-mile self-guided interpretive trail, and an RV dump station.
Recreation: Boating, water-skiing, sailboarding and swimming are the biggest recreational draws. Fishing is known for largemouth bass, coastal cutthroat, tiger muskie, yellow perch, northern pike minnow, Chinook salmon, Coho salmon, and rainbow trout. The tiger muskie is unique to Mayfield Lake, being sterile hybrids between the northern pike and muskellunge introduced to control the pesky northern pike minnow. Tiger muskies can grow to over 50" and are catch-and-release only.

Campsites (103 back-in and pull-through sites for tents or RVs up to 60', including 72 with full or partial 30/50-amp hookups, 2 H/B sites, 8 cabins, all reservable): Sites are organized into 4 loops. Loop A (sites 1-41) is closest to the prettier Tilton Arm and has full hookups 30 amp at every site. Sites 14-28 are back-ins with lake access. They are wooded/shaded and large with average to excellent privacy. Loop B (sites 42-72) has water & electric 50-amp hookups in every site, and is closer to the Cowlitz River Arm. These sites are wooded and large with only average privacy. The 2 H/B sites are located between these two loops. Loop C (actually a spur) contains the 8 cabins. Each has an ADA-accessible deck. Loop D (sites 74-101) is good for tents or small RVs with no hookups. These are near the tip of the peninsula with no direct lake access but are large and wooded with average privacy and peek-a-boo views of both the Cowlitz River and Tilton River Arms of the Lake, giving a more open feel.

Trip notes: If you drive into this place and feel like you're surrounded by water, there's a reason -- you ARE surrounded by water. The State Park sits in a peninsula where the Cowlitz River and Tilton River Arms of Mayfield Lake (reservoir) join to fill a larger basin behind Mayfield Dam. Water is not visible from most sites, but as you move around the Park you suddenly see water in just about every direction. Keep in mind that the Lake is a reservoir, so the shores are uneven and have little time to season. The real beauty here is the forest, which also surprised us at every bend, and the Day Use Area seemed just as popular with the local deer as it did with the campers. We saw deer swimming in the swimming area, standing idly by in the campground, and holding up traffic as they crossed the roads. So enjoy the forest and wildlife and, if watching the water isn't enough, grab a boat and some water skis and have a ball.

Local Alternatives: Mayfield Park is a former county park now operated by Tacoma Power. It contains 55 sites for tents and RVs under 35' due to narrow roads, with many sites right on the Lake. However, sites are smaller with limited privacy.

Willapa Hills/Upper Chehalis Valley Area

The Willapa Hills form the lowest upland region of the entire Pacific Coast Range, gently lifting much of Pacific Co. and far western Lewis Co. They are the source of many rivers, including the Willapa River, Grays River, the Naselle River and, most notably, the Chehalis River.

Rainbow Falls/Willapa Hills Trail S.P. (Lewis Co.'s BEST *BIKE-IN CG*)
Beautiful it certainly is, but take the term "Falls" with tongue placed firmly in cheek as there are no falls to speak of. It is instead a misty, tumbling portion of the Chehals River surrounded by an even prettier campground.

Overview: This resilient campground is located 16.9 miles west of Chehalis and 7 miles east of Pe Ell near Doty/Dryad on 139 acres at 273' elevation, open year-round; GPS 46.6339, -123.2341.

Facilities: This adequately equipped facility includes bathrooms with showers, potable water, picnic tables, fire grills, horseshoe pits, a softball field, a fuchsia garden, camp hosts, and an RV dump.

Recreation: The southern cut of the park is intertwined with 10 miles of hiking trails and 7 miles of biking trails. The main campground area in the northern cut has quick access to the Willapa Hills Trail with 56 miles of hiking/biking trails, extending all the way to Willapa Harbor (see below). Bird watching, swimming and fishing for catfish, eel, salmon, steelhead and trout are popular.

Campsites (53 sites for tents or RVs up to 20', 8 with full hookups 30-amp, 3 horse sites, 3 H/B sites, several walk-in sites, and one group camp for up to 60.

Reservations are for the Kitchen Shelter only): Sites vary in size from small (H/B) to large. The park is old, made primarily for tents and smaller RVs. Privacy is good, as sites are surrounded by old growth forest, but depends on the occupancy of the park. The best sites for privacy and quiet are 6 and 47. Established by the Civilian Conservation Corps in 1935 (several log structures remain). This park is skirted on two sides by the Chehalis River with 3400' of freshwater shoreline. The "Falls" is really a 10' drop in a very pretty stretch of the Chehalis River that empties into a pool that is good for swimming. Of note, this is the only public park in a 21-mile radius.

Trip Notes: This park experienced a major transformation in December of 2007 when the Chehalis River flooded this area, washing out the iconic footbridge across "the Falls," as well as the motor vehicle bridge providing direct access from Highway 6. The footbridge had a reputation among daredevils who, against park policy, jumped off the bridge into the small pool below. The park was also known to be inhabited by weekend partyers who often disturbed the peace and quiet during summer weekends. This is no longer true. It was decided, for both safety and funding reasons, not to replace the footbridge; rather, access is through the tiny town of Dryad toward the north end of the campground. The park rangers also state they are committed to preserving a peaceful environment. The only noise you will hear now is a small amount of road noise.

The Willapa Hills Trail: Accompanying these developments is the inclusion of the Willapa Hills Trail S.P., which comes within a hundred yards of the park. This 56-mile trail originates in Chehalis and ends at the western end of South Bend on Willapa Harbor in Pacific County. It currently has no campgrounds of its own, except for Rainbow Falls S.P. It is a work in progress intended for hikers, bikers, and equestrians. The path follows the old Pacific Northern Railroad, and most of the old railroad bridges have been fully repaired. The trail itself is being paved in small sections as funding allows.

For more photos of Lewis Co. CGs, HIKE-IN, BOAT-IN, or GROUP CGs, consult
campeverycountywa.com

LINCOLN COUNTY (Davenport/Hartline/Odessa)

Cut from the so-called channeled scablands formed by Ice Age floods and later transformed by irrigation, this is farming country. It is very flat, except for rolling hills along Lake Roosevelt, which makes up most of its northern border. This is where recreation thrives, with 27 campgrounds in the Lake Roosevelt Recreation Area alone.

Lower Lake Roosevelt

Lake Roosevelt is a 130-mile lake of the Columbia River created by the Grand Coulee Dam. Named after President Franklin D. Roosevelt, it is part of the Lake Roosevelt National Recreation Area and managed by the National Park Service. The Lower Arm runs east-west from Fort Spokane to the Grand Coulee Dam, separating Lincoln Co. from Ferry and Okanogan Counties. There are dozens of campgrounds along on this Lake, making it a veritable camper's smorgasbord.

Spring Canyon CG (Lincoln Co.'s *MOST APPEALING CG TO THE SENSES, BEST BIKE-IN CG* and includes *BEST GROUP CG*)
This is the closest public campground to the Grand Coulee Dam which is in clear view. Roosevelt Lake is at its widest and deepest here, making it an inviting place to cool off in the intense summer heat.
Overview: This hillside campground is located 47 miles northwest of Davenport and 2.5 miles east of Grand Coulee, managed by the NPS at 1500' elevation, open year-round; GPS 47.93306, -118.93907.
Facilities: This moderately well-equipped campground includes vault toilets, running water (shut off during winter months), a huge Day Use Area along the Lake, a playground, a good boat launch/dock, swimming area, RV dump, and camp hosts.
Recreation: Boating and water sports on Lake Roosevelt take center stage here. This comes with abundant wildlife and birds, including eagles and osprey.

Dozens of species of fish inhabit the lake. For walkers and hikers, the Bunchgrass Prairie Nature Trail offers a short interpretive walk through sagebrush and bunch grasses.

Campsites (74 sites for tents and RVs of any size, no hookups, two small group sites for 25 people each, all reservable): There are two distinct loops in this campground. The lower loop is closer to the water with green but minimal shade trees and average privacy from good site spacing. Sites on the uppermost loop have carport-like shade covers built over the paved parking pads.

Trip Notes: Sometimes campers complain about dogs off leash, wandering through other people's sites. I did too, at 5:00 a.m. as I watched a large, sniffing creature dig its nose into the door of one of my camp-panion's tents. Then I realized... that was no dog. I remembered the advice from my favorite book "How to Stay Alive in the Woods," and explained in a calm, monotone voice that eating Sherry and Ron would be a very, very bad thing. The bear looked up and meandered over to another campsite where fish had been left overnight in the back of a boat in 90+ degree heat. Just remember when it comes to camping, you have nothing to fear except fear itself. And bears.

Local Attraction: A nearby attraction is Northrop Canyon, which provides hiking with great views of the area and Northrup Lake.

Keller Ferry CG (Lincoln Co.'s MOST UNIQUELY WASHINGTON CG)
You can get there by car, by boat, or by the only Washington State Ferry in Eastern Washington. But best of all -- the ferry is FREE. An 8- minute crossing takes you from prairie to the lush forest.

Overview: This magnificent little campground is 55.6 miles northwest of Davenport and 6 miles north Wilbur on lower Lake Roosevelt, operated by Dakota Columbia Houseboat Adventures at 229' elevation, open year-round; GPS 47.9285, -118.6942.

Facilities: This nicely equipped campground comes with vault toilets, running water, boat launch/dock, marina, swimming area, RV dump, and camp hosts. There is a store, restaurant and snack bar on site.

Recreation: As with most Lake Roosevelt campgrounds, boating and water sports loom large.

Campsites (55 sites, 2 group camps for up to 25 people each, no hookups, reservable): Sites are shady, grassy, and well-spaced, and, despite some puzzling reviews, completely level. The campground is in a transition period, previously run by the NPS. As of 2014, it is run by Dakota Columbia, the same company that operates Seven Bays Marina, a wonderful day use facility just up the Lake. New upgrades and development are promised by the new company. The new marina is already showing vast improvements.

Trip Notes: Dropping down those steep, sharp switchbacks from Wilbur into Keller Ferry made this lovely campground seem all the more peaceful, but somehow still buzzing with quiet activity. The ferry runs non-stop all day long, while the people resting in their lounge chairs on the grassy campsites were doing something I'd been meaning to do for quite some time -- RELAXING. Everything was just so easy. When we finally decided to cross the mighty Lake Roosevelt to our favorite Ferry County (no pun intended), it took all of 20 minutes. I couldn't help but look back for as long as possible.

Hawk Creek CG (Lincoln Co.'s *BEST RUSTIC CG*)

This campground is well-loved by nature lovers but under-appreciated by luxury seekers. Backed by Hawk Creek Falls, which plunges 50' into a bathing pool just behind the rustic campground, trails lead to the "Great Bend" of Lake Roosevelt, with panoramic views of the 130-mile long lake. Or you can climb the hills to view the same from basalt caves formed by Ice-Age floods. But don't come looking for well-manicured lawns or 5-Star restaurants. You'll need to look elsewhere for those.

Overview: Located 14 miles north of Davenport on the Hawk Creek spur of Lake Roosevelt, operated by the NPS at 1305' elevation, open year-round; GPS 47.8157, -118.3255.

Facilities include vault toilets, pumped water, gravel pads, and a boat ramp.

Recreation: Fishing for bass and walleye gets two fins up. Fishing trails lead to views of the "Great Bend" of Lake Roosevelt, the basalt Hawk Creek Caves, and several small canyons filled with wildlife. Fifty-foot Hawk Creek Falls is located at the end of the campground. Canoeing, swimming, and wildlife viewing are also popular.

Campsites (21 sites for tents or RVs up to 25', no hookups or reservations): Sites are rustic but well-shaded, and small to medium in size. Privacy can be limited when the campground is full on weekends. This is offset by the beauty of Hawk Creek, best visited in late winter or early spring when the waters of Lake Roosevelt are
lowest, and the Creek is in its most natural condition. The waterfall offers swimming and bathing opportunities in the plunging pool. Be aware that cacti and thorny vegetation occur away from the campground and creek bed.

Fort Spokane CG (Lincoln Co.'s *BEST CG FOR ENTIRE FAMILIES*)

The Park sits at the confluence of the Spokane River and Lake Roosevelt. Fort Spokane operated as a military fort from 1880 until the beginning of the Spanish-American War to keep peace between early settlers and American Indians. It was later used as the Fort Spokane Indian Boarding School with disastrous results. Displays through the Park illustrate this confluence/conflict of two cultures.

Overview: This very unique campground is located 23 miles north of Davenport on the Spokane River Arm of upper Lake Roosevelt, operated by the NPS at 1417' elevation, open year-round; GPS 47.9046, -118.30915.

Facilities: This uniquely equipped campground contains ADA-accessible flush and vault toilets, drinking water (shut off in winter), picnic tables, fire grills, campfire circles, amphitheater, playground, boat ramp and dock, visitor center, fish cleaning stations, an RV dump, and camp hosts. Unique to this campground is the historic, restored Fort Spokane Interpretive Center just across SR 25 from the campground.

Recreation: Boating, swimming, and viewing the self-guided tour of Fort Spokane (open summer only) are the most popular activities. Fishing is good for bass, rainbow trout, salmon, and walleye. Fort Spokane also boasts some of the best bird habitats in the Lake Roosevelt National Recreation Area. Birders often see bald eagles, blue herons, finches, golden eagles, ospreys, and even peregrine falcons. Wildlife viewing is also excellent -- you won't have to go out and find it -- the deer will come to you, as they seem to be everywhere.

Campsites (67 sites for tents and RVs up to 40', 2 group sites for up to 45 people each, no hookups, reservable): Campsites are large and shaded, but lack privacy. There is little vegetation apart from the Ponderosa pines, so the campground tends to be noisy when it is full.

Trip Notes: Two things surprised us on our first visit here. First, old Fort Spokane is entirely separate from the campground, connected by a 0.5-mile walking trail. The campground in 2015 was under severe fire watch, so all ground vegetation was removed, and even the pine needles were meticulously swept away to reduce the danger. This left us with a rather sterile view of the campground, but upon reflection, we badly want to go back and camp during a less dry season.

The Keller Ferry is the only Washington State Ferry to operate in Eastern Washington. It connects Lincoln and Ferry Counties.

The Sage-Steppe Channeled Scablands

The Telford-Crab Creek Tract of the channeled scablands in Lincoln Co. is a 40-mile wide swath of devastation known for its curving grooves worn into the landscape by Ice Age Floods. This is reflected in the many lakes that remain. Rock Lake and Coffeepot Lake were the deepest cut, but all the lakes show this long, curved, slightly crescent-shaped pattern. This is interspersed by many flood-scoured, wide ringed circular moats or "craters" that lie in wait for exploration by those inquisitive enough to come and find them.

Coffeepot Lake CG (Lincoln Co.'s *BEST FREE CG*)
This is arguably the most popular lake in the Lincoln Co. portion of the channeled scablands. It is larger than most lakes, and, thanks to Ice Floodwaters that cut well below the water table, one of the deepest. Now it sits in the prettiest of canyons, with a beautiful campground resting on a rock bench at the base of the canyon. For once, those Ice Age Floods did us one big favor.
Overview: This delightful campground is located 29 miles southeast of Davenport and 15 miles west of Harrington on 310-acre Coffeepot Lake, operated by the BLM at 1818' elevation, open year-round; GPS: 47.499567, -118.557197.
Facilities: Limited facilities include rest rooms, drinking water, picnic tables, a covered picnic site, trash cans, and a fishing dock. The boat launch is occasionally closed due to muddy conditions, and boats may need to be hand-launched.
Recreation includes boating, canoeing/kayaking, and fishing (March 1st to September 30th) for largemouth bass, black crappie, rainbow trout, and yellow perch. This is also known as a good canoeing and kayaking lake. Wildflowers include serviceberry, chokecherry, and mock orange shrubs.
Campsites (6 campsites for tents and RVs up to 35', no hookups or reservations, FREE of charge): Sites are small here, but each is separated by cottonwood trees with some shade. They sit on a bench, so are quite flat. They tend to be green in the spring, and not so green in the summer, plus close to the water and nestled nicely in the steep canyon.
Trip Notes: Just why this place is named Coffeepot Lake seems a mystery. The Lake is certainly not shaped like any coffeepot we've ever seen, nor does it bubble, boil, or blow off steam. It just sits there quietly like so many other lakes in the scablands. What we DID experience, located as it is in this vertical basalt canyon, was waking up early in the morning, nursing an entire pot of coffee for several hours, as the morning moisture slowly lifted, studying the more delicate blotches of color and subtle sounds of this hearty but fragile geological wonder as it slowly gave way to the heat of the day.
Local Alternative: Other recommended FREE CGs in Lincoln Co. (not already listed above) include Twin Lakes CG, with its 3 grassy sites and one additional site

on a grassy knoll. Each site contains a table and fire grate. There is also a toilet and boat launch; GPS 47.529749, -118505917.

Sprague Lake

This mostly Lincoln County lake stretches so for far along Interstate 90 that it crosses over the Adams County line to the west. The area was first formed by lava flows about 16 million years ago, laying down a thick bed of basalt. Then, about 16,000 years ago, the floods from Lake Missoula covered the area in 200 feet or more of raging water. When the floods receded, carving out much of the basalt, we were left with numerous basalt mesas, coulees and basins, including the Sprague Lake that we know and love today.

Sprague Lake Resort (Lincoln Co.'s *BEST EQUIPPED/BEST CG FOR RVs*)
This private resort lies on the eastern end of Sprague Lake, where it is quieter and less windy than the windsurfing-ready west end. The State of Washington regularly stocks the Lake with game fish of all kinds.
Overview: This very established resort lies 39 miles south of Davenport and 2 miles southwest of Sprague on 1841-acre Sprague Lake, privately operated at 1903' elevation, open seasonally, usually April through November; GPS 47.2878, -118.0215.
Facilities: This well-equipped campground comes with bathrooms, showers, boat dock, Wi-Fi, Cell phone service is adequate to strong at all points along the Lake.
Recreation: Fly fishing is at its best here, especially for bluegill, channel catfish, black crappie, yellow perch, rainbow and cutthroat trout, and largemouth bass.
Campsites (55 sites for tents and RVs of any size, including 34 with full hookups 30-amp, reservable): The grounds are immaculate and shady with old growth cottonwoods that tower over the campground. Sites are grassy with grass pads, but a little "lumpy," so bring leveling blocks. Most sites face the Lake. There is less train noise here that at Four Seasons Resort on the west end of the Lake.
Trip Notes: Check your expectations before you arrive, and camp here with an open mind. The approach may lead you to believe that you've driven up a dead-end road of houses whose owners have given up maintaining their properties. And when you arrive, even though meticulously maintained, the resort is really quite small. No playgrounds, Kamp Stores, or swimming pools you may find at other resorts, but a very quiet campground on the end of a lake managed by an extremely helpful friendly host. You can rest here, enjoy the lake, and be assured that you will be undisturbed with a helpful host just a short walk away.

For more photos of Lincoln Co. CGs, or more on BOAT-IN or HIKE-IN CGs, consult campeverycountywa.com

Mason County (Shelton/Belfair/Hoodsport)

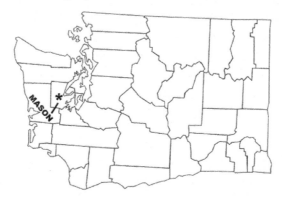

This may be the smallest county on the Olympic Peninsula, but it proudly boasts its place as gateway to the Olympic Rain Forest, the Skokomish Valley, and captivating Hood Canal. Originally named Sawamish County in 1854, it was later renamed after Charles H. Mason (1830-1859), the territory's first Secretary of State and acting governor. It was built up first by logging, then by railroads, and soon after by tourism, due to its many waterways, inlets, mountains, lakes and virgin forests. It maintains its pioneer spirit, with some of the most unique camping in Washington.

Southshore of Hood Canal

Belfair S.P. (Mason Co.'s *BEST CG FOR ENTIRE FAMILIES*)
When Hood Canal hits this southernmost point at "The Heel" and hooks sharply east, it forms the "Southshore," a more sheltered, gentler waterway giving way to incredible wetlands and streams at "The Toe," better known as Belfair S.P.
Overview: Located 3 miles west of Belfair on 65 acres with saltwater shoreline on Hood Canal at 19' elevation, Beach Loop open year-round; GPS 47.42972, -122.87556.
Facilities: The park comes equipped with bathrooms with showers (both ADA), picnic tables (ADA), fire rings, a playground, sports field, a Kitchen Shelter, camp hosts, and an RV dump.
Recreation: The gentle breezes and calmer waters at this southernmost tip of Hood Canal lend themselves to kite flying, windsurfing, and kayaking. Clam and especially oyster harvesting are good, while both freshwater and saltwater fishing are fair. Be mindful that WA state licenses are required. Stream and saltwater swimming are also popular. Birding is excellent (see below).

Campsites (167 sites, including 47 with full hookups 50 amp, 8 cabins, 3H/B sites, reservable): Sites are in three loops. The Main Loop (sites 49-62, 73-82, 99-111, C1-C4 for cabins, and T2-T19 for hookups) is a relatively open and borders Big Mission Creek. The grassy Beach Loop (sites 83, 98, 101, and T20-T47 for hookups) also borders Big Mission Creek. Both this and the Main Loop are best for swimming. The Forest Loop (sites 113-184) is the prettiest of the 3 Loops, situated along Little Mission Creek, but can only accommodate RVs up to 30', so is best for tenters. It is set among extremely large conifers acting as a wind break and providing shade.

Trip Notes: The South Shore of Hood Canal has always had a calming effect on me - a great amalgam of wetlands and forest. It is superior to nearby Twanoh S.P. and Potlatch S.P. both which have beautiful waterfronts but are congested and bisected by busy highways.

Local Attraction: The Theler Wetlands is a series of wetland trails and boardwalks at the tip of Hood Canal where it meets the Union River. It is noted for excellent bird watching (no dogs allowed here). Frequently observed birds include the American bald eagle, American wigeons, buffleheads, goldeneyes, golden-crowned kinglets, green-winged teals, horned grebes, northern pintails, ospreys, red-breasted mergansers, red-necked grebes, and red-tailed hawks.

South Fork Skokomish River Region

The South Fork of the Skokomish River forms one of the most bucolic, idyllic, Fairy Tale valleys in all of Washington. It has also battled flooding, due to upstream logging and other industries. In the meantime, we can take the high ground (literally) and find remarkable camping opportunities upstream along this much-loved river.

Brown Creek CG (Mason Co.'s *BEST RUSTIC CG*)
This is one of the most sustainable, people-pleasing campgrounds in Washington. Why? Because it had been "unofficially" used by locals for decades. This was never Party Central -- this was used for fishing, hunting, and river camping for so long that the USFS finally recognized the need, took control, and developed it into one of the best getaways in the area.

Overview: This Olympic National Forest beauty is located 23.7 miles northeast of Shelton and 15 miles up the Skokomish Valley Road at the confluence of Brown Creek and the South Fork Skokomish River at 600' elevation, 6 sites are open year-round; GPS 47.412121, -123.322013.

Facilities are minimal, but comes with vault toilets, drinking water (summer only), fire rings, and picnic tables.

Recreation: Hiking, tube floating, and fishing are the mainstays here. The 0.8-mile Brown Creek Nature Loop Trail #877 is a beautifully forested walk around the donut-shaped wetland within the park, allowing wildlife and bird viewing. Wading and tubing in the South Fork Skokomish River get rave reviews. Fishing for Chinook, Coho and chum salmon round out the highlights.

Campsites (13 back-in sites for tents or RVs up to 21', plus 9 pull-through sites for larger RVs, one site is ADA, no hookups or reservations): Sites are located in 3 unnamed sections: (1) Sites 1-6 (open year round) are the most rustic and back up to the river; (2) Sites 7-11 have a more developed, groomed appearance along the campgrounds' paved roadway. It is a small loop meandering through a stand of white barked conifers and alders with a "deep woods" feel offering good to excellent privacy; and (3) Sites 12-22 comprise a larger loop in a stand of maples, Douglas fir, and hemlock with an open, airy feel with fair to good privacy.

Trip Notes and Directions: This remote campground was a pleasant surprise with some of the largest and most private campsites we have seen. It is a little difficult to find: We recommend you be prepared to always veer to the right, and you should be fine. When the Skokomish Valley Road finally forks, take the right fork onto Forest Rd 23. This will alternate between paved and gravel surfaces for about 15 miles until you come to the Brown Creek Bridge. Once over the bridge, make a very sharp right, hugging the river, and you'll drive right to it. This "driving by karma" as we call it, is less stressful than following maps or uncertain GPS in unfamiliar territory. Another warning regarding maps: Brown Creek Pond is not really the donut-shaped little lake that appears in drawings of the campground. Rather, it is a beaver pond wetland with a grove of trees in the middle. The hiking trail around the pond (above) is terrific, but the pond won't support any boats. Leave your canoes and kayaks at home, or you'll find yourself up Brown Creek without a paddle.

Local Attraction: The "steel bridge," the only named ascribed to this towering structure over the South Skokomish Gorge, is a logging bridge that has captured the respect of local folks in the Shelton area. If you're a guest of the locals, you'll be taken to see this before the sun sets. Be nice, it's worth a look and a walk across. From here you can also see Vincent Creek Falls, a narrow 125' high tumble of water into the Skokomish River.

Local Alternative: Those looking for something less remote and less rustic might try Cedar Arms CG along the South Skokomish River just one mile from Hwy 101. It has just 5 individual tent sites, including one group site. Swimming is excellent in the beautiful, slow-moving stretch of the River. This is largely a "boutique-ing" campground, as each site is highly individualized, with strings of Mexican prayer flags colorfully decorating each custom site. GPS coordinates are 47.334° N, 123.27°W.

North Fork Skokomish River Region

Most campers get very little opportunity to see the North Fork of the Skokomish River, except for the portions that form Lake Cushman. This river has been claimed by both the Tacoma Power Company and the Skokomish Tribe for over a century, but due to an arduous series of negotiations, much of the land has been returned to the Tribe, while leaving the dams in place. The result is that camping is much improved in the area, showcased by the Tribe as their pride and joy.

Skokomish Park (Mason Co.'s *MOST APPEALING CG TO THE SENSES, and includes BEST GROUP CG* within North Camp)
Formerly known as Lake Cushman S.P., this land was returned to the Skokomish Tribe in settlement for land lost due to the damming of Lake Cushman. The Tribe has transformed a fairly good park into one of the very best in Washington.
Overview: This well-appointed campground is proudly located 22.7 miles north of Shelton and 7 miles northwest of Hoodsport on 600 acres with 41,500' of shoreline on 4,010-acre Lake Cushman, operated by Skokomish Indian Tribal Enterprises at 1000' elevation, South Camp Loop is open year-round; GPS 47.4633, -123.2178.
Facilities: Featured are bathrooms with coin-op showers in each loop, picnic tables, fire rings/grills, hand-hewn benches, 9 miles of trails, camp hosts, and an RV dump.
Recreation: Kayaking and canoeing are excellent, with kayak, stand-up paddle board, paddle boat, and mountain bike rentals in the South Loop. Swimming is also exceptional, though the water can be cold. Water skiing on this large lake tends not to be disturbing to campers. Hiking at nearby Staircase Recreation Area and Big Creek CG is highly recommended, including the hike to the top of Mt. Elinor. The Lake Cushman Gold Course provides links for golfers without leaving the Cushman environment.
Campsites (60 sites for tents and RVs of all sizes, including 30 with full hookups 30/50 camp, 2 H/B sites, 1 small group camp for 20 and one large group camp for 80 in the North Loop, reservable): Sites are divided into South and North Camp Loops. Both are excellent and well maintained by the Skokomish Tribe, who add hand-hewn benches and other touches not seen at other parks. The South Camp Loop is more manicured, has access to supervised swimming and boating areas, and is preferable for campers with children. The North Camp Loop is preferred by some parties without children, is intentionally more rustic, more heavily wooded, and includes the larger of the Group Camps, adding more private, unrestricted access to the Lake. Both loops accommodate RVs of any size, but the only the South Camp Loop has hookups. This is clearly superior to nearby Big Creek CG which is dusty and brushy despite recent upgrades compared to the evergreen coolness of Skokomish Park. It is also superior to Cushman Resort, which is

extremely congested, and another example of "camping in fast motion." Dow Creek RV Park and CG remains the best local alternative.

Trip Notes: Some of my camp-panions will tell you emphatically that this is their favorite campground in Washington. I could easily add it to my top 10 based on privacy, and the lush atmosphere of the Olympic foothills. The personal touches added by the Tribe, and the complexity and positioning of the sites are near perfection. In short, this is a "park on a lake that's not about the lake" -- it's about the camping. And this is our ultimate criteria for campgrounds. The beaches are fine -- they offer good mountain and lake views -- but the campsites themselves put this park among our favorites.

Washington History: The Antlers Hotel was built in 1895 on the shores of Lake Cushman as a luxury getaway for seasoned outdoorsmen. In 1903 Theodore Roosevelt was invited to stay here in order to secure his signature to open up the land to logging. He did not do so, but focused instead on the local elk, which were nearly wiped out. By 1909 he created the 610,000-acre Mount Olympus National Monument inside the Olympic National Forest. This led to the preservation of the "Roosevelt Elk" and set the stage 30 years later for the creation of the Olympic National Park by another President Roosevelt (see WA History under Willaby Campground, Grays Harbor Co.). Incidentally, the Antlers Hotel was flooded by the newly dammed Lake Cushman in 1924, but Teddy's legacy remains.

Lake Cushman is breathtaking from any view, on or off the Lake

Staircase CG at ONP (Mason Co.'s *MOST UNIQUELY WASHINGTON CG* and includes *BEST HIKE-IN CAMPSITES*)

The name Staircase" was first used in the 1890 diaries of the O'Neil Expedition. In mapping and exploring this southeastern corner of the Olympic Peninsula, they felled logs in zig-zag trails and covered them with moss and brush for the mules to cross a rock bluff that was otherwise impassible -- thus "staircase." Today the name staircase is used to describe the series of regular recurring rapids one mile upstream from the campground.

Overview: This Olympic National Park campground is located 31.2 miles northwest of Shelton on 8 acres on the North Fork of the Skokomish River at 1066' elevation, open year-round weather permitting. GPS 47.515, -123.328.

Facilities: There are flush toilets and potable water during summer season only, but pit toilets and no water in off-season. Other amenities include picnic tables, fire grills, animal-proof food lockers, an amphitheater, a vintage Ranger Station, equestrian trails, hiking trails, and camp hosts.

Recreation: While visitors enjoy fishing, biking, swimming, boating, canoeing, kayaking, picnicking and wildlife viewing, this campground is famous for its direct access to splendid hiking. The Staircase Rapids Loop is an easy flat 2-mile trail that winds through old growth forest to a 200' suspension bridge over the North Fork of the Skokomish River. From this bridge hikers can veer off an additional 1.2 miles to where Four Stream meets the Skokomish in a red cedar forest. Shady Lane Trail is flat and only 0.9 miles to the Four Stream Road and Lake Cushman. The first 0.1 mile along the River is wheelchair accessible. More strenuous hikes include the Wagonwheel Lake Trail at 2.9 miles with an elevation gain of 3,365'. The Flapjack Lakes Trail is a 7.8-mile one-way hike with a 3,115-foot elevation gain. The two lakes lay side by side just below tree line at the base of the Sawtooth Range. Note that no dogs are allowed on these trails, and a camping permits are required.

Campsites (49 sites for tents and RVs up to 21', with a few for up to 35', some ADA, 5 sites are walk-ins, no hookups or reservations): Campground sites are set in old growth forest, and are heavily shaded, even damp at times. Many sites have river access, most are flat. They are fairly large but can lack privacy from other sites. Alternatively, this closer spacing can be an advantage for larger groups. Parking is on native material. The campsites on the less strenuous trails are dispersed, but always surrounded by water and mountains.

Trip Notes: The recently upgraded campground can surprise visitors with the beauty of the Skokomish River and the sudden shift to a more rain forest feel. It would be easy to stand on top of the concrete bridge and stare down at the translucent blue flowering river water, free of pollution, damming, and human interference. It surrounds the campground on two sides, giving it its irresistible draw. The vintage Ranger Station adds a sense of nostalgia and timelessness. This has been a go-to hike-in camping spot for my brothers and I, as the quicker access up the flat trails left more time for the camping experience.

<u>Dow Creek RV Resort/CG</u> (Mason Co.'s *BEST EQUIPPED/BEST CG FOR RVs*)
Sometimes, rarely, you find a campground that is about the Creek. Well, you found it: small, bubbly, winding through moss and vine maples. Sometimes we need nothing more.

<u>Overview</u>: This facility is strategically located 18.1 miles north of Shelton and 2.7 miles west of Hoodsport, operated by Sunrise Resorts at 641' elevation, open year-round; GPS 47.411877, -123.190665.

<u>Facilities</u>: The RV section is equipped with bathrooms with showers, fire rings, picnic tables, sections of cut logs for seating/tables, a playground, sports court, laundry, vintage picnic shelter, camp hosts, and is a short walk to Lake Cushman Grocery.

<u>Recreation</u> includes tennis, walking/hiking trails at adjacent Hoodsport Trail (formerly a S.P.), and golfing 1 mile away at Lake Cushman Golf Course. Hood Canal itself provides shellfish harvesting, boating, and scuba diving. Great hiking is nearby at Staircase, Big Creek, Mount Elinor, and other trails within the Olympic National Forest and ONP.

<u>Campsites</u> (94 sites for tents or RVs of any size, 17 with full hookups and 50 with electric & water hookups 50 amp, 5 cabins, reservable): The RV sites in the main park are wooded and well-spaced, particularly those on the back loop furthest from N. Lake Cushman Rd. The tent sites (open summer only) are detached just down the road, across from the Lake Cushman Golf Course. These sites are large, wooded, and private. There is some evidence of logging just beyond the treeline but does not detract from the simple beauty of the place. The tent sites (10 in all) are more rustic, with vault toilets, picnic tables, and fire rings. They are also quieter, but closer to walking trails and the golf course.

<u>Trip Notes</u>: This park was the surprise of the year. It just felt good. Dow Creek runs through the park, one of the prettiest creeks anywhere, pristine and gentle, eventually flowing to Lake Kokanee ("Lower Lake Cushman"). Vintage remnants of older campgrounds are visible throughout the park. This fit our ultimate criteria for a good campground: we didn't want to leave when our time was up and extended our stay. Twice.

<u>Local Attractions</u>: The Hoodsport Winery in Hoodsport is popular with wine connoisseurs.

Tahuya State Forest

The 23,000-acre Tahuya State Forest strikes a delicate balance of providing sustainable revenue for public services through timber production and leaving undeveloped land as habitat for native plants and animals, water retention and water quality benefits. Campers will find some areas popular with motorized off-road vehicles and equestrians, with the remainder being a very natural and unspoiled habitat for the campers themselves.

<u>Aldrich Lake CG</u> (Mason Co.'s *BEST FREE CG*)
This is rustic campground is sometimes called Aldridge Lake. Its old world feel and isolation make it a campworthy find at any price.
<u>Overview</u>: This remote campground is tucked away 38.2 miles north of Shelton and 14.7 miles west of Belfair on 10.6-acre Aldrich Lake, operated by the DNR at 448' elevation, open April 15 to Sept. 15; GPS 47.432623, -123.0822558 (see directions below).
<u>Facilities</u>: These are limited to a concrete pit toilet plus two older pit toilets, picnic tables, metal fire rings, and an unimproved boat launch.
<u>Recreation</u>: Mushroom gathering and berry picking are a big deal here, and in the area generally. Swimming is popular at the Lake, despite snags in the water. Fishing is fair, with some rainbows and bluegills caught here. There are also other lakes close by for fishing, plus an extensive system of hiking trails throughout the Tahuya Forest.
<u>Campsites</u> (5 sites for tents or truck-mounted campers; no hookups, water or reservations, FREE with Discover Pass): The spacious sites wrap around the north side of this small lake, with site 5 at the turnaround at the end of the road. A small creek runs between sites 2 and 3. The sites are forested with Douglas fir, pines, dogwood, and wild rhododendrons. Sites 2 and 3 are pull-throughs, but not level enough for RVs. The back-in sites are more level. Site 1 is adjacent to the boat launch and small Day Use Area, giving it more space. All campsites face the Lake. Take note: the small lake is shared by the Boy Scout Camp Hahobas on the southwest corner of the Lake.
<u>Trip Notes</u>: The addition of dogwood and wild rhododendrons, plus modern, clear signage to the campground were big surprises. I would recommend camping on weekdays, however, as this is often full on summer weekends. Overall, this is a little rustic, but very campworthy, in a wonderful forested area.

Puget Sound Islands

The Mason County islands of Puget Sound form an administratively interconnected series of marine parks that are both magnificent and underutilized. They vary in size from tiny 11.5-acre McMicken Island to noteworthy 1,194-acre Harstine Island. What they offer is a quieter, less crowded alternative to the San Juans with similar boating, camping, and bicycling opportunities.

<u>Jarrell Cove S.P. Drive-In/Boat-In</u> (Mason Co.'s *BEST BIKE-IN* CG)
This place is both a haven for boaters, and a miniature marine playground for campers, while Harstine Island itself is popular with bicyclists who enjoy 18.6 square miles of sweeping marine views and quiet country roads.

Overview: This quirky Harstine Island campground is located 15 miles west of Shelton via a bridge over Pickering Passage on 43 acres with 3500' of saltwater shoreline, open year-round; GPS 47.284, -122.885.

Facilities include bathrooms with showers, picnic tables, fire grills, 2 fire circles, 2 kitchen shelters, a horseshoe pit, one mile of hiking/biking trails, an amphitheater, a sports court, 650' of boat dock, 682' of moorage, 14 mooring buoys, a marine pump-out station, and camp hosts.

Recreation: Kayaking and boating are perfect here. Hiking is available at Hartstine Island S.P., which is connected to Jarrell Cove by a 0.5-mile trails. Bird watching is also popular. Birds seen and heard here include brown creepers, common goldeneyes, Downy woodpeckers, Hutton's vireos, Pacific-slope flycatchers, red-breasted mergansers, red-breasted nuthatches, red-throated loons, ring-billed bulls, and surf scoters.

Campsites (22 sites for tents and RVs up to 34', one ADA site, no hookups, one walk-in group camp for up to 45 with a kitchen shelter, reservable, open year round): Sites are in two areas: the grassy flat area as you drive into the campground, and walk-in/boat-in sites above the entrance dock on the shoreline (keep in mind that most campers arrive by boat). Only a few of the grassy sites are separated by vegetation but are large enough to give average to good privacy. The walk-in sites near the entrance dock are terraced with good views of the Cove and are more private. These are also more wooded, compared to the grassy sites that are open but surrounded by forest on 3 sides.

Trip Notes: It's official -- this place is charming; a word I hate, but Jarrell Cove is just that pretty. There are two large docks, each nestled into its own arm of the Cove. One arm looks across at another dock on the far shore; the other is just beneath the walk-in campsites. Together, you begin to feel what boaters feel when they approach the land from the water, feeling nature bumping up against nature. Various short trails lead to the Group Camp, another to Harstine Island S.P. (a Day Use Camp), and two others to the docks. Small, compact, surrounded by water and... charming.

Local Attractions: Jarrell Cove administers 5 satellite parks: Hope Island S.P. (see website), Harstine Island S.P. (also above), McMicken Island S.P. (a boat-in Day Use Park with a land bridge accessible at low tide that's noted for great harvesting of Manila clams, butter clams, and horse clams), Stretch Point S.P. (another boat-in Day Use Park12 miles north of Shelton), and Eatle Island S.P. (a 10-acre Day Use Park between McNeil and Anderson Islands in Thurston Co.).

For more photos of Mason Co. CGs, or more about BOAT-IN CGs, consult campeverycountywa.com.

OKANOGAN COUNTY (Okanogan/Omak/Winthrop)

Washington's largest county was also the last to be settled, driven by gold and silver booms in the late 1800s. It is home to Old West towns, ghost towns, river towns, the Omak Stampede, and much of the Colville Indian Reservation. It proudly maintains its reputation as unspoiled, independent and unrestrained.

Methow Valley Region

The Methow River Valley sits just east of the North Cascades National Park, finally emptying into the Columbia River at Pateros. It is one of Washington's most revered natural playgrounds extending over 80 miles through the Western-themed town of Winthrop with its many resorts and tourist attractions, and Twisp, with its own history of colorful antiheroes. Camping is equally rich, set among snow-capped alpine peaks, mountain lakes, and the inviting but treacherous waters of the Methow River.

Pearrygin Lake S.P. *(Okanogan Co.'s BEST CG FOR ENTIRE FAMILIES and BEST EQUIPPED CG/BEST CG FOR RVs)*

This lovely park was named after B.F. Pearrygin, an early settler on the Lake whom history remembers in very unflattering terms, dubbing him as a rowdy western "pirate." Ironic, given how much this lake and campground are loved by campers from all over Washington and beyond. It is near the equally popular Wild West town of Winthrop.

Overview: This family-friendly campground is located 4 miles northwest of Winthrop on 743 acres with 11,000' of lakefront on 183.2-acre Lake Pearrygin at 1768' elevation, open April to October; GPS: 48.4866, -120.1459.

Facilities: This well-equipped spot includes bathrooms (ADA) with showers, running water, picnic tables, fire grills, boat launch, 60' of boat dock, amphitheater, a Junior Ranger Program for children, Camp Store, RV dump, and camp hosts.

The popular Day Use Area includes a bathhouse, 4 barbecue stands, a marked swimming beach, volleyball court, and large lawn with shade trees.

Summer Recreation: The Lake provides opportunities for swimming, fishing, wildlife viewing, boating, and good water-skiing. For hikers, the Rex Derr Trail is a 3.1-mile loop on a shrub steppe hillside above the Lake that skirts the old Graves Homestead. Fishing is best for rainbow trout.

Winter Recreation: This was named an official non-motorized Sno-Park in 2015. Nordic skiing, snow shoeing, and cross-country skiing are excellent.

Campsites (183 sites, including 77 with full hookups 30/50 amp for RVs up to 60', 2 cabins & 1 vacation house, reservable): Sites are in two loops, East and West; sites in East Loop are more wooded with average to good privacy and shade from willow and ash trees; many sites in West Loop lack privacy and shade, but have better lake access. Campers with children might prefer the West Loop. Sites 86-104 and 138-148 are especially suited to those with young swimmers. The West Loop cabins sleep four, and have kitchenettes and air conditioning, a welcome amenity during the typically hot summers.

Trip notes: Lovely lake, very inviting for boating and, for the kids, swimming. The West Loop was a beehive of activity with enthusiastic kids running back and forth (usually through our campsite) to the lake. There were marmots everywhere, and beautiful, healthy deer with just enough survival instinct to stay out of the campsites. Gotta tell you, though, the 107-degree temperature cut our stay short. Next time we'll be staying in the East Loop, with or without kids. It's just too hot and exposed otherwise. Late spring, early summer, or early fall visits might be best.

Washington History: The refurbished Wild West town of Winthrop has a wild and varied history. Of B.F. Pearrygin it was said "he sold his soul to the devil but never collected the pay!" On the other, Winthrop founder Guy Waring was a cum laude graduate of Harvard and a classmate of President Theodore Roosevelt. In 1891 he opened Waring's Methow Trading Post, around which grew the town that catered to cattle ranchers and miners. In 1971, with news of the opening of North Cascade Highway, local merchants put up the capital to restore the town to its original Western mining look. The original building of Waring's Methow Trading post still stands proudly (although renamed Last Trading Post) as do most of the original buildings.

Heart of the Okanogan Region

This region is characterized by the Cariboo Trail, where cattle drives followed the Okanogan River to the hungry mining camps of the British Columbia gold boom of the 1860s. U.S. 97 now follows this north-south trail, but the area maintains a distinctly cattleman flavor, much like the better known Chisholm Trail delivering beef-on-the-hoof from Texas ranches to Kansas railheads.

<u>Conconully S.P.</u> *(Okanogan Co.'s MOST UNIQUELLY WASHINGTON CG)*
Conconully, a town of just over 200 people, has been everything from the rip-roaring silver town of "Salmon City" (its former name), to the Okanogan county seat, to the little town between the reservoirs that gave up its old schoolyard to build the now arboretum-like State Park. Spend a few minutes in this little western town, and it will charm your spurs off.

<u>Overview</u>: The Park is located 15 miles north of Omak in the town of Conconully on 81 acres with 5400' of freshwater shoreline on Conconully Reservoir and Conconully Lake at 2303' elevation, open March 15 to December 1; GPS 48.5558, -119.751.

<u>Facilities</u>: The park is equipped with ADA flush toilets, ADA showers, running water, picnic tables, fire grills, a playground with wading pool, 2 boat launches, 1 dock for smaller boats, Park Store, one kitchen shelter, campground hosts, and an RV dump.

<u>Recreation</u>: Bird watching (hawks, herons, ospreys), boating, swimming, water-skiing, and especially fishing are popular here. Described as a "fisherman's paradise," the lakes provide kokanee salmon, largemouth bass (no limit), and rainbow trout. Another popular activity is "ghost towning," as this is the center of the Okanogan Silver Boom of the 1890s. Gold-panning is best on the Similkameen River to the north, but also good just beyond the ghost town of Ruby. Hiking is limited to a half-mile nature trail, and access to the Golden Stairway, a 6-mile hike above Conconully Reservoir. Wildlife-viewing is extensive, and includes coyotes, mule deer, elk, and muskrats.

<u>Campsites</u>: (69 tent sites, 15 RV sites with water & electric 50-amp hookups, 4 small and 1 large cabin w/electric & water for rent, reservable): Sites are grassy w/adequate privacy. RV sites 56D-60D are the only reservable RV hookup sites. The trees are large and well-manicured, including weeping willow, big leaf maple, Douglas fir, Ponderosa pine, poplar, and scrub oak.

<u>Washington History</u>: This Park was built in 1910 by the Bureau of Land Reclamation Project in Central Washington. Replicas of the town's original schoolhouse and courthouse are on the grounds. The park became a state park in 1945.

<u>Trip Notes</u>: The amazing thing about Conconully is that the State Park and the town are like a single unit. Mule deer graze in the park, then cross the street to graze in private yards. You will meet your fellow campers at the General Store sitting on the colorful Adirondack chairs eating ice cream cones and discussing fishing, history, you name it. Conconully Lake stretches for about 5 miles into the forest, making the entire "Park"-- including both reservoirs, the compact little town, and the park itself -- stretch for 7 miles or so. And best of all, Conconully isn't so much "wild west" as it is "old west." It is very peaceful, very engaging, and a place that is hard to leave.

<u>Osoyoos Lake Veterans Memorial Park</u> (Okanogan Co.'s *BEST BIKE-IN CG*)
Osoyoos is the native word for "narrowing of the waters," as the Okanogan Highlands on both sides of the Okanogan River dip down nearly 3000' for this long lake that backs up well into British Columbia. The American Legion donated most of the campground land, giving it the designation of the Veterans Memorial Park.
<u>Overview</u>: This bike-accessible Park is located in the City of Oroville on 300' of lakefront on the southern shore of 12-mile long Lake Osoyoos, operated by the City of Oroville Parks at 932' elevation, Open mid-March to October; GPS 48.935032, -119.436943.
<u>Facilities</u>: These include a bathhouse with showers, picnic tables, fire rings, concession stand, 40' fishing dock, railed lake trail for shore fishing, and an RV dump.
<u>Recreation</u>: Fishing is fair for smallmouth bass from spring to fall. Other fish include Chinook trout, kokanee, and yellow perch. Canoeing and kayaking are ideal here due to the still lake waters.
<u>Campsites</u> (86 tent and RVs up to 35', 13 sites have water & electric 30-amp hookups, 6 walk-in sites, and 2 ADA sites): These campsites seem designed for that "one big happy family" atmosphere, lacking privacy but creating a festive mood. Those seeking more solitude will find solace at the 40' fishing dock, the huge grassy Day Use Area, or canoeing/kayaking on the lake. The most private campsites are the hookup sites on the lakeshore.
<u>Trip Notes</u>: This was a very happy environment, and quite lush for our May visit. It was nice to withdraw from the arid Okanogan Valley and find this green oasis. It is certainly "everybody-oriented," but those who need more privacy and solitude might want to explore Blue Lake or Bonaparte Lake.
<u>Local Attractions</u>: Those camping with or without children need to set aside the better part of a day to drive 12 miles east into the Okanogan Highlands to visit the nearly 4000' Nine Mile Loop. Its best feature is the reassembled ghost town of Old Molson. This town sprang to life in the early 1900s until, a year or so later, they learned they had built their town on someone else's legal homestead. They abandoned everything, moving the new town one-half mile north. All of the original buildings were left intact, along with farm equipment, a bell tower, and some houses/cabins all open to public view. The Loop also includes the original sites of those towns Circle City and Sidley, British Columbia (borders were much less well defined in those days).

<u>Crawfish Lake CG</u> (Okanogan Co.'s *BEST FREE CG*)
This pretty lake provides the perfect home for those tasty little miniature lobsters we call crawfish. Or at least they did at one time. Once crawling with them, the lake

has been so overfished that they are now hard to find. All that is left is the perfect camping lake.

Overview: This Okanogan National Forest campground is located 20 miles east of Riverside on the northeast shore of 80-acre Crawfish Lake at 4500' elevation, open mid-May to October, weather permitting; GPS 48.4838, -119.2146.

Facilities include vault toilets (ADA-friendly), picnic tables, fire rings, wooden benches, and a gravel boat launch. There is no water or garbage service.

Recreation: Fishing is fair for rainbow and eastern brook trout. Note that the southern end of the Lake is on the Colville Indian Reservation, and special fishing permits are required. Boating is allowed with electric motors or human-powered boats. Crawfishing is possible, but overfishing has made them scarce. This is a natural lake with good swimming.

Campsites (19 sites for tents or RVs up to 35', 11 sites have lakefront, 2 are double sites, FREE with NW Forest Pass): Ponderosa pines and mixed conifers provide both mixed shade and a buffer from the Indian lands, so that those unfriendly "no trespassing" signs won't be found here. The best campsites are 1, 2, 13, and 18. If you come on a weekday, you should easily get a lakefront site. Most of the off-lake sites, however, are nicely forested with good privacy, and may be preferred by some.

Trip Notes: This little azure gem is not as remote as critics claim (if you've traveled extensively in Okanogan Co., 20 miles from the nearest town is pretty typical). The road is mostly paved, except for the last 2 miles, which were flat gravel roads without potholes, but a bit washboardy. I was also surprised to find houses around most of the lake, making it remote, but certainly not wilderness. Each campsite was delightfully different from the rest, and the lake seemed to have a natural blue glow about it. This has great general appeal, rating high on the "everybody-friendly" list and a good all-around getaway.

Loomis-Loup Loup State Forest Region
This often-overlooked area of Okanogan County sits on a forested mountain pass separating the Methow and Okanogan Valleys. Most of us know it as Highway 20, the shortcut between the Winthrop-Twisp and Okanogan-Omak areas. Slow down, look around, pitch your tent, and grab your fishing poles and hiking boots.

Leader Lake CG (Okanogan Co.'s *BEST RUSTIC CG*)
This is not only the closest campground to services in Okanogan, it is also the best campground in the region: Quiet, natural, welcoming, and prized by locals. It is also just off Highway 20, with easy bicycle access.

Overview: Located 8.8 miles west of Okanogan on the shore of 155-acre Leader Lake (reservoir) on 159 acres, managed by the DNR at 2293' elevation, open year-round; GPS 48.3617, -119.6973.

<u>Facilities</u> include vault toilets, picnic tables, fire rings, 2 boat launches, a fishing platform, and a wooden deck with bench for lake viewing.

<u>Recreation</u>: Fishing is good for bass, bluegills, crappie, and rainbow trout. The great hiking here is less known. The Ray Trail is a 1.0-mile long wilderness trail of average difficulty. The Beaver Lake Trail is more strenuous at 4.1 miles and 1877' elevation gain leading to a mile-high lake that invites foot and body soaking. Granite Trail is more strenuous at 11 miles of hard hiking that most make a 2-day trek. All give clear views of the Loup Loup Forest and Okanogan Valley.

<u>Campsites</u> (14 sites for tents and RVs up to 30', no hookups, water, or reservations, FREE with Discover Pass): Campsites are in two areas. Sites on the Northshore are dry and lack shade, with at least one site suitable for larger RVs. The Southshore sites are more shaded but require a rather uneven and rough paved road around a steep hill to get there, and most RV'ers might want to avoid this area. Pads are on native material. This campground is close to services in Okanogan, which seems many miles away.

<u>Trip Notes</u>: We found the lake far more beautiful than anticipated, with diverse shoreline, vegetation, and very "Old West" looking barns and houses. The Northern campsites are the most accessible to bicyclers. There is one semi-concealed site at the northwest corner of the earthen dam that has a culvert of water running past with excellent shade that we strongly recommend for weary bicyclers.

Okanogan Highlands/Five-Mountains Region

Ever heard of the Bonaparte Mountains? Small wonder, very few have. Reason: almost no one lives there. This remote northeastern corner of Okanogan County is "inhabited" by such towns as Wauconda, Bodie, Old Toroda, and Chesaw -- all of which are listed as ghost towns. What is left behind is an unspoiled mountain chain with high altitude lakes and perfect camping getaways.

<u>Bonaparte Lake CG</u> (Okanogan Co.'s *MOST APPEALING CG TO THE SENSES*)

In the shadow of 7257-foot high Mount Bonaparte lies little Bonaparte Lake, the gem of the series of 5 lakes, with the campground on the south shore and Bonaparte Resort on the north shore.

<u>Overview</u>: This Okanogan National Forest campground is located 36 miles east of Tonasket on the south shore of 80-acre Bonaparte Lake at 3567' elevation, open mid-May to late September; GPS 48.79246, -119.05742.

<u>Facilities</u>: This uncharacteristic USFS campground includes both vault and flush toilets, drinking water, grey water disposal, picnic tables, fire rings/grills, a sand play area, boat launch, a wheelchair-friendly fishing pier, and camp hosts. There are plans for a swimming dock and new group site with a covered picnic shelter.

Recreation: As most would expect, fishing looms large, producing lake trout, rainbow trout, and smallmouth bass. Only electric boat motors are allowed with a speed limit of 10 mph, so quiet is king. Swimming is available. Hiking is the best way to see this part of Washington, particularly the 4.5-mile (each way) Bonaparte Mountain Trail #306. The mountain rises 3500' above its surroundings, making it somewhat difficult going up, but leads to an historic lookout tower and cabin built in 1914 and now on the National Register of Historic Places. It gives 360-degree panoramic views of Tiffany Mountain (8245') and Copper Butte (7140'), the Kettle and Selkirk Mountains.

Campsites (27 sites for tents and smaller RVs, including multiple sites, no hookups or reservations): Tamarack and Douglas fir trees provide ample shade, but ground vegetation and privacy are minimal. Sites are organized into two loops. The smaller loop has only vault toilets, while the larger loop has both flush and vault toilets. Some parking aprons are paved, others are on native material. Both loops have sites on the water's edge, and all have good lake views. The sites are very individual, including 2 triple sites, 7 double sites, 14 single sites, 3 walk-in tent sites, and 1 group site. This gives flexibility to any sized group, a rarity among USFS campgrounds.

Trip Notes: Here we go again, with the perfect little USFS campground on the perfect little lake -- so you know I'm smitten. This campground has getaway written all over it -- sites on the lake, nice mountain views, quiet, good paved roads to get there, and a perfectly pristine lakeshore. The lake was even nice enough to form itself into a dumbbell shape, separating it from the busier campers at Bonaparte Lake Resort. This one is calling you.

Local Alternatives: Bonaparte Lake Resort has RV hookups (electric 20 and 30 amp), cabins, showers, and boat rentals, but is cluttered and even shabby. Campgrounds at Beaver Lake, Beth Lake, and Lost Lake, the other lakes in this 4-lake Bonaparte chain, have better than average campgrounds that appeal to hunters, fisherfolk, hikers and, of course, campers.

Columbia River Region

This southern border of Okanogan County stretches from Pateros to the Grand Coulee Dam. It is difficult to call this the "Columbia River," as the majority of the water is taken up with Rufus Woods Lake and Lake Pateros, two exceptionally wide reservoirs created by Chief Joseph and Wells Dams. As such, this area provides diverse aquatic recreation and fascinating geological features: the place where cowboy sagebrush meets the inland ocean.

Bridgeport S.P. (Okanogan Co.'s *BEST EQUIPPED/BEST CG FOR RVs*)
The Chief Joseph Dam, just one mile from Bridgeport State Park, backs up the Columbia River for 51 miles, known by the assumed name of Rufus Woods Lake.

Hey! It's hot here! Walk barefoot through the lush grassy meadows and take a dip in the Columbia... I mean, Rufus Woods Lake.

Overview: This unusual campground is located 4 miles northeast of Bridgeport on 748 acres with 7500' of Columbia River shoreline at 850' elevation, open March to October; GPS 48.0156, -119.6082.

Facilities include bathrooms with showers (ADA), picnic tables, fire rings/grills, 2 boat ramps, 240' of boat dock, designated swimming area, RV dump and camp hosts.

Recreation: The 9-hole Lakewoods Golf Course is adjacent to the Park. After hitting the links, swimming is excellent. Fishing (most by boat) is fair for walleye, rainbow trout, and silvers. A Colville Tribe fishing license is required for shore fishing. The Dunes Trailhead provides four miles of hiking trails. Bird watching is good for chukar, quail, pheasant, eagles and hawks.

Campsites (34 sites, including 20 with water & electric 30-amp hookups for RVs up to 45', one group camp for 20-72, reservable): All sites rest on 18 acres of rolling, manicured lawn spotted by shade trees and odd little "haystack" rock formations. Privacy is still average, as the sites are quite large and well-placed.

Trip Notes: We first stumbled upon this oasis of a campground on an escape from an ill-fated trip to nearby campground that proved too hot to handle. It was so refreshing to take a drive in our air-conditioned van and stumble across Bridgeport State Park, and to feel the coolness of the verdant green grass and wide spot in the Columbia in the middle of a very hot and dry July. People at the park seemed to be genuinely enjoying themselves, interacting with neighbors, while their children seemed happily entertained by the lush willow trees, the odd rock formations, and the shoreline of the Lake. We soon made this one of our favorite camping destinations. Lesson learned: this is the best campground in the area, which is probably best visited in spring and fall.

Geological History: This campground's most unique feature is the series of "haystacks," a series of 20' basalt formations deposited by ancient glaciers that are popular for climbing, photographing, and viewing the park from above.

Local Attractions: The Park sits just behind Chief Joseph Dam, the second largest hydroelectric power producing dam in the United States. It is 51 miles downstream from Grand Coulee Dam and has a free tour that offers a better view of its powerhouse and inner workings than Grand Coulee.

For more photos of Okanogan Co. CGs, or more about HIKE-IN, BOAT-IN, or GROUP CGs (and more!), consult campeverycountywa.com

Pearrygin Lake S.P. is the best CG
in Washington for Entire Families

The pristine shoreline of Lake
Bonaparte

Conconully S.P. sits between a
reservoir and lake on the edge of the
Old West town of Conconully

Leader Lake is close to the town of
Okanogan and Loomis-Loup Loup
Forest

Think of Osoyoos as a peaceful lake
on a crowded campground

PACIFIC COUNTY (South Bend/Raymond/Long Beach)

This is among the earliest counties in Washington to be carved from a much larger unit; it is also sparsely populated and undeveloped, untouched by major industry apart from fishing, oyster farming, tourism, and what remains of the logging industry. This may be a good thing, as the county wraps around one of the world's largest and purest saltwater estuaries (Willapa Bay), which is the county's most enduring claim to fame. Its rural, natural character may ensure the continued purity of its shallow tidal waters and ocean beaches.

Cranberry Coast/South Beach Area

The lesser known South Beach on the Washington coast is often overlooked for Ocean Shores to the north and Long Beach to the south. It offers 18 miles of sandy beaches stretching from the fishing port of Westport to the historic town of Tokeland jutting out into the north end of Willapa Bay. Along the way, thousands of acres of cranberry bogs started by Finnish farmers 150 years ago give this stretch of the coast a weathered, broken-in feel that makes for great camping Northwest style.

Grayland Beach S.P. (Pacific Co.'s *BEST EQUIPPED/BEST CG FOR RVs*):
Gray land as far as the eye can see... and this is only the second longest beach in Pacific County.
Overview: This newer, well-designed campground is located 31.8 miles northwest of South Bend in the town of Grayland on 412 acres with 7,449' of Pacific Ocean shoreline, open year-round; GPS 46.78889, -124.09167.
Facilities: This park is nicely equipped with bathrooms, showers, flush toilets, running water, picnic tables, fire grills, an amphitheater, good cell phone reception, camp hosts and an RV dump.

Recreation: The beach lends itself to kite flying, beach combing, clamming, crabbing, surfing, and deep-sea fishing.

Campsites (120 sites, including 96 with hookups, 4 ADA sites, 16 yurts - some pet friendly, 10 of which are ADA-accessible, reservable): The campground is divided into interconnected loops of 10 sites each (Loop 3 contains 2 yurts), plus two beach strips with small loops, back-in sites, pull-through sites, and 10 of the 12 yurts.

Trip notes: The Pacific County ocean beaches are unique in that they are 100% sand, and seem endless, with few landmarks to give a sense of time or distance. Long Beach has been dubbed "World's Longest Driving Beach," and the South Beach (incorporating Tokeland, Grayland and Westport) is close behind. This park seems especially inviting for groups, if an entire loop were reserved. The campground itself rivals the best on the Washington coast, with modern facilities and five different paths to an incredible ocean beach. There are no bad sites, and privacy is guaranteed.

Local Attraction: Don't forget to explore the tiny town of Tokeland, including the historic Tokeland Hotel opened in 1889. It is on the National Register of Historic Places.

Willapa Bay Area

Willapa Bay covers over 260 square miles of tidelands, separated from the Pacific Ocean only by the narrow 30-mile Long Beach Peninsula. Early settlers called it Shoalwater Bay, named for its shallow, slow-moving, ever-changing character.

Bay Center/Willapa Bay KOA *(Pacific Co.'s MOST UNIQUELY WASHINGTON CG)*

The peninsula and small island town of Bay Center cranes its neck right out into the middle of Willapa Bay, surrounding itself with tidewaters and the briny hint of shellfish.

Overview: Located 14 miles southwest of South Bend and 1 mile southwest of Bay Center on 5 acres with 1000' of saltwater shoreline, open April 7 to November 8; GPS 46.621376, -123.953483

Facilities: Familiar KOA facilities include bathrooms with showers and running water, picnic tables, fire pits, a playground, laundry, Kamp Store, game room, horseshoes, pet area, Wi-Fi, cable TV (limited channels), camp hosts, and an RV dump. There are also personal touches here, from pet hitches fashioned from driftwood to local marine details in the landscaping.

Recreation: Kayaking is extraordinary and unique on the tidal estuaries of the Bone, Palix, and Niawakum Rivers, with its wildlife viewing. These coastal wetland and estuary ecosystems are the highest quality examples remaining of native coastal salt marsh communities in Washington. Softshell clam digging on muddy or sandy beaches where these streams meet the Bay include cockles, bent-noses, butters, and gapers. On the gravelly bayshore itself, clam digging includes the Manila clam.

Campsites (58 sites for tents and RVs up to 65', including 42 with partial or full hookups 20/30/50 amp, 4 cabins, 2 yurts, reservable): Sites run the gamut from poor to good privacy, all surrounded by a tall canopy of conifers and deciduous trees, with lush foliage between some sites. Sites are back-ins and pull-throughs, with some pull-through patio sites available. Pads are typically gravel or natural material.

Trip Notes: When camping on Willapa Bay, keep a few things in mind: this is not Hawaii; this is not the coast of Maine; this is not even the ocean. Rather, this is a primal, evolving, and endless stretch of pristine tidewater that can be glassy and still one moment, and a series of delicate, brackish tidepools and rivulets the next. This is in fact one of the largest and most well-preserved saltwater estuaries in the world. It was the feature story on several episodes of Charles Kurault's television program "Sunday Morning" on CBS. It is an area that lead him and his viewers to look over the primitive landscape and think deeper thoughts about the creation of the cosmos and life itself. But it is not for everyone. Less reflective individuals might better appreciate one of Pacific County's ocean beaches. That having been said, this lovely KOA park is nicely laid out, providing many amenities in a very isolated and unique environment. The service from owners Iris and Ken is exceptional, not based on the awards they have won, but from details ranging from helping people park their RVs to running a well-stocked Kampstore with prices comparable to a regular store. The Park is somehow cozy and rustic without being primitive: showers, laundry room, and sites are all well-maintained, even in inclement weather. You'll feel at home here.

Bruceport Co. Park *(Pacific Co.'s BEST BIKE-IN CG)*
The sole inhabitants of the once promising town of Bruceport are seagulls and campers. Decades of erosion destroyed the town but created indescribable camping vistas of one of a kind Willapa Harbor.

Overview: This rolling campground is located 5 miles southwest of South Bend on 42 acres on a bluff overlooking Willapa Bay with limited saltwater shoreline, operated by Pacific Co. Parks at 141' elevation, open mid-May to Labor Day weekend; GPS 46.68615, -123.88775.

Facilities: Ample amenities include bathrooms with showers, running water, picnic tables, fire rings, a covered shelter (reservations required), camp hosts, and an RV dump.

Recreation: The Bay offers oyster harvesting (license required), plus kayaking on the tidal estuaries of the Bone, Palix, and Niawakum Rivers.

Campsites (45 sites for tents or RVs up to 30', including 8 sites with full hookups 30/50-amp, 5 group sites -- A1, A2, A13, A14, A15 -- requiring reservations): Tall

"Older Growth" spruces and firs line the campground, with a large rolling grassy pasture in the middle. Pads are on grass or native material. Note that while the signs say "RV Park" this is a better campground for tents or small trailers, as the hookup sites are side-by-side and in full sun (some RV campers may prefer the better-appointed Willapa Bay/Bay Center KOA just south). Several sites have a view of Willapa Harbor. Both fans and critics will point out that each site is unique in size and shape with privacy depending upon occupancy. A short trail leads down to the shoreline. Bicyclers have the advantage here, as the park is just off Highway 101, close to services in South Bend/Raymond, and most sites are first come, first served. It lies 5 miles beyond Willapa Hills Trail S.P., making it a camping destination for bicyclers and hikers coming from as far away as Chehalis.

Trip Notes: The park has a beauty and uniqueness not typical of county parks. Keep in mind that views are of the Harbor, not the more tidal Willapa Bay to the south. While beach viewing is available via a beach trail, beach walking on the muddy shore is limited. It is, however, the best forested campground in the county, where sea and shore sit marvelously on top of one another.

Local Attractions: Visit the historic Pacific County Courthouse in South Bend with its stained-glass dome and gardens. The Carriage Museum and metal sculptures along Highway 101 in Raymond are also worth a look-see.

Long Beach Peninsula

At 30 miles long, and as narrow as one mile wide, the Long Beach Peninsula proudly proclaims itself the "World's Longest Beach." With land at a premium, camping is largely restricted to tight RV parks and small groups of cabins -- with tent camping limited to the large State Parks and private camping resorts. But as they've said since the sixties, the beach goes on...

Cape Disappointment S.P. (Pacific Co.'s MOST APPEALING CG TO THE SENSES and BEST CG FOR ENTIRE FAMILIES:

This is the land largely reclaimed from the sea at the point where the tumultuous 4-mile wide Columbia River dumps into the normally peaceful Pacific Ocean. Many ships have met their end here, but campers over many decades have been able to face nature head-on, experiencing the sheer beauty and violent nature of land versus ocean and river.

Overview: This iconic campground is located 43.8 miles southwest of South Bend and 3 miles west of Ilwaco on 1882 acres with over 2 miles of ocean and Columbia River shoreline, open year-round; GPS 46.29139, -124.07083.

Facilities: Good facilities include bathrooms with showers (4 ADA), picnic tables and fire grills, a Camp Store and restaurant, the Lewis and Clark Interpretive Center Museum, 2 amphitheaters, a boat ramp, 135' of boat dock, camp hosts, and an RV dump. This park also includes not one, but two lighthouses within the campground: the iconic postcard star 65' North Head Lighthouse perched 194' above the Pacific Ocean, and the older, 53' Cape Disappointment Lighthouse resting 220' above the Columbia River.

Cape Disappointment Lighthouse shines north toward the Northhead Lighthouse where both protect and shine down on the State Park

Recreation: Both lighthouses are accessible by 8 miles of hiking trails within the park. Trails include the McKenzie Head Interpretive Trail (0.25 miles, the Benson Beach Trail (0.45 miles), the North Head Trail (1.5 miles), the Coastal Forest Loop Trail (1.5 miles), and the extensive Discovery Trail. Beach combing is popular along kid-friendly Waikiki Beach and Benson Beach. Ship watching and salmon fishing are popular off the jetty. Razor clam digging is excellent along the Long

Beach Peninsula. An appropriate fishing license is required for both fishing and clamming. Check with the WDFW before setting out.

Campsites (220 sites for tents or RVs up to 45', including 60 with full hookups and 1 with water & electricity 50-amp hookups, 5 ADA sites, 5 H/B sites, 3 cabins & 13 yurts, reservable): Sites are in two general areas. Near the entrance, sites border small Lake O'Neil, but have little foliage, less privacy, and are smaller. Their popularity stems from close proximity to Waikiki Beach, which is popular with families. Sites in the 5 Loops are forested with pine, Douglas fir and spruce, and rest among former sea stacks once surrounded by water. These sites are larger and more private, with good access to 2-mile long Benson Beach.

Trip Notes: I have long since encouraged campers to "experience Washington from the Ground Up." Here, however, campers will experience Washington from the ocean up. Our sites (151-152) were nestled at the base of the highest sea stacks, when the construction of the North Jetty stabilized the shifting sand, adding 600 acres of land to the Park. Camping on former ocean, these rocks towered over us, inviting climbing by our 11-year old camper who magically persuaded me to join him. There is obviously some kind of mojo at work here. My dog Boca and I walked the entire length of Benson Beach, mesmerized by the lighthouses that framed the beach like bookends. Magic, indeed.

Washington History: This campground is part of the greater Lewis and Clark National Historic Park, which continues into NW Oregon. This was the spot where Lewis and Clark first viewed the Pacific Ocean. Later, the area became a major military defense on the Columbia River, as evidenced by nearby Fort Columbia S.P., which was active from 1896 until the end of WWII.

Local attractions: Nearby Fort Columbia S.P. attests to the area's military past, which has been largely obliterated at Cape Disappointment S.P. (formerly Fort Canby). Leadbetter S.P. and Wildlife Refuge at the end of the 30-mile Long Beach Peninsula is second to none for wildlife viewing, with saltwater marsh on the bay side, open ocean on the other, and a major nesting place for many bird species, including the Snowy Plover. The beach town of Long Beach includes arcades, shops, restaurants, and Marsh's Free Museum, featuring the Jake the Alligator Man, a two-headed goat, and the World's Largest Frying Pan.

Radar Ridge/Naselle Valley Area

The Finnish influence in Pacific Co. is evident from north to south -- and that brings us to the Naselle Valley. Finnish immigrants began sailing up the Naselle River in the 1880s to clear mammoth trees for farms, with trees always "falling, falling, falling." Like the people, the campgrounds are few, but the thick forests above the Valley, where the campgrounds sit, have survived the tenacious swing of Scandinavian axes.

Snag Lake CG *(Pacific Co.'s BEST RUSTIC and BEST FREE CG):*
Radar Ridge, a now defunct Cold War Aircraft Control Warning (AC&W) facility, gives panoramic views of the Naselle River Valley, Willapa Bay, the Long Beach Peninsula, the Pacific Ocean and the Columbia River. But half-way up the hill is the perfect little campground on the perfect little pond in the woods that provides both good fishing and unspoiled camping.

Overview: This tiny campground is located 5 miles west of Naselle, operated by the DNR at 100' elevation, open year-round; GPS 46.423762, -123.821788.

Facilities: Minimal amenities include a vault toilet, picnic tables, fire grills, and a boat ramp (single wide). Two fishing platforms allow fishing poles to maneuver the snags, which attract fish seeking food and shade. No drinking water or garbage service is provided.

Recreation: Fishing is popular from April through October (the ponds are stocked) for rainbow trout and cutthroat. Most campers make the short drive up to Radar Ridge to take in panoramic views of SW Washington and NW Oregon. Trails connect Snag Lake to Western Lake, which is also stocked for fishing.

Campsites (8 sites: 2 drive-ins and 6 walk-ins, no reservations, FREE with Discover Pass): The two drive-in sites are big enough for small self-contained RVs for those who dare taking them up the 4-mile rocky road. The walk-in sites, however, are the star, located in good forest that also has good visibility of the Lake. All sites are well shaded, and most are very private. A low, even breeze seems to keep mosquitoes in check, but come prepared.

Trip Notes: Most reviewers refer to this as "a snag-filled pond in the woods." They nailed it; but watch the faces of the little boys running along the trails with fishing poles, and even the adults roasting their catch over charcoal, and the charm of this place will sink in.

Washington History: Radar Ridge was a fully manned U.S. Air Force facility built to stave off Soviet threats during the Cold War following WWII. It operated from 1950 until 1964 and became the site for radar weapon testing of U.S. aircraft and as well as "war games" for practice in case of enemy attack. It was one of three such sites in Washington. At the summit, satellite and radar equipment are still used for area businesses. At the base, the former officer quarters have been converted into the Naselle Youth Camp, a state juvenile rehabilitation institution. The lakes were later developed by the DNR for local recreation.

For more photos of Pacific Co. CGs, or more about BOAT-IN CGs, consult campeverycountywa.com

PEND OREILLE COUNTY (Newport/Metaline Falls)

Pronounced "pawned array," this remote northeastern corner of the state became the last county created in Washington. The origin of the name is controversial but is possibly a shortened version of the expression "pendant oreille" coined by French-Canadian trappers referring to the "ear hangings" or shell earrings worn by native peoples. History has never confirmed this. Regardless, this is a very singular county with moose, caribou, caves, north-flowing rivers, and wildlife that are rare or non-existent in the rest of the state.

The Pend Oreille River Water Trail
Pend Oreille County's most unique feature is its river of the same name that runs north -- a natural, physical oddity -- flowing out of Idaho's Lake Pend Oreille into Canada. Lumberjacks in the northern forests couldn't float their logs to mills in the south of the county, which led to railroads becoming the chief means of transport. But that leaves more river for us -- namely, 70 miles of river exploration, running with the current from Newport to one mile from the Canadian Border at Boundary Dam, sharing all the unique brand of beauty that only this county can provide.

#All campgrounds featured below on the Pend Oreille River Water Trail are accessible by motor vehicle#

Boundary Dam CG (Pend Oreille Co.'s *MOST UNIQUELY WASHINGTON CG*):
Here you can camp at the upper edge of a major Dam with almost total quiet, camp on a small island, or camp near multiple beautiful waterfalls upstream.
Overview: Located 12 miles northeast of Metaline on 17 mile-long, 1793-acre Boundary Dam Reservoir, operated by Seattle City Light at 1995' elevation, open mid-April to Labor Day; GPS 48.985662724 -117.3418.

Facilities: Well-kept and friendly, the campground contains restrooms with flush toilets and running water (sorry, no showers, though there are plans for the future). The staff of the dam has been known to chop firewood for campers (?!). And as the name would imply, they have a pretty swell boat launch. The restored Old Miner's Cabin is within the campground but is for viewing only and is not for rent.

Recreation: This site is the northern terminus of the Pend Oreille River Water Trail, which covers 70 miles of the Pend Oreille River, beginning in Oldtown, ID, then follows the river north the length of the county all the way up to the Boundary Dam Campground and Boat Launch. Several "unofficial" campsites have also developed, and Seattle City Light plans to expand camping areas in the future. For now, most people prefer to canoe or kayak the 12-mile northern stretch starting beneath the Box Canyon Dam, past the deep canyon walls, through the twisting Z Canyon, and onto the flat water of Boundary Reservoir to view 200' Peewee Falls. Wildlife viewing is remarkable at the Flume Creek Mountain Goat Viewing Area (see below). Hiking is possible in the Salmo-Priest Wilderness Area.

Campsites (8 sites for RVs up to 36' and 12 tent sites, no hookups or reservations, FREE of charge): The sites themselves are just 0.1 miles behind Boundary Dam and are forested. There are additional primitive boat-in sites near Z Canyon and the "Island" that some take as overnight side trips while camping here.

Trip Notes: This very flat, very open campground has the look of being newly discovered, and about to explode with popularity. Seattle City Light has already installed Paul Bunyan-sized picnic tables, beautiful concrete pads, and have kept the campground spotless. While it may appear more appealing to adults, we also saw kids having fun. Giggly, energy burning, full grin fun. This place is gonna be a star.

Boundary Dam Itself: The Dam is a 42-inch thick arched concrete structure between two rock cliffs. It contains 265,000 horsepower turbines and supplies 45% of the electricity for Seattle City Light in faraway western Washington. There is an observation platform at Vista House Observation Area. A Visitors Gallery is built within a massive limestone cavern.

Local Alternatives: The most accessible is Campbell Park/Box Canyon Dam CG (four sites for tents or small RVs, operated by the Pend Oreille PUD, FREE). This is a small but beautiful forested area adjacent to a grassy area around a small swimming pond ideal for younger children. One campsite has a bridge across a small creek, while another has a waterfall within the campsite. This would be an excellent getaway for a young family where the kids would be entertained all day at the swimming pond but always within view.

Local Attractions include the Box Canyon Dam, which represents the only break in the Pend Oreille River Water Trail, a monolithic structure that is owned by the county PUD. Box Canyon Dam requires a portage. The North Pend Oreille Lions Club Excursion Train ride runs 6 weeks a year between Ione and Metaline Falls. It provides views of the Box Canyon Dam, plus rock cliffs and tunnels not seen from the highway. Flume Creek Mountain Goat Viewing Area provides an opportunity to observe mountain goats, bighorn sheep, moose, woodland caribou, and white-tailed and mule deer. Even further north, Crawford S.P. features Gardner Cave, a 1055' limestone cave discovered by a local bootlegger in 1899, where guided tours are given up to four times daily. The bootlegger has since moved on.

Panhandle CG (Pend Oreille Co.'s *BEST BIKE-IN CG*)

This beautiful eastern shore campground combines features from both the River and the Kalispell Indian Reservation, where traditions survive, and the public is welcome.

Overview: Located 30 miles north of Newport near Usk on 20 acres on the east bank of Pend Oreille River adjacent to Leclerc Creek Wildlife Area, operated by the USFS at 2100' elevation, open Mid-May to mid-September; GPS 48.5099, -117.2715.

Facilities include ADA-friendly vault toilets, running water, picnic tables, fire pits, tent pads, a swimming area, boat launch, and camp host in summer months.

Recreation: Fishing is notable for smallmouth bass. ORVs are prohibited in the campground and on the trail. A walking trail between Usk and Cusick follows the Pend River on the western side with great river viewing. The many abandoned pilings in the river have been reclaimed by local ospreys for nests and photographic opportunities for birders.

Campsites (13 sites for tents or RVs up to 45', no hookups, reservable): Grass and gravel sites are large and open but wooded and private. These are the best riverfront sites on the Pend Oreille River.

Trip Notes: The good news: this is a great campground for viewing a great river. The bad news: while it sits right on the River on one side, it is just off the busy Le Clerc Road on the other. I would be uncomfortable having very small children here, as a quick escape from parents could end in disaster. What is good for the big folks isn't so great for the tiny ones. Edgewater CG (below) might be a better choice.

Local Alternative: Edgewater CG (20 sites for tents and RVs up to 70', operated by the USFS, reservable, open seasonally) is closer to activities in Ione (across the beautiful Red Bridge) but further from Kalispell tribal activities. The campsites above the River are nicely spaced with an architectural flare, but those away from the River are bordering on shabby due to the condition of the forest here. All campsites are on a single road that parallels the River. The only river access is at the end of the spur in the Day Use Area.

Local Attractions include the Manresa Grotto, a system of caves still used by the Kalispell Tribe for sacred ceremonies. The Kalispell Tribal Center is home to their yearly powwow in August, with fields of buffaloes always grazing as if unaware of adoring tourists.

Pioneer Park (Pend Oreille Co.'s *MOST APPEALING CG TO THE SENSES*)

This little park sprung into existence in 2006 as a southern kayak/canoe put-in to the Pend Oreille River Water Trail. It combines perfect forest campsites with a short but remarkable river walk, fusing the best of both. This pretty place may be just the bit of perfect camping you're looking for, even if boating is not on your agenda.

Overview: This newbie is located 3 miles west of Newport on 5 acres on the eastern shore of the Pend Oreille River, operated by the US Forest Service at 2000' elevation, open mid-May to mid-September; GPS 48.2129, -117.0542.

Facilities include vault toilets, running water, picnic tables, fire pits, a picnic shelter, boat launch, boardwalk trail to the River, and a dog swimming beach (dogs are not allowed elsewhere on the River). There are camp hosts in the summer.

Recreation: Fishing is good for largemouth and smallmouth bass. The 0.3-mile Pioneer Park Heritage Trail #321 unfolds the history of the Kalispell Tribe through twelve artistic, interpretive displays, plus dramatic views of the Pend Oreille River. Water-skiing and boating (35 mph limit) are popular, as the River is a short walk from the campground. This is near the southern boundary of the Pend Oreille River Water Trail, where kayakers and canoers can float and paddle as far north as Box Canyon without requiring portage. This is the most popular put-in along the Water Trail.

Campsites (16 sites for tents and RVs up to 40', no hookups, reservable): Sites are arranged in a single loop forested with western white pine and western cedars, with deciduous trees closer to the River (no riverfront sites). Privacy is good here, with spacious sites equipped with gravel tent pads divided by good vegetation, including wild roses and thimbleberry.

Trip Notes: Oh, so this is what a modern campground looks like. Enough room to turn your vehicle around at the boat launch. Separate dog and people swimming beaches so others don't have to tolerate your overly eager Labrador retriever. Large, spacious campsites that don't look directly across from each other. Interpretive trails signs about things that matter (and not another description of the northwest huckleberry). Vintage-looking rockery added so that the Park doesn't have that all too familiar cookie-cutter look. It engages the senses and should be many people's go-to campground.

Colville National Forest

The Colville National Forest is living proof that not all of Eastern Washington is flat. In fact, this 1.5-million-acre forest includes the Okanogan, Kettle River, and Selkirk Mountain ranges, which are considered foothills of the Rocky Mountains.

East Sullivan Lake (Pend Oreille Co.'s *BEST CG FOR ENTIRE FAMILIES*)

Sullivan Lake is a reservoir created by Sullivan Dam, built in 1911. A second dam north of the Lake on Sullivan Creek created Mill Pond and included a hydroelectric plant (now abandoned) and interrupted a habitat for native fish species, as well as covering a remarkable stretch of whitewater rapids that could provide remarkable recreational opportunities. In 2013, after a long court battle, approval was granted to remove Mill Pond Dam and restore Sullivan Creek for improved outdoor recreation. Stay tuned. In the meantime, enjoy this very fun set of campgrounds.

Overview: Located 7.2 miles south of Metaline Falls on the north end of 1291-acre Sullivan Lake, operated by the USFS at 2592' elevation, open mid-May through October; GPS 48.8391, -117.2795.

Facilities include ADA-friendly vault toilets, running water, picnic tables, fire rings, tent pads, swimming area, boat launch, an Air Strip, and camp hosts. The Group Camp is open from Memorial Day Weekend through Labor Day Weekend.

Recreation: Swimming and boating are the biggest recreational draws. Hikers and horses alike enjoy the 4.2-mile Lakeshore Trail with access to Salmo-Priest Wilderness (a designated National Scenic Trail) and a 0.6-mile Interpretive Trail. Gold panners have had luck on nearby Sullivan Creek, where an area is set aside for panning and prospecting.

Campsites (38 tent/RV sites for RVs up to 28', one group camp for up to 40, no hookups, reservable): Sites do not have a direct view of the Lake but can see it through the trees. The campground has three loops (Fir, Cedar, and Pine) with sites tucked into a stand of mixed conifers including cedar and Douglas fir. Fir Loop is the largest and closest to the boat ramp. Pine Loop is close to the swimming beach and has numerous double wide campsites but shorter parking aprons. Cedar Loop has all the campground's pull-throughs which are designated double sites. The Group Camp is a tight loop of campsites very near the Sullivan Lake boat launch, with good all-around access to the Lake.

Trip Notes: So, we walk into a grocery store in Metaline Falls, a bit road weary and unable to find maps for sale and ask for directions to Sullivan Lake. Suddenly, half a dozen customers come up to us and proceed to tell us all about the campgrounds at the same time. Sullivan Lake is obviously the favorite local campground of this magnificent little community. That can be good and bad. It can certainly be one of the liveliest, funnest campgrounds around, but also the busiest. East Sullivan clearly has the best campsites of the 3 Sullivan Lake campgrounds (see below).

Local Alternatives: A better choice for some RV'ers would be Noisy Creek CG, 2 miles south of East Sullivan CG, also run by USFS (19 sites including 10 ADA sites, no hookups, one Group Camp for up to 40, reservable, open weekend before Memorial Day weekend through mid-Sept.). Facilities feature a swimming area and boat ramp. Campsites are in two loops, Eagle and Bighorn, on the terraced slopes of south Sullivan Lake. None face the Lake, but a few face "noisy" Harvey Creek. A second alternative is West Sullivan CG near East Sullivan CG, also run by USFS,

Elevation 2592' (10 tent/RV sites, no hookups, reservable, open mid-May through mid-October). Facilities include a floating swimming platform. There is still evidence of its Civilian Conservation Corps beginnings in structures such as the bathhouse. Campsites consist of two overlapping sections in a stand of mixed conifers, including cedar, tamarack, and some birch. They do not, however, compare to the perfect campsites at East Sullivan.

Big Meadow Lake CG (Pend Oreille Co.'s *BEST FREE* and *BEST RUSTIC CG*)
This is the campground that named itself. Originally named Heather Lake, as flood control from Aladdin Mountain, this very unique reservoir was simply referred to by locals as "the big meadow lake," and the rest is history.
Overview: Located in a lovely meadow area just 6.6 miles west of Ione with 17 acres on 82.6-acre man made Big Meadow Lake, operated by the USFS at 3400' elevation, open the 4th Saturday in April through October; GPS 48.7293, -117.5636.
Facilities include vault toilets, fire pits, picnic tables, tent pads, the Hess Cabin Day Shelter, a boat ramp and fishing dock.
Recreation features fishing for burbot, lake trout, and sockeye salmon; Terry Trail (interpretive), Meadow Creek Trail #125 (1.5 miles and ADA-friendly), Lakeside Trail #126 (1.5 miles) and Homestead Trail (0.5 miles). A special feature is the Wildlife Observatory reclaimed from a dismantled fire lookout and reassembled on this site; from here may be viewed cougars, ducks, geese, elk, moose, and osprey.
Campsites (17 tent/RV sites for RVs of any size, one shelter, no hookups or drinking water, FREE with NW Forest Pass): Sites wrap around the south side of the Lake tucked in among aspen, tamarack, white fir, larch, and mixed conifers. Some sites are private, other have lake views, and are sufficiently dispersed to provide privacy and even isolation if desired.

Trip Notes: Visiting Big Meadow Lake is a lot like visiting your grandparents' small farm as a kid. Everything is in order, but not so manicured and mechanized to be mistaken for a commercial farm. It has character. There is no barn with a hayloft, but there is a lookout tower rescued from an old fire watch. There are no cows to feed, but moose wander through at will to feed in the marshes below the dam. And there are no electric fences to trick your little brother into touching, but decades old grape stake fences pop up everywhere, their original purpose long forgotten. This is the place to relax, feeling like your grandparents are making sure you are well fed and have an extra blanket.
Local attractions: None whatsoever. But then again, you won't be looking for any.

Southern County/Lakes Area

Pend Oreille Co. may not be the land of 10,000 lakes, but it does have nearly 60 named lakes, many of which lie in the accessible region between Spokane and Newport. Most of the homes in this area belong to people of a very outdoors state of mind, so campers are always in good company.

<u>Newport/Little Diamond KOA</u> (Pend Oreille Co.'s *BEST EQUIPPED/BEST CG OR RVs*)

The irony of this campground is that there really is no Little Diamond Lake. There is the very well-known Diamond Lake, which follows Highway 2 for several miles between Spokane and Newport. The lake in question is a pretty little thing with the unfortunate name of Mallard Marsh. But this is no swamp. In this case we have to agree with the promoters -- the lake is a little diamond.

<u>Overview</u>: This beautiful KOA is located 7 miles southwest of Newport with access to 30-acre Little Diamond Lake on 360 acres at 2,428' elevation, open April 15 to October 3; GPS 48.1428, -117.2221.

<u>Facilities</u>: Typical of KOAs, this Kampground is well-equipped with bathrooms/showers, Wi-fi, a swimming pool, hot tub, spa, lodge, baseball diamond, barbecue circle, playground, picnic shelter, recreation room, pool tables, pet area, boat ramp, walking trails, a golf driving range, a Disc Golf course, Kamp Store, and RV dump.

<u>Recreation</u>: Fishing is good for bass, Kamloops trout, and rainbow trout. Human-powered boating is popular, with rentals for paddleboats, canoes and mini-kayaks. Golfers will enjoy the driving range and disc golf.

<u>Campsites</u> (112 sites for tents and RVs of any size with hookups for water & electric 30/50-amp, reservable): Sites are average in size, wooded and shady. There is some privacy due to the careful inclusion of trees and foliage. Tent sites on the periphery have the most space. There are also open, grassy spaces that divide the campsites up into smaller groups, reducing any feeling of congestion.

<u>Trip Notes</u>: I love many of the KOAs, and most of the USFS campgrounds. This seems to combine both. It has great amenities, well-manicured lawns, and wide appeal. The addition of the golf driving range and disc golf course makes the park much larger than most; plus, this KOA, much to its credit, has left the foliage, trees on the periphery, and the Lake very much in their natural state. It's not so much a compromise as it is a very well thought out fusion of the best of two worlds.

For more photos of Pend Oreille Co. CGs, or more about HIKE-IN CGs, consult
campeverycountywa.com

PIERCE COUNTY (Tacoma/MRNP)

PIERCE

This county has so many distinct regions surrounding the rugged City of Tacoma that you may need to camp several different places before you can grasp its complexity. Start with Mount Rainier National Park, the Key Peninsula, Chinook Pass, and the Nisqually River Plateau before venturing into more remote areas.

Mount Rainier National Park (MRNP)

Mount Rainier among the most recognizable mountain peaks, plus the most glaciated peak in the contiguous U.S.A. It is ranked third of the 128 ultra-prominent mountain peaks of the United States, and spawns six major rivers (the Carbon, Cowlitz, Mowich, Nisqually, Puyallup, and White Rivers). More to the point, it forms the backdrop for much of the recreation in Pierce County and beyond.

Cougar Rock CG at MRNP (Pierce Co.'s *MOST UNIQUELY WASHINGTON CG*)

Set at the southwest corner of 14,410' Mount Rainier, location is the word here, as this semi-rustic campground is close to MRNP's most popular destinations, including Paradise Lodge, Narada Falls, and Longmire.

Overview: Located 14 miles east of Ashford and 2 miles east of Longmire on the Nisqually River at 3180 elevation, open late May to late September; GPS 46.7674, -121.7927.

Facilities: Moderate facilities include bathrooms with flush toilets, drinking water, picnic tables, fire grills, RV dump station, and a General Store 2 miles away in Longmire. The Nisqually River is accessible from the Day Use Area across Highway 706.

Recreation: Hiking is spectacular here, and we strongly recommend acquiring a topographical map of the area. Hiking trails accessible directly from the campground include the 0.7-mile Trail of Shadows (easy); the 2.2-mile Carter

Falls/Madcap Falls Loop Trail, the 4.6-mile Rampart Ridge Loop Trail (both moderate); and the 93-mile Wonderland Trail (strenuous) that encircles Mt. Rainier, passing through Longmire, Paradise, and Indian Henry's Hunting Ground. Many other trails start a short drive from the campground, including Christine Falls 4.5 miles east of Longmire (easy), 2-mile Kautz Creep Loop Trail 2.2 miles east of Longmire (moderate), 5.6-mile Comet Falls/Van Trump Park Trail and 7.2-mile Eagle Peak Saddle Loop Trail near Longmire (strenuous).

Campsites (173 sites for tents or RVs up to 35', no hookups, 5 group sites for up to 12 people each, reservable): Sites are small to medium, most with average privacy, many pull-throughs, most hemmed in by trees. The quietest campsites, however, are in Loop E, which does not allow generators. The campground contains one lookout at the Mountain, borders the Nisqually River, and has the best access to Paradise Lodge. In short, this campground is the best in MRNP for location, but Ohanapecosh CG at MRNP (see under Lewis Co.) is the best for camping.

Trip Notes: This campground has a vintage, Boy/Girl Scout Summer Camp feel. The amphitheater has an especially strong yesteryear feel, and the accessibility of hiking trails is extraordinary (but no hiking trails for Fido).

Mowich Lake CG at MRNP (Pierce Co.'s *BEST FREE* and *RUSTIC CG*)
It may take some determination to drive here over the bumpy roads, but once you get here you will find the largest and deepest lake in MRNP, as well one of its most scenic locations.

Overview: Located off Highway 165 six miles inside the Mowich Entrance of MRNP at 4955' elevation, open early July to early October; GPS 46.939, -121.862.

Facilities include vault toilets, tent platforms, secure food storage, and picnic tables at 10 of the campsites.

Recreation: Kayaking/canoeing on Mowich Lake is a must. This is also a good launching point for many trails in the Mt. Rainier Wilderness. The 93-mile Wonderland Trail, which circles Mt. Rainier, is accessible from the campground. Other options are the 5.6-mile round-trip to the Tolmie Peak Lookout which passes the alluring Eunice Lake; and 6-mile round-trip Spray Park Trail with its 354' cascading waterfall. Both are accessible from the campground.

Campsites (21 walk-in sites for tents, including 3 group sites, no hookups or reservations, FREE with America the Beautiful Pass or Park entrance fee): All sites require a 200-yard walk. All sites are close together with only a modest amount of shade. What you have is camping next to a beautiful, pristine lake with a picture-perfect reflection of MRNP. The only bad reviews from those who could not manage the 17-mile bumpy dirt road to get there. Camper beware.

Highway 410/Chinook Pass Region

This stretch of Highway 410 is commonly known as the Stephen Mather Memorial Parkway, and includes the beautiful Chinook Pass Scenic Byway. It travels through the Mt. Baker-Snoqualmie National Forest and Mount Rainier National Park with spectacular views of Mount Rainier, dense forests, towering peaks, old growth forests, and lush subalpine meadows. Hey campers -- don't just make this a drive-by! Take off your shoes and stay awhile.

<u>Silver Springs CG</u> (Pierce Co.'s *BEST BIKE-IN CG*)
Trees seem to grow in every direction here -- up, down, angled, sideways, and sometimes floating above the ground. No, this is not Avatar, but a heavily forested, natural campground where fallen trees are often left in their natural positions as nature intended.
<u>Overview</u>: Located 32 miles east of Enumclaw and 7 miles east of Greenwater on the White River, operated by the USFS at 2500' elevation, open April through September; GPS 46.9938, -121.5321.
<u>Facilities</u> include flush and vault toilets, drinking water, picnic tables, fire grills, and camp hosts.
<u>Recreation</u>: The main hiking trail accessible from the campground is the Crystal Lakes Trail, which starts near the Crystal Creek Guard Station near the east end of the campground along Highway 410. This is a 5.7-mile round trip hike passing alpine meadows, plus Lower and Upper Crystal Lakes and contains dispersed camping sites (see separate entry above). Other activities are close by in the northeast corner of MRNP, including the Sunrise Lodge.
<u>Campsites</u> (55 sites for tents and RVs up to 42', no hookups, 1 group site for 20-50, reservable): Sites are spacious and secluded. Natural forest hems in each campsite, providing excellent privacy. It is very shady, cooler in summer heat, but can take on a bit of a chill in cold weather. The most private sites are in the Loop with sites 36-42.
<u>Trip Notes</u>: This campground reminds you quickly that the White River, which marks the boundary of MRNP, is not far from its source at the Emmons Glacier on Mount Rainier. The riverbed is a rocky floodplain, with a braided river containing many gravel bars. The river struggles to find a single channel here, set between subalpine forest and rolling foothills. But that's its charm, and why it is so "White," still roiling and pushing ahead, inviting exploration. The forest also calls for a closer look. The roots of every tree -- interesting. The way the woodland creek winds its way through the forest and campground -- even more interesting. The many foot bridges across the creek -- nice touches that draw you back into the trees. It is also in close proximity to the lodge and activities around Sunrise with less use and less restrictions than the campgrounds within the National Park.

Local Alternative: The Dalles CG is located 2 miles east of Greenwater at the confluence of Minnehaha Creek and the White River, operated by the USFS at an elevation of 2200', open the Thursday before Memorial Day through Labor Day.

Key Peninsula Region
The Key Peninsula is a 16-mile long finger of land that sits in the middle of Puget Sound in the westernmost point of Pierce County. Its history is one of isolation with no roads, but residents traveling via the "Mosquito Fleet" of privately-run ferries. The community of Home began as an anarchist community that kept lawmakers on their toes for decades. The historic Glencove Hotel provided housing for "drummers" who sold their wares (some legal and some not) throughout the Peninsula. But "the boys" have settled down now, and with the building of roads and the passage of time, the "Key" has joined the mainstream of rural communities with some exceptional recreational opportunities.

Penrose Point S.P. (Pierce Co.'s *MOST APPEALING CG TO THE SENSES*)
Overview: This marine campground is located on a narrow channel near Lakebay on the Key Peninsula on 152 acres with 2 miles of saltwater shoreline on Mayo Cove and Carr Inlet, open year-round; GPS 47.259, -122.744.
Facilities include flush toilets, running water, showers, picnic tables, fire rings, 2 covered shelters, dock and moorage, 2.5 miles of hiking trails plus a 0.2-mile interpretive trail, and camp hosts.
Recreation: Shellfish digging is excellent here, as the area has been enhanced with Manila clams and oysters. Native littleneck clams, butter clams, horse clams, cockles and eastern softshell clams are also found on this beach.
Campsites (82 sites, no hookups, one group camp for 20-50, reservable): The best sites are 7, 8, 18, 36, 49, 52, 63, 65, 68, and 69. All are wooded, none on the water. They have average to good privacy, and shady or partly shady.
Trip Notes: The biggest surprise was the uniqueness of the campsites -- each is very different from the others -- no cookie-cutter state park sites here. Some were long and deep to accommodate large RVs, others were nestled into the rain forest-like vegetation, while others were terraced with steps built into the slope. For me, this is as good as camping gets. The madrona trees and the great picnic area/marina added special touches of color.

Nisqually River Region
The Nisqually River has its source at the Nisqually Glacier on Mount Rainier. It carves its way through the landscape for 81 miles, emptying into Puget Sound, and forming the border between Pierce County and Thurston County to the south. Along the way, Indian reservations, hydroelectric dams, and rural communities look to it for life, sustenance, and even recreational opportunities.

Alder Lake Park (Pierce Co.'s *BEST EQUIPPED/BEST CG FOR RVs, BEST CG FOR ENTIRE FAMILIES,* and *BEST GROUP CG*)

This is the best of the Tacoma Power Parks, the others being in Lewis Co. This Park is actually five different campgrounds: Main, Group Sites, Osprey, Elk Plain, and Rocky Point. It is definitely a family-oriented park with enough room and diversity for everyone.

Overview: Located near Eatonville/Elbe on 161 acres along 3,065-acre Alder Lake (reservoir), operated by Tacoma Public Utilities at 1227' elevation, open Jan. 1 to Dec. 20 yearly; GPS 46.7997, -122.2976.

Facilities: Extensive facilities vary according to campground. All sites have picnic tables, fire rings, and water faucets and bathrooms. There are 3 playgrounds (Elk Plain CG, Sunny Point Day Use, and Stacel Point Day Use). Some contain ADA-accessible bathrooms. There is a 20-slip boat moorage dock (Stacel Point Day Use) and 2 boat launches (Main CG and Rocky Point CG). Camp hosts are present during summer months.

Recreation: Fishing is good for rainbow and cutthroat trout, kokanee, largemouth bass, yellow perch, black crappie and bullhead catfish. Swimming is good, particularly at the Main CG/Stacel Point Day Use and Sunny Beach Day Use Areas. 330-foot high Alder Dam gives tours in summertime, but always gives the best views around.

Campsites (173 sites for tents or RVs of any size, plus 5 group camps; 111 sites have partial or full hookups 30/50 amp, all are reservable): For more information, see below.

Main CG: 78 sites, 74 with water & electric, plus 37 with full hookups 30/50 amp. The 16 tent sites have poor privacy, are small and sometimes uneven. Tent sites are best reserved in clusters of 2, the best being 55/56, 61/62, 63/64, 65/66. The RV sites have average privacy but can also be small and poorly designed, but with good pad maneuverability. Most sites are pull-throughs.

Group Camps: There are five small group camps of varying sizes: the largest has 15 individual sites, the smallest has 5 individual sites. The largest has 3 shelters and 3 fire rings. All but one group site has its own bathroom, which it shares with an adjoining group site. All group camps are grassy, well-maintained, and open at the expense of privacy.

Osprey CG includes 44 tent sites with no hookups. Many are designated as walk-in sites and tend to be small. Best sites are 236, 237, 238, 239, and 242. This campground has a walking trail to the picnic area on the Lake (Stacel Point). There is some road and pedestrian noise (it is adjacent to the Group Camp) but is the best tent-only area in the park. (see comments below)

Elk Plain CG includes 25 sites, 24 with water & electric hookups 30/50-amp, plus one walk-in site (#308, which may be the best single site, and the only one allowing tents, but has much foot traffic to the Lake). But this one is a quandary. It has the campsites closest to the water, but it is essentially a small tight triangle centered around a children's play area. It is so tight, in fact, that many people fired up their charcoal grills right on the narrow road, making it only a matter of time before they get knocked over and someone gets hurt. For the more careful campers who enjoy fishing, and who find it beneficial to have their children in view, I think it can work. Other fisherman might want to consider Rocky Point CG.

Rocky Point CG includes 25 RV sites, all with water & electric hookups 30/50-amp. No tents are allowed. This is close to Highway 7 and has the most highway noise of the four campgrounds. Best sites are 407, 408, and 409. The strength of the other sites is the easy lake access, taller trees and vegetation, and reasonable privacy for sites on the periphery (the sites in the center are closer together). It is located about 4 miles from the main campground. It not only has the best fishing (feeder streams enter the lake here), but also very wooded, some with lake views, many of which have good privacy. If you are a fisherman, you might consider camping here first. The kids will also like it, as there is plenty to do.

Trip Notes: We have mixed feelings about Alder Lake, some very good (the Group Sites and Osprey CG in particular), and others less positive. The Main CG was designed a long time ago, with sites wide and shallow, following the contour of the roads, rather than extending back into the woods. It is the first camping experience when we felt intruded upon by other people's children. This was due more to the design of the campsites, than the individuals in question (most of whom were great neighbors). I can only recommend camping for those with families and RVs (the tent sites are far too open to recommend) or those who don't mind the higher level of activity. Camper beware.

On a more positive note, the Group CG and Osprey CG (which are adjacent to one another) are the park's strength. The excellent group camps are grassy, well designed, and spacious, but lacking privacy. I recommend these for large, mixed groups, as the bathrooms and shelters are quite good. For tent campers, this is where you want to be. The walk-in sites are extremely well designed on a hillside, but all terraced and flat, albeit somewhat small. The parking is designed so that you won't have to carry your equipment far, and, unlike the main campground, the sites are surrounded by tall trees and vegetation, making for average to good privacy with good shade, keeping the temperatures cooler in hot weather. It also has a footpath directly to the beach.

For more photos of Pierce Co. CGs or more about HIKE-IN CGs consult
campeverycountywa.com

SAN JUAN COUNTY (Friday Harbor/Eastsound/Lopez)

Paradise! 172 named islands, 4 islands with camping accessible by ferry, 16 boat-in only campgrounds, 4 DNR campgrounds, picturesque villages, gorgeous harbors, restaurants, luxurious resorts, primitive fishing camps, and all of it surrounded by pristine water. Paradise!

Orcas Island

This horseshoe-shaped island is the largest in the San Juan Chain providing every form of recreation from the most primitive and natural (Doe Bay) to fine dining and lodging (Rosario Resort). Most, however, will find the simpler accommodations at Deer Harbor and Moran State Park every bit as inviting.

Moran S.P. Ferry-In (San Juan Co.'s *BEST CG FOR ENTIRE FAMILIES*)
This sweeping State Park, founded in 1921, is the fourth largest in Washington. Its development by the Civilian Conservation Corps (CCC) in the 1930s make it arguably the most iconic in the entire State Park System.
Overview: This historic park is located on the east side of 57.7-square mile Orcas Island on 5,252 acres at elevations from 932' to 2409', open year- round; GPS 48.65956, -122.85796.
Facilities: The Park contains over 20 vintage structures built by the CCC. The most memorable is the Mount Constitution observation tower, which gives sweeping views of the San Juans and the mainland. The 3 Cascade Lake campgrounds (North End, Midway, South End) include picnic tables, fire grills, running water, bathrooms, showers, a snack bar, a formal swimming area, seasonal boat rentals, camp hosts, and an RV dump. There is a rentable Vacation House at Camp Moran. Other facilities vary among the 6 campgrounds (see more below).
Recreation: The Park includes two large freshwater lakes. 175.8-acre Cascade Lake is surrounded by a hiking trail. 194.5-acre Mountain Lake is warm for

swimming (by northwest standards) and good for kayaking. Both are stocked with rainbow, cutthroat, and kokanee trout. Smaller freshwater lakes (accessible on foot) include Twin Lakes and Summit Lake. Trails include 6 miles for horses, 11 miles for bikes, and 38 miles for hikers. There are 2 boat ramps (one on each lake) for non-motorized boats.

Campsites (117 sites for tents or RVs up to 45' and 34 sites for tents only, no hookups, plus a Group Camp for up to 56 people, reservable): There are 6 campgrounds within Moran S.P., the first three of which are set on Cascade Lake.

1. North End CG contains 52 sites near the entrance with a swimming area and log kitchen shelter. It is also near the RV dump, and less private with partial shade. Sites are slightly sloped with gravel pads. Three sites are pull-throughs. There is some traffic noise.

2. The 49 sites of Midway CG are the favorite of the Camp Every County Crew, due to its ideal setting on Cascade Lake and proximity to the boat launch. The few sites on the Lake (24-30) are the most private, and the best sites overall.

3. South End CG has 11 lake shore sites, including one ADA site with ADA accessible bathroom. This is the most popular and private camping.

4. A 6-site H/B campground lies just beyond Cascade Lake and is more primitive with an Adirondack Shelter and vault toilet. Campers with vehicles are not allowed. There are no reservations.

5. Mountain Lake CG is more rustic than camping on Cascade Lake. It has 19 sites in a single loop on a small peninsula surrounded by the Lake. Sites are relatively flat with partial shade and pads of native material. It has picnic tables, fire grills, and a vault toilet.

6. Group Camp - A single loop located near Mountain Lake, this 7-site campground features the Mt. Lake Picnic Shelter with a stone fireplace, and a plumbed bathroom.

Trip notes: This CCC-era campground greets you with a concrete arch that welcomes campers into a little piece of paradise. You will find yourselves so charmed by tree-lined Cascade Lake that you may not notice at first that the Park is made entirely out of native materials. The deer, who wander everywhere at will, will make you feel like you're part of the very landscape. On Mt. Constitution you'll find the Park's centerpiece -- the stone observation tower -- that is the highest point of the San Juan chain. On a clear day you'll be able to view Mt. Baker on the mainland with Vancouver Island Canada to the east.

Shaw Island

This pint-sized island, the smallest of the four islands connected by WA State ferries, lies at the geographical center of the San Juan Chain. As such, it is not to be overlooked, as island residents claim the San Juans revolve around Shaw.

<u>Shaw Island Co. Park Ferry-In</u> (San Juan Co.'s *BEST RUSTIC CG*)
Note that the Washington State Ferries make only irregular stops at Shaw Island, so plan accordingly.

<u>Overview</u>: This sandy, hidden away campground is located on the south end of 7.7-square mile Shaw Island at 54' elevation, open year-round; GPS 48.572323, -122.95212.

<u>Facilities</u>: These include a vault toilet, picnic tables, fire grills, water spigots in season, a boat launch, picnic shelter, baseball diamond, and sandy beaches.

<u>Recreation</u>: In addition to beach combing, boating, and baseball, you may want to delve into a little island combing. The island is very private (with 165 privacy-loving residents) but is interspersed with great photographic opportunities. These include island marine views, the one-room schoolhouse (still in operation), the museum fashioned out of the old log cabin post office, and the modern but rustic-looking library designed by Shaw Island resident Coonie Cameron.

<u>Campsites</u> (11 sites for tents only, including 2 H/B and one group site for up to 8 people, no hookups, reservable): Like the Island, the sites are quite small -- too small for RVs or trailers. Six sites rest on the bluff.

<u>Trip Notes</u>: Sure is a compact little thang. After staying on Orcas, the first thing we noticed about Shaw is there are no restaurants, B&Bs, motels, hotels, gas stations, boutiques, hardware stores, movie theaters, fast-food joints, sidewalks or streetlights. This, for us, is what gives it a rustic character. It's just camping here! We managed a one-nighter in our small tent trailer but won't bring it next time. This is for tenters only. What we have here is an island that is rustic on the outside but filled with curious and adventuresome people.

Lopez Island

The gentle topography of Lopez sets it apart from the rocky bluffs of San Juan Island, and the hills and mountains of Orcas Island. This is roughly 30 square miles of rolling farmlands, quiet bays and driftwood-strewn beaches, where sheep look up at you with curiosity, bicyclers are given the right-of-way, and residents wave at you from their cars. Lopez has been dubbed "the Friendly Isle."

<u>Spencer Spit S.P. Ferry-In</u> (San Juan Co.'s *MOST APPEALING CG TO THE SENSES*, and *BEST BIKE-IN CG*)
The 1/4-mile-long spit grows, shrinks, and disappears, depending on the tide. Views of Orcas Island, an old homestead for picnicking, and walk-in campsites make this a great camping destination.

<u>Overview</u>: This unique campground with its "disappearing beach" is located on the northeast side of Lopez Island on 200 acres, open year-round; GPS 48.534265, -122.861056.

Facilities: These include 2 bathrooms (no showers), running water, picnic tables, fire grills, 3 picnic shelters, one of which is old Spencer's 1913 homesteading cabin, a 15-table picnic area on the Spit, kayak and bike rentals, kayaking tours, 11 mooring buoys, 2 miles of hiking trails, camp hosts, and an RV dump station.

Recreation: Bicycling is king here, as Lopez offers the perfect conditions: quiet, flat roads, low traffic, and great rest stops at Lopez Village and Richardson. You will also find kayaking, crabbing, clamming, saltwater fishing, swimming, diving, and bird watching.

Campsites (37 sites for tents or small RVs, including 7 walk-in sites, including site 6 with an Adirondack shelter, plus 7 H/B sites, one Cascadia Marine Trail site, 3 group camps for 24-50 people each including the G1 site with an Adirondack shelter, no hookups, reservable): Sites are medium-sized with good privacy. Nine of the tent/RV sites are pull-throughs and popular with campers in small RVs, others are back-ins. Group Camp 2 is the largest of the 3 group tenting sites. Sites are separated by thick marine vegetation. All sites are flat with parking on gravel.

Trip notes: The Spit itself is fascinating, with views of nearby islands and passages. The island is perfectly flat, making it great for bicycling, passing fields of sheep and llama, and many bed & breakfasts. Camping was comfortable enough, but somewhat cramped, so people need to leave their campsites to appreciate the place to its fullest. The kayaking opportunities are good in the passage between Lopez and Decatur Islands. I must confess that, other than bicycling, I spent the majority of my time watching the fascinating beach and lagoon, which seemed in a constant state of change with the tide, sun, and clouds making it seem very much like a slowly turning kaleidoscope of iridescent colors.

Local Alternative: Odlin Co. Park sits near the Lopez Ferry terminal and offers 31 sites (10 of which are on the beach), vault toilets, and potable water. The sites accommodate RVs better than Spencer Spit, but there are no hookups.

San Juan Island

This, the second largest island in the San Juan Chain, is home to the quaint village of Friday Harbor, the upscale resort town of Roche Harbor, plus many small lakes, gravel beaches, rocky bluffs, and unobstructed marine views.

San Juan Co. Park (San Juan Co.'s *MOST UNIQUELY WASHINGTON CG*)

Rocky bluffs and gravel beaches overlook Haro Strait and with views of the Strait of San Juan de Fuca, the Olympic Peninsula, and Vancouver Island. It is also the site of the only west coast war with Britain, the Pig War of 1859, but now it is a peaceful place (no more pigs or bullets, please).

Overview: This small but popular campground is located on the west side of 55.5-square mile San Juan Island on 12 acres with 300' of rocky beach on Smallpox Bay, open year-round; GPS 48.5416, -123.1597.

Facilities: Included are flush toilets, running water, picnic tables, fire grills, a small picnic shelter, historic and newly restored Brann Cabin, a pebbly beach, boat launch, and camp hosts.

Recreation: Historic English Camp is adjacent to the Park (see below). San Juan Island is known for whale watching, sea kayaking, bicycling, and fishing.

Campsites (19 sites for tents or RVs up to 25', plus one H/B/kayaker site, a walk-in group camp for up to 20 people, no hookups, reservable): Most sites have water views across an open meadow surrounded by trees. There are no barriers between sites, so privacy is compromised, though sites are large enough to minimize this. There are no waterfront sites. Parking pads are on grass.

Trip Notes: My oldest memory of this Park was camping here as a child with my family. I wandered down to the small, protected harbor to see, 20 or 30 yards offshore beneath the crystalline waters, the distinct shape of a giant conch shell. Wanting this shell for myself, I kept my discovery from my family and especially my two aggressive brothers. I awkwardly asked the park host about low tide, in the roundabout way only a 9-year old could muster, and set my sights on 6:00 a.m. I snuck out of bed the next morning, sleeping little all night long, and wandered down to the shore undiscovered. I looked out into the surf. There it was, the object of my desire, the one thing that I thought would earn me permanent bragging rights with my brothers, but... it wasn't a conch shell in the TRUEST sense. Not quite. But it stared back at me, with its two giant eyes, neither judging nor mocking me, with a woeful empathy. No, the giant fish head I mistook for a conch shell seemed certain to keep my guilty little secret forever. I have never told my family his story, but now they can laugh all they like.

Historic Notes: The old 1890s cabin of homesteader Lewis Brann has been accurately preserved to its original condition, sitting among the campsites to remind campers of the Park's historic past.

Local Attractions: Lime Kiln S.P. is a 36-acre day use only park that is considered one of the best whale watching spots on earth. From the safety of a 1919-era lighthouse on a sea cliff, visitors are greeted from below by spouting Orcas, slap-happy gray whales, barking sea lions and splashing porpoises.

Adjacent to San Juan Co. Park is the historic English Camp where, in 1849, the killing of a pig brought England and the Unites States to the brink of war over ownership of the Island. The American Camp is located 5 miles south, as both Camps co-existed peacefully until the 1872 when the Island was declared the territory of the U.S. A few buildings, a formal garden, and a cemetery remain in the English Camp, along with a 45-minute loop through woodland and along the bay. There are also interpretive programs throughout the year.

<u>Lakedale Resort</u> (San Juan Co.'s *BEST EQUIPPED/BEST CG FOR RVs*)
This Resort is surrounded by three long-armed spring fed lakes, providing glamping opportunities for campers and jetsetters alike.

<u>Overview</u>: This best-equipped of campgrounds is privately owned on 82 acres between the towns of Roche Harbor and Friday Harbor, open Mar 1 to Oct 31; GPS: 48.57617, -123.082258.

<u>Facilities</u> include picnic tables and fire pits, bathrooms with showers, chemical toilets, running water, boat rentals, sport courts, a General Store, a Mess Tent for Cabin and Cottage guests (continental breakfast), Wi-Fi, and camp hosts. Lodging includes 21 luxury canvas cabins, 1 canvas bunkhouse, 6 log cabins, 7 yurts, a 10-room hotel/lodge, and 1 on-site Airstream rental.

<u>Recreation</u>: On-site recreation includes lake fishing, boating, swimming, and volleyball.

<u>Campsites</u> (41 tent sites, 5 sites with water/electric sites 50 amps for RVs of any size, all reservable): I will comment only on the tent and RV sites, as the management of most private resorts prefer to speak for themselves on their lodging facilities (http://www.lakedale.com). Many of the tent sites have lakes views, but the RV sites do not. The RV sites are well spaced, flat, and very private. The tents sites are more unevenly space, with privacy ranging from average to very good. Both RV and tent site are well-shaded with mature trees.

<u>Trip Notes</u>: I'll give this place credit. It struts its jet-set/glamping facilities rather gracefully. All facilities, including camping and RV sites, are set among trees within view of these finger lakes. The various groups of campers (yurts vs. cabins. vs. campsites, etc.) seem to peacefully co-exist like a mosaic, with only occasional awareness of the other. On the other hand, these are the priciest camping facilities in the island chain, but still a good value for all that is offered. For specific information, contact lakedale.com/family-camping-and-RV-site-on-San-Juan-island/ as rates are subject to change.

<u>Local Alternative</u>: The San Juan Co. Fairgrounds are located less than one mile from downtown Friday Harbor, GPS 48.526157, -123.016118. Here you'll find restrooms with showers, camp hosts, with RV waste disposal available in Friday Harbor. There are 8 RV pedestals for RVs up to 45' with water/electric 20/30 amps, 1 tent site with no hookups, with reservations strongly encouraged.

<u>OTHER CAMPGROUNDS</u>: There are no FREE drive-in CGs in San Juan Co. that we can recommend at this time.

For more photos of San Juan Co. CGs, or more about HIKE-IN or BOAT-IN CGs, consult campeverycountywa.com

SKAGIT COUNTY (Mount Vernon/LaConnor/Concrete)

From Rosario Strait, across the tulip fields, and up the mighty Skagit River to the craggy peaks of the North Cascades, this county is a study in diversity.

Highway 20/Skagit Valley/North Cascades Highway
State Route 20 is the northernmost route across the Cascade Mountain Range in Washington, and the state's longest highway stretching 436 miles across the northern regions of Washington. The Skagit Co. portion of this primarily follows the Skagit River from Puget Sound to the North Cascades National Park (NCNP). So, your recreational options divided between raging rivers (Rasar S.P.) and pure mountain streams (Marble Creek Campground), great choices for any camper.

Marble Creek CG (Skagit Co.'s *BEST RUSTIC CG*)
The Cascade River, on which this campground rests, is a tributary of the Skagit River, and a designated National Scenic River. It is hemmed in by several wildlife areas, and populated with mountain goats, coyotes, pine marten and a variety of migratory birds. If you want nature and seclusion, get on up here.
Overview: This Mt. Baker-Snoqualmie National Forest campground is located 8 miles east of Marblemount on 12 acres with riverfront on Cascade River/Marble Creek at 900' elevation, open mid-May 18 through late September. GPS 48.5293, -121.2738.
Facilities: These include vault toilets, picnic tables, fire rings, a boat ramp, and camp hosts in summer.
Recreation: There is an 8.1-mile hike to the Skagit River confluence and the NCNP.
Campsites (22 sites for tents or RVs up to 22', no hookups or potable water, reservable): Sites are large and private, along the shores of both the ever-changing Cascade River, and the smaller, rushing Marble Creek in old growth forest. Reserve one of the sites 1-12 that are along the Cascade River. The best site is

clearly site 12, which has its own road and best riverfront, and could be used as a double site. There is no road noise, only the sound of the River and Creek.

Trip Notes: This place was less remote than we had imagined. The road (up to the park at least) was paved, and a short distance from Marblemount. The sites themselves were more primitive, but that milky blue Cascade River won us over. Like many parks in this day and age, it could have used a thorough going over with a machete and a lawn mower, as well as some additional gravel on the park road. But this is primitive camping I could really live with, possibly for several days at a time.

Rasar S.P. (Skagit Co.'s *BEST EQUIPPED/BEST CG FOR RVs* and *BEST BIKE-IN CG*)

Overview: Located 17.3 miles east of Sedro Woolley and 8 miles west of Concrete on 169 acres with 4000' of Skagit riverfront at 100' elevation, open year-round; GPS 48.5177, -121.9025.

Facilities include flush toilets, picnic tables, fire grills, running water, showers, a playground and amphitheater, a cooking shelter, 3.7 miles of hiking trails, 1 mile of ADA-accessible hiking trails, and campground hosts.

Recreation: As above, hiking around the Park itself very good. Wildlife viewing is said to be good, though many of us saw more tracks and evidence of animals bedding down than actual wildlife. Birding, especially eagle watching, is best in fall or winter. Fishing is best for steelhead.

Campsites (38 back-in and pull-through sites for tents and RVs of any size, including 20 with water & electric 30 amp hookups, 2 ADA sites, 3 H/B sites, 2 Adirondack shelters, 3 cabins, 3 group camps for 20-80 each, all reservable): Sites are wooded and large with good privacy, concrete parking pads, and no street noise. Best per campsitephotos.com are: 2, 4, 6, 8, 16, 23, 29, 34, 35, and 36, and we think they were on point. Sites also include walk-ins, hiker/biker sites, and ADA sites. The best of the 3 group camps is the Elk Camp. Each group camp has its own playground and cooking shelter.

Trip Notes: We drove into Rasar about 1:45 for a 2:30 check-in, unaware how close the Park was to Sedro Woolly. We found that our camp-panions John and Tom had arrived at 8:30 a.m. and sweet-talked the rangers into setting up early. We were told that at 8:30 our double site was under water from the rain, but no rain or flood now. The land is more resilient than I am. All I knew was that the stresses of working full-time, taking care of two houses, and family concerns were looming large. By the time we set up, I could feel the place drawing the tension out of me, and I mostly slept for the first day and a half. The place was as relaxing as I remembered from last summer's visit. It wasn't until the third day that I realized the extent of the walking trails, including 3/4 of a mile along the Skagit River. This River evolves and changes every few hundred yards. In the meadows, you could see where the elk had bedded down each night. The trees are almost freakish, reflecting a long history of logging, and transformation of the land by the flooding river. Though this was not declared a State Park until 1997, and not completed until 2010, there is a sense of history here that is right underfoot.

Puget Sound and Fidalgo Island

The best recreational opportunities in the Puget Sound portion of Skagit County occur on Fidalgo Island, home of the City of Anacortes and the San Juan Ferries. Fidalgo is connected to Whidbey Island in the south by the Deception Pass Bridge, and to the tulip fields of LaConner to the east by the LaConner Rainbow Bridge across the Swinomish Channel. Fidalgo's 41 square miles offer 8 major lakes, two campgrounds on saltwater (below), and ferry access to the San Juan Islands and Vancouver Island, British Columbia.

Bowman Bay CG at Deception Pass S.P. (Skagit Co.'s *MOST APPEALING CG TO THE SENSES*)

This former Samish Indian Village, turned military park, then turned fish hatchery, was later converted to this beautiful park by the Civilian Conservation Corps.

Overview: This stunningly beautiful campground is located 7 miles south of Anacortes on Fidalgo Island with 77,000' of saltwater shoreline on Rosario Strait, on the north shore of Deception Pass, and is the northern end of Deception Pass S.P., open seasonally.

Facilities include bathrooms with flush toilets, showers, running water, playground, 2 cooking shelters, boat launch, campground host. This is the smallest of the 3 campgrounds.

Recreation includes gray whale watching, hiking, and beachcombing.

Campsites (20 sites for tents or small RVs, 1 CMT site for boaters, no hookups, reservable): Best sites for privacy are 274, 276, 277, 279, 282. Sites 284-285 are a double site w/average privacy. Sites 287-289 are a triple site w/poor to average privacy. Vegetation is light within the campground, but is surrounded by madronas, cedars, and firs outside the campsite area. This campground has the added bonuses of the Maiden of the Sea statue, as well as Rosario Head with its elaborate tidepools.

Trip Notes: Here you will find beauty at every turn. Touches include the stone bathrooms, cooking shelters, and even a bronze statue of a CCC worker. The history and complexity of this place is apparent as soon as you pass through the gates. All of the sites have a view of the Bay, and the trail to Rosario Head has the most dramatic madrona and fir trees anywhere. The Maiden of the Sea statue was smaller than I imaged, but no less impressive. When I return to camp at Deception Pass S.P., I will choose this campground, as it is brighter and more scenic than those at Cranberry Lake.

Local Folklore: The Samish legend of the Maiden of the Sea believes that princess Ko-Kwal-alwoot married the Spirit of the Sea in order to guarantee that seafood would always be plentiful. The statue is located at Rosario head adjacent to Bowman Bay.

Washington Park (Skagit Co.'s *MOST UNIQUELY WASHINGTON CG* and *BEST CG FOR ENTIRE FAMILIES*)

This is the part of Fidalgo Island that most people never see -- beyond the City of Anacortes, beyond the ferry docks, and on to the most breathtaking, magnificent precipice around -- Fidalgo Head. And in the middle of this marine wonderland lies a little old campground with the simple name of Washington Park.

Overview: This exceptional campground is located within and operated by the City of Anacortes on 220 acres with over 2 miles of saltwater shoreline at 135' elevation, open year-round; GPS 48.4992, -122.6929.

Facilities include flush toilets, showers, running water, a day use picnic sites and 3 rentable picnic shelters, a playground, boat launch, an overnight single car parking lot, camp hosts, and an RV dump station.

Recreation: The most popular recreation is standing and staring for hours at the marine view. This is best accomplished along the hiking and walking trails, but a single 2-lane road also circles the peninsula with many designated viewpoints.

Campsites (68 back-in and pull-through sites for tents and RVs of all sizes, including 46 with water & electric 30-amp hookups, 1 group tenting area for up to 30, reservable): The sites can be said to be in three intertwining loops. Sites are wooded and private, but not always level (remember your leveling blocks). All sites are heavily wooded, of average to large in size, and with average privacy. The camping area is not as well engineered as many of our state parks or better private parks, but still very campworthy.

Trip Notes: The precipice of Fidalgo Head, surrounded by beaches, coves, bluffs, and killer marine views, makes the perfect place to build a campground. The trees were the most fascinating: madronas, firs, and cedars reflected against the backdrop of the pristine waters of Burrows Bay, Rosario Strait, and the San Juan Islands -- all picture-perfect views. We spent the majority of our camping time at the bluffs and designated viewpoints taking in marine views that are perhaps the best we've ever seen -- and we've seen quite a few -- but these have remained the most firmly etched in our minds.

OTHER CAMPGROUNDS: There are no FREE CGs in Skagit Co. that we can recommend at this time.For more photos of Skagit Co. CGs, or more about HIKE-IN or BOAT-IN CGs, consult campeverycountywa.com

SKAMANIA COUNTY (Stevenson/Northwoods)

Two major icons make this county famous: Mount St. Helens and Beacon rock; but the real star is the Gifford Pinchot National Forest with its 22 USFS campgrounds. Be prepared! Most of this county is gravel roads, but all of them lead to something extraordinary.

Columbia River Gorge
You don't often see a river running through an entire mountain range, but this is Washington, folks. More correctly, the Columbia River was here first, with the Cascade Range forming later, but rising slowly enough for the River to kept eroding it, cutting 4000' in some places. What we have today is a clear division between east and west -- between the dry side and wet side of Washington, all visible from singular vantage points. It is now a designated National Scenic Area, shared by both Washington and Oregon.

Beacon Rock S.P. (includes Skamania Co.'s *BEST BIKE-IN CG, BEST GROUP CG*, and only *BOAT-IN CAMPSITES*)
The centerpiece of the Park is Beacon Rock itself, the 848-ft basalt core of an extinct volcano whose softer materials were washed away by the Missoula floods. The trail to the top includes 15 switchbacks, handrails, and several small bridges.
Overview: This iconic park is located 9.8 miles southwest of Stevenson on 5100 acres with 9500' of Columbia River waterfront. Its highest point is 1968', and is open year-round; GPS 45.662598, - 121.901801.
Facilities: The Park is well equipped with flush toilets, showers, running water (hot and cold), picnic tables, fire pits, a playground in the Day Use Area, a marina on the Columbia River, and camp hosts.

Beacon Rock is a must-climb camping experience

Recreation: Rock climbing is a given, but the park also boasts 20 miles of hiking/biking/equestrian trails. Windsurfing is excellent at nearby Spring Creek Hatchery S.P. Rentals are available in Hood River, Oregon.

Campsites (Woodard Creek CG has 5 sites for RVs up to 40', all with full hookups; Main Campground has 26 sites, no hookups, mostly for tenters or small RVs; Group Camp for up to 200 people with 2 Adirondack shelters, 2 equestrian sites at the trailhead, Group Camp is reservable, main campground closed in winter): Sites in the Main CG are moderate in size, but heavily wooded, shady, and relatively private. They are on a hillside away from road noise but are typically flat. Woodard Creek CG consists of 5 RV sites close to both Highway 105 and the railroad. There are also two tent sites at the marina to accommodate boat-in campers. Best sites are 21, 22, and 23 (all in the Main Campground). The large Group Camp is a dispersed grassy area with Adirondack shelters, each of which can accommodate 8 people.

Trip Notes: We were very surprised at the complexity of this park. The Group Camp was among the best we have seen with nooks and crannies where individual campers can get some privacy from other campers. This is a mecca for geologists, rock climbers, hikers and, yes, even campers.

Timberlake RV Park (Skamania Co.'s *BEST EQUIPPED/ BEST CG FOR RVs*)

The land on which this park sits is itself a synopsis of the history of this area. Norwegians settlers named it "Heim Dal," later translated as Home Valley in 1894 when the Swedish Bylin family homesteaded the region. They survived the 1902 "Yacolt Burn" forest fire by standing in the Anderson Slough, losing all but their lives. They rebuilt, and the homestead stayed in family hands until 2006, when one of the Bylin-Anderson clan neared retirement, designating part of the land as a campground high above the bustling Columbia Gorge. Founder and former owner Leroy Anderson built this Park to give campers the opportunity to experience the peacefulness of their best homesteading years.

Overview: This well-appointed campground is located 8.3 miles east of Stevenson and 4 miles north of Home Valley on 22 acres, privately operated at 871' elevation, open March to November; GPS 45.7332, -121.7641.

Facilities: This well-appointed campground is equipped with bathrooms and showers, picnic tables, well-designed fire pits, Wi-Fi, good cell phone reception, a dog park (unfenced), helpful camp hosts, and an RV dump.

Recreation: The Park was built as a centralized location for all activities in the Gorge, including fishing on the White Salmon River, golfing at one of the many courses in Stevenson, windsurfing on the Columbia, and simply enjoying nature in an undisturbed form.

Campsites (22 back-ins and walk-ins for tents, 43 back-in RV sites for RVs of any size including 25 sites with full hookups and 18 with water & electric 20/30/50-amp hookups, reservable): Sites are in two large loops, a larger double loop (RV sites 19-43, tent sites T1-T2 and T-13 to T-22) and a smaller single loop (RV sites 6-13 plus tents sites T3-T-9), with some side-by-side RV sites in between (RV sites 2-5 and 14-18). All RV sites have gravel pads, while tent sites are walk-ins. Some water & electric sites are uphill and somewhat hard to maneuver, but the full hookup sites are level with easy maneuverability. There is no train or highway noise. Reservations are recommended for RV'ers, but the tent sites are often available.

Trip Notes: This is a high energy RV Park with real camping for tenters, dominated by long, slender, colorful wind surfing boards mounted on top of cars, campers, trucks, and even trailers. The Columbia Gorge provides the activities, and campers here take full opportunity. But it can also be restful, with tent sites set low in the middle of a heavily forested loop, or high on the banks above the roads. One site saw wind surfers manically waxing their boards, while in the next site hammocks and reading were the name of the game. This place lives up to the promise to deliver both peacefulness and access to all that that the Gorge can offer.

Local Attraction: Beacon Rock is an 848-ft basalt core of an extinct volcano whose softer materials were washed away by the Missoula floods. The trail to the top includes 15 switchbacks, handrails, and several small bridges.

Wind River Road (Highway 30)

The Wind River originates in the Cascades and flows 30 miles south where it meets the Columbia near the town of Carson. Highway 30 follows this path, and is a popular ride for motorcyclers, due to its sweeping turns, old growth forest, wilderness areas, and beautiful campgrounds. You don't necessarily need a motorcycle, but you definitely need to go camping here.

Panther Creek CG (Skamania Co.'s *MOST APPEALING CG TO THE SENSES*)

This woodland oasis that doubles under the assumed name of Panther Creek draws you a few miles off the Wind River Highway, then seduces you into a camper's coma so that you'll never want to leave. It is beautiful, but it is evil. Campers beware.

Overview: This campground is beautifully located 12.2 miles northeast of Stevenson and 5 miles north of Carson, operated by the USFS at 988' elevation, open early May through mid-September; GPS 45.821, -121.876.

Facilities: These include vault toilets, water by spigot, hiking and equestrian trails with access to the Pacific Crest Trail, and camp hosts.

Recreation: Panther Creek Falls Trail #137 is less than one mile long and leads to one of the most beautiful waterfalls in the U.S. with a total height of 136' and a 102' drop, and 100' in width with tiered horsetails. Added bonuses are the Carson Hot Springs and the historic St. Martin Hotel.

Campsites (33 back-in sites including 6 double sites for tents or RVs up to 25', no hookups, equestrian staging area with one site, all reservable): Sites are large, spread out and private. Sites 5, 9, 18, 23, 26 and 27 are multi-sites.

Trip Notes: It is a wonderful feeling to pull into a new campground and your immediate impression is that it's perfect, the sites are perfect, the creek is perfect, it's just the right size... Yep, this is the place. Extremely peaceful, quiet, shady, and the kind of creek in which you can spend all day wading. There are also horse and hiking trails right from the campground, ensuring that you will never be bored -- unless, of course, that is your goal.

Camping Alternatives: Beaver CG, USFS (23 sites, no hookups, reservable) - Sites large, wooded and shady, mostly with maple trees, 2 pull-throughs. Fishing is allowed in the Wind River. An added bonus is Government Mineral Springs, whose original guard station is still available for rent. Paradise Creek CG, USFS, 1600' elevation (42 sites, no hookups, reservable) - Sites large and private. 20 miles north of Carson near Columbia Gorge, all paved roads. Nice!

Indian Heaven Wilderness

Indian Heaven is a 20,600-acre wilderness within the southern Gifford Pinchot National Forest. It is a gentle plateau mosaic of wildflower meadows, about 175 small lakes, panoramic views, volcanic fields, and volcanic craters turned into lakes. Native peoples have been using this property for sacred and cultural purposes for at least 9,000 years, and it still elicits indescribable awe.

Forlorn Lakes CG (Skamania Co.'s BEST RUSTIC CG)
"Forlorn" is an odd designation for such a happy place. The small lakes invite fishing, human powered boats, lakeshore sunbathing, and play (remember that word?).

Overview: This collection of campgrounds is located 32 miles northeast of Stevenson and 17 miles west of Trout Lake, operated by the USFS at 3700' elevation, open mid-June to mid-September; GPS 45.95893, -121.757005.

Facilities: Scattered amenities include vault toilets (some ADA), fire grills, picnic tables, and camp hosts.

There is nothing forlorn about the charming Forlorn Lakes

Recreation: The area is excellent for mountain blueberries (wild huckleberries) that ripen in late August. Swimming and kayaking are good in the various small lakes. Cave exploring is popular in the Natural Bridges, which are actually lava tubes. Guler Ice Caves are also lava tubes formed by the freezing of dripping water. Bird Creek Meadows and the Indian Heaven Wilderness also provide endless hiking and exploring.

Campsites (24 sites for tents or small RVs, no hookups or reservations, no water on site): Sites wind for 1.7 miles around five campgrounds with 16 lakes, perfect for canoeing. Parking aprons are irregular, and only campgrounds 1, 2 and 3 accommodate RVs. Others are best for tents or truck-mounted campers. Despite this, the sites offer excellent privacy, quiet, and heavy vegetation. Most sites have lakefront views; others have short trails to lakes. The forest here is a blend of Eastern and Western Washington, including Douglas fir, Engelmann spruce, and lodgepole pine.

Trip Notes: There is a sense of deep forest excitement here. We spent hours exploring the various lakes, some of which were pristine blue, others shallower and more brackish. There is a 3.9 mile stretch of gravel road as you approach the campground from the town of Trout Lake (the only route we recommend). Access through Carson and the Wind River Hwy leads to severely rutted gravel roads that may damage some vehicles.

Local Alternatives: Peterson Prairie CG has the advantage of having all paved roads, located just west of the very helpful Trout Lake Ranger Station. Lost Creek Ditch bisects the campground in two, satisfying some peoples' need to seek out the unusual. Goose Lake CG, which comes with a popular fishing lake just west of the Forlorns, is especially good for children, and offers walk-in tent sites.

Takhlakh Lake CG (Skamania Co.'s *MOST UNIQUELY WASHINGTON CG*)
Just 7 miles west of Mt. Adams lies a lake. But not just any lake. This is a magnificent alpine lake elusively named from the Native American word "takh" which means meadows. But there are no meadows here. Instead, this is a pristine, nearly round lake just the right size to capture the perfect reflection of majestic Mt. Adams. Ever wanted to appear in a picture postcard? Set foot or boat on this lake, and you'll do just that.

Overview: This awe-inspiring campground is located 98 miles northeast of Stevenson and 46 miles southeast of Randle on 32.6-acre Takhlakh Lake, operated by the USFS at 4449' elevation, open when the snow clears in June to late September, weather permitting; GPS 46.278, -121.599.

Facilities: This rugged campground includes vault toilets, picnic tables, fire grills, and camp hosts. Kayak/canoe launching is easy at several points along the lakeshore.

Recreation: There is a walking trail around the entire Lake full of magnificent photo opportunities. More restless hikers seek out the trails around Mt. Adams. Canoeing and kayaking are unparalleled (no motors allowed on the Lake). Fishing is good for brown, cutthroat, eastern brook, and rainbow, trout.

campeverycountywa.com

Takhlakh Lake captures the perfect reflection of Mount Adams

Campsites (62 sites for tents or RVs up to 30', no hookups or potable water; reservable): Sites are shady and wooded w/adequate privacy. Most sites are back-ins (some hilly) with a few pull-throughs. Access through Randle (from the north) or Trout Lake (from the south).

Trip notes: Finding the perfect campground on the perfect lake and the perfect mountain view means travelling for miles on grated, dusty, gravel roads and trusting that you'll eventually get there without getting lost. But we made it. We had difficulty situating our pop-up trailer in the driveway of site 30, which was a long mound sloped on 3 sides and inches from large trees – kind of like trying to park on the top of a large loaf of bread. But again, we made it. We assumed at first that Mt. Adams was shrouded with clouds, as our sense of direction was compromised from the switchback roads the last few miles to the park entrance. When I finally walked the campground, and suddenly saw the reflection of Mt. Adams framed by old growth trees around the large round lake, it literally took my breath away. On the water were multi-colored "human-powered" boats: a small blue canoe, a red kayak, two matching bright orange pontoon boats, and a large green canoe with raised ends reminiscent of Hiawatha. Another camper, seeing my reaction, stated, "Yeah, this is why clichés are made." And so it goes. The pictures just can't capture the beauty of this place. Put this one on your bucket list, even if you've been here before.

Local Camping Alternatives: (1) Olallie Lake – close to Takhlakh, a smaller lake with a similar view of Mt. Adams. Sites were fewer and smaller, and most of the park was covered with oily gravel, as it is otherwise rather dusty. Had only 2-3 good sites. (2) Council Lake – Beautiful, alpine lake (bigger than Olallie, smaller than Takhlakh, but longer and narrower).

Lower Falls Rec Area (Skamania Co.'s *BEST CG FOR ENTIRE FAMILIES*)
Seclusion is the word here, in a brilliant campground tucked away far up the Lewis River, with river boardwalks, viewing platforms, access stairwells, and some of the most dramatic waterfalls anywhere.

Overview: Located 53 miles north of Stevenson and 61 miles east of Woodland, operated by the USFS at 1535' elevation, open May to late October;
GPS 46.15664, -121.87845.

Facilities: Reasonable facilities include composting toilets, picnic tables, fire rings, paved roads, a large Day Use Area, and camp hosts.

Recreation: Hiking is popular on Lewis River Trail #31, Quartz Creek Trail #5, and Wright Meadows Trail #80. Waterfall viewing is the big draw here at Lower Lewis River Falls, Curly Creek Falls, Big Creek Falls, and Middle Falls. Fishing (catch and release only) is good for bull trout, cutthroat trout, rainbow trout, and whitefish. Swimming is strongly discouraged, as the currents and heavy under tows beneath Lower Falls are deceptively dangerous.

<u>Campsites</u> (42 back-in and pull-through sites, including 2 double sites, for tents and RVs up to 60', no hookups, reservable): Sites are divided into two loops, Upper and Lower. All sites are wooded, private, and quite large. The Lower Loop has the best access to the River and is closest to the Falls.

Lower Falls Campground sits on the edge of one of the most complex and mesmerizing waterfalls in Washington

<u>Trip Notes</u>: These incredible, complex, mesmerizing falls are closer to the campground than we expected (1/8 to 1/4 mile away by trail). And the Falls are not just a single flow of water, but dozens of distinct cascades of water -- some raging torrents, others narrow flows that tumble the entire height of that mighty set of rocks, others that rumble down fissures in the rock bank. Still others free fall nearly the entire height, until they hit benches of rock that pulverize the water into a fine mist that can be felt from the shore of the river below. Combine all these with a fine USFS campground in a family friendly environment, and this rates high, high, high on the list of best camping facilities in Washington.

Local Alternative: Twin Falls CG – just east of Lower Falls, has only a few sites, all of them walk-ins, so tents only. Two sites are right on the Lewis River, and very idyllic. The river here is narrower and deeper with rapids and nice falls. Is a very shady and more private spot than the other local parks.

Council Lake CG (Skamania Co.'s *BEST FREE CG*)
This is a surprisingly cozy campground in an area of many small beautiful lakes. There's just something sturdier about this little lake, with an equally sturdy campground to match.
Overview: This lovely, rustic campground is located 41.3 miles north of Stevenson and 35.3 miles east of Cougar on beautiful alpine Council Lake (43.7 acres), operated by the USFS at 4225' elevation, open May to October; GPS 46.266884, -121.629982.
Facilities: Limited facilities include a pit toilet (no TP!) and fire rings. There is no water or garbage service.
Recreation: This includes fishing for rainbow, eastern, brown, and cutthroat trout. Good boating for human-powered boats only. Hiking is available on the 1.3-mile Council Bluff Trail - an old lookout road - leading to a great vista overlooking volcanoes with room for 3-4 tents.
Campsites (7 sites for tents and the smallest of RVs, no hookups or reservations, FREE with NW Forest Pass): The sites are arranged in a narrow dumbbell-shaped pattern that puts the center sites in close proximity, but the old growth trees give some privacy.
Trip Notes: This beautiful blue-green lake is long and rectangle-shaped, pointing toward great mountain peaks beyond. This is one of the more pristine smaller campgrounds in the area -- no oiled gravel or evidence of recent fires or blow downs. This is a great place for quiet and focusing on camping and floating on that peaceful lake.

For more photos of Skamania Co. CGs, or more on HIKE-IN CGs, consult
campeverycountywa.com

SNOHOMISH COUNTY (Everett/Granite Falls/Darrington)

This is one of the fastest-growing counties in Washington, but still has some of the most confusing and wonderful back roads. From the "cut off" campground at Troublesome Creek to the variety of campgrounds on the Mountain Loop Highway to Puget Sound, there are treasures around every bend.

Mountain Loop Highway 92/FR 20

The paved State Highway 92 stretches from Granite Falls to Barlow Pass, where the pavement ends, and one-lane graveled Forest Road 20 stretches to Darrington. Most car campers stick to the paved portion, while the more adventurous choose to follow the gravel road deeper into the wilderness. In truth, the Mountain Loop Trail is only a half loop, extending from Granite Falls to Darrington. The second half traverses the non-mountain towns of Oso, Arlington, and Jordan.

Verlot CG (Snohomish Co.'s *BEST CG FOR ENTIRE FAMILIES*)

This compact campground is nestled between Hwy 92 and the South Fork Stillaguamish River, with Benson Creek flowing through the west end, providing the kids with a safe place for unsupervised adventures in this small forested creek. Adults will enjoy the low rumble of the River, and the mixed shade and sun.

Overview: This popular Snoqualmie National Forest campground is located 11.1 miles west of Granite Falls on the South Fork of the Stillaguamish River at 1004' elevation, open year-round with services provided April 27 through October 30; GPS 48.0904, -121.7778.

Facilities: Familiar USFS amenities include ADA-friendly vault toilets, picnic tables, fire grills, and 6 water spigots. Close by is the Verlot Service Center which can provide information and written materials.

Recreation: The river provides fishing for trout, plus limited wading and tubing. The Mountain Loop Trails are close at hand for hiking and mountain biking.

Campsites (8 sites for tents only, 17 sites for tents and small RVs, no hookups, reservable): Sites are arranged in two small loops with sites 1-3 and 6-18 on the Stillaguamish River. Sites 4-5 are on the Benson Creek, while sites 19-26 are higher and quite shady. All sites are back-ins, have gravel parking pads, and tent pads on native material. There is only low road noise here, despite being close to Hwy 92.

Trip Notes: The most unique feature is the series of wooded bridges and boardwalks that allow exploration across Benson Creek into the deeper forest, without danger of kids crossing the highway. They will have to use their imaginations here, but all the building blocks are provided for great adventures.

Local Alternatives: Turlo CG is just 0.2 miles west of Verlot and consists of a very shady single loop along the Stillaguamish. It may be quieter here, but some campers find it too shady. Red Bridge C.G. is 7.1 miles east just beyond (you guessed it) the big red bridge over the Stillaguamish. There is better tubing here, but no potable water, making it a deal breaker for some.

campeverycountywa.com

Verlot CG, just off the Mountain Loop Highway, has a deep woods feel

Barlow Pass Boondocking Sites (Snohomish Co.'s *BEST FREE CAMPSITES*)
The prettiest part of the Mountain Loop Highway is overlooked by most, when drivers stop exploring when the paved road ends at Barlow Pass. But the next 8 mile stretch of gravel road, between Barlow Pass and Bedal CG, reveals the prettiest mountain peaks, marshes, waterfalls, and campsites in the entire Loop.

Overview: This initial 8 mile stretch of FR 20 is located 16 miles southeast of Darrington and stretches to Barlow Pass 30.5 miles east of Granite Falls, operated by the USFS at 1250' - 2300' elevation, open late May to early September; GPS for Barlow Pass is 48.026927, -121.443853.

Facilities: These beautiful campsites have no amenities except those provided by Mother Nature.

Recreation features hiking the Mountain Loop Trails, in particular the short Barlow Point Trail #709 to the Barlow Point Lookout; and the 8-mile round trip Monte Cristo Trail #53 to the incredible ghost town of the same name. At Monte Cristo itself, other hiking trails include the 11-mile round trip Silver Lake Trail #708, and the Twin Lake Trail #708.1 just beyond (add an additional 6 miles round trip).

Campsites (Approx. 12 riverside sites for tents and 3 non-riverside sites for tents and small RVs, non-reservable, FREE with NW Forest Pass): The sites are varied, with some resting on the River as a singular unit. This was the exception, as most were on 2-3 levels, one for parking, one for tenting, and yet another for cooking. At one site at the Deer Creek Road 4052 (marked by a USFS sign), campers will find a large parking lot normally used for winter sports. Here there is a large, lovely campsite just off the lot (GPS 48.085163° N, 121.552699° W). This site has been used by RVers. There will be some daytime road noise in all sites, but the rush of the River will largely neutralize it.

Trip Notes: This was the most unexpected find for the summer of 2017. We finally went camping at Bedal, but along the way were distracted by the beautiful South Fork of the Stillaguamish River, and the individual campsites that dotted it. There were a small number of sites off the river suitable for small RVs such as ours. Bedal was great, though crowded on the holiday weekend, and made us long for the relative solitude of the boondocking sites along FR 20.

Bedal CG (Snohomish Co.'s *BEST RUSTIC CG*)

It isn't quite a wilderness campground but resembles the prettier parts of Appalachia in this remote, single-lane gravel road area settled by Tarheels from North Carolina. No Hatfields, no McCoys, no banjos in the distance, just a lovely, primitive spot on a sharp turn of the babbling North Sauk River; GPS 48.0968, -121.3869.

Overview: Located 16 miles southeast of Darrington at the confluence of the North and South forks of the Sauk River, operated by the USFS at 1253' elevation, open late May to early September.

Facilities: You'll find vault toilets (but no drinking water), picnic tables, fire rings, a boat launch for non-motorized boats, garbage service, an 18' by 18' Adirondack shelter built of old growth timber, and camp hosts. There is an RV dump at Clear Creek CG 8 miles to the north.

Recreation: Featured are hiking and whitewater rafting/kayaking. The Bedal Creek Trail follows a mining trail to Bedal Basin and on to Sloan Peak where you may see mountain goats, but will definitely see meadows filled with trillium, asters, and bleeding hearts. A less ambitious hike is to North Sauk Falls, just one mile from the campground. The whitewater section between Bedal and White Chuck Put-In to the north is recommended for beginning paddlers who go with more experienced paddlers.

Campsites (22 back-in and pull-through sites for tents or RVs up to 21', no hookups, reservable): The sound of rushing water can be heard from every campsite. Sites are shady and private, especially those by the River. All sites have tent pads on native material, parking pads are graveled.

Trip Notes: When is second growth forest better than old growth forest? The politically correct answer, of course, is NEVER! But now that we've kept the absentee critics at bay, campers have to marvel at the many old growth stumps with multiple second growth trees growing large and in charge. The old growth was cut well over 100 years ago, so this campground is bursting with mature, healthy native trees that provide shade in this most rustic setting.

Directions: Take I-5 North through Everett to Exit 194. Follow Highway 2 for about two miles. Stay in the left lane and merge onto Lake Stevens Highway 204. Follow for two miles to Highway 9. Take the left onto Highway 9 toward Lake Stevens, continue for just under two miles and take Highway 92 to Granite Falls. Take a right and follow for about nine miles to the Mountain Loop Highway.

Washington History: The Campground is named after an early pioneer family led by James Bedal, who married the daughter of the last Sauk Indian chief. Their children became trail guides, fire lookout keepers, and remarkable historians of the Sauk-Suiattle Tribe. The resulting hamlet of Bedal grew into a small logging settlement with a schoolhouse and nearby store. The campground is on part of the homestead, and remnants of Harry Bedal's cabin can still be found at the base of Sloan Peak.

Port Susan on Puget Sound

The most campworthy stretch of Puget Sound in Snohomish Co. is its northern half, stretching from the Tulalip Indian Reservation to the mouth of the Stillaguamish River near Stanwood. This shoreline borders Port Susan, a strait and bay bounded by Camano Island to the west and the mainland to the east. This seemingly enclosed body of water features many resorts, Bed & Breakfasts, RV parks and, best of all, one of the Camp Every County Crew's favorite campgrounds.

Kayak Point Co. Park (Snohomish Co.'s BEST EQUIPPED/BEST CG FOR RVs and MOST UNIQUELY WASHINGTON CG)
County Parks aren't supposed to be this good... Great job, Snohomish County! Great waterfront, lush campsites, terrific rentals... amazing.

Overview: This luxuriant campground is located 13 miles south of Stanwood on 670 acres with 3300' of Puget Sound waterfront, open year-round; GPS 48.136987, -122.363743.

Facilities: Included are flush toilets, running water, showers, picnic tables, fire rings/grills, a boat ramp and 300' pier. Featured is a huge, elaborate, plus an inviting playground for the kids (and adults, if no one is watching).

Recreation: Windsurfing, fishing, and boating are the main event. Kayak Point Golf course is just 1 mile away.

Campsites (32 sites for tents and RVs up to 25', 23 with water & electric 30-amp hookups, 10 yurts, one cabin/cottage, 2 ADA sites, reservable): Sites are spacious with shade trees, none on the water, but quiet and well patrolled. Premium sites are 7, 8, 9, 11, 13, and 15. Included are 23 pull-through sites. The Park gets heavy day use on summer weekends. It has an extensive yurt village plus Kayak Kottage (available for rent).

Trip notes: This was a last-minute change for us. We had reservations at Gold Basin, but the campground was closed down to repercussions of the Oso landslide. So, we were stunned when we drove into this beautiful, lush park and scored the biggest and best site (site 15). Green flowed everywhere, with beds of ivy stretching back from the open area, and trees forming a thick canopy over us. A County Park? This was as nice or nicer than many State Parks, reminiscent of Manchester S.P. My dog Boca and I ventured down the steep trails to the common area many times, enjoying the party atmosphere down below. A wedding and a birthday party were held during our stay. This was the best surprise of the summer. One caution: we were told by rangers that the Park is completely booked on weekends (we were there on a weekday). Stay during the week if you can to ensure a quieter stay.

Kayak Point Park's luxuriant campground is matched
only by its magnificent shoreline

218

Stevens Pass Greenway Scenic Byway (Highway 2)

The Greenway follows the historic Great Northern Railway's Iron Goat Trail, connecting Everett with Stevens Pass, and a friendly collection of rustic communities along the way. Visitors can hike, ski, white water kayak, enjoy views of snow-capped spires, or pitch their tents in some great campgrounds settled among the mountain peaks.

Beckler River CG (Snohomish Co.'s BEST BIKE-IN CG)

Beckler River is a tributary of the South Fork of the Skykomish River. At only 8 miles long, the Beckler exhibits numerous cascades and rapids in narrow channels and a rocky river bottom with many boulders. It owes its crystalline water to a lack of development along its shores.

Overview: This pristine campground is located 2.1 miles east of Skykomish on 12 acres with extensive shoreline on the Beckler River, operated by the USFS at 1100' elevation, open May 26 - September 6; GPS: 47.7326, -121.3332.

Facilities: Unique amenities include ADA vault toilets, picnic tables, fire grills, drinking water by solar-powered spigot, and camp hosts.

Recreation: This is a campground known as a quiet getaway, and not so much for its activities. Swimming and tubing are common in the River, and fishing is limited to brook and rainbow trout. Gold panning is good nearby, but red garnets are most unique here. Hiking is accessible, including the Beckler River Trail, which gives a vista of the Skykomish Valley and leads to remains of a trapper's cabin. There is also access to the Pacific Crest Trail. Iron Goat Trail #1074, a short drive from the campground, leads to the ghost town of Wellington, decimated by a massive deadly avalanche in 1900.

Campsites (27 back-in and pull-through sites for tents and small RVs including 2 ADA sites, no hookups or reservations): Sites are wooded and spacious, allowing good privacy with old growth Douglas fir, Western red cedar, Western hemlock, and vine maple. Many sites are near the River.

Trip Notes: This compact campground was much tidier and better laid out than nearby Money Creek and Miller River Group (both in King Co.). The sites are larger, with picnic tables situated further back into the trees. Some of the pull-through sites were ridiculously large. Many sites had direct river access. The river itself had stunning sections of crystalline water said to be laden with gold and red garnets. Bring out your gold pans and find out for yourselves!

Troublesome Creek CG (Snohomish Co.'s *MOST APPEALLING CG TO THE SENSES*)

Turn up the color wheel, Mother Nature, this is a remote campground with amenities, a great river, great hikes and... must I repeat myself? Great color everywhere!

Overview: Located 18 miles northwest of Skykomish at the confluence of the North Fork of the Skykomish River and Troublesome Creek, operated by the USFS at 1243' elevation, open mid-May to mid-September; GPS 47.89778, -121.4025.

Facilities: Here you will find vault toilets, drinking water, picnic tables, fire rings, garbage pickup, a sturdy footbridge across Troublesome Creek, and camp hosts.

Recreation: Fishing is good for steelhead and salmon. The 3.5-mile hike to Blanca Lake is highly recommended. This beautiful lake has stunning blue-green water fed by glacier melt.

Campsites (25 back-in and pull-through sites for tents and RVs up to 25', no hookups, reservable): Sites are in three sections: the upper loop (sites 11-13 and 21-25) has the best privacy and heaviest forest but can be dark and too shady for some. The middle spur (sites 14-20) sits above pretty Troublesome Creek and may be the nicest sites for those who don't want to access the Skykomish River. The lower loop (sites 1-6 and walk-in sites 7-10) has average to fair privacy but is your best bet for those who want access to the North Fork of the Skykomish, either for fishing, or to have the sound of the gentle current lull you to sleep at night. Both loops and the spur can accommodate small RVs; no RVs in sites 19-25.

Trip Notes: The drive to Troublesome Creek explains its low use. The original road from Index was washed out in 2006 and was beyond repair and remains permanently closed. Access is now through Skykomish with 18 miles of mostly gravel roads. They are passable, however, and well worth the patience and white knuckling to get there. The Skykomish River and Troublesome Creek (don't swim in the creek, some have had "trouble" with its deceptive currents) are exceptionally inviting and welcoming, a real delight to the senses. The colors here are exceptional, from the deep green-black of the upper loop, to the gentler greens of the salmon berries, ferns, vine maples, silver firs, hemlocks, and big leaf maples of the lower loop. The Creek offers a glimmering azure blue to the middle spur, while the River is clear and crystalline, with green rocks reflected in the filtered sunlight. So, don't turn around and give up on the gravel roads -- you will have missed a one of a kind campground.

Local Alternative: San Juan CG sits just 3 miles east. This has 9 campsites and rests right on the Skykomish River.

For more photos of Snohomish Co. CGs, or for more about GROUP or HIKE-IN CGs, consult campeverycountywa.com

SPOKANE COUNTY (Spokane/Liberty Lake/Cheney)

There is no denying that the City of Spokane dominates this smallish county of the same name. Outside the City are mostly small fishing resorts, an Air Force base, and college campuses; but inside, along the Spokane River, on Mount Spokane, and even nestled among the suburbs, you'll find some pretty worthwhile camping.

Riverside State Park

This 12,000-acre park stretches along the Spokane and Little Spokane Rivers with a lot of help from the Civilian Conservation Corps with multiple campgrounds. As such, it is the epicenter for just about every camper, hiker, equestrian, and naturalist in the entire county.

Bowl and Pitcher CG at Riverside S.P. (Spokane Co.'s *MOST UNIQUELY WASHINGTON CG*)

Riverside S.P. began here, built by the CCC in the 1930s. It still retains that vintage charm, most notably in the iconic suspension bridge over the roiling and churning Spokane River.

Overview: Located 6 miles from downtown Spokane at 1707' elevation, open year-round; GPS 47.696, -117.4944.

Facilities include bathrooms with flush toilets, picnic tables, fire grills, a CCC Picnic Shelter (rentable), an amphitheater, camp hosts, and an RV dump station.

Summer Recreation include swimming, fishing, boating, horseback riding, whitewater rafting, and hiking. The Centennial Trail offers 37 miles of biking and hiking trails, then, for those who won't be confined to the State Park boundaries, continues through downtown Spokane, the Spokane Valley, and on to Couer d'Alene Idaho. See other Riverside S.P. campgrounds for more recreational information.

Winter Recreation includes cross-country skiing, snowshoeing, snowmobiling and all-around snow play.

Campsites (32 back-in sites for tents and RVs up to 45', including 17 with water & electric 30/50-amp hookups, reservable): Sites are lightly forested with Ponderosa pine with graveled pads. Sites are small to average, level and open with poor to average privacy. Sites 1-14 have less shade but are larger and have a view of the river, all have hookups; sites 15-17 are hookup sites that are smaller with better shade, and the best RV sites overall; sites 18-33 are tent sites that are smaller with better shade. Sites 32 and 33 are the best tent sites overall.

Trip Notes: The big draw is the Spokane River with its spire-like geological formations and the foot bridge originally built by the CCC. It has since been rebuilt for easier and safer crossing. This leads to great hiking beyond (including the Centennial Trail), but the view from the bridge alone is worth the trip. As most RV sites (1-14) get full sun, be sure to bring a canopy. When we camped here, I spend much of my time in a lawn chair by the River, shaded by the rock formations, and reading a good book.

The iconic footbridge at Riverside S.P.
was originally built by the CCC but later replaced for safer crossing

Local Alternatives: An Equestrian CG lies to the south across the River with 21 sites, restrooms, an-ADA mounting platform, a newly renovated riding arena, and gateway to miles and miles of trails. The campground is located just off Aubrey L. White Parkway. Also see Nine Mile Recreation Area (below).

Nine Mile Rec Area/CG at Riverside S.P. (Spokane Co.'s *BEST CG FOR ENTIRE FAMILIES*)
This is a unique gem where the Lake makes the campground, scattered on the edge of beautiful Lake Spokane with its shimmering waters and yellow lily pads.

Overview: Located 9 miles north of downtown Spokane on 4,748-acre Lake Spokane at 1624' elevation, open May 15 to Sept. 15; GPS 47.793, -117.5674; GPS 47.793, -117.5674.

Facilities: This this well-equipped beach area includes bathrooms with showers, a bathhouse, 3 large Kitchen Shelters with electricity (2 also have fireplaces), a swimming beach, 1 mile of ADA trail and 55 miles of hiking and biking trails, boat ramp, 2 docks, kayak and canoe rentals, and an RV dump.

Recreation also Includes fishing, rock climbing, water-skiing, plus lake and whitewater kayaking. The nearby Little Spokane Natural Area features a self-guided trail connecting the Indian Painted Rocks area with the mouth of the Little Spokane River. The Spokane House Interpretive Center at Nine Mile Falls tells the history of the early fur trade in the area.

Campsites (24 back-in sites for tents and RVs up to 45' with water & electric 30/50-amp hookups, reservable): Campsites occupy a large, flat, level grassy lawn with little vegetation. Sites are mostly side-by-side and small to average in size.

Trip Notes: This campground will not appeal to everyone. It is not the little wooded campground on the little lake (look to USFS campgrounds for that). Instead, it is a side-by-side grassy campground on a beautiful 25-mile lake with excellent facilities. It is great for people who are active all day long, but not so much for people that want to sit quietly in the shade and read (look to Lake Roosevelt campgrounds for that). Even those who camp elsewhere will be drawn by the ongoing beach party here, or by the simple beauty of the Lake.

Mount Spokane State Park

Located on 13,919 acres, Washington's largest state park was largely inspired by the Civilian Conservation Corps (CCC) in the 1930's, leaving behind remnants in the form of stone and log lodges, historic cabins, heritage sites, and picnic shelters. But nature created the biggest inspiration of all, namely 5,883-foot Mount Spokane, from which visitors can see Idaho, the City of Spokane, and the entire Selkirk Mountain Range. Hikers and snow shoers find a complex system of trails, skiers find ski slopes that are sometimes open into June, and campers find small campgrounds nestled between this whirlwind of possibilities.

Bear Creek Lodge CG (Spokane Co.'s *BEST BIKE-IN CG*)
When Bear Creek Lodge opened in 1952 it was touted as the widest single span wood structure west of the Mississippi. Major improvements began in 2001 by the original Linder family, and it remains a family-run business.

Overview: The cozy lodge and campground are located 25 miles northwest of Spokane at the entrance to Mt. Spokane S.P., family-operated at 3100' elevation, open May to mid-October; GPS 47.8825° N, 117.1352° W.

Facilities: These include two unisex bathrooms with showers, drinking water, picnic tables, fire grills and a camp host. The Lodge itself features 15 rooms, high speed internet service (AirPipe), restaurant serving American-style cuisine (chicken and country-style barbecued pork ribs, vegan and gluten-free dishes).

Recreation: See Bald Knob CG (website). A horse unloading dock is located one-quarter mile inside the S.P. entrance.

Campsites (13 sites for tents or RVs of any size, water & electric 110-volt hookups, reservations are recommended): Sites are small to medium in size with shade trees and average privacy. Level sites are good for RVs, providing both good access to the Lodge and quiet camping.

Trip Notes: It's a family thing. Is everything perfect at every moment? Of course not, but it will be attended to, and it will be done well. The welcome sign at the entrance to the tubing hill tells it all -- Welcome! And once you get used to feeling welcome, go to the Lodge and have a nice dinner. The s'mores can wait until tomorrow.

The Spokane City Suburbs

A few Spokane suburbs make up the remainder of Spokane County. South of Cheney lies the Turnbull National Wildlife Refuge, which is great for wildlife viewing, but not camping. Just west of Spokane is the Medical Lake Area -- great for fishing and boating, but again, not for camping. And the Spokane Valley? No camping here. For suburban camping, we must turn to the communities of Cheney, Deer Park and Liberty Lake.

Dragoon Creek CG (Spokane Co.'s *BEST FREE* and *BEST RUSTIC CG*)
Funding from the Discover Pass re-opened this much-loved campground near Deer Park. Wade in the stream, stroll through the piney forest, and enjoy rustic camping near great facilities.

Overview: Located 14 miles north of Spokane off Hwy 395 on the banks of Dragoon Creek (a tributary of the Little Spokane River), operated by the DNR at 1971' elevation, maximum 3-day stay, open May to September; GPS 47.8884, -117.4433.

Facilities include vault toilets, drinking water, picnic tables, fire grill, picnic shelters, grassy meadows near the Creek, camp hosts.

Recreation: This includes trout fishing, wading in the Creek and its pools, kite flying and Frisbee throwing. The Deer Park Golf Course is nearby.

Campsites (23 back-in sites for tents or RVs up to 40', no hookups or reservations, FREE of charge with Discover Pass): Sites are in 2 loops, upper and lower, are well-spaced with good shade trees.

Trip Notes: This campground is about location, located just north of the Spokane city limits surrounded by multiple family farms. It has that shaggy DNR look, where nothing is quite perfect, nor does it strive to be, but provides a rustic and comforting camping experience. There is little access to Dragoon Creek itself, but its rippling waters provide coolness in the summer heat and will lull you to sleep at night.

Ponderosa Falls CG and RV Resort (Spokane Co.'s *BEST EQUIPPED/BEST CG FOR RVs*)

As you wander around the myriad of tent and RV sites, cabins, bungalows, playgrounds, and miniature golf lanes, you will occasionally find glimpses of cartoon bear images that tweak the memories of the older but may be lost on the younger. That is because this is a former Yogi Bear's Jellystone Park, modeled after the old children's cartoon, now retrofitted for modern campers. Ironically, you will find far more adult campers than children, who are more drawn to campgrounds like Nine-Mile and Liberty Lake, where they have more room to roam, trees to climb, and their own adventures to create.

Overview: Located 10 miles west of Spokane near Cheney, operated by K/M Resorts at 2535' elevation, open year-round; GPS 47.584609, -117.540926.

Facilities: This well-equipped facility includes bathrooms with showers, a heated indoor pool and sauna, workout room, playground, miniature golf, sports courts, community fire pit, laundry, Wi-Fi, Cable TV, Camp Store, RV dump, and camp hosts.

Recreation: It's playtime, campers. Put down the fishing poles, hiking boots, and body boards, and just play.

Campsites (28 tent sites,156 RV sites with full hookups 30/50-amp, 5 bungalows, 7 cabins, reservable): The Park is becoming surrounded by suburban sprawl, visible through the chain link fence that surrounds the campground on two sides. RV sites are a mixture of back-ins and pull-throughs on gravel or sandy pads. Tent sites are walk-ins with parking close by. Our favorite sites are those on the hillside interspersed with the cabins and bungalows. Some have camping decks that overlook the rest of the Park. This small area has its own bathrooms and a dish washing sink and affords more privacy than the rest of the Park.

Trip Notes: This one is rather commercial, but that's its strength, provided that's what you're looking for. Some RV sites on the upper level have decks that look out over the rest of the Park. The cabins and bungalows have similar views. And it's hot over here -- an indoor pool can be a relief; plus, they have separate times for children, adults, and families. Miniature Golf adds another dimension but is a "sport" only the most hopeless of competitors will take too seriously. Yes, the falls are artificial, but you're not in the wilderness, you're in the suburbs near Cheney. Take a load off, loosen up, and have a little fun.

<u>Liberty Lake Regional Park</u> (Spokane Co.'s *MOST APPEALING CG TO THE SENSES* and *BEST HIKE-IN SITE at Camp Hughes Cabin*)

One of the largest county parks in the State of Washington, Liberty Lake Regional Park comprises over 3,591 acres of wetlands, lakeshore, rain forest-like wetland forests, irrigated turf, and conservation areas.

<u>Overview</u>: This ever-evolving park is located 17 miles southeast of Spokane on 696-acre Liberty Lake, operated by Spokane County Parks at 2073' elevation, with camping for the main campground open May 1st to Sept. 30th; camping along the Liberty Lake Loop Trail is open year-round; GPS (see below).

<u>Facilities</u>: These include bathrooms with showers, picnic tables, fire grills, a Picnic Shelter, swimming beach with lifeguards, BBQ area, playground, 7 miles of hiking trails, nearby WDFW boating access, RV dump, and camp hosts.

<u>Recreation</u>: Here we start with fishing for trout, large and small mouth bass, and bluegill. Also popular are swimming, volleyball, and especially hiking. The Liberty Lake Loop Trailhead is just off the RV area, the start of an 8.5-mile round-trip hike up to waterfalls, shaded forest, and cedar groves. The trail is well maintained and considered of moderate difficulty with a 1483' elevation gain. Diamond spikes and trekking poles are recommended. Mountain biking is also permitted. The equally long Edith Hansen Riding Trail shares the same forests but is reserved exclusively for horseback riders. The trailhead is located near an equestrian-friendly parking area off of S. Idaho Road.

<u>Campsites</u> (9 tent sites, 17 sites for RVs of any size, water/electric 30-amp hookups, 2 Lake View cabins plus the Camp Hughes Cabin, 1 Group Site, reservable): Tent sites 4-13 sit on the edge of marshy grasslands once covered by lake water. The area was drained a century or so ago for pastureland and is now being restored to its original ecosystem. Sites here are back-ins and reasonably spaced with views of the distant lake. Sites 1-3 sit higher up and were closed for restoration during our stay. RV sites have gravel pads and are all long side-by-side pull-throughs. Privacy is only average with partial shade. The Lake View cabins are very new and modern, with excellent lake views. The most famous cabin, known as the Hughes Cabin, makes for the best hike-in campsite in the area.

<u>Trip Notes</u>: It took a second stay here to finally get it -- this is a live, evolving ecosystem. On our first trip, we wondered why the camping area was not on the Lake; on this, our second stay, we realized that those verdant green pasture lands were originally the south end of the lake, when the pragmatic needs of this once rural area meant draining it for livestock. Maybe if we come back in a few decades, our sites will be lakefront once again. Until then, it is an interesting, quirky place that the kids love, and where adults can find plenty of R & R.

STEVENS COUNTY (Colville/Kettle Falls/Chewelah)

This county encompasses some of the earliest exploration in Washington. Salmon harvesting, mines, and refineries have largely been replaced by tourism and recreation. The campgrounds here express their communities more than any other county, tied together by history and community bonds.

Northport Area

The town of Northport, just 7 miles from the Canadian border, was the heart of a late 1800s mining boom. Its towering smelter, combined with connections with the railroad and Columbia River, helped make it "one of the rowdiest mining towns in the west." The smelters are shut down now, and the community has survived decades of quiet desperation during hard times, but it has come out as one of the friendliest and most cohesive communities in Washington, making a great backdrop for equally welcoming camping.

Sheep Creek CG (Stevens Co.'s *BEST FREE CG*)

Thank you, town of Northport, for saving Sheep Creek Campground!

Overview: Located 30 miles north of Colville and 6 miles northwest of Northport, operated by the DNR at 1650' elevation, open seasonally; GPS: 48.9602, -117.8336.

Facilities: Limited facilities include pit toilets, drinking water by hand pump, picnic tables, fire rings, a large picnic shelter, and a viewing platform over Sheep Creek.

Recreation: Fishing in the spring and summer, hunting in the fall. There are also hiking trails nearby.

Campsites: (11 back-in sites for tents and smaller RVs, no hookups or reservations, FREE with Discover Pass): Sites are large, private, wooded, and lush on dirt pads. Two sites are very close to the Creek. The best campsites are beyond the Day Use Area in the loop at the end of the road. The campground is situated along noisy Sheep Creek and equipped with a fishing deck and viewing benches. A bridge crosses the creek, dividing the campground in two. The sites before the bridge are private but experience some logging truck noise. You'll find more quiet on the other side.

Trip Notes: This is the perfect getaway campground, with its babbling brook, wooden bridge, hand hewn picnic shelter, and natural setting. The friendly town of Northport also provides access to groceries, hardware, and food. Be sure to visit the Mustang Grill for breakfast or lunch.

Washington History: This campground was slated for permanent closure in 2009 due to budget cuts. Rather than have their community meeting spot left to deteriorate, the City Council and citizens of Northport adopted it, and managed in regularly until 2011 when they were awarded a grant to further improve the campground, and the DNR resumed management. Hurray for civic pride!

Little Pend Oreille Lakes Region

This small section of the Colville National Forest along Highway 20 straddles the Stevens County-Pend Oreille County line. It includes a small chain of 5 lakes ranging in size from 26 acres (Sherry Lake) to 163 acres (Lake Thomas). All 5 lakes are connected by the slow-moving Little Pend Oreille River. This forms a white lily channel between the lower four lakes that can make for a spectacular paddling adventure. Six different campgrounds sprinkle the five lakes.

Lake Thomas CG (Stevens Co.'s *BEST BIKE-IN CG*)

Lake Thomas is the quietest campground in a very pretty series of lakes that are known for ORV use. This lake is special, being not only the largest, but also the only lake in the chain that does not allow ORVs. They have their fun far away, while we have our camping fun right here, right now.

Overview: This beautiful terraced lake campground is located 26 miles east of Colville and 8 miles south of Ione on 163-acre Lake Thomas, operated by the USFS on 43 acres at 3290' elevation, open Memorial Day to Labor Day; GPS 48.6238, -117.5358.

Facilities: Good facilities include pit toilets, running water, fire pits, picnic tables, tent pads, bear-proof garbage bins, boat launch, and camp hosts who drive through daily.

Recreation: This spot is known for fishing for large-mouth bass, black crappie, yellow perch, brook trout, and rainbow trout. This lake chain is in the middle of an extensive network Off-Road Vehicle (ORV) Trails. Hiking is popular at Rufus Trail #148. The sandy lakeshore makes for good swimming. This is also located along a popular bicycle route from Colville to the Pend Oreille Valley, and is a good bicycle stop over with adequate services for resupplying.

Campsites/Trip Notes (16 back-in and pull-through sites for tents or RVs up to 16', no hookups or reservations): Lake Thomas has the advantage of being the largest of the lakes, and does not allow ORVs to be driven in or out of the campground, though it is near ORV trails. It is quiet most of the time. Sites are located on a wooded hillside, most along the Lake. Note that the lower lakes (Heritage, Thomas, and Gillette) share the shore with private residences, and their campgrounds are not recommended due to motorboat and ORV noise. Lake Thomas is quieter than the rest, which is immediately noticeable.

Nearby alternatives: There are two reasonable camping alternatives in the Little Pend Oreille chain. Beaver Lodge Resort (38 sites for tents or RVs up to 40' including water and electric 30-amp hookups and 10 cabins) has the most amenities but is quite busy. Lake Leo (8 sites, no hookups or reservations, across the county line in Pend Oreille Co.) is detached from the rest and is clearly the quietest campground in this chain of lakes, making good camping for those seeking less activity.

Lake Thomas is the largest and quietest lake in the Little Pend Oreille chain

Colville Area

The history of the City of Colville is really the history of Fort Colville, which was located at 3 different locations at various times. The original Fort Colville was built north of Kettle Falls by British agents for the Hudson's Bay Company and lasted until the 49th Parallel was established as the border between Canada and the U.S., ceding the land to American soldiers. The U.S. Army then built a new Fort Colville in Pinkney City, just one mile from the present-day Douglas Falls Grange Park. As a more promising city was platted 3 miles away, and Fort Colville was slated for closure, developers were encouraged to change its name from Belmont to Colville, so that the county seat could be moved to this location -- and the rest is history.

<u>Douglas Falls Grange Park</u> (Stevens Co.'s *BEST CG FOR ENTIRE FAMILIES*)
This campground dates from 1855, when Pioneer R.H. Douglas harnessed the 60-foot Mill Creek Falls first as a sawmill, then, when that failed, as a distillery. That means spirits, folks. The City of Colville has used the grounds for community gatherings ever since, with athletic fields and picnic shelters adjoining the campground. It has become a popular meeting place, even when the spirits aren't flowing.
<u>Overview</u>: This unique campground is located 3 miles northeast of Colville with 120 acres on Mill Creek, operated by the DNR at 1823' elevation, open April through November; GPS: 48.61665, -117.90535.
<u>Facilities</u>: Numerous facilities include vault toilets, drinking water, picnic tables, fire rings, a ball field, and a picnic shelter, and camp hosts.
<u>Recreation</u>: The 0.2-mile Douglas Falls Grange Park Nature Loop Trail is a delight and allows campers to see the Falls on Mill Creek both from above and below.
<u>Campsites</u> (12 sites back-in sites for tents or small RVs, no hookups or reservations, FREE with Discover Pass): Sites are wooded with grass pads and good privacy, albeit somewhat primitive. This is best for tent campers, and very close to the city of Colville. It includes a 0.2-mile walk to the 60' waterfall on Mill Creek, plus a cable walking bridge, giving this park a very remote feeling.
<u>Trip Notes</u>: This campground is very steeped in history -- not in an academic sense, but in a way that takes you back to the feeling of pioneer times. Everything has a hand-made, custom feel. The Day Use Area is used by the community of Colville, and the pastoral areas around the park are left very natural. Don't come here expecting Disneyland, just good, natural camping, and an experience of vintage Washington.

Upper Lake Roosevelt

Lake Roosevelt is a 150-mile long reservoir formed from the Columbia River behind Grand Coulee Dam. The Upper Arm, separating Ferry and Stevens Counties, runs north-south from north of the Canadian border to roughly Fort Spokane. During the spring, the reservoir water level decreases substantially, and the appearance of the many campgrounds in the shallower Upper Arm changes accordingly. Yet, the campgrounds remain popular throughout the year, showcasing their resilience and timeless beauty.

<u>Kettle Falls CG</u> (Stevens Co.'s *MOST UNIQUELY WASHINGTON CG* and includes *BEST GROUP CG*)
The campground occupies the original townsite of Kettle Falls. The falls were submerged by the creation of Lake Roosevelt after the completion of Grand Coulee Dam, and the townsite moved to higher ground in 1938.

<u>Overview:</u> This underrated campground is located 3 miles west of the current city of Kettle Falls, managed by the NPS at 1631' elevation, open year-round; GPS 48.28638, -118.12003.

<u>Facilities:</u> This extensive campground includes vault toilets, running water (seasonal), picnic tables, fire rings, picnic shelters, a playground, an amphitheater, softball fields, a boat launch/dock, fish cleaning stations, a marina with a "floating bathroom," houseboats for rent, camp hosts, and an RV dump station.

<u>Recreation:</u> Boating, fishing and water skiing are popular here, although the Lake is not very accessible to swimmers.

<u>Campsites</u> (77 sites for tents and RVs up to 30', no hookups, 2 Group Camps for 50-75, reservable): Sites are level with many asphalt back-ins. The vegetation is primarily Ponderosa pine, providing average privacy, as the sites are of average size. Caution: There is some daytime noise from a nearby mill.

<u>Trip notes:</u> My campanion Tom, who arrived at the campground several hours before me, dubbed the campground as "rather boring, just 3 camping loops and a dry marina." True, Roosevelt Lake levels were at an all-time low, but I decided to take my dog Boca and explore the entire campground myself. The famed houseboats and "floating bathroom" were stranded on dry ground, but I was impressed that other boats were still able to launch (not true of nearby Evans, Marcus Island, or other campgrounds). Then we spotted a simple sign that said "Trail," pointing away from the marina. We found ourselves in a stunning Locust Grove, worlds apart from the familiar coastal firs and spruces of my hometown. Soon we came to another sign that said, "Group Camp." We entered from the backside, preferring to stay among the locust trees and off the asphalt road. Suddenly, I spotted another sign. This said "Gust Weigelt, Manufacturer and Importer, Harnesses and Saddles..." I saw remnants of the foundations, sidewalks, and steps to the businesses that lined the main commercial streets of pre-1938 Kettle Falls. I became mesmerized by the feeling that I had been transported back 80 years. I stayed until nearly dark, just taking it all in. This was the ultimate experience of "experiencing Washington State from the ground up," the very purpose of this project. When you visit this campground, do not miss this part of the experience.

Kettle Falls CG is built of the original townsite of Kettle Falls

Local Alternatives: A nearby alternative is Evans CG to the north (46 sites, no hookups or reservations). Its one advantage over Kettle Falls is a swimming beach, open when lake levels are higher. Marcus Island CG is intriguing when the water levels are high, and the entire park turns into a long, narrow island with a causeway to the mainland; when the levels are low, it looks like a narrow-wooded ridge and loses some of its charm. Check lake levels before heading out.
Local Attractions: Include Saint Paul's Mission and Fort Colville.

Deer Lake CG/RV Resort (Stevens Co.'s *BEST EQUIPPED/ BEST CG for RVs*)
Deer Lake is the largest and most pristine of the natural lakes in the Colville Watershed, surrounded by lush forests, abundant wildlife, and mountain peaks. The Resort manages to meld a perfect mixture of luxury, nature, and a good time to be had by all.
Overview: This large campground is located 35 miles north of Spokane and 35 miles south of Colville on 1,146-acre Deer Lake, privately operated on 195 acres at 2474' elevation, open (March 1 through October 3; GPS 48.11176, -117.58663.
Facilities: This well-equipped resort includes picnic tables, fire rings, laundry, Wi-Fi, an amphitheater, a swimming area, Country Store, the Country Griddle Cafe, Mini Golf, organized Water Sports, boat slips, boat rentals (motor boats, row boats, paddle boats, and kayaks), boat launch and docks, trash pick-up, excellent camp hosts, and an RV dump.
Recreation includes fishing for black bass, largemouth bass, smallmouth bass, crappie, perch, kokanee salmon, and rainbow trout. Boating, hiking, sailing, cross-country skiing, swimming, wildlife viewing, birding, and kayaking are also popular.
Campsites (16 tent sites and 65 RV sites with full hookups 30/50-amp, 3 Regular Cabins, 1 Loft Cabin, 4 Camp Wagons, 2 Condos, 1 House with 2 units, all reservable): RV sites are both pull-through and back-in, and closely spaced. Tent sites are more wooded and spread out. Privacy may be a challenge here, and shade is at a premium, as the tent sites are dispersed on a large lawn, and the RV area has very little vegetation between sites.
Trip Notes: We preferred this lake and campground to the others in the watershed for its natural feel. You know immediately that it is a natural, spring fed lake, as its crystal waters mirror the mountain peaks and thicker forests to create the backdrop for mesmerizing sunsets. Unique to this place are the Camp Wagons, which are small covered wagon-like tents that can sleep a small family -- very novel -- and the Water Sports -- organized games on the Lake. Families definitely love this place. Note that it is very busy in the summertime, so be prepared to have lots of company.
Local Alternatives: Nearby Winona Beach Resort sits on 472-acre Waitts Lake/Reservoir with plenty of old-world charm, but also has a large number of long-

term residents. This well-equipped facility includes bathrooms with flush-toilets and showers, picnic tables, fire rings, a playground, Wi-Fi, a swimming beach, 5 boat docks, boat rentals, boat launching facilities, a snack bar, antique store, general store, and an RV dump. It has 64 sites for tents and RVs up to 40', 57 with full and partial 30/50-amp hookups, with 8 cabins.

Hunters CG (Stevens Co.'s *MOST APPEALING CG TO THE SENSES*)
This campground rests on a blunt prominence of Lake Roosevelt where it takes a short but sharp turn to the east. As such, it has a wide vista of views for very long stretches. Every time you walk a few yards or turn your head, you will see something different and wonderful.
Overview: This panoramic campground is located 41 miles southwest of Colville and 3 miles west of Hunters with extensive Lake Roosevelt shoreline, managed by the NPS at 1314' elevation, open year-round; GPS 48.12463, -118.3119.
Facilities: This nicely equipped campground includes vault toilets, running water (seasonal), picnic tables, fire rings, a massive boat launch/dock, a great swimming area, an RV dump, and camp hosts.
Recreation: Sure, there are fishing, boating, and other water sports on the Lake, but these views could easily mesmerize most campers into just staring for days.
Campsites: (37 individual sites plus 3 group sites for up to 25 people each, no hookups, reservations required for group sites): Individual sites along the water are flat, whereas those away from the Lake can be slightly sloped. Privacy is moderate to good, and all have some shade trees. The best sites are along the River, although these are few in number, and weekdays may be better for arrival, since there are no reservations for individual sites. The group sites are all flat. Note that the group sites are not on the Lake but have partial lake views. This is one of the more developed group sites, although its popularity can work against it in terms or privacy.
Trip Notes: The view of Lake Roosevelt is phenomenal from here, as the campground sits where the Columbia River takes a sharp 90-degree turn, and we felt as if we were staring at two different arms of the River at the same time. We could see this sweeping view from the individual campsites, which were a surprise for us, as only the group campground gets attention. The 3 group camps were way too close together for our liking, and our tendency might be to reserve all three at one time with a larger group.

Spokane River
The Spokane River drains beautiful Lake Coeur D'Alene in northern Idaho and empties into the Columbia River/Lake Roosevelt near Fort Spokane. Along the say, especially along the River's north shore, campers find a reprieve, far from the city lights of Spokane or the larger or more commercial parks along the way.

Lake Spokane CG (Stevens Co.'s *BEST RUSTIC CG*)

Lake Spokane, also known as Long Lake, is a 25-mile long reservoir running between Nine Mile Falls Dam and Long Lake Dam to the west.

Overview: This pretty little campground is located 22.1 miles northwest of Spokane on the north shore of 4,748-acre Lake Spokane, owned by DNR and operated by the Avista Corp. in cooperation with Riverside S.P. at 1700' elevation, open April 15 to October 15; GPS: 47.9046, -118.30915.

Facilities: Limited facilities include vault toilets, drinking water by hand pump, picnic tables, fire grills, a two-lane boat launch, swimming beach, cell phone service, and camp hosts.

Recreation: These include swimming, fishing for bass and trout, and boating activities of all kinds including water skiing, windsurfing, sail boating, and kayaking/canoeing.

Campsites (12 sites for tents or RVs up to 30', only site 10 has hookups and is reservable): Sites retain that shaggy DNR appearance -- very functional but natural, surrounded by Ponderosa pine, overlooking Lake Spokane from a small bluff. Site 10, unlike the other sites, comes equipped with full hookups, a private toilet, and a killer view of Lake Spokane from the edge of the bluff.

Trip Notes: This rustic gem is used primarily by boaters entering Lake Spokane. The campground may be rustic, but the Day Use Area shines brightly, well equipped and well-manicured. The day users come and go, but then we campers have the place all to ourselves, overlooking the seemingly endless lake from our folding chairs and our cold beverages without a care in the world. Balance is good, and you'll find it right here.

For more photos of Stevens Co. CGs, or info on HIKE-IN or BOAT-IN CGs, consult campeverycountywa.com

THURSTON COUNTY (Olympia/Nisqually/Littlerock)

THURSTON

From the many-fingered waterways of southern Puget Sound, to the amazing Nisqually National Wildlife Refuge, to the glacial prairies at the base of the Capital State Forest, this small county provides a wide variety of camping and recreational opportunities.

Nisqually River Region

The Nisqually River has its source at the Nisqually Glacier on Mount Rainier, but makes its grand exit at the Nisqually River Delta in northern Thurston Co. Its 81-mile journey crisscrosses the Nisqually Indian Reservation and is their territorial center. Tribal influences make recreation here more solitary and natural than much of the County.

Riverbend CG/RV Park (Thurston Co.'s *MOST UNIQUELY WASHINGTON CG*)
This at first appears like an RV Park with some long-term residents but look deeper. On the edge of the campground, on the sandy shores of the Nisqually River, are some of the nicest, most natural tent sites in all of Washington. The campground is also under new management with vast improvements. Warning: don't confuse this with Riverbend RV Park in Okanogan Co.
Overview: This gated campground is located 12.2 miles east of downtown Olympia and 3.5 miles south of I-5, privately operated on 25 acres at low elevation, open year-round; GPS 47.04804, -122.69429.
Facilities: Updated amenities include bathrooms with showers (ADA), pit toilets near the River, some picnic tables and fire pits, laundry, a playground, picnic area, a boat ramp, Club House with library/games/TV, a mini store, Wi-Fi and cable TV at some sites, a pet play area, friendly camp hosts, and an RV dump.
Recreation: Disc Golf, horseshoes, and outdoor games are available. Check fishing regulations before setting out, as these change from year to year.

Campsites (93 sites for tents and RVs up to 60', including 15 tent sites on the River, a mixture of pull-throughs and back-ins with full and partial 30/50 amp hookups, reservable): Sites are large, level and shady on gravel or sand pads, but subject to railroad and military plane noise. The tents sites on the River are rustic and natural, and also the most private. The RV sites surround beautifully manicured grounds. On the edge of the RV area is farmland with llamas who seem to keep many campers entertained.

Trip Notes: This campground is best for longer stays, those stopping over along I-5, or for tent campers who are less bothered by train or plane noise. The long-term campers are reported as very nice and unobtrusive by most reviewers, and our experience was the same. The crowning jewel is the Nisqually River itself -- very uniquely Washington -- with its opalescent water, easy wading, camping on the sandy beach.

Local Attraction: The amazing Billy Frank Jr. Nisqually National Wildlife Refuge occupies the Nisqually River Delta, where the River meets Puget Sound. Covering 3,114 acres, this is home to over 300 species of birds, mammals, reptiles, and amphibians.

Thurston County's Prairie Region

Thurston Co. is unique among Puget Sound counties with its sprawling prairies. Those travelling north of Olympia to shop at Cabela's must take the Hawks Prairie exit, but most prairies lie further south where towns are smaller and more scattered. Still, less than 10% of the area's prairies still exist, with only a fraction of that suitable to support its many endangered species. Camp well here, but also appreciate what a remarkable opportunity you have to share this land.

American Heritage CG (Thurston Co.'s *BEST EQUIPPED CG/BEST CG FOR RVs*)

Despite what is often published, this is not a KOA Park or franchised park, but an independent, family-run operation, with its own attention to the details of a good camping experience.

Overview: This tidy but natural campground is located 7.6 miles south Olympia on 25 acres, private/family operated at 174' elevation, open year-round for RVs (tents are summer only); GPS 46.946439, -122.926398.

Facilities: This campground comes well-equipped with bathrooms, showers, running water, picnic tables, fire rings, laundry, Wi-Fi, an on-site store, swimming pool, a play field and playground, volleyball and horseshoe pits, a paved bicycle track, an animal viewing farm, camp hosts, and an RV dump.

Recreation: Most recreation occurs within the park.

Campsites (86 sites, including 72 back-in RV sites with 30-amp hookups, one wonderful cabin, all reservable): The RV sites are formed into two loops surrounded by a larger loop; the tent sites have a separate, more isolated, grassier loop. Most sites are wooded and private. The Park seems oriented to families, and the staff (the Heck family) make great efforts to accommodate everyone. The noise of coyotes and wolves can be heard at night, owing in part to its proximity to Wolf Haven. Though the parks sits close to I-5, most freeway sound is buffered by pristine stands of mature trees and vegetation. Of note, many campers come here generation after generation, including entire families, groups of friends, and more solitary campers, owing to the welcoming environment of the staff.

Trip Notes: The City of Tumwater is slowly encroaching on this park, but don't judge it until you are inside the campground itself. It does not have the feel of a suburban park, as the lush, high vegetation and trees provide a great escape. The sites are very deep and large and can accommodate even the largest RVs. The tent sites are also large enough for those Goliath tents you see occasionally. More to the point, the Heck Family was extremely welcoming, and this is reflected in every detail of the Park. On that note, however, I must add that the Park is showing its age and could use a little more maintenance. Maybe their growing children will follow in their parent's footsteps and get it done.

Millersylvania S.P. (Thurston Co.'s *BEST CG FOR ENTIRE FAMILIES*)
This park was originally called "Miller's Glade," after the Miller family that donated the land. The name was later changed to Millersylvania, or "wooded glade," due to its striking forest, lakes, and prairie land. Its construction by the CCC in 1935 gives it the vintage character of the era, with its brick bathrooms, kitchen shelters, and other stone and wooden buildings.

Overview: Vintage in every way, this campground is located 11.7 miles south of Olympia on 842 acres with 3,300' of freshwater shoreline on 38.8-acre Deep Lake at 210' elevation, open year-round; GPS 46.91278, -122.90972.

Facilities: Vintage with modern updates, campers will find bathrooms with showers (ADA), picnic tables, fire grills, 4 kitchen shelters, a boat launch, 100' of dock, a Park Store, concession stand, boat rentals, 8.6 miles of hiking trails, 7.6 miles of biking trails, camp hosts, and an RV dump station.

Recreation: This includes swimming, boating (speed limit 5 mph, no gas motors), fishing, hiking, and "glamping."

Campsites (120 tent spaces, 48 full utility sites for RVs up to 45' with full hookups 30 amp, 5 "glamping sites" in the Pampered Wilderness, one group camp for 20-40, the Environmental Learning Center for 150-160, Lakeside Cottage, all are reservable): The tent sites, while shaded and beautiful amid old growth forest, are connected by a series of difficult to maneuver roads, and large vehicles should reserve sites in the RV loop. The most shaded/wooded RV sites are 201-227 and 246-248, others are in full sun. The 5 Pampered Wilderness sites feature furnished hand-made canvas and log cabins with king-sized beds, electricity, mini-fridges, microwaves, gourmet coffee, barbecues with utensils, continental breakfasts, wine glasses, and even s'mores. The Group Camp is wooded and shady, with a group fire pit and kitchen shelter. The Environmental Learning/Retreat Center features a furnished wood lodge with dining hall and equipped kitchen, 19 heated cabins (2 with bathrooms) for 6-8 people each, 4 trailer/RV sites, 2 outdoor classrooms, bathrooms with showers, and an amphitheater.

Trip Notes: The 1930s-1940s feel of this campground strikes you the minute you enter the camping areas. It is easy to imagine movie stars -- Katherine Hepburn, Humphrey Bogart, and even Mae West -- glamping in the Pampered Wilderness, sipping wine, wading in Deep Lake, and sitting around their respective campfires, while their servants bring them boeuf bourguignon and caviar, before being tucked in beneath the silk sheets of their candlelit canvas tents. Exaggeration? Sure, but this place retains a vintage, Hollywood-type glamor that is a real treasure.

campeverycountywa.com

Lost lake is the centerpiece of Millersylvania S.P.

Capital State Forest

The 91,650-acre Capitol State Forest is a "working forest" providing both timber and recreation. These are trust lands managed to provide sustainable revenue in support of schools, state universities and local county public services. These Black Hills lands also provide the majority of the County's trails for ORVs, mountain biking, horseback riding, and hiking, laced with some of the most regenerative campgrounds in Washington.

Margaret McKenny CG (Thurston Co.'s *BEST FREE/RUSTIC CG*, *MOST APPEALING CG TO THE SENSES*, and *BEST BIKE-IN CG*)
This campground was named for the noted ecologist of the same name and reflects her love of forest preservation in every way.
Overview: This greenest of campgrounds is located 14 miles southwest of Olympia and 3 miles northwest of Littlerock, managed by the DNR at 292' elevation, open May to November; GPS 46.9265, -123.0628.

Facilities: Campers at this DNR-equipped site can expect vault toilets, picnic tables, fire rings, horse corals in the equestrian loop, and camp hosts. There is no potable drinking water at this time.

Campsites (21 back-in sites for tents and RVs up to 45' plus 8 walk-in sites, one loop dedicated to equestrians, no hookups or reservations, FREE with Discover Pass): The campground consists of 3 loops (see more below). Sites are wooded but primitive, and of variable size.

Parking pads are gravel. Second growth Douglas fir, Sitka spruce, big leaf maple and alder provide both privacy and quiet. There is a campsite host during the summer months - very important, as vandalism is on the rise in all areas. Unlike nearby campgrounds, this one does not allow ORVs, and is seldom used by hunters. This Is a good base for hiking, mountain biking, and horseback riding -- all activities compatible with relaxed camping.

Trip Notes: Even as you enter the Park, you see that its strong suits are as a trailhead for hiking, and dedicated campsites for horse campers. The regular camping sites, however, are also beautiful and diverse. It has some of the smallest and largest campsites of any local campground. The C Loop is the most attractive, as it has immediate access to Waddell Creek and surrounds a grassy circle. This is the first time we have camped in a "no fee" campground. I like not having a check-in or check-out time, as it was more relaxing. We had 180 degrees of pure, second growth forest around us, plus enough space to pitch at least 3 additional tents. The horse campers in Loop B were extremely quiet and friendly. Those in Loop A were a great mixture of people, some who used only homemade hemp rope and hand-made camping gear, others who kept to themselves but friendly when approached. We camped with several families in Loop C, and enjoyed watching the kids play in the large, grassy loop.

Historical Note: Here we will quote the campground's historical sign #1: Miss Margaret McKenny for whom this site is named, an ardent conservationist, author of many wildlife books, and a noted mushroom authority and photographer, has given freely of her time to conservation causes and to the teaching of children...

Nearby Attractions: The Mima Mounds Natural Preserve is just south of the campground on Mima Rd. The old logging ghost town of Bordeaux was unlike the other "log towns" of its era, as it was built by the French who preferred brick-and-mortar construction to the less permanent log construction of their counterparts. Remains of buildings still stand in the forest just off Bordeaux Rd.

For more photos of Thurston Co. CGs consult
campeverycountywa.com

Cathlamet describes itself as "a drinking town with a fishing problem"

The sand dunes at Skamokawa

The town of Skamokawa was built on a series of canals

Teepees are a big draw at Skamokawa Vista Park

The Grays River Covered Bridge in Wahkiakum County

WAHKIAKUM COUNTY (Cathlamet/Skamokawa)

WAHKIAKUM

Small, isolated, and mysterious, this county was accessible only by river or canal until the 1930s when the first trans-county highway was built. A backwater county of covered bridges, ghost towns, and Columbia River boat traffic, this makes a damn interesting place to visit.

Cathlamet/Puget Island Area

Described by locals as a "quaint drinking village with a fishing problem," the historic river town of Cathlamet draws tourists who want to step back in time. Its riverboat character, museums, and historic buildings beckon back to a time when life was more deliberate, and camping was more a way of life.

Elochoman Slough Marina RV Park (Wahkiakum Co.'s *BEST BOAT-IN* and *BIKE-IN CG*)

Camp here, and you'll experience this unique part of Washington up close and personal, surrounded by boats, immersed in the Columbia River life, and surrounded by one of the quaintest and most historical towns in Washington.

Overview: This small and bustling marina campground is located in the river town of Cathlamet on the Columbia River, operated by Wahkiakum Port District 1, open year-round; GPS 46.198928, -123.380174.

Facilities: These include bathrooms with showers, picnic tables, fire grills, laundry, a picnic area with barbecue, a concession stand, launch ramps, camp hosts, and an RV dump station.

Recreation: Water-focused activities include fishing, boating and, for campers, binge boat watching.

Campsites (21 back-in tent sites, 7 hookup sites with water & electric 30/50-amp hookups for RVs of any size, 4 cabins, 2 yurts, reservable): Tent camping is divided into two sections. The best sites are on the dike road, a long, narrow peninsula dividing the marina from a small forested barrier island. Here boats must slowly travel the length of the peninsula before turning into the marina. These sites are small with some vegetation and privacy, but quiet and peaceful. The "waterfront sites" sit precariously on the edge of the parking lot and the unobstructed Columbia River. These will be enjoyed by the binge boat watchers less concerned with privacy. The RV sites are pure utility, set on gravel with zero privacy or vegetation. These can be recommended only for those who come purely for marina business. The cabins are nestled into the edge of town, set on a hillside overlooking the marina, and get very high ratings. The yurts seem older but sit at the end of the dike road with the best boat watching.

Trip Notes: This is a very unique campground in the most unique of small towns. Campers will be immersed in the river life of Cathlamet and the Columbia River generally. But... if you come to camp here, travel light! Bring the smaller vehicle and the smaller tent and leave all the extras at home. The marina will supply all that you need.

Local Alternative: Camping and Moorage is located on Puget Island (a residential island connected to Cathlamet by bridge) and is a newer but smaller alternative.

Skamokawa Area

This town was not settled by Venetians, nor does it resemble Venice in Italy, except of course for the series of natural canals on which it was built. In fact, the town resembles "Who-Ville," depicted by Dr. Seuss, with the buildings much higher than wide, all built around canals, and leaning just a bit. Even if you're simply driving past on Highway 4, this unique and historic town will leave a whimsical and lasting impression that will bring you back.

Skamokawa Vista Park (Wahkiakum Co.'s *MOST UNIQUELY WASHINGTON CG, BEST CG for ENTIRE FAMILIES,* and *BEST EQUIPPED CG FOR RVs*)
This is Wahkiakum Co.'s premier camping park set within the historic town of Skamokawa, sometimes called "Little Venice," as the town was built on a series of natural canals. Add a white sand beach on the Columbia River, and you'll be drawn into the endearing character of this town and park.

Overview: This remarkable park is located within the river town of Skamokawa on 75 acres on the Columbia River, operated by the Port of Wahkiakum No. 2 at 20' elevation, open year-round; GPS: 46.269373, -123.460765.

Facilities: Generous amenities include bathrooms with showers, picnic tables, fire pits, 2 playgrounds, 2 teepees for rent, day use shelters, a basketball court, horseshoe pits, a tennis court, sports fields, a public library at the entrance, Wi-Fi, camp hosts, and an RV dump station.

Recreation: The disparate activities available include beach combing, kayaking, visiting the historic buildings of Skamokawa, wildlife viewing, fishing, field sports, and boat watching.

Campsites (59 sites total for tents or RVs up to 35' with consideration for larger RVs. Five sites have yurts. Twelve are primitive sites for tents. RVs sites include 27 with partial and 15 with full 20/30/50-amp hookups. All are reservable): The layout of the campground resembles the old school yard on which it sits. The large, flat sports field lies in the middle, with sites arranged around the Columbia River and into the wooded and beach areas. Sites 27-33 are full hookup sites nestled in the trees, and the best for larger groups, and the most private overall.

Trip notes: Can a campground move the earth? A silly question you say, but in this case, they moved tons of white sand onto the shore of this Columbia River gem. A bank of trees protects campsites from the wind of the Columbia River. On weekends, dozens of multi-colored kayaks line the sandy beach, as this is a popular spot for many WA and OR kayak clubs, who enjoy the many canals on which the town of Skamokawa is built.

Local Alternative: County Line CG, near the Wahkiakum-Cowlitz Co. line on the Columbia River, offers riverfront tent camping (3 sites) and RV camping (18 sites with electric hookups only). It provides good fishing and boat watching.

Local Attraction: The Julia Butler Hanson Refuge for the Columbian White-Tailed Deer is just a short drive to the east. These are the only white-tailed deer west of the Cascades, whose population became so low they were once considered extinct. About 300 of these shy creatures now live on the refuge and surrounding communities, though they are known to occasionally wander into the Vista Park.

Grays River/Deep River Area

Deep River is 2 miles downstream from Grays River, both of which empty into Grays Bay. Several small towns, past and present, line both rivers, along with numerous houseboats and boat launches. It is rustic and natural, with a muddy, backwater feel and character all its own.

Rose Creek Retreat (Wahkiakum Co.'s *MOST APPEALING CG TO THE SENSES*)

There is camping, and there is glamping, but here we have what we might call "boutique-ing." This retreat was handcrafted out of land long misused by loggers and factories. Now campers are greeted by the scents of heirloom roses, the sights of eagles and ships floating by, and the hoots of owls as the sun sets over Grays Bay.

Overview: This boutique camping retreat is located 27 miles northwest of Cathlamet and 8.5 miles south of Grays River, privately operated, open year-round; GPS unknown, see directions below.

Facilities: Tent campers will find restrooms (ADA accessible), a fire pit in the Rose Garden Site, a Day Use area with picnic tables and a fire pit, a Visitor Center, and most notably their own individual wildlife park in each site.

Recreation: Activities feature relaxing or foraging for mushrooms, huckleberries and wildflowers. Birding, hiking, paddle boarding, canoeing, and kayaking are also popular.

Campsites (3 sites for tents only, reservations are required): Rose Creek Retreat is unique in that each site is an individually conceived and crafted garden-like camping experience. Here is the breakdown: The Creekside Garden Site features private camping in a restored forest, intersected by Rose Creek, and interspersed by native trees and hundreds of native roses, providing a lush and serene environment. The Orchid Garden Site is the most secluded site, underneath canopies of maples, spotted with wild orchids, and interspersed by huckleberry bushes ripe for the picking. It features a hand-built wigwam/wickiup, terrariums and trails. The Rose Garden Site rests right on the Columbia River with a restored cool, babbling creek running through. Over 30 varieties of tea roses give this site a more formal feel, while still being the best birding site, ensuring that it appeals to all the senses simultaneously. It contains a sleeping gazebo for those seeking a little more luxury.

Trip Notes: A personal tour from operator Sol Mertz was very telling of the hospitality you will receive here. More telling is the simultaneous scent of the old roses on the bank dropping down to the Altoona-Pillar Rock Road, part of the original residence once located on this spot. One can take in the intoxicating scent of the past, while observe eagles swooping down from the trees onto the mighty Columbia River in search of fish, while taking in the multicolor sunsets rising out of the west. Furthermore, land that was once taken for dead is now being restored to the "Real Washington," making it the most uniquely Washington camping areas in the County, if not the entire State.

Historical Note: This area has long been home to indigenous peoples, later visited by Lewis and Clark, and more recently became the site of two ghost towns, Altoona and Cottardi Station. The decline of the salmon industry meant the demise of these towns, and the land was heavily logged and left to be overrun by invasive species. The owners stepped in and began using ecological forestry processes to restore the habitat, with the return of several species, including native trees, birds, and other wildlife. The land is now dominated by multiple gardens that showcase the natural beauty of the area.

OTHER CAMPGROUNDS: There are no Hike-In or Group CGs in Wahkiakum Co. that we can recommend at this time. For more photos on Wahkiakum Co. CGs, please consult campeverycountywa.com

WALLA WALLA COUNTY (Walla Walla/Burbank)

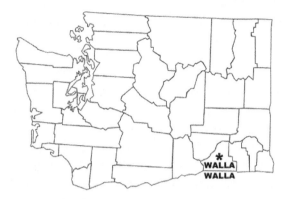

Even locals have fun with the name "Walla Walla." Celebrities are given names like Little Chief Twice Nice (the Walla Walla Brand Vegetable Mascot), and Walla Walla Wine Wine Woman Woman (PEMCO Insurance Northwest Profile #96). The name of the city and county actually derived from the Nez Perce Indian word Wallah, meaning water. Wallah Wallah, in turn, means "running waters," referring to the Touchet, Walla Walla, Columbia and Snake Rivers plus their many tributaries.

Snake River/Lake Sacajawea Area
The irony here is that while "Wallah Wallah" meant "running waters" in the Nez Perce tongue, this section of the Snake River no longer flows at all. It is now a series of lakes/reservoirs created by the Ice Harbor, Lower Monumental, Little Goose, and Lower Granite Dams. Now we have Lake Sacajawea, Lake West, Lake Bryan, and Lower Granite Lake. But whether you're pro-running waters, pro-lakes, or just want to forget the whole thing and go camping, you'll find that recreation here is pretty exceptional.

Charbonneau Park (Walla Walla Co.'s *BEST CG FOR ENTIRE FAMILIES*)
You can see the Ice Harbor Dam from the campsites here, as Lake Sacajawea extends east. The marina sets this campground apart, located in the widest and deepest part of the Lake, overlooked by this very nice campground on a knoll named after John Baptiste Charbonneau, the son of Sacajawea, and well-known American explorer, fur trapper trader, and military scout.
Overview: This campground is located 9 miles west of Pasco and 40.7 miles northwest of Walla Walla on 244 acres with extensive Lake Sacajawea shoreline,

operated by the US Army COE at 453' elevation, open mid-May through Labor Day; GPS: 46.256261, -118.845421.

Facilities: This nicely appointed Park is equipped with bathrooms with showers, picnic tables, fire grills, a large detached Day Use Area with two shelters, a swimming area, playground, concession stand. a boat ramp, a marina, volleyball courts, RV dump, and camp hosts.

Recreation: Popular are boating, swimming, fishing for salmon, steelhead, sturgeon, trout and smallmouth bass. Stargazing is also popular.

Campsites (37 sites for tents and RVs of any size,15 with full hookups and 22 with water & electric 50-amp hookups, reservable): Sites are grassy with adequate privacy. Put simply, while Windust Park (Franklin Co.) has the privacy, and Fishhook Park has the nicest campsites, Charbonneau has the SPACE. Unlike the other parks, Charbonneau also has a marina, and is named one of the top 100 Family Parks in WA (sometimes a mixed blessing).

Trip Notes: The camping section of this park occupies the same amount of acreage as Fishhook, with the same number of sites, but arranges them on a large "hill," which means more sites look down on others, and not all sites have views of the Lake. On the positive side, some have views of the marina and the Ice Harbor Dam, but others have views of desert or marsh. The Day Use area is separated from the camping area, making it less accessible to campers. While the Park occupies 244 acres, it seems smaller. There is some train noise. I can still understand why this campground is more popular with families, as campers are positioned to interact with each other, but also why Fishhook is more popular with those who value privacy. The truth is, they are both lovely parks.

Local Attractions include the Ice Harbor Dam itself, the Hopkins Ridge Wind Farm near Touchet, and the Three Rivers Winery near Walla Walla.

Fishhook Park (Walla Walla Co.'s *MOST APPEALING CG TO THE SENSES, BEST EQUIPPED/BEST CG FOR RVs,* and *BEST BIKE-IN CG*)

The park was named for Fishhook Rapids, which were once nearby, where Lewis and Clark spent time in October 1805. They described this as the most beautiful section of the Snake River. The rapids are now underwater after the building of the Ice Harbor Dam, but we have this beautiful park to commemorate both the rapids and the Lewis and Clark Expedition.

Overview: This terraced campground is located 19 miles southeast of Pasco and 41 miles northwest of Walla Walla on 46 acres, operated by the US Army COE at 460' elevation, open mid-May through Labor Day; GPS 46.315, -118.76611.

Facilities: This beautifully organized Park has bathrooms with showers, picnic tables, fire grills, picnic shelters, a swimming area, two playgrounds, a boat ramp, RV dump and camp hosts.

Recreation: Boating, swimming, fishing for salmon, steelhead, sturgeon, trout and smallmouth bass are popular, as well as stargazing.

Campsites (11 walk-in sites for tents, plus 41 for tents or RVs of any size with water & electric 50 amp hookups, reservable): Compared to Charbonneau Park, which uses roughly the same acreage for the same number of campsites, Fishhook Park's camping area is long and narrow, with all sites having a lake view. Sites are grassy with privacy guaranteed by their sheer size. The walk-in sites on the lawn are perfect for bicyclers. The strength of this campground is the uniqueness, variety, and quality of the sites. This is a great balance of solitude, relaxation and lushness.

Trip Notes: This is the most beautiful park on Lake Sacajawea, with sites extremely spacious, very green, and all having water views, where I can imagine staying for days without needing to leave the campground. One negative note is the closeness of the trains, which blows their crossing whistle when passing through the Park. The sound was somewhat muffled by the trees, but still disturbed some of those in our party.

Ayer Boat Basin (Walla Walla Co.'s *BEST FREE AND BEST RUSTIC CG*)
In a county that has only 6.4% public land, it is difficult to find many public parks. It is particularly difficult to find FREE public campgrounds. But this one is unique in its own right, set on a small bay from the Snake River beneath velvety hillsides.

Overview: This stark gem is located 45 north of Walla Walla and 45 miles west of Pasco on Lake Sacajawea, operated by the US Army COE on 170 acres at 541' elevation, open year-round; GPS 46.5845869, -118.3719198.

Facilities: Primitive facilities include vault toilets, covered picnic tables, and a 2-lane boat launch.

Recreation: These are limited to fishing, boating, swimming, and stargazing.

Campsites (Four sites for tents, and dispersed sites for tents or RVs up to 40', no hookups or reservations, FREE of charge): The four marvelous tent sites sit the furthest from the railroads along the Snake River. Two of these sites rest directly on the small bay, and two of the sites have covered picnic tables to provide shade. One of the bay sites has shade trees. Smaller RVs may be able to occupy the tent sites. Larger RVs have dispersed sites at the opposite site of the bay and in the parking area. The boat-in site is just inside the small concrete channel from the River. There will be some railroad noise here.

Trip Notes: Dropping down toward the Snake River from the hills of northern Walla Walla Co., we were met with fish jumping, pelicans feeding, and hills of velvet. This place is a rare find indeed, both for tent campers looking for a one-of-a-kind camping experience, and RV campers wanting to get away from the crowds. The covered picnic tables in the camping area provide some relief from the sun, and the cool water relief from the heat. Good camping here!

Columbia River/Lake Wallula Area

This area is defined by a complex series of waterways formed by McNary Dam near the Confluence of the Columbia and Snake Rivers. It is a water world in the desert, providing outdoor activities around every bend.

Hood Park (Walla Walla Co.'s *MOST UNIQUELY WASHINGTON CG*)

Hood Park may not have the polish of Charbonneau or Fishhook Parks, but that's what gives his park its own unique character. Furthermore, this arm of Lake Wallula backs up to the Ice Harbor Dam, making campers think they're on the Snake River, not the Columbia. What is clear is that there is much more to explore here than other area parks.

Overview: Located 3 miles south of Pasco and 42.5 miles west of Walla Walla, operated by the US Army COE at 364' elevation, open mid-May through Labor Day; GPS 46.21372, -119.013.

Facilities include bathrooms with showers and running water, picnic tables, fire grills, sun shelters, a swimming beach, amphitheater, one Group Picnic Shelter, a playground, basketball courts, horseshoe pits, a boat ramp, fishponds, an RV dump and camp hosts.

Recreation: Campers enjoy fishing in Lake Wallula and the fishing ponds with the park, boating, swimming, and bird watching at the adjacent McNary Wildlife Refuge, with 15,000 acres of sloughs, ponds, streams and islands important to migratory waterfowl, shorebirds and songbirds.

Campsites (67 sites for tents or RVs up to 30' with water & electric 30/50-amp hookups, reservable): These large sites come with level asphalt parking pads and are reasonably spaced with good privacy. The many mature trees in the Park are exceptional, providing shade, songbirds, and windbreaks.

Trip Notes: The Park has a stunningly beautiful Day Use Area and boat launch, set on a wide stretch of the Snake River just above the Ice Harbor Dam. The shade trees provide the most shade of the Snake and Columbia River campgrounds. The one small drawback is lack of unobstructed lake views from the campground, which required walks toward the boat launch -- a walk we made many times. This still remains one of the best campgrounds in the larger area.

For more photos of Walla Walla Co. CGs consult
campeverycountywa.com

WHATCOM COUNTY (Bellingham/NCNP/Mount Baker)

The Canadian influence is obvious here the moment you pound your tent stakes into one of the many and varied Whatcom County campgrounds. In fact, access to two of them require passage through Canada. But this only adds to their charm, eh?

Salish Sea/Georgia Strait

No, Georgia Strait is not the name of a female country singer, but part of an intricate network of coastal waterways between Vancouver Island in Canada and the mainland that includes the northern coast of Whatcom County. Georgia Strait, the Strait of Juan de Fuca, and Puget Sound interconnect to form the Salish Sea, named for the Coastal Salish people that once inhabited this land. But the Georgia Strait washes many more Canadian than Washington shores, giving this area its strong Canadian connections.

Birch Bay S.P. (Whatcom Co.'s *BEST EQUIPPED/BEST CG FOR RVs*)

The town of Birch Bay was named for the many species of birch noted by the earliest European explorers. From its inception, this area has been known for its flora, fauna, and recreational activities.

Overview: This secluded wooded saltwater park is located 20.3 miles northwest of Bellingham and 7.5 miles south of Blaine on 194 acres with 8,255' of saltwater shoreline and 14,923' of freshwater shoreline on Terrell Creek, open year-round; GPS 48.9043, -122.7643.

Facilities: Here you'll find extensive picnic and Day Use facilities, including a Kitchen Shelter with water & electricity, plus 120 unsheltered picnic tables. Campground facilities include 8 bathrooms (1 ADA), 18 showers (2 ADA), picnic tables, fire grills, a boat ramp, an amphitheater, a basketball court, camp hosts, and an RV dump.

Recreation is quite varied. The waters off Birch Bay are warmer than normal, making for good swimming. Clamming, crabbing, and oyster harvesting are popular (a WDFW recreational license is required). beach combing, swimming, boating, bird watching, and the 0.5-mile Terrell Marsh Interpretive Trail are also popular. The Terrell Creek Marsh is one of the few remaining saltwater/freshwater estuaries in north Puget Sound. It winds throughout the campground hugging the shoreline just a hundred yards or so away, as if the park were built around it. Here you can view all manner of birds and wildlife, including blue herons.

Campsites (169 sites, including 20 sites with water & electric 30/50-amp hookups for RVs up to 60', a primitive group camp for up to 60 people, two group camps with 5 sites each, reservable): Sites consist of standard sites in 3 conjoined loops (the A side, sites 75-167), a utility loop for RVs (the B side, sites 1-74), and an unnamed loop for the group sites. The A loop consists of heavily forested back-in sites that are flat with great privacy. The less forested B loop is made up of back-in sites for tents or RVs, with the hookup sites smaller with average privacy. Note that sites 40 through 74 on the B side are tent sites without hookups, so are the closest tent sites to the beach. The best sites overall are 7, 9, 11, 18, 23, 24, 27, 29, 51, 54, 56, 74, 78, 80, 84, 92, 103, 104, 113, 115, 108, and 127.

Trip notes: We in Western Washington are used to wooded campgrounds, and those set on saltwater, but Birch Bay is still full or surprises. Terrell Creek seems to be everywhere you go with its birds and unidentified furry creatures. The beach is very accessible and watching the sailboats on the Bay seemed to occupy much of our time. We found good clam digging for native littleneck and Manila clams in the sandy gravel as well as butter clams, cockles and horse clams on lower tides. We finally gave in to the temptation, threw some in our pot, and sat back enjoying the local flavor.

Larrabee S.P. (Whatcom Co.'s MOST UNIQUELY WASHINGTON CG)
Overview: Located 6 miles south of Bellingham (Fairhaven) on Chuckanut Drive on 2,683 acres with 8100' of saltwater shoreline on Samish Bay, open year-round; GPS 48.6552, -122.4914.

Facilities include bathrooms with showers (ADA), picnic tables, fire grills, 2 picnic shelters (reservable), playground, amphitheater, boat launch, Kamp Store, camp hosts, and an RV dump.

Recreation: This is a great location for boating, fishing, and sailboarding. There are also 13 miles of biking trails, and 15 miles of hiking trails that include the Interurban Trail, the iconic Fragrance Lake Trail (trailhead located just outside the main State Park entrance), and Lost Lake Trail (trailhead 0.5 miles south of entrance).

Campsites (51 standard tent sites, 26 full utility sites 30/50 amp for RVs up to 60', 8 walk-in sites, and one Group Camp for up to 40): Sites range in size from very small to large. Tent sites are wooded, and often built into the rocky terrain. RV sites are side-by-side, and often in full sun, the best being site T1. The primitive walk-in sites are among the best and recommended for bicyclists. The Group Camp is beautiful but located very close to the noisy railroad tracks. Privacy is best in the small loops containing sites 1-7 and 42-49.

Trip Notes: I first visited this Park several years ago and found it terribly small. Not in overall acreage, of course, but with a very compact camping and day use area. It seemed like a miniature version of a Washington State Park presented as a display at a World Fair or theme park. This preyed on my mind for years before I took an extended stay here. What I now understood is that it has been largely preserved from its original 1915 character, in the days before aircraft-sized SUVs, tents large enough to envelope some African villages, and RVs larger than the homes in which many of us were raised. This is what makes it utterly unique. Everything is accessible. The Fragrance Lake Trail begins just across Chuckanut Drive from the Park Entrance. The beach and Wildcat Cove are both accessible by foot. Even the bicycle trails to Lost Lake are a short hop away. Additionally, everything was in perfect repair. The rangers, camp hosts, and their assistants were constantly keeping everything meticulously manicured. Yet, many of the sites were built in and around rock outcroppings and vegetation that kept it feeling very natural.

A couple of downsides: yes, the trains are as frequent and loud as the Park Service says. Upside: there is a muralled trail under the tracks that takes you safely and colorfully to the beach area. Downside: boat launching is only possible at high tide. Upside: The boat launch at Wildcat Cove is within walking distance, but far enough away from the camping area to be noise-free.

Conclusion: I think that every Washington camper should camp here at least once in their lifetime. Its diminutive size and preservation of 100-year old structures makes it more quaint than practical, but like me, your stay here will prey on your mind for many years.

Washington History: Larrabee became the first official Washington State Park in October of 1915 after 20 acres of land was donated by Frances Larrabee. The family eventually donated an additional 1500 acres in 1937, while smaller donors gave an additional 1000-plus acres. Historic Chuckanut Drive, built along the base of the Chuckanut Mountains in 1895, was the first road built to connect Bellingham with Mt. Vernon. First built as a dirt logging road, it parallels the path of the Great Northern Railway. It was graveled and finally paved following the establishment of Larrabee S.P. In 1931 it was established as a Washington State Scenic Byway, designated as State Route 11. To this day, it gives unparalleled views of the Samish Bay and the many islands beyond.

Mount Baker/Nooksack River Region (Highway 542)

Highway 542, better known as the Mount Baker Highway, is a designated State Scenic Highway and National Forest Scenic Byway. It follows the stunning Nooksack River from Bellingham Bay to Mount Baker and Mount Shuksan in a scenic byway that is second to none.

Silver Lake Co. Park (Whatcom Co.'s *BEST CG FOR ENTIRE FAMILIES*)
This is the park that you thought disappeared with the coming of overcrowded and over pruned National and State Parks in the 1940s. Nosiree Bob, this one has stayed under the radar, and will charm the bobby socks right off your feet.
Overview: Located 40 miles west of Bellingham and 2.5 miles north of Maple Falls on 157.3-acre Silver Lake, operated by Whatcom Co. Parks on 412 acres at 646' elevation, open year-round; GPS 48.9719, -122.07.
Facilities include flush toilets, a bathhouse with showers, drinking water, picnic tables, fire rings, a boat launch, camp hosts, and an RV dump.
Recreation includes but is not limited to hiking, swimming, boating, fishing, horseback riding, and visiting the good people at the Black Mountain Forestry Center.
Campsites: The Park consists of a complex of campgrounds and day use facilities.
-Maple Creek CG: This, the largest campground at the Park, consisting of six loops with 47 sites. Sites with water & electric 50-amp are 1-6, 25-27, and 29-42 for tents and RVs of any size. Sites 19-24, 28, and 44-46 have water & electric 30-amp hookups. This is also the busiest and most popular campground, near the south end of the Lake on tiny Maple Creek. Sites range from rustic to larger and more developed, and most are shaded. Cascade Cabin, the smallest and most private of the cabins, is near the entrance.
-Cedar CG: This campground has only 15 sites in a single loop for tents, truck campers, vans, and small self-contained RVs. It is the prettiest of the campgrounds, near 6 vintage cabins from the 1940s era that sit right on the central portion of the Lake. It also has the best access to the beautiful "bay" and Day Use Area and shelter rentals. The cabins here are perhaps the best of any campground in Washington. Sites are well-spaced and shaded.
-Red Mountain CG (do not confuse this with the campground of the same name on the Cle Elum River in Kittitas Co.): This detached campground is connected to the lake by hiking and equestrian trails. It has 28 sites, all with water and electric 50-amp hookups, and is better known as the "Horse Camp," as it boasts two horse stables. It may also be the quietest of the campgrounds, and the best suited for large RVs. The kids, however, may want to be closer to activity on the Lake. Sites have partial shade with fair to good privacy, and often have space available.
-Group Camp: Compact and cozy, this 37-site camp with water & electric hookups

circles a community shelter. It is removed from the Lake, and is most popular with privacy-oriented, cohesive adult groups such as church and service organizations.

Day Use Area: This includes the boat launch, the bridged "bay" that is popular with kayakers and canoers, the playground, and both the Silver Lake and Lakeside Lodges (for rent). This beautiful area has the look of a Japanese garden, but with northwest foliage. Here you will find children at play, ducks sleeping undisturbed near the shore, and human-powered boats drifting quietly in and out.

-Black Mountain Forestry Center: This remarkable Interpretive Center sits just outside the main entrance to the Park. Visit the Gerdrum House -- a pioneer house built out of a single cedar tree and broad-bladed ax -- and talk to Phil Cloward and other volunteers who have decades of interesting and varied forestry and conservation experience. This is a unique, friendly opportunity to learn about logging methods from the "insiders" while enjoying the many displays -- among which is a 400-year old Nooksack Indian canoe found floating in Silver Lake in pioneer times.

Trip Notes: This is the oldest continuously running set of campgrounds in Washington, which is apparent the minute you enter the grounds. The cabins have a very 1930s/1940s vintage feel and are continuously upgraded and maintained. I can think of no better place to take campers out of the modern, mechanized world for a while and just plain play.

Washington History: A road was built from the Gerdrum House to the Lake in 1902, which marks the beginnings of Silver Lake Park. New buildings, including a hotel were built to attract tourists. Mr. Gerdrum transported them from the train station in Maple Falls to the Lake by horse and wagon. Private ownership of the Park continued until 1967, when it was sold to Whatcom County. The original founders still have an involvement in the Black Mountain Forestry Center.

Douglas Fir CG (Whatcom Co.'s *BEST RUSTIC CG*)

Imagine camping so far from the lights of the city that the darkness sucks the light right out of your flashlight. That place would be called Douglas Fir Campground. It has the advantage of nearby services in Glacier and Maple Falls and is also is clearly the best campground in the Mt. Baker National Forest with access to Mt. Baker and Mt. Shuksan.

Overview: This Mt. Baker-Snoqualmie National Forest campground is located 37.2 miles east of Bellingham and 2 miles east of Glacier at 1200' elevation, open mid-May until late September; GPS 48.902, -121.9133.

Facilities: The campground is rustic, with only a hand pump for water and ADA vault toilets, which adds to its charm. Each site includes a picnic table and fire ring. Vintage CCC-built stonework and a picnic shelter were recently refurbished for use.

Recreation: The campground has access to Picture Lake and Artist Point giving great views of Mt. Baker's north slope and Mt. Shuksan. A nearby launching site exists for rafts and kayaks (no motorized boats allowed) for whitewater boating. The most popular hiking trail is Horseshoe Bend #687, accessible from the campground. Gold panning is available at several locations, including Nugent's Corner, Nooksack Falls, and the Great Excelsior Mine.

Campsites (29 sites for tents or RVs up to 57', no hookups, some sites are reservable): Many sites lie on the North Fork of the Nooksack River, all sit among old growth Douglas fir, silver fir, and western hemlock. Most are large, private, and unique. There is some concern for leveling RVs >30'. Among the best sites are site 1 (the most secluded), and sites 8, 12, 13, 14, 17 (off-river). The best riverside site is site 4. Note that only 18 of the sites are reservable.

Trip Notes: As a big fan of the USFS campgrounds, I'm please to find a campground that rivals those in the Gifford Pinchot National Forest in Skamania County. The real difference here, aside from the obvious proximity to Heather Meadows and Artist Point (with views of Mt. Shuksan and Mt. Baker) is the Nooksack River itself. This section of the River had a milky green gem-like sparkle from the glacial waters. Rockhounds have told me this is the color of the gemstone aventurine, which is ironic given the popularity of white water rafting in the area. This is simple and pure camping at its best.

Local Alternatives: The obvious alternative is Silver Fir CG closer to Heather Meadows, but at the time of this writing it has been heavily gravel-led, with an immense amount of vegetation removed as hazard trees. We cannot recommend this as long as sites are available at Douglas Fir.

Nooksack River/Boyds Creek Campsites (Whatcom Co.'s *BEST FREE CAMPSITES*)

This decommissioned campground no longer has an official name but continues to be used and maintained by campers who appreciate the natural beauty and rustic nature of these campsites. This type of camping is commonly called "boondocking," although officials prefer the term "dispersed camping."

Overview: These campsites are located 7 miles east of Glacier on Forest Road 37 on the south bank of the North Fork of the Nooksack River, operated by campers in co-operation with the USFS at 906' elevation, open as long as the roads passable; GPS is unreliable in this locale.

Facilities: None, except for the vault toilets generously provided by the USFS for sanitation purposes. Previous campers have also built huge river rock firepits in all 8 sites.

Recreation: This features fishing on the Nooksack River. The 0.25-mile Boyd Creek Interpretive Trail is just one mile before the campsite area. Skyline Divide Trail, a 2-mile hike with 1000' elevation, lies 7 miles beyond the camping area at the end of Forest Road 37. Nine miles from Glacier is a paved one-lane road that leads to the best vistas of Mt. Baker in the area and is highly recommended. The Great Excelsior Gold Mine provides opportunities for both ghost towning and gold-panning/sluicing. The entrance is located 0.5 miles beyond the last campsite. Look for road maker 031 on the left and hike in one mile to the mine, where the open entrance is still visible.

<u>Campsites</u> (8 sites for tents or RVs of any size willing to travel the gravel road, no hookups or reservations, FREE with NW Forest Pass): sites range from small to extra-large, the site at the end of the spur being a double site we are calling sites 7 and 8, all are very private and shaded. Seven of the eight sites are on the riverbank.

<u>Trip Notes</u>: I don't usually trust boondocking sites, having bad experiences with campers being disruptive and destructive. So, I visited this site on a Saturday morning, just as it was filling up, and again on Monday afternoon to check on the carnage. You know what? I couldn't so much as find a bottle cap or a scrap of paper left behind. That guy who was going to town with his chainsaw ended up cutting vine maple branches that were encroaching on the campsites, plus left behind cut up firewood for other campers. This gives a sample as to why these campsites have operated for several decades, and why the USFS has been willing to donate precious time to help them out. Co-operation, self-policing, and contributing to the maintenance -- all in a beautiful rustic setting? Now I know this can work and work quite well. Just be mindful that this spot fills up early on summer weekends.

The best views of Mt. Baker can be found south of Glacier off Forest Road 39

Baker Lake Region

While the Mount Baker Highway extends west of Mount Baker, beautiful Baker Lake extends due south and extends a full 9 miles. It is in fact a reservoir forged from the Baker River behind the Upper Baker Dam. At 4800 acres it is quite narrow with plenty of developed campgrounds on the western side and views of Mount Baker and the North Cascades that will make you want to kick back and stay awhile.

Panorama Point CG (Whatcom Co.'s *MOST APPEALING CG TO THE SENSES*)
This is not the largest campground on Baker Lake, nor is it the most developed, but it is certainly the most beautiful with a fairy tale quality even on cloudy days.
Overview: This Mt. Baker-Snoqualmie National Forest campground is located on the west shore of Baker Lake on approx. 20 acres 17.2 miles north of Concrete at 730' elevation, open mid-May to late September; GPS 48.724, -121.6731.
Facilities: Limited facilities include vault toilets, piped water, garbage bins, picnic tables, fire grills, a gravel boat ramp, camp hosts, and an extensive canopy of trees.
Recreation: Kayaking and canoeing are ideal here, as motorboating is limited by the park's location at the narrow "knuckle" of the Lake. Water-skiing is more popular in wider sections of Baker Lake. There are multiple hiking trails on the east side of the Lake. Fishing is very good for kokanee salmon, Dolly Varden trout, and cutthroat trout.
Campsites (15 sites for tents and small RVs, 3 of which are multiple sites, no hookups, 9 of the 15 sites are reservable): Sites are average to large, lush, private, the best being 1, 5, 6, 22, 13, 14. Sites are smaller than nearby Horseshoe Cove, but most are close to the Lake. Parking pads are gravel. This campground gives spectacular views of the south face of Mt. Baker, in addition to the recreational opportunities of Baker Lake. Douglas firs have largely replaced the old growth forest due to natural forest fires in the 1840s. It's still fine forest, and in the springtime they bring about an explosion of wildflowers, including coralroot, foamflower, twinflower, twistedstalk, and western trillium.
Trip Notes: Wow. Since we camped on a series of cloudy days, we expected to be underwhelmed. Granted, the views were blunted by clouds, but it was the vegetation that drew us in. It was whimsical. Fascinating. Engaging. Be sure you choose one of the sites close to the "point." For us, it's the vegetation, not the views, that will bring us back.
Local Alternative: By far, the best local alternative is Horseshoe Cove CG just three miles south. This campground is larger and more developed (flush toilets!) than Panorama Point with better lake access, but less spectacular views of Mt. Baker. The Day Use Area is a bit primitive, but has great lake access, overlooking a small island and the fishermen launching their boats from the "point" jutting out into the Lake. Anglers may prefer this campground. That campsites are also larger for those who prefer more space for their "stuff."

Local Attraction is the Shadows of the Sentinels Trail, a 0.6-mile board-walked trail which is handicap-accessible. It isn't the Avenue of the Giants or the Trees of Mystery, but it is worth the short drive for the short walk.

North Cascades National Park (NCNP)

Welcome to Washington's newest and least known National Park. But hidden away in its remote 500,00 acres is a larger than life alpine wilderness with jagged peaks covered with over 300 glaciers, cascading waters, and crystalline lakes of clear sapphire blue.

Colonial Creek CG at NCNP (Whatcom Co.'s *BEST BIKE-IN CG*)

It's true confession time. We dislike most of the large campgrounds in the NCNP. They seem poorly engineered, hastily built, and poorly executed. But this one campground, nestled between beautiful Diablo and Ross Lakes, with access to the best trails in the National Park, assures us that this was the developer's "baby," with all their expertise and attention to detail poured into this one near perfect campground.

Overview: This camping gem is centrally located 15 miles east of Newhalem on Lake Diablo at 1200' elevation, open seasonally; GPS 48.69023, -121.09793.

Facilities: Good facilities include bathrooms with flush toilets, potable water, picnic tables, fire grills, a fishing pier, boat launch, garbage and recycling service, evening Ranger Programs, and an RV dump station.

Recreation: This includes swimming, boating, and hiking.

Campsites (142 back-in and pull-through sites for tents and small RVs, no hookups, the South Loop is reservable): Sites are wooded and private. The North Loop (north of Hwy 20) has 42 sites and affords more privacy with better access to hiking, while the 100 sites of the South Loop (south of Hwy 20) have better lake access, better access to swimming and boating, but more activity. Sites 64-73 have the best lake access. RVs will want to book a site in the South Loop, although our pop-up trailers did fine in the North Loop.

Trip notes: The campground is divided by the North Cascades Highway (Hwy 20). We stayed in the quieter, more heavily forested North Loop, which made a cooler getaway from the 107-degree temperatures of Eastern Washington in July. The four of us, our two dogs and two cockatoos, stayed in the cool dense forest, with great forest exploring the smaller streams and bridges leading to trails. The greatest part was visiting the nearby town of Diablo and the unique Diablo Dam. It has a tram up the mountainside, and boat trips up Ross Lake. We will have to save these side trips for next time. And there will certainly be a next time.

WHITMAN COUNTY (Colfax/Pullman)

Just south of Spokane is this delightful county where most of the many small towns have huge school yards that are the town centers. The County's biggest employer is Washington State University, and everyone lives on a huge family wheat farm. That means that most of the public land is tied up with education, while the private land is tied up with wheat fields, leaving very little for campgrounds. But not to worry! We've picked out the camping gems for you.

The Palouse Region

This is Palouse Country, a region of rolling, asymmetrical hills without continuous valleys or ridges, not shaped by rivers and streams, but by a series of wind dunes. When spring comes, and the colors explode, you won't be able to take your eyes off of it.

<u>Kamiak Butte Co. Park</u> (Whitman Co.'s *MOST UNIQUELY WASHINGTON* and *MOST APPEALING CG TO THE SENSES*)

Kamiak Butte was named a National Natural Landmark based on its unique geology, incredible views, 170 plant species, 130 bird species, and 30 mammal species. How good does the campground have to be for this place to still be great?

<u>Overview</u>: This amazing county park is located 17 miles east of Colfax and 2 miles south of Palouse on 298 acres, operated by Whitman County Parks at 3631' elevation, open year-round; GPS 46.8905, -117.1360.

<u>Facilities</u>: This park comes well-equipped with picnic tables, fire grills/pits, a playground, amphitheater, 3 small shelters for up to 35 people each, and one large shelter for up to 100 people.

<u>Recreation</u>: The park's claim to fame is its 5 miles of trails. The 3.5-mile Pine Ridge Trail is part of the National Trails System, reaching an elevation of 3641'.

The Sunset Trail circles around and below the campground itself, making itself available to campers at just the right time of day. Birding watching includes warblers, woodpeckers, nuthatches, flycatchers, black-headed grosbeaks, Rufous-sided towhees and the occasional gray catbird.

Campsites (9 sites for tents or small RVs, no hookups or reservations): Sites are wooded and private, arranged in a single loop. The best sites are 3 and 4 (site 4 can accommodate a large RV). The campground and north face of the butte are covered in mature Ponderosa pine, Douglas fir and western larch, and said to be the largest forested tract in all of Whitman County.

Kamiak Butte Trail leads to panoramic views of the rolling hills
of the Palouse Country

Trip Notes: It's a wonder how some of these smaller counties can come up with such magnificent county parks. Of course, it helps to have a National Natural Wonder in your back pocket, but this place exceeded our camping expectations. This well-kept campground, entirely detached from the Day Use Area, has a lush, manicured charm that makes it well worth the trip.

Washington History: The park is named after Chief Kamiakin, the leader of the Yakama, Palouse, and Klickitat peoples who staged an uprising known as the Yakima Wars of 1855-1858. He was defeated and fled, but later returned peacefully to his native homeland.

Geological History: The Butte itself is an "island," consisting of Precambrian quartzite projecting approximately 1,000 feet above the surrounding wheat fields. The reddish rocks once formed the bed of an ancient sea, and the grains of sand embedded in them act as suncatchers, causing them to glitter in the Palouse sun.

The Columbia River/Lower Granite Lake Region

The southern border of Whitman County spills out along a long and lonely stretch of the Snake River made slower by the Little Goose and Lower Granite Dams. But with dams come the required recreational facilities, and fortunately a few campgrounds are quite campworthy.

Wawawai County Park (Whitman Co.'s *BEST CG FOR ENTIRE FAMILIES and BEST BIKE-IN CG*)

Wawawai (pronounced Wa-WAA-Wee) was a native village for hundreds of years, giving way to a premier orchard community on the Snake River, until it was inundated by the creation of the Lower Granite Dam in 1975. The park now occupies the site of the original post office, but now you'll have to buy your stamps elsewhere.

Overview: This cohesive little county park is located 29 miles south of Colfax on Lower Granite Lake (Snake River) on 49 acres, operated by Whitman County Parks at 791' elevation, open year round; GPS 46.6359, -117.3728.

Facilities: You'll find vault toilets, drinking water from mid-April through mid-October, covered picnic tables, fire grills, a playground, a fishing pond, a nearby boat launch at Wawawai Landing, one large reservable group shelter for up to 100 people with 10 picnic tables and a barbecue grill, and a half-mile interpretive trail ending at a bird-viewing platform. A special feature is an underground earth-sheltered house built right into the hillside that serves as the park ranger's home.

Recreation: The park features a small bay off the confluence of Wawawai Creek and the Snake River appropriate for non-motorized boats and fishing. Fishing is best on the Snake River itself and includes summer steelhead. Bird watching includes wrens, goldfinches, California quail, song sparrows and white-crowned sparrows, red-tailed hawks, robins, and black-billed magpies. There are also numerous shaded walking areas around the park.

Campsites (5 pull-through tent sites including 2 with sand tent pads, plus 4 pull-through RV sites, no hookups or reservations): All 9 sites are large and paved with adequate privacy. All sites are shady and relatively flat.

Trip Notes: This Park is known for such icons as the earthen house and the Picnic Pavilion, but the camping area is every bit as beautiful, separated from the hilly Day Use Area by a concrete path. The shade trees, and the Whitman County Parks' attention to detail with the placement of its covered picnic shelters and interpretive signs make this stand out as one of the best county parks in Washington.

Washington History: The Palouse and Nez Perce tribes occupied this site for thousands of years before the coming of the settlers from the east. The original name was Wawawa, which means "talk, talk," or council grounds. The area is now known as a wine producing area.

The iconic Picnic Pavilion is the centerpiece of Wawawai Co. Park

Boyer Park and Marina (Whitman Co.'s *BEST EQUIPPED/BEST CG FOR RVs*)
Boyer Park was built in 2013 to fill an RV camping void in this remote Snake
River region. But don't let its remoteness fool you! This place has modern,
upscale facilities and, despite being known as an RV park, is equally inviting to
tent campers.
Overview: This lush park is located 24 miles southwest of Colfax on the Snake
River, privately operated on 140 acres at 640' elevation, open year-round; GPS
46.6791, -117.4457.
Facilities: This well-equipped park includes bathrooms with showers, picnic
tables, barbecue pits, laundry, garbage collection, a swimming area, playground,
volleyball court, boat launch and marina, meeting rooms, a bike/jogging path,
Convenience Store, the Snake River Grill, and an RV dump.
Recreation: The many recreational opportunities include boating, fishing,
swimming and hunting.
Campsites (3 walk-in tent sites, plus 28 full-hookup 20/30/50-amp RV sites, 28 of
which are long-term sites for winter or spring, and 20 water & electric 30-amp RV
sites. There are also 4 motel rooms and 4 rustic wood cabins. All sites, motel
rooms, and cabins are reservable): The Park is divided into 3 campgrounds. The
Main Campground (28 full hookup sites plus 3 walk-in tent sites) are mostly
occupied by longer-term RV campers in the winter and spring. The Central Park
(13 sites, water only) were occupied exclusively by tent campers. The South Park
(20 sites partial hookups) seemed to be the newest loop and occupied mostly by
smaller RVs. Sites are average in size with average privacy, but lush and green.
Trip Notes: This is a textbook example of how irrigation can make the desert
bloom. Bright and shiny, great food, an entire one-third of the Park (Central
Park) reserved for tent campers, remarkable beach with an explorable island,

and a quirky gift shop that will make you chuckle. The wind can be very strong here, despite the tall trees that lessen the blow. There are no places like this anywhere else in the area, with a wide variety of services, standing head and shoulders above its competitors. Hey! Get your camp on and get set for a great time.

Nisqually John Landing Rec Area (Whitman Co.'s *BEST FREE* and *BEST RUSTIC CG*)

"Who was Nisqually John? Why, he's an historical figure," was the answer we got whenever we asked about the naming of this campground. All we know is that this guy named John once landed his craft on the Snake River here, that he had some connection to Nisqually, and was lucky enough to have one of the nicest campgrounds in the area named after him.

Overview: This primitive campground is located 44 miles south of Colfax and 14 miles west of Clarkston on 8 acres on Lower Granite Lake, operated by the US Army COE at 659' elevation, open all year; GPS 46.4766, -117.2354.

Facilities: Limited facilities include a vault toilet, picnic tables, metal fire grills (fires prohibited mid-June to mid-October), a Day Use Area, a one-lane boat launch, and garbage service.

Recreation includes hiking up to the 3,07-acre Nisqually John Habitat Management Unit and Nisqually John Canyon (1.9 miles each way), kite flying, and steelhead fishing.

Campsites (several dispersed tent sites, no hookups or reservations, FREE of charge): This rarely camped-in campground is right on the Snake River/Lower Granite Lake, nestled into a small canyon with a small bay nearby. The grassy sites are walk-ins, but many enjoy camping on the edge of the gravel parking area. There is some train noise.

Trip Notes: I guess nobody told these campers that they're not supposed to have this much fun in a FREE campground. The tent campers were tucked away in their little alcove sites on the River, while the RV campers parked on the edge of the parking lot, spreading out their bounty on the well-manicured lawns. It is an astonishingly simple but brilliant layout for a campground, and perhaps others should follow their example.

Local Alternatives: The best single FREE alternatives in Whitman Co. are operated by US Army Corps of Engineers and are located along the north shore of the Snake River. These include (west to east) Riparia (aka Lake West Park), North Shore Tailrace, Wawawai Landing, and Blyton Landing. Nisqually John Landing lies east of these campgrounds.

For more photos of Whitman Co. CGs consult
campeverycountywa.com

YAKIMA COUNTY (Yakima/Chinook Pass/White Pass)

The complexity of this, Washington's second largest county, comes from one of the world's most "fruitful" agricultural valleys surrounded by the mountainous Norse Peak Wilderness to the northwest, the William O. Douglas Wilderness to the west, the Mount Adams Wilderness to the southwest, and the Wenas Wildlife Area to the east. There is definitely something for everybody.

Yakima Valley

Don't let the velvety brown hills of the Yakima Valley seduce you into overlooking the verdant valley of orchards at your feet. In fact, since the Yakima Reclamation Project completed irrigation of the Valley in 1910, Yakima County has become the leading global producer of apples, hops, mint, and asparagus, with quality wine production increasing every year. Furthermore, commercial promoters tout the City of Yakima as "The Palm Springs of Washington" (more about that below).

Yakima Sportsman S.P. (Yakima Co.'s *BEST EQUIPPED/BEST CG FOR RVs*)
Described as an "oasis in the desert," this park was created by the Yakima Sportsman's Association for wildlife preservation and game management. It rests along the beautiful Yakima River surrounded by orchards, ranches, and the city of Yakima. There are over 140 species of birds here, in addition to other wildlife. Just sit back, buy some local fresh fruit or wine, and enjoy.
Overview: This fine natural campground is located on the outskirts of the City of Yakima on 277 acres at 1066' elevation, open year-round; GPS 46.5919, -120.4555.
Facilities: Well-equipped and well-appointed, campers will find bathrooms with showers, running water, a playground, ponds for bird watching and wildlife viewing,

a Park Store, camp hosts, and an RV dump. The Juan A. Alvarez Living Classroom includes a short, paved ADA-accessible trail. It includes ponds, wooden bridges, and a viewing platform that affords visitors an inside look into a living, working wetland.

Recreation: Birders will find black-capped chickadees, wood ducks, great blue herons, belted kingfishers, black-billed magpies, great horned owls, screech owls, Bewick's wrens, and downy woodpeckers. The park connects to the Yakima River Greenway Trail with 18 miles of paved walkways providing fishing lakes, picnic areas and river access, all open to the public free of charge year-round.

Campsites (70 sites for tents and RVs up to 60', 36 with 30-amp full hookups, reservable): The sites are divided into three groups. The center group consists of 3 rows or "islands." The first island is the main RV strip where sites are side-by-side, similar to most standard RV parks, but very grassy and well-manicured. The middle strip is a tree-lined green space, while the third is a lightly used tent strip that is also popular with truck-mounted campers and camping vans. It is also tree lined and provides more shade. The main tenting area (sites 37-64) forms a half circle around the three islands. These sites get the most privacy and the least traffic, with sites that are treed and of average to large in size. The Camp Every County Team's favorite sites are the two loops near the Greenway Trail and the River (sites 17-26 and 27-36). Each of these sites had its own huge shade tree, had relatively little car traffic, and seemed larger, being on the campground's edge.

Trip Notes: Yakima is one of our favorite cities; yet, we found it amusing that promoters dub it the "Palm Springs of Washington." No, very few think this campground is like Palm Springs, and we couldn't be happier! Yakima Sportsman is lush and verdant with a lot of depth and diversity.

Ahtanum State Forest

This 75,000-acre working forest provides habitat for native plants and animals, water retention for much needed irrigation, and diverse recreational opportunities. Ecosystems range from shrub-steppe in the eastern portion to high alpine in the western area with year-round activities including camping, bird watching, hiking, horseback riding, off-road vehicle riding, mountain biking, snowmobiling, hunting, and sightseeing.

Clover Flats CG (Yakima Co.'s *BEST FREE CG*)
Rule of Thumb: if you want the best wilderness camping, you have to drive until the road is impassible. This rings true of Yakima County and Clover Flats, but you'll be on top of the world, surrounded by summer wildflower displays that only the high desert can provide.

Overview: This high-elevation campground is located 43 miles west of Yakima, operated by the DNR at 6345' elevation, open year-round, except during heavy snows; GPS 46.507, -121.177.

Facilities: Better than expected facilities include pit toilets, drinking water, picnic tables, fire grills, and garbage cans.

Recreation: The most prevalent activities are hiking in the summer and snowmobiling in the winter. Photography is also popular, being in the shadow of 6,981' Darland Mountain, with unobstructed views of Mt. Jefferson, Mt. Hood, Mt. Adams, Mt. St. Helens and Mt. Rainier. Eagle Nest Vista, an overlook just one-half mile east of the campground, provides dramatic views of the North Fork Ahtanum drainage, Dome Peak, and the Goat Rocks Wilderness Area.

Campsites (9 sites for tents or RVs up to 24', no hookups or reservations, FREE with Discover Pass): Be aware that the last 3.2 miles to the campground is a one-land gravel road with a steep 12% grade. This stretch is recommended for (but not limited to) high-clearance vehicles without trailers, though we pulled our pop-i[trailer quite successfully in August. The campsites provide tent pads on native material, surrounded by subalpine vegetation, meadows, and mountain peaks. Note also that snow may remain in patches well into June but should not be a deal breaker.

Trip Notes: Wow, surprise beauty of the summer! The expansive meadows are a carnival of yellow and purple wildflowers beneath the tall, slender, and architecturally layered alpine trees that create statuesque silhouettes against the blue summer sky. We were so entranced we never left for Darland Mountain, though we spent some time at Eagle Nest Vista on the trip out. Clover Flats is a delight to the eyes, olfactory glands, and even to the skin, where the balm of the alpines is like menthol that stays with you long after you leave.

Local alternative: A nearby but busier alternative is Tree Phones CG, which is on the Middle Fork of Ahtanum Creek and has more hiking opportunities, but also is the center for organized marathon runs and All-Terrain Vehicle (ATV) activity. Most campers will find Ahtanum Meadows CG, near the end of the paved road up to Clover Flats, the best and prettiest all-around camping alternative.

Chinook Pass Scenic Byway/Hwy 410

The Eastern portion of this, Washington's premier scenic byway, takes you up and over 5430' Chinook Pass with spectacular views of Mt. Rainier, towering peaks, caves and river canyons, all the way to the fertile Naches Valley. Along the way, you will follow the American, Bumping, and Naches Rivers, plus campgrounds that will make you want to stop and stay awhile.

<u>Hell's Crossing CG</u> Yakima Co.'s *MOST APPEALING CGs TO THE SENSES*)
Don't let the off-putting name intimidate you -- this campground is named for the hellish difficulty pioneers had crossing this section of the Cascades back in the day. These days our state highway system makes it easier, at least in the summer months. It is far from heaven, but some find it pretty close.

<u>Overview</u>: This Wenatchee National Forest Campground is located 14.3 miles northeast of Chinook Pass and 52 miles northwest of Yakima on the American River at 3268' elevation, open late May through mid-September; GPS 46.9648364, -121.266476.

<u>Facilities</u>: Rustic amenities include vault toilets, picnic tables, and drinking water.

<u>Recreation</u>: Trout fishing, swimming, and rafting are popular on the American River. Goat Creek Trail #205 (accessible from the campground) is a 5.5-mile loop that offers a breathtaking view of Goat Peak. Pleasant Valley Trail #999 is a 5.4-mile loop, also accessible from the campground and relatively flat, that takes hikers into the William O. Douglas Wilderness and Pleasant Lake.

The American River bisects Hells Crossing CG inviting campers on both sides to come out and play

<u>Campsites</u> (6 tent sites plus 12 sites for tents or RVs up to 20', no hookups, reservable): Sites are in two sections, each with its own entrance. Sites 1-10 lie on the east side of the American River, with sites 11-18 on the west. Each section ends in a sharp loop, where the best sites are found (sites 10 and 18). Most sites are back-in with only a single pull-through (site 9). They are flat and well-spaced with moderate shade. East side sites have gravel parking pads, west side sites are dirt and rock. Some sites are perched high above the riverbanks, others rest right on the shore. All others are a short walk from the river.

<u>Trip Notes</u>: The American River seems to envelope campers here, being so visible and tangible to every campsite. This is a campground for river lovers, a real

showpiece, with the river running down the middle like a long, straight, wide and wet dividing line to give the sites more distance from each other, inviting campers on both sides to come out and play.

Local Alternative: While Hells Crossing is for river lovers, nearby Lodgepole CG is a forest campground for lovers of Ponderosa and lodgepole pines, old growth Douglas fir, and western red cedar. It is more developed than Hells Crossing with paved parking pads but is at higher elevation and across Hwy 410 from the American River.

White Pass Scenic Byway/Highway 12

Yakima County has a second National Scenic Byway and, although this mountain pass is of lower elevation and less "White" than Chinook Pass, the recreational possibilities include mountains, lakes, rivers and, if you're a devoted camper, one rip-roaring good time.

Indian Creek CG (Yakima Co.'s *BEST CG FOR ENTIRE FAMILIES*)

Remnants of vintage park, eagles in tall trees, and a broad creek flowing through a rocky creek bed just begging to be splashed... Ah, I'm a kid again.

Overview: This Wenatchee National Forest gem is located on Rimrock Lake east of White Pass at 3000' elevation, open late May until early September; GPS 46.645, -121.2425.

Facilities include vault toilets, drinking water, picnic tables, fire rings/grills, picnic shelter, and camp hosts.

Recreation: Fishing on Rimrock Lake produces primarily kokanee salmon and trout. Swimming is possible where Andy Creek runs into Rimrock Lake. Motorized and non-motorized boating are popular. Wildlife viewing includes bald eagles, black bear, deer, gray wolves, grizzly bear, mountain goats, and the northern spotted owl.

Campsites (38 sites, no hookups, reservable): Sites are wooded, spacious, and private. None border Rimrock Lake, which is reachable by short trails. Located on the eastern side of the Cascades, it is heavily forested with Ponderosa Pines, and less arid than campgrounds just a few miles east. when making reservations, however, as some of the websites have mis-numbered the campsites

Trip notes: I love this place. It is nestled against Silver Beach Resort, one of those tiny, congested, frenetic, unreasonably popular RV parks that I regard as "camping in fast motion." Just steps away, Indian Creek is the opposite: quiet, spacious, and uncrowded with great forest and vegetation. There are hidden remnants of vintage park everywhere, as this park has seen better days. But I loved wading in rocky Indian Creek, following it to Rimrock Lake, looking up and seeing eagles high in the trees, and feeling like a kid again. Isn't that what camping should be about?

Indian Creek CG makes you lose your sense of time
so you want to stay forever

<u>Hause Creek CG</u> (Yakima Co.'s *BEST BIKE-IN CG*)
This river is wild. The Tieton River, that is. And not "wild" as in "wilderness." That crazy river tumbles, buckles, changes flow, and changes back again every 50 or 60 yards -- a welcome and refreshing relief in this otherwise arid campground.
<u>Overview</u>: This Wenatchee National Forest campground located 4 miles east of Rimrock Lake on the Tieton River at 2600' elevation, open April 20 to Sept. 26. GPS 46.67556, -121.07639.
<u>Facilities</u> include flush toilets, drinking water, picnic tables, fire rings/grills, and camp hosts.
<u>Recreation</u>: Whitewater rafting is the most exhilarating activity here, particularly in September when the Bureau of Land Reclamation releases extra water from Rimrock Lake into the Tieton River. This is also close to great hiking opportunities, including the Boulder Cave National Recreation Trail and the Goat Rocks Wilderness.
<u>Campsites</u> (42 sites, no hookups, reservable): The campground is located east of and below Rimrock Lake Dam, bordered on one side by the Tieton River. Trees within the campground include larch, aspens, alders and, of course, Ponderosa pine. This is more developed than most of the other campgrounds on the eastern slope of the White Pass Highway, with good river access and well-spaced campsites ensuring good privacy with shade trees.
<u>Trip Notes</u>: Yes, this campground is about the River. Loved it, liked the big, spacious campsites cooled by the light spray of the River. There are signs everywhere of people having fun. At one site, a camper erected a makeshift sculpture of a sea serpent out of dry tree roots, expressing his/her fanciful feelings about what else the river might hold. I suspect that person was having a good time, the true mark of a good campground.

268

Local alternatives: Willows CG is a perplexing popular campground just 3 miles east. To us it seemed ordinary and "messy," although there were 2 or 3 good sites on the Tieton River. Six miles further east lies quiet, breezy Windy Point CG, with most sites (10 in all) on a calmer stretch of the Tieton River. A tall, slender waterfall is very visible on the opposite shore. As daytime temperatures can soar, the low, constant breeze is welcome relief. Other advantages include less extreme day/night temperature changes due to lower altitude. Windy Point can accommodate tents or RVs up to 37'.

Clear Lake Rec Area (Yakima Co.'s *MOST UNIQUELY WASHINGTON CG*)
This recreation complex is a series of named and unnamed campgrounds, boat launches, and day use areas. It stretches between the dam and spillway of Clear Lake to the western edge of Rimrock Lake. Don't let its complexity deter you -- it is underutilized, and a delight to those of us looking for uniquely Washington camping.
Overview: This Okanogan-Wenatchee National Forest camping area is located 7 miles west of White Pass on 232-acre Clear Lake and the North Fork of the Tieton River at 2994' elevation, open Memorial Day weekend through Labor Day; GPS 46.63111, -121.26667.
Facilities: Scattered amenities include vault toilets, picnic tables, fire rings, drinking water at Clear Lake South, garbage service, two fishing platforms in the detached Day Use Area (more below), a boat launch (a fee is charged), camp hosts, and an RV dump.
Recreation: The campground offers all manner of water adventures, including fishing for eastern brook and rainbow trout, canoeing, kayaking, and no-wake motorboating. There is no swimming in Clear Lake itself, though it is good in the outlet creeks from the Lake that re-join to resume the Tieton River below.

The main spillway from Clear Lake is the centerpiece for uniquely Washington camping between the Rimrock and Clear Lake Reservoirs

<u>Campsites</u> (59 sites for tents or small RVs, about 4 dispersed walk-in sites, 1 group site for up to 40 people requiring reservations, no hookups, no reservations for individual sites): The sites are set in a rich forest of Ponderosa pine, grand fir, and hemlock. They are distributed as follows:

-<u>Clear Lake North</u>: This, the first camping area, is divided into two campgrounds. Three-Day CG (not recommended) is far from the River and fairly cramped. Spring CG rests on a flat bench above the River, with steep trails to the bottom, providing both swimming opportunities and views of Rimrock Lake. These sites are large, spread out, and uniformly wooded. The two campgrounds have a combined 36 sites, 3 of which are doubles, no hookups or reservations.

-<u>Group Camp</u>: This perfectly flat camping area is separated from the River below by rock outcroppings that make good climbing, but a dangerous temptation to kids who might want to jump off into the water (don't try it!). It can be seen from FR 740 above, and Fish Hawk CG across the River. This closely rivals Indian Flat Group Camp on Chinook Pass (above), lacking only in less than perfect privacy. It can accommodate up to 40 campers, with a group fire ring, three large group picnic tables, and vault toilets. There are no hookups, but reservations are required.

-Clear Lake South : The sites fall into 4 distinct areas: 1) One drive-in site and several dispersed walk-in sites on the small hill just before that marvelous spillway giving campers the most direct access to Clear Lake (very popular!); 2) A small Day Use area on an "island" between the spillway and the outlet creek from Clear Lake Dam; 3) Fish Hawk CG, the best of the individual camping areas, rests along the combined outlet creeks from the spillway and the dam (the re-formed Tieton River) with good views of both; 4) Cold Creek CG is a series of developed but scattered sites closer to the dam, on the road to the private Prime Timer CG (for special needs kids and adults) and the boat launch. Some will like the privacy of the sites, but we found them rather ordinary. Sites 15 and 16 have a direct view of the dam. The two combined campgrounds have 22 sites for tents or RVs up to 22', no hookups or reservations.

-Clear Lake Boat Launch: This is a Day Use Area that charges a fee for boat launching. It may be the best single spot overall for viewing the Lake, rivaled only by the detached Day Use Area on the west shore of the Lake (below).

-Clear Lake Day Use Area: This larger no barrier Day Use Area sits on 7opposite (west) shore of Clear Lake, with a large picnic shelter, paved trails, fishing, nature walks, wildlife viewing, picnic areas, and non-motorized boating. The two fishing platforms and unobstructed view of the Lake make this a destination for most campers.

Trip Notes: Clear Lake could really be called Upper Rimrock Lake, as it is part of Rimrock, but sits higher, with about one mile of waterways connecting the two. The minute we saw that many-layered spillway, we were hooked! It was like camping IN the Tieton River, surrounded by it, part of it, and it part of us. You could safely wade or swim in the cold water and follow it all the way to Rimrock. We camped here in August, when we expected water levels to be at their lowest -- we were glad to be wrong! Water levels were at their highest point. You might check before heading out, though. The camping is likely less dramatic if no water is pouring out of the spillway.

Yakama Nation Mt. Adams Recreation Area

This is the only area within the Yakima Reservation forested western boundary that is open to non-Yakamas -- and as close to Mt. Adams as non-tribal campers can get. It is an entirely unique camping world, with primitive campgrounds and views of Mt. Adams from the east that most of us would never otherwise see. Add this one to the top of your bucket list. But don't wait too long -- public access to this breathtaking land has been under dispute.

<u>Bird Lake CG</u> (Yakima Co.'s *BEST RUSTIC CG and BEST CG FOR ENTIRE FAMILIES*)

It is refreshing to find rustic campgrounds that are also great for families. Nestled at the eastern foot of 12,280' Mt. Adams, with family-friendly hiking trails that are among the best in Washington, breathtaking views, and good fishing all come together here in the forested boundary of the Yakama Reservation.

<u>Overview</u>: This uniquely beautiful rustic campground is located 135 miles southwest of Yakima on Bird Lake operated by the Yakama Nation Tribe at 5,597' elevation, open early July to September; GPS 46.141285, -121.440683.

<u>Facilities</u>: Limited facilities include vault toilets, picnic tables, fire grills, and garbage cans. Water is available, and firewood is provided free of charge.

<u>Recreation</u>: Fishing is notable for largemouth bass, smallmouth bass, spotted bass, striped bass, white bass, catfish, crappie, eastern brook trout, and walleye. Fishing permits required (available at campground). Hiking includes the Bird Lake - Crooked Creek Falls - Bluff Lake Loop Hike (4-mile loop), the amazing Bird Creek Meadows Trail (3-mile loop), also known as the Trail of Wildflowers, and the spur to Hellroaring Canyon viewpoint. No mountain bikes, ATVs, or motorcycles are permitted on the trails. This is considered one of the best family hikes in Washington.

<u>Campsites</u> (21 sites for tents, no hookups or reservations, tribal camping permits required - available at campground): These beautiful but primitive sites are set in old-growth Douglas fir and Ponderosa pine. Most have quick shore access, or at least a view of the lake. Only electric motors are allowed on the lake.

<u>Directions</u>: Start in the town of Trout Lake in Klickitat Co. Head due north on the Mount Adams Recreation Highway/Road #23 for 5 miles. Turn right/northeast onto Forest Road 82 for another 5 miles, when the road will merge with Forest Road 8225. After one mile, bear left onto Bench Lake Road/Tribal Route 285. Continue for 4 miles to Mirror Lake C.G. where you can self-register for a required entry permit to the area. Turn left onto Bird Lake Road and continue 1.77 miles to Bird Lake CG. Note that all roads after the Mount Adams Recreation Highway are gravel and dirt, and extremely rough, only suitable for 4-wheel drive trucks or high clearance vehicles.

<u>Trip Notes</u>: It had been years since we camped at delightful Bird Lake, so we were disappointed when we eagerly set out, only to be stopped by a rather prominent "ROAD CLOSED" sign. Stay tuned, as optimists are predicting re-opening very soon. Check status before setting out.

For more photos of Yakima Co. CGs, or info on HIKE-IN or GROUP CGs (and more!), consult campeverycountywa.com

APPENDIX 1
Campworthy Campgrounds by Category

campgrounds with ADIRONDACK SHELTERS

These are wooden 3-sided shelters with bunkbeds, most of which are located in Group Camps. Sleeping in these seems like summer camp when you were a kid.

1. Battle Ground Lake S.P. Group - Clark
2. Beacon Rock S.P. Group - Skamania
3. Bedal - Snohomish
4. Cranberry Lake (Deception Pass) - Island
5. Kanaskat-Palmer S.P. Group - King
6. Moran S.P. (primitive CG) - San Juan
7. Scenic Beach S.P. - Kitsap
8. Seaquest S.P. Group - Cowlitz
9. Rasar S.P. (walk-in sites) - Skagit
10. Spencer Spit S.P Group - San Juan

best campgrounds for BERRY PICKING

Berries were such a staple of the native peoples that it seems only fitting that is be part of the camping experience. We will gladly eat a blackberry pie in the outdoors to show respect to those who went before us. It's the least we can do.

1. Aldrich Lake (blackberries) – Mason
2. Bird Creek (huckleberries) – Yakima
3. Bear Creek Lodge (huckleberries) - Spokane
4. Big Meadow Lake (same) - Pend Oreille
5. Cold Creek Camp (huckleberries) – Clark
6. Fields Spring S.P. (huckleberries) - Asotin
7. Forlorn Lakes CG (huckleberries) - Skamania
8. Iron Creek CG (huckleberries) - Lewis
9. Manchester S.P. (blackberries) - Kitsap
10. Tucquala Meadows (huckleberries) – Kittitas

best campgrounds for BIRD WATCHING

Birds are often the first sound you hear in the morning, and the last sound you hear before dropping off to sleep. They are the heart of the wildlife in your camping area, and deserve a look see.

1. Belfair S.P. - Mason Co.
2. Conconully S.P. - Okanogan Co.
3. Dungeness Rec Area – Clallam Co.
4. Lyle Lake/Seep Lakes - Adams Co.
5. Kalaloch CG, ONP - Jefferson Co.
6. Potholes S.P. - Grant Co.
7. Rasar S.P. - Skagit Co.
8. Riverbend CG - Thurston Co.
9. Steamboat Rock S.P. - Grant Co.
10. Wenatchee Confluence S.P. - Chelan Co.

best campgrounds with CABINS

Can't wait until summer to go camping? This may be your best winter option (for yurts and teepees, see below)

1. Battle Ground Lake S.P. - Clark Co.
2. Boyer Marina - Whitman Co.
3. Fields Spring S.P. (Tamarack Cabin) - Asotin Co.
4. Ike Kinswa S.P. - Lewis Co.
5. Kayak Point Regional Park - Snohomish Co.
6. Lincoln Rock S.P. - Douglas Co.
7. Ponderosa Falls Park - Spokane Co.
8. Potholes S.P. - Grant Co.
9. Rasar S.P. - Skagit Co.
10. Silver Lake County Park - Whatcom Co.

CIVILIAN CONSERVATION CORPS campgrounds

These campgrounds, built with the assistance of the CCC in the 1930s and early 1940s, have a vintage style marked by permanence, sturdiness, and hand-hewn determination. Well of course they do -- they're still here and lookin' good!

1. Bowl and Pitcher (Riverside S.P.) – Spokane
2. Bowman Bay (Deception Pass S.P.) - Skagit
3. Cranberry Lake (Deception Pass) – Island
4. Lewis and Clark S.P. – Lewis (website)
5. Lewis and Clark Trail S.P. – Columbia Co.
6. Kalaloch CG in ONP – Jefferson Co.
7. Millersylvania S.P. – Thurston Co.
8. Moran S.P. - San Juan Co.
9. Rainbow Falls S.P. - Lewis Co.
10. Wanapum Rec Area - Kittitas Co.

campgrounds with CLAM/OYSTER HARVESTING

How about a little clam chowder for your campfire supper? And in case you're doing the cooking, I prefer the Manhattan style to the New England. Thanks for asking.

1. Belfair S.P. – Mason Co.
2. Birch Bay S.P. – Whatcom Co.
3. Cape Disappointment S.P. – Pacific Co.
4. Fort Townsend S.P. – Jefferson Co.
5. Grayland Beach S.P. – Pacific Co.
6. Kalaloch CG ONP – Jefferson Co.
7. Ocean City S.P. - Grays Harbor Co.
8. Pacific Beach S.P. – Grays Harbor Co.
9. Penrose S.P. – Pierce Co.
10. Twin Harbors S.P. - Grays Harbor Co.

perfect forested campgrounds on perfect CREEKS

We had to include this category, because these are the unsung campground heroes of Washington. They don't include snow-capped peaks, pounding ocean surf, or volcanic activity. All they offer is... perfection.

1. Brown Creek – Mason Co.
2. Cold Creek – Clark Co.
3. Campbell Tree Grove - Grays Harbor Co.
4. Dow Creek RV Park/CG – Mason Co.
5. Johnny Creek – Chelan Co.
6. Panther Creek – Skamania Co.
7. Pataha Creek – Garfield Co.
8. Sheep Creek – Stevens Co.
9. Silver Falls – Chelan Co.
10. Tucannon - Columbia Co.

campworthy campgrounds with great FISHING

Fishing and camping have always been the perfect partner. Fishing doesn't have to overshadow camping, and good camping doesn't have to mean poor fishing. Here are 10 of the best combos.

1. Coppermine Bottom – Jefferson Co.
2. Four Seasons CG/RV Resort – Adams Co.
3. Ike Kinswa S.P. – Lewis Co.
4. Panorama Point – Whatcom Co.
5. Pearrygin Lake S.P. – Okanogan Co.
6. Potholes S.P. – Grant Co.
7. Rasar S.P. – Skagit Co.
8. Swan Lake – Ferry Co.
9. Tucannon CG – Columbia Co.
10. Walupt Lake CG – Lewis Co.

best campgrounds for GLAMPING

We are including only glamping facilities in campgrounds already deemed campworthy by our panel of experts (meaning us). There are plenty of glamping/lodging facilities out there, but these are beyond the scope of this manual.
1. Columbia Hills S.P. – Klickitat Co.
2. Kayak Regional Park (yurt village) – Snohomish Co.
3. Lakedale Resort – San Juan Island/Co.
4. Millersylvania S.P. – Thurston Co.
5. Moran S.P. – Orcas Island in San Juan Co.
6. Rose Creek Retreat – Wahkiakum Co.

best campgrounds for HIKING

Most of the time hiking is just hiking. But whether you want to see the magnificent peaks of the North Cascades, the ghost town of Monte Cristo, or the amazing Kamiak Butte, it adds a big fat juicy cherry to your camping experience.

1. Bird Creek – Yakima Co.
2. Campbell Creek Grove – Grays Harbor Co.
3. Colonial Creek CG in ONP – Whatcom Co.
4. Kamiak Butte Co. Park – Whitman Co.
5. Lower Falls – Skamania Co.
6. Moran S.P. – San Juan Co.
7. Steamboat Rock S.P. – Grant Co.
8. Staircase CG in ONP – Mason Co.
9. Tucquala Meadows – Kittitas Co.
10. Walupt Lake – Lewis Co.

best campgrounds steeped in HISTORY

We all survived the boring high school history teacher, making you memorize all those names and dates without knowing what they meant. But learning history by living it, experiencing it, being entranced by it, helps you finally understand what all the fuss was about.

1. Cape Disappointment S.P. – Pacific Co.
2. Conconully S.P. – Okanogan Co.
3. Douglas Falls Grange – Stevens Co.
4. Fort Flagler S.P. – Jefferson Co.
5. Fort Spokane – Lincoln Co.
6. Kettle Falls – Stevens Co.
7. Lewis and Clark Trail S.P. – Columbia Co.
8. Salmon La Sac – Kittitas Co.
9. Salt Creek Rec Area – Clallam Co.
10. San Juan Co. Park – San Juan Co.

best campgrounds for KITE FLYING

Illegal in Afghanistan, treasured by children, but long forgotten by adults, kite flying can add a lightness to the camping experience that will make your cares disappear into thin air.

1. Belfair S.P. - Mason Co.
2. Cape Disappointment S.P. - Pacific Co.
3. Cascade Park and CG - Grant Co.
4. Crow Butte Park - Benton Co.
5. Fay Bainbridge Park and CG - Kitsap Co.
6. Garfield Co. Fairgrounds - Garfield Co.
7. Grayland Beach S.P. - Pacific Co.
8. Kalaloch CG, ONP - Jefferson Co.
9. Ocean City S.P. - Grays Harbor Co.
10. Taidnapam Park - Lewis Co. (website)

best campgrounds on (smaller) natural LAKES

Smaller lakes may lack the impressive shorelines and vistas of the larger lakes, but what they offer is a cozy, safer, and quieter option where the boats are usually human powered, and the swimming far more inviting for children and adults alike.

1. Battle Ground Lake S.P. - Clark Co.
2. Bird Lake CG – Yakima Co.
3. Bonaparte Lake CG - Okanogan Co.

4. Forlorn Lakes CG - Skamania Co.
5. Millersylvania S.P. (Lost Lake) - Thurston Co.
6. Swan Lake CG - Ferry Co.
7. Takhlakh Lake CG - Skamania Co.
8. Moran S.P. (Cascade Lake) -San Juan Co.

best campgrounds on (larger) natural LAKES

Camping on a large lake is quite different than small lakes and ponds. Larger lakes have an atmosphere of their own, including wakes from boats, fog, cloud formations, and much longer vistas. But these campworthy campgrounds rival the quality of their lakes, making for a great pairing.

1. East Sullivan CG on Sullivan Lake - Pend Oreille
2. Fairholm CG, ONP on Lake Crescent – Clallam
3. Lake Chelan S.P. - Chelan Co.
4. Lake Curlew S.P. - Ferry Co.
5. Lake Pearrygin – Okanogan Co.
6. Lake Wenatchee S.P. - Chelan Co.
7. Liberty Lake Regional Park - Spokane Co.
8. Merrill Lake CG - Cowlitz Co.
9. Skokomish Park, Lake Cushman – Mason
10. Walupt Lake CG - Lewis Co.

QUIRKIEST of the campworthy campgrounds

Camping should not be taken too seriously, as this defeats its purpose - to achieve clarity of mind, to find balance, and to reconnect with nature. Sometimes the builders of these campgrounds got a little carried away... or were they just having a carefree good time?

1. Boundary Dam CG - Pend Oreille Co.
2. Clear Lake Recreation Area - Yakima Co.
3. Daroga S.P. - Douglas Co.
4. Kamloops Island CG - Ferry Co.
5. Lighthouse Park on Point Roberts - Whatcom Co. (website)
6. Seal Rock CG - Jefferson Co.
7. Skamokawa Vista Park - Wahkiakum Co.
8. Taidnapam Park - Lewis Co. (website)

9. Wawawai Co. Park – Whitman Co.
10. Tolt-MacDonald Co. Park - King Co.

best campgrounds on SALT WATER

1. Cape Disappointment S.P., Pacific Co.
2. Dungeness Spit Rec. Area, San Juan Strait - Clallam Co.
3. Grayland Beach S.P., Pacific - Pacific Co.
4. Kalaloch CG/ONP, Pacific – Jefferson Co.
5. Kayak Point Regional Park, Puget Sound - Snohomish Co.
6. Manchester S.P., Puget Sound - Kitsap Co.
7. Ocean City S.P., Pacific - Grays Harbor Co.
8. Salt Creek Rec Area, San Juan Strait - Clallam Co.
9. Scenic Beach S.P., Hood Canal - Kitsap Co.
10. Washington Park, Puget Sound - Skagit Co.

campgrounds with TEEPEES

1. Columbia Hills S.P. - Klickitat Co.
2. Fields Spring S.P. - Asotin Co.
3. Skamokawa Vista – Wahkiakum Co.

campgrounds with YURTS

1. Bay Center KOA - Pacific Co.
2. Cape Disappointment S.P. - Pacific Co.
3. Coho CG - Grays Harbor Co.
4. Grayland Beach S.P. (some allow pets) - Pacific Co.
5. Kanaskat-Palmer S.P. - King Co.
6. Kayak Point Regional Park - Snohomish Co.
7. Paradise Point S.P. - Clark Co.
8. Seaquest S.P. (some allow pets) - Cowlitz Co.
9. Skamokawa Vista Park - Wahkiakum Co.
10. Twin Harbors S.P. - Grays Harbor Co.

APPENDIX 2

The Camp Every County Washington Crew's Favorite Campworthy Campgrounds
(all listed alphabetically)

John's Top 10 Campgrounds

John hales from Boston and lends an East Coast perspective to camping. He says he hates everything yet is often the voice of reason and keeps the rest of us on track. He is content to remain in his campsite and can pick campworthy campgrounds out of a lineup.

1. Cape Disappointment S.P. - Pacific Co.
2. Conconully S.P. - Okanogan Co.
3. Cranberry Lake (Deception Pass) Island Co.
4. Douglas Fir CG, USFS - Whatcom Co.
5. Grayland Beach S.P. - Pacific Co.
6. Lake Easton S.P. - Kittitas Co.
7. Lake Wenatchee S.P. - Chelan Co.
8. Moran S.P. - San Juan Co.
9. Potholes S.P. - Grant Co.
10. Steamboat Rock S.P. - Grant Co.

Tom's Top 10 Campgrounds

Tom grew up in the sprawl of the Puget Sound Area, and has come to value privacy, space, and quiet above all else. If working on this project with Tom has taught us one thing, it's that he knows how to pick out campsites through the sometimes deceptive reservations systems. He has never let us down.

1. Cape Disappointment S.P. - Pacific Co.
2. Coho, USFS - Grays Harbor Co.
3. Colonial Creek CG in NCNP - Whatcom
4. Crow Butte Park, Port of Benton - Benton
5. Fishhook Park, US Army COE - Walla Walla Co.
6. Iron Creek CG, USFS - Lewis Co.
7. Kalaloch CG, ONP - Jefferson Co.
8. Lake Wenatchee S.P. - Chelan Co.
9. Moran S.P. - San Juan Co.
10. Potholes S.P. - Grant Co.

Gary's Top 10 Campgrounds

Gary was the oldest member of the Camp Every County Crew and grew up in Tacoma. True to his sentimental and often superstitious nature, he passed away just days after our final camping trip at Walupt Lake. He is known for having a big heart (sometimes the source of unintentional humor), and for being the first to pick up the mood or "energy" of a campground. He is missed, but no camping trip will ever be complete without Gary stories.

1. Ike Kinswa S.P. - Lewis Co.
2. Indian Creek CG - Yakima Co.
3. Johnny Creek CG, USFS - Chelan Co.
4. Kanaskat-Palmer S.P. - King Co.
5. Larrabee S.P. - Whatcom Co.
6. Manchester S.P. - Kitsap Co.
7. Ohanapecosh CG at MRNP - Lewis Co.
8. Panorama Point CG, USFS - Whatcom Co.
9. Scenic Beach S.P. - Kitsap Co.
10. Wanapum/Gingko S.P. - Kittitas Co.

Brendan's Top 10 Campgrounds

Brendan is the token impractical science nerd of the Crew from just outside of Raymond (yes, it's in Washington). His ideal campground might be described as "The perfect USFS campground on the perfect little lake." But if it's not perfect, he leans toward the quirky.

1. Coho, USFS - Grays Harbor Co.
2. Johnny Creek CG, USFS - Chelan Co.
3. Kalaloch CG, ONP - Jefferson Co.
4. Lake Curlew S.P. - Ferry Co.
5. Lake Wenatchee S.P. - Chelan Co.
6. Manchester S.P. – Kitsap Co.
7. Salmon La Sac CG, USFS - Kittitas Co.
8. Scenic Beach S.P. - Kitsap Co.
9. Skokomish Park, Skokomish Tribe - Mason Co.
10. Steamboat Rock S.P. – Grant Co.

Top 10 MOST UNIQUELY WASHINGTON CAMPGROUNDS

Many campgrounds are utterly unique to the State of Washington. The moment you enter them, you experience the magic that no other place can replicate. Here are the 10 most unique.

1. Conconully S.P. - Okanogan Co.
2. Hoh Rain Forest CG, ONP - Jefferson Co.
3. Kamiak Butte County Park - Whitman County
4. Keller Ferry CG, NPS - Lincoln Co.
5. Larrabee S.P. - Whatcom Co.
6. Ohanapecosh CG, MRNP - Lewis Co.
7. Palouse Falls S.P. - Franklin Co.
8. Scenic Beach S.P. - Kitsap Co.

9. Steamboat Rock S.P. – Grant Co.
10. Takhlakh Lake CG, USFS - Skamania

Top 10 BEST CAMPGROUNDS
FOR THE ENTIRE FAMILY

"Family-friendly" doesn't have to mean for the kids only. The perfect balance is everybody-friendly campgrounds -- those for the entire family. We've named one for each of the 39 Washington counties, but here are the 10 best.

1. Battle Ground Lake S.P. - Clark Co.
2. Cape Disappointment S.P. - Pacific Co.
3. Columbia Hills S.P. - Klickitat Co.
4. Lake Chelan S.P. - Chelan Co.
5. Lake Easton S.P. - Kittitas Co.
6. Lena Lake Hike-In CG, USFS - Jefferson
7. Millersylvania S.P. - Thurston Co.
8. Pearrygin Lake S.P. - Okanogan Co.
9. Scenic Beach S.P. - Kitsap Co.
10. Silver Lake Co. Park - Whatcom Co.

Top 10 BEST EQUIPPED/
BEST CAMPGROUNDS FOR RVs

Travel trailers, 5th Wheels, teardrop trailers, tent trailers, camping vans -- all of these are a big part of the camping scene. But even tent campers occasionally like extra amenities -- electricity, showers, or, at the very least, a picnic table and fire grill. Here are the 10 campgrounds we found to be the best equipped:

1. American Heritage CG, private – Thurston Co.
2. Beebe Bridge CG, Chelan PUD - Douglas Co.
3. Boyer's Marina CG, private – Whitman
4. Cranberry Lake CG/S.P – Island Co.
5. CBRA, Grant PUD - Grant Co.
6. Grayland Beach S.P. - Pacific Co.
7. Ike Kinswa S.P. - Lewis Co.
8. Maryhill S.P. - Klickitat Co.
9. Rasar S.P. - Skagit Co.
10. Yakima Sportsman S.P. - Yakima Co.

Top 10 BEST FREE CAMPGROUNDS

Free campgrounds are not just affordable to all. They afford the opportunity to be creative, home-spun, and free from commercial overload. Sometimes the most creative people make the best camping neighbors.

1. Ayer Boat Basin CG, US Army COE - Walla Walla
2. Big Meadow Lake CG, USFS - Pend Oreille Co.
3. Campbell Tree Grove CG, USFS - Grays Harbor
4. Clover Flats CG, DNR – Yakima Co.
5. Cold Creek CG, DNR - Clark Co.
6. Lyle River CG, DNR - Clallam Co.
7. Margaret McKinney CG, DNR - Thurston Co.
8. Merrill Lake CG, DNR - Cowlitz Co.
9. Tucannon CG, USFS - Columbia Co.
10. Windust Park, US Army COE - Franklin Co.

Top 10 BEST RUSTIC CAMPGROUNDS

Take away the heavy pruning, the landscaping, the concrete, and the cheap commercial buildings, and what do you get? Nature in its purest form.

1. Bird Lake CG, Yakama Nation – Yakima Co.
2. Collins CG, USFS - Jefferson Co.
3. Douglas Creek Rec Site, BLM – Douglas Co.
4. Douglas Fir CG, USFS - Whatcom Co.
5. Forlorn Lakes CGs, USFS – Skamania Co.
6. Hawk Creek CG, NPS - Lincoln Co.
7. Klahowya CG, USFS - Clallam Co.
8. Marble Creek CG, USFS - Skagit Co.
9. Owhi CG, USFS - Kittitas Co.
10. Silver Falls CG, USFS - Chelan Co.

Top 10 BEST BIKE-IN CAMPGROUNDS

Sometimes getting to your campground is a big part of the experience. When you want to get entirely away from the mechanized, noisy, fossil fuel burning world, get out the two-wheeler and start your adventure from your doorstep.

1. Bear Creek CG, DNR - Clallam Co.
2. Columbia Hills S.P. - Klickitat Co.
3. Daroga S.P. - Douglas Co.
4. Fishhook Park, US Army COE - Walla Walla Co.
5. Garfield County Fairgrounds - Garfield Co.
6. Keller CG, Confederated Tribes of the Colville Reservation - Ferry Co.
7. Rainbow Falls S.P./Willapa Hills S.P. – Lewis
8. Rhododendron County Park - Island Co.
9. Seaquest S.P. - Cowlitz Co.
10. Spencer Spit S.P. - San Juan Co.

Index of Campgrounds